Eileen Chang: The Performativity of Self-Translation

Sinica Leidensia

Edited by

Barend J. ter Haar
Nicolas Standaert

In co-operation with

P.K. Bol, D.R. Knechtges, E.S. Rawski,
W.L. Idema, H.T. Zurndorfer

VOLUME 172

The titles published in this series are listed at *brill.com/sinl*

Eileen Chang: The Performativity of Self-Translation

By

Jessica Tsui-yan Li

BRILL

LEIDEN | BOSTON

Cover image: Eileen Chang, Shanghai, 1944. USC Digital Library. Ailing Zhang (Eileen Chang) Papers Collection.

Library of Congress Cataloging-in-Publication Data

Names: Li, Jessica Tsui-yan, 1975- author.
Title: Eileen Chang : the performativity of self-translation / by Jessica
    Tsui-yan Li.
Description: Leiden ; Boston : Brill, 2025. | Series: Sinica leidensia,
    0169-9563 ; volume 172 | Includes bibliographical references and index.
    | Identifiers: LCCN 2025003343 (print) | LCCN 2025003344 (ebook) | ISBN
    9789004727175 (paperback ; acid-free paper) | ISBN 9789004730052 (ebook)
Subjects: LCSH: Zhang, Ailing–Translations into English–History and
    criticism | Self-translation. | LCGFT: Literary criticism.
Classification: LCC PL2837.E35 Z727 2025 (print) | LCC PL2837.E35 (ebook)
    | DDC 895.13/51–dc23/eng/20250409
LC record available at https://lccn.loc.gov/2025003343
LC ebook record available at https://lccn.loc.gov/2025003344

Typeface for the Latin, Greek, and Cyrillic scripts: "Brill". See and download: brill.com/brill-typeface.

ISSN 0169-9563
ISBN 978-90-04-72717-5 (hardback)
ISBN 978-90-04-73005-2 (e-book)
DOI 10.1163/9789004730052

Copyright 2025 by Jessica Tsui-yan Li. Published by Koninklijke Brill BV, Plantijnstraat 2, 2321 JC Leiden, The Netherlands.
Koninklijke Brill BV incorporates the imprints Brill, Brill Nijhoff, Brill Schöningh, Brill Fink, Brill mentis, Brill Wageningen Academic, Vandenhoeck & Ruprecht, Böhlau and V&R unipress.
Koninklijke Brill BV reserves the right to protect this publication against unauthorized use. Requests for re-use and/or translations must be addressed to Koninklijke Brill BV via brill.com or copyright.com.
For more information: info@brill.com.

This book is printed on acid-free paper and produced in a sustainable manner.

To my parents

Li Ming Yee and Chan Yuet Chun

∵

Contents

Acknowledgements   IX

Notes about Chinese Romanization and Translation   XI

List of Illustrations   XII

Introduction: The Practice of Self-Translation in Eileen Chang's Works   1

1   Eileen Chang as a Self-Translator   3

2   Translation History in China   11

3   Theories of Self-Translation   15

4   Summary of Each Chapter   27

PART 1
Translating the Self

1   **Rewriting the Self in Memoirs**   33

2   **Reimagining the Self in Eileen Chang's Semi-Autobiographical Novels:** *Xiaotuanyuan* 《小團圓》 (*Little Reunions*), *The Fall of the Pagoda*, and *The Book of Change*   52

3   **Self-Translation as a Performative Act:** *Duizhaoji – kan lao zhaoxiangbu* 《對照記——看老照相簿》 (*Mutual Reflections – Looking at Old Photo Albums*)   69

PART 2
Paradoxical In-Betweenness

4   **Interdependence: "Jinsuoji"** 《金鎖記》 ("The Golden Cangue"), *The Rouge of the North, Yuannü* 《怨女》 (*Embittered Woman*), and "The Golden Cangue"   87

5   **Authorship: "Shame, Amah!" and "Guihuazheng – A Xiao beiqiu"** 〈桂花蒸——阿小悲秋〉 ("Steamed Osmanthus Flower: Ah Xiao's Unhappy Autumn")   108

6   **Re-Evaluation: "Deng"** 〈等〉 ("Waiting") and "Little Finger Up"   118

VIII   CONTENTS

7   Recontextualization: "Stale Mates – A Short Story Set in the Time
    When Love Came to China" and "Wusi yishi – Luo Wentao sanmei
    tuanyuan" 〈五四遺事——羅文濤三美團圓〉 ("Regret after the
    May Fourth Movement – The Reunion of Luo Wentao and the Three
    Beauties") 128

8   Metacommentary on "Xiangjianhuan" 〈相見歡〉 ("A Joyful
    Rendezvous") and "She Said Smiling" 136

    PART 3
    Cultural Translation

9   Interpretation: "Demons and Fairies" and "Zhongguoren de zongjiao"
    〈中國人的宗教〉 ("The Religion of the Chinese") 157

10 Distanciation: "Still Alive" and "Yangren kan jingxi ji qita" 〈洋人
    看京戲及其他〉 ("Westerners Watching Peking Opera and Other
    Issues") 172

11 Transformation: "Chinese Life and Fashions" and "Gengyiji" 〈更衣記〉
    ("A Chronicle of Changing Clothes") 184

    PART 4
    Political Ambivalence

12 Authenticity Reconsidered: *The Rice-Sprout Song – A Novel of Modern
    China* and *Yangge* 《秧歌》 203

13 Postmodern Intertextuality: *Chidi zhi lian* 《赤地之戀》 (*The
    Romance of the Redland*) and *Naked Earth – A Novel about China* 224

14 Transcultural Hospitality: "A Return to the Frontier" and "Chongfang
    biancheng" 〈重訪邊城〉 239

15 Transgressing Boundaries: "The Spyring or Ch'ing k'ê! Ch'ing k'ê!" and
    "Se, Jie" 〈色，戒〉 ("Lust, Caution") 249

    Conclusion: The Performativity of Eileen Chang's Self-Translation 263

    Bibliography 274
    Index 297

Acknowledgements

The publication of this book would not have been possible without the great support and advice of many people, institutions, and organizations. Some chapters of this book are derived from my second Ph.D. dissertation, completed at the Centre for Comparative Literature at the University of Toronto in 2007. I had been studying the self-translation of Eileen Chang's works for over twenty years. During the writing, rewriting, and revising processes, I felt in love with the work, particularly when new material would appear, and did not realize at first that two decades had passed.

I am grateful to my first Ph.D. supervisor Kwok-kan Tam for his precious teaching in the fascinating field of Comparative Literature at the Chinese University of Hong Kong, and for continuously supporting my academic pursuits since my graduate studies. I am also thankful to my second Ph.D. supervisors, Linda Hutcheon and Johanna Liu, for their indispensable guidance and moral support in the writing and completion of my dissertation on Eileen Chang at the University of Toronto. Moreover, I would like to express my gratitude and appreciation to Atsuko Sakaki and Ming Xie, the committee members for my dissertation on Eileen Chang, for their valuable comments and suggestions for improving the quality of my work. I had the honour of receiving a visiting scholar position in the Department of East Asian Languages and Civilization at Harvard University in 2020–2021. Unfortunately, I was not able to take up this position due to the outbreak of the COVID-19 pandemic. Nevertheless, I was so blessed to receive the very insightful advice from my supervisor David Der-wei Wang. I would like to thank Christopher Lee, Hsiu-Chuang Deppman, and Susan Ingram, who devoted their precious time to, and made great effort in, commenting on individual chapters.

I presented some of my chapters at annual conferences, meetings, workshops, seminars, and talks for the following organizations and institutions: Association for Asian Studies, Association for Asian Studies in Asia, Association for Asian Studies New England Region, American Comparative Literature Association, Canadian Asian Studies Association, Canadian Comparative Literature Association, International Conference of Institutes and Libraries for Chinese Overseas Studies on Chinese through the Americas, International Congress of the Federation for Modern Languages and Literatures, Modern Language Association, Society for Cinema and Media Studies, Brock University, Chinese University of Hong Kong, Hang Seng University of Hong Kong, Harvard University, Kyungpook National University, National Taipei University of Technology, Pennsylvania State University, University of British Columbia, University of Calgary, University of California, Los Angeles, University of

London, University of Hong Kong, University of Ottawa, University of Toronto, and York University.

I am very thankful to my colleagues, friends, and participants in conferences, meetings, workshops, seminars, and conversations for their very generous and helpful suggestions, questions, and comments: Albert Braz, Yu Chang, Pietro Giordan, Doris Hambuch, Carole Hoyan, Nicole Huang, Karen Kingsbury, Kaby Kung, Wendy Larson, Charles Andrew Laughlin, Leo Ou-fan Lee, Pei-yin Lin, Christopher Lupke, Kam Louie, Yue Meng, Paul Morris, Kenny Ng, Andrew Parkin, Markus Reisenleitner, Tze-Lan Sang, Haun Saussy, Shuang Shen, Elena Siemens, Mingwei Song, Josh Stenberg, Mark Terry, Chialan Sharon Wang, Jiwei Xiao, Terry Siu-han Yip, and many colleagues and friends too numerous to mention here; my apologies to those whose names are not listed.

I would like to express my gratitude to Xiao-He Ma, Librarian for the Chinese Collection, Harvard-Yenching Library at Harvard University, for going above and beyond in helping me to obtain materials on Eileen Chang Studies. I also thank the staff members of Shanghai shi dang'an guan (Shanghai Municipal Archives), the University of Southern California Libraries, and the University of Hong Kong Libraries for facilitating the acquiring of Eileen Chang archival materials. I also thank my research assistants, Jiashuo Li, Ada Wang, and Yuting Shi, from York University, for their work in data collection.

My special thanks to Qin Higley, former Senior Acquisition Editor of Asian Studies, and Stephanie Carta, Associate Editor of Asian Studies, both from Brill Academic Publishers; to the anonymous reviewers for their critical and productive comments; and to the staff members of the Press involved in this project.

I thank Alicia Filipowich, the coordinator of the York Centre for Asian Research at York University, for her help with all my grant applications and reimbursement for this book project. I am very grateful to Cindy Chopoidalo for her meticulous and excellent copyediting of my book manuscript. I really appreciate her efficiency, dedication, and professionalism. I am indebted to the Social Sciences and Humanities Research Council of Canada and York University's Faculty of Liberal Arts and Professional Studies for sponsoring the publication of this book.

I would like to express my greatest gratitude to my parents for their appreciation of and faith in me. I am particularly thankful to my husband Jack Hang-tat Leong for his tremendous support, love, and care in my everyday life. I am so grateful for my two precious children who are the greatest blessing in my life. Above all, I thank God for the beautiful sunrise, wonderful sounds of nature, and the delicacy of snowflakes that inspire me with faith, joy, and peace to enjoy happy moments and persevere through the difficult times of my life.

Notes about Chinese Romanization and Translation

The Hanyu Pinyin romanization system is generally used in this book. Some Chinese names of places, people, and other proper nouns that are well established in other forms are also used. For Pinyin spellings, apostrophes or hyphens are usually not used; however, when syllables are connected together, an apostrophe will be used. For Chinese given names and words that are connected to make new meanings, the Pinyin romanizations are joined together without a space. Transliterations of Chinese words may be italicized. All translations are mine unless otherwise stated.

Illustrations

1 The College Preparatory Course, St. Mary's Hall, Shanghai, 1937
   Shanghai Shi Dang'an Guan (Shanghai Municipal Archives)   5
2 Changde Apartment sign, Shanghai (Photo taken in August 2013)
   Photo credit: Jessica Tsui-yan Li   42
3 Changde Apartment, Shanghai (Photo taken in August 2013)
   Photo credit: Jessica Tsui-yan Li   42
4 University of Hong Kong Fung Ping Shan Library, Hong Kong (Photo
   taken in July 2023)
   Photo credit: Jessica Tsui-yan Li   65
5 Zhang Maoyuan, Eileen Chang, and Niuer
   Photo credit: USC Digital Library. Ailing Zhang (Eileen Chang) Papers
   Collection   70
6 Nephew, Zhang Zhiyi, Nephew, Huang Suqiong, Zhang Maoyuan, Tianjin
   Photo credit: USC Digital Library. Ailing Zhang (Eileen Chang) Papers
   Collection   71
7 Huang Suqiong, London, 1926
   Photo credit: USC Digital Library. Ailing Zhang (Eileen Chang) Papers
   Collection   73
8 Eileen Chang and Zhang Zijing, West Lake, Hangzhou
   Photo credit: USC Digital Library. Ailing Zhang (Eileen Chang) Papers
   Collection   73
9 Eileen Chang's maternal grandmother, Changsha, Hunan
   Photo credit: USC Digital Library. Ailing Zhang (Eileen Chang) Papers
   Collection   74
10 Li Juou, Eileen Chang's paternal grandmother
   Photo credit: USC Digital Library. Ailing Zhang (Eileen Chang) Papers
   Collection   76
11 Zhang Peilun, Eileen Chang's paternal grandfather
   Photo credit: USC Digital Library. Ailing Zhang (Eileen Chang) Papers
   Collection   76
12 Yanying and Eileen Chang, Shanghai, 1944
   Photo credit: USC Digital Library. Ailing Zhang (Eileen Chang) Papers
   Collection   78
13 Eileen Chang and Li Xianglan, Shanghai, 1943
   Photo credit: USC Digital Library. Ailing Zhang (Eileen Chang) Papers
   Collection   79
14 Eileen Chang, Hong Kong, 1954
   Photo credit: USC Digital Library. Ailing Zhang (Eileen Chang) Papers
   Collection   82

ILLUSTRATIONS

15 Eileen Chang, San Francisco, 1961
Photo credit: USC Digital Library. Ailing Zhang (Eileen Chang) Papers
Collection 82

16 Eileen Chang, Washington, D.C., 1966
Photo credit: USC Digital Library. Ailing Zhang (Eileen Chang) Papers
Collection 83

17 Chang, Eileen. "She Said Smiling" unpublished manuscript
Photo credit: USC Digital Library. Ailing Zhang (Eileen Chang) Papers
Collection 138

18 Chang, Eileen. *The Rice-Sprout Song – A Novel of Modern China.* New
York: Scribner's, 1955
Photo credit: Jessica Tsui-yan Li 207

INTRODUCTION

The Practice of Self-Translation in Eileen Chang's Works

Self-translation, in a specific sense, refers to a linguistic and cultural activity in which authors/self-translators transmit, facilitate, and negotiate meanings across at least two different linguistic and cultural systems for their own text, articulating the formation of a multilingual and fragmented identity as opposed to a unified and static monolingual one. In a restorative sense, self-translation enables authors to express a sense of displacement, to revisit the past, and to heal traumatic experiences. In terms of transcultural innovations, this literary and translation practice calls for new genres and writing techniques in comparison and contrast to well-established literary and translation conventions. It also promotes new concepts and words for a different reading public by challenging traditional hermeneutics (Hokenson and Munson 12–14; Klimkiewicz 198–199; Li, "The Politics of Self-Translation: Eileen Chang" 100–101; Stavans 3–10).

I further argue that self-translation, in a broad sense, can be regarded the translation of the author's self from their internal mentality into external articulation, as well as from their self to others. Rather than simply discovering or revealing the true self, authors/self-translators performatively create their self and construct their identity through the meaning-making activity of self-translation. Moreover, self-translation is the authors/self-translators' expression of the sociohistorical and political conditions in which the work and/or the translation is created, as they use their languages to understand and interpret the world around them. Self-translation allows the authors/self-translators to explore and illuminate the various factors that they use to construct themselves in terms of gender, social changes, cultural practices, and global politics.

In translation studies, research and debate on self-translation have become more vigorous and contentious in the twenty-first century, thanks to the flourishing discourses of postcolonialism, globalization, migration, and diasporic studies. The practice of self-translation, however, is underexamined in both literary and translation studies, due to its indispensable requirement of high proficiency almost equally in more than one language for both self-translators and scholars, in addition to its threat to nationalism based on a single lingua franca, a unified culture, and a misconception of its association with idiosyncratic

© JESSICA TSUI-YAN LI, 2025 | DOI:10.1163/9789004730052_002

minority migrants. This book enriches current studies of self-translation by proposing a new hypothesis of theorizing self-translation as a performative act, characterized by its in-betweenness and by the aesthetic freedom that the self-translator enjoys, contextualized within larger debates about translation and the specific practice of self-translation in Chinese history in comparison to its Western counterpart.

This book focuses on the self-translation of Zhang Ailing 張愛玲 (Eileen Chang, 1920–1995), one of the most important Chinese writers of the twentieth century. Although this point is overlooked in most studies of her work, Chang's literary achievements are attributed in part to her ongoing lifelong self-translation of her life experiences and family sagas as well as to her bilingualism and practice of self-translation, which means that her work engages mainly with two languages and their related literary traditions, cultures, and critical traditions; her expertise in Chinese, her mother tongue, is almost matched by her skill in English, her second language. As a Chinese and English bilingual writer and self-translator, she both preserves and transgresses the Chinese and English literary and cultural conventions that provide the larger contexts of this study.

Modern Chinese translation underwent tremendous changes at the turn of the twentieth century with the modernization movement that accompanied the shifting of political powers in China. Western ideas imported to China gradually took shape even as traditional Chinese customs remained. Hybridizations of Chinese and Western literary ideas and techniques appeared in Chinese translation during this era. Growing up in a transcultural aristocratic family during the Republican period (1912–1949), Eileen Chang depicts the cultural negotiation in modern China of the early twentieth century in her self-translations. After moving to Hong Kong in 1952 and then to the United States in 1955, Chang produced self-translations that bridged philosophical divergences and cultural disparities during the Cold War period (1947–1991). Incorporating her autobiographical anecdotes and family sagas against a backdrop of swift sociohistorical transformations in modern China, Chang reveals much in her self-translations about representations of identity construction and agency as alternative practices to the mainstream May Fourth nationalistic discourse and the later political schism of the Cold War, thus constituting part of the legacy of Chinese literary and cultural modernity in translation.

Rather than evaluating whether Eileen Chang's self-translation can truly capture the representations in her earlier texts as would exact copies of "original" texts, in this book I argue that Chang's self-translation is indeed her re-creation, in which she revisits the ideologies embedded in the

INTRODUCTION   3

previous texts from a critical distance, and constructs her notion of cultural in-betweenness through the implicit and explicit re-contextualization of her texts in their different linguistic and cultural systems. Though readers cannot truly reach the author's intention and the text may have an "after-life" of its own, I nonetheless suggest that Chang's intention does occupy a crucial position in her re-interpretation of her own works, though it cannot totally control their meaning. Her self-translations and translated works form an interdependent relationship and suggest a pluralist and non-hierarchical structure for the process of self-translation. Given the examples of Chang's self-translation as a life-long process, I further argue that Chang's self-translation is a performative act that produces representations of identity and agency, which allows her to interpret various aspects of herself constituted by gender, social, cultural, and political circumstances in the world where she resided.

In order to understand precisely the characteristics of Eileen Chang's self-translation, I address the following questions: How does Chang depict and demonstrate identity construction through rewriting her personal stories, family tales, and historical circumstances in her self-translation? What is the relationship between her former texts and self-translations with regard to the hybridized aesthetic ideals that flourished in modern Chinese society in the early twentieth century? How does Chang perform the role of cultural translator in her writing and self-translation? How does Chang execute her power of authorship as self-translator to portray the Cold War imaginary of global modernity in her political fiction and self-translation? This book investigates how and why Chang's self-translation produces representations of identity and agency in their specificities aligned with various political and historical circumstances, ideological presumptions, social institutional forces, linguistic diversities, gender and class power relations, and ethnic and regional experiences.

1 Eileen Chang as a Self-Translator

Eileen Chang's name reflects her transcultural background and experience. Her birth name was Zhang Ying 張煐 (Z. Zhang 319). She was born and raised in Shanghai and lived in Tianjin between 1922 and 1928. Her mother renamed her Eileen Chang when she entered Huang's primary school in Shanghai at the age of ten. The Chinese transliteration of *Eileen* is *Ailing*; *Zhang* is a romanization of her family name in Hanyu Pinyin, while *Chang* is an English transliteration of her family name. Her Chinese name then became Zhang Ailing. She also used pseudonyms such as Shi Min 世民, Liang Jing 梁京, Shuang Lu 霜廬, Fan Siping 范思平, Zhang Aizhen 張愛珍, and Aizhen 愛珍.

Chang's aristocratic family history, associated with the Qing court and army, was an important part of her transcultural upbringing. She was born in Shanghai to a wealthy family with an army and court background. Her grandmother's father was Li Hongzhang 李鴻章 (1823–1901), one of the most influential statesmen of the Qing dynasty. Li was responsible for initiating various kinds of military, industrial, and cultural institutions, as well as signing a number of unequal treaties with foreign countries for the Qing court. Her grandfather was Zhang Peilun 張佩綸 (1848–1903), a high Qing court official known for his advocacy of war against foreign invasion, his criticism of corruption, and his classical Chinese scholarship. Following the downfall of his office, Zhang was recruited to Li's office and married his daughter Li Juou 李菊耦 (1866–1912). Her father, Zhang Zhiyi 張志沂 (Zhang Tingzhong 張廷重 1898–1953), was a classical Chinese language and literature scholar, but was also a morphine and opium addict and a domestic tyrant. Her mother, Huang Suqiong 黃素瓊 (Huang Yifan 黃逸梵 1893–1957) was the daughter of Huang Yisheng 黃翼升 (1818–1894), a naval official in the late Qing dynasty. Huang Suqiong was an avid student of Western art and culture.

Chang was influenced by both Chinese and Western cultures and literatures thanks to her parents' influence and her educational background. Her father specialized in Chinese culture and classical literature, and was also well versed in English, having worked as an English secretary in the Tientsin-Pukow Railway Bureau in Tianjin between 1922 and 1927. Her mother was passionate about Western art and culture, and also had a solid background in Chinese culture and classical literature, teaching her Tang poetry when she was two years old. Beginning at age three, Chang studied classical Chinese literature with a private teacher at home. She finished reading the classical Chinese novel *Hongloumeng* 《紅樓夢》 (*Dream of the Red Chamber*, 1791), at the age of eight. When she was ten years old, she went to Huang's primary school and went immediately into grade four. In 1932, she studied at St. Mary's Hall, which catered especially to upper-class Chinese students in Shanghai with a focus on an English curriculum, and also studied with a Russian piano teacher. Though she was admitted to the University of London with a full scholarship in 1939, she was not able to go there because of the war in Europe. In August 1939, she went to the University of Hong Kong to study literature. Before she could finish her degree, however, she was forced to return to Shanghai, due to the Japanese occupation of Hong Kong between 1941 and 1945 (see Huang, *Hong Kong Connections*). After that, she started to live independently as a writer.

FIGURE 1   The College Preparatory Course, St. Mary's Hall, Shanghai, 1937
SHANGHAI SHI DANG'AN GUAN (SHANGHAI MUNICIPAL ARCHIVES)

Chang's two marriages, the first to a Chinese husband in Shanghai and the second to an American husband in the United States, also became part of her transcultural experience and her transcendence of ideological, linguistic, cultural, and national boundaries. She married Hu Lancheng 胡蘭成 (1906–1981) in 1944 but divorced him in 1947, mainly due to his extramarital affairs. Hu was a famous scholar who collaborated with the Japanese, working in the Propaganda Ministry of the Wang Jingwei 汪精衛 (1883–1944) government in China during the Second Sino-Japanese War in the late 1930s and early 1940s. In February 1956, she met Ferdinand Reyher (1891–1967) in Peterborough, New Hampshire, and married him in New York that August. Reyher was a communist who had been formerly married to Rebecca Hourwich (1897–1987), a famous American feminist. He was also friends with German communist playwright Bertolt Brecht (1898–1956), film director John Huston (1906–1987), and Nobel Literature Prize winner Sinclair Lewis (1885–1951).

As a bilingual writer and self-translator, Chang wrote in both Chinese and English, and translated her own works from Chinese into English and vice versa. Some of her early English publications include "The School Rats Have a Party" (1932), "The Sun Parlor" (1936), "Sketches of Some Shepherds" (1937), and "My Great Expectations" (1937), which appeared in *The Phoenix*, a yearbook published annually by St. Mary's Hall (Wu 59). When she was eighteen, *Shanghai Evening Post* published her English autobiographical essay, "What a Life! What a Girl's Life!" (1938),[1] which she self-translated into Chinese as "Siyu" 〈私語〉 ("Whispers," 1944). In wartime Shanghai, she published three cultural critiques and six film reviews in English in the magazine *The XXth Century* in 1943, and subsequently self-translated them into Chinese. Adopting foreign perspectives to examine her own culture, she wrote three critical essays, "Chinese Life and Fashions" (1943), "Still Alive" (1943), and "Demons and Fairies" (1943), which she later translated into Chinese with more subtlety and irony as, respectively, "Gengyiji" 〈更衣記〉 ("A Chronicle of Changing Clothes," 1943), "Yangren kan jingxi ji qita" 〈洋人看京戲及其他〉 ("Westerners Watching Peking Operas and Other Issues," 1943), and "Zhongguoren de zongjiao" 〈中國人的宗教〉 ("The Religion of the Chinese," 1944). As an enthusiastic movie fan, she had six film reviews published in the "On the Screen" column in 1943: "Wife, Vamp, Child," "The Opium War," "'Song of Autumn' and 'Clouds over the Moon,'" "Mothers and Daughters-in-Law," "'On with the Show' and 'The Call of Spring,'" and "Educating the Family." She translated the first and the last of these film reviews into Chinese as "Jieyindeng" 〈借銀燈〉 ("Borrowing the Silver Spot-light") and "Yingong jiuxueji" 〈銀宮就學記〉 ("Attending a Film School"). These early autobiographical essays, cultural critiques, and film reviews helped to establish her career of self-translation.

Chang rendered her personal experience, family tales, and historical events into works of fiction and self-translation that have remained popular among Chinese readers worldwide to this day. *Liuyan* 《流言》 (*Written on Water*, 1945), *Chuanqi* 《傳奇》 (*Romances*, 1944), and *Zhangkan* 《張看》 (*Chang's Outlook*, 1976) collect most of her essays and several novellas that provide glimpses of her worldviews on various subjects, such as women, gender relations, writing, language, music, dance, and urban lifestyle from her early adulthood to her middle age. Her university studies and lived experience in Hong Kong provided her with much of her literary inspiration. Her "romances of Hong Kong" are featured in seven novellas, including "Qingcheng zhi lian"

---

1 According to her younger brother Zhang Zijing 張子靜 (1921–1997), Chang wrote the essay "What a Life! What a Girl's Life!" at age eighteen to retell the traumatic experience of her teenage years, and published it in the *Shanghai Evening Post* in 1938 (107). In his introduction to Chang's *The Fall of the Pagoda,* David Der-wei Wang explains that the *Shanghai Evening Post* was a Shanghai English-language newspaper run by the Missouri-born newspaperman Carl Crow (1884–1945) (v).

〈傾城之戀〉 ("Love in a Fallen City," 1943), which she based on the life experiences of her family and friends; it was adapted into a stage production in Shanghai in 1944, and many other adaptations have since been produced in Hong Kong and mainland China from the 1980s to the present day. She also reconstructs her childhood and adolescent years in *Duizhaoji – kan lao zhaoxiangbu* 《對照記：看老照相簿》 (*Mutual Reflections – Looking at Old Photo Albums,* 1994), and in her posthumously published semi-autobiographical novels *Xiaotuanyuan* 《小團圓》 (*Little Reunions,* 2009), *The Fall of the Pagoda* (2010), and *The Book of Change* (2010). These essays, short stories, family photo album, and semi-autobiographical novels all inform each other, present different aspects of Chang's identities and agency, and illuminate the performative characteristics of her self-translation.

Exercising her power of authorship as self-translator, Chang produced works of translation and self-translation that provide visions of global integration in the face of the Cold War, after she left mainland China in 1952. During her brief stay in Hong Kong between 1952 and 1955, Chang worked in the United States Information Service (USIS), a regional branch of the United States Information Agency (USIA) that aimed to curb the spread of communism. In the 1950s and 1960s, she actively translated a number of American poems, essays, short stories, novels, and works of literary criticism into Chinese. For example, she translated Ernest Hemingway's (1899–1961) *The Old Man and the Sea* (1952) as *Laoren yu hai* 《老人與海》, published under the pen name Fan Siping 范思平 by *Xianggang Zhongyi chubanshe* 香港中一出版社, in 1952. She used her Chinese name, Zhang Ailing, for the third edition of *Laoren yu hai,* published in 1955. She also translated Marjorie Kinnan Rawling's (1896–1953) *The Yearling* (1938) as *Xiaolu* 《小鹿》 published by *Xianggang Tianfeng chubanshe* 香港天風出版社 in 1953, and retitled *Luyuan changchun* 《鹿苑長春》 when it was republished by *Jinri shijie chubanshe* 今日世界出版社 in 1963. Other translations include part of Ralph Waldo Emerson's (1803–1882) *The Portable Emerson* (1881) as *Aimoshen xuanji* 《愛默森選集》 published by *Xianggang Tianfeng chubanshe* in 1953; and Edward L. Beach's (1918–2002) *Submarine!* as *Haidi changzheng ji* 《海底長征記》, published under the pen name Ai Zhen 愛珍 by *Zhongnan ribao* 《中南日報》 in 1954. She also co-translated Washington Irving's (1783–1895) "The Legend of Sleepy Hollow" (1820) as *Wutou qishi* 《無頭騎士》, published by *Jinri shijie chubanshe* in 1954, and translated the discussion of "Ernest Hemingway" in William Van O'Connor's (1915–1966) *Seven Modern American Novelists* (1964) as "Ouniesi Haimingwei" 〈歐涅斯 · 海明威〉 in *Meiguo xiandai qida xiaoshuojia* 《美國現代七大小說家》, published by *Jinri shijie chubanshe* in 1967. When she was "commissioned" to write two novels featuring anti-communist ideology, she used rhetorical literary techniques to navigate her rather critical position in the debate over Cold War polarization in *The Rice Sprout Song – A Novel of Modern China* (1955), translated into Chinese as *Yangge* 《秧歌》 (*The Rice-Sprout Song*, 1954);[2] and *Chidi zhi lian* 《赤地之戀》 (*The Romance of the Redland*, 1954), translated into English as *Naked Earth – A Novel about China* (1956). Her translations of American works into Chinese, and her writing and self-translation of her two novels in both Chinese and English, demonstrate her position as both a linguistic and a cultural translator navigating between the divisions in the Cold War.

Chang continued to work on several translation projects, with institutional support, after moving to the United States in 1955. In 1956, she was awarded a creative writing scholarship from the Edward MacDowell Colony and the Huntington Harford Foundation, which provided her with space to translate her story "Jinsuoji" 〈金鎖記〉 ("The Golden Cangue," 1943) into English as *Pink Tears*.[3] Based on this story, she wrote *The Rouge of the North* (1967) and its self-translation into Chinese, *Yuannü* 《怨女》 (*Embittered Woman*, 1966), and her translation of "Jinsuoji" into English as "The Golden Cangue" (1971). Her multiple revisions and translations of this tale demonstrate the paradoxical relationship of in-betweenness in all of its versions. Some of her other works written in both Chinese and English include "Stale Mates: A Short Story Set in the Time When Love Came to China" (1956), translated into Chinese as "Wusi yishi – Luo Wentao sanmei tuanyuan" 〈五四遺事——羅文濤三美團圓〉 ("Regret after the May Fourth Movement: The Reunion of Luo Wentao and the Three Beauties," 1957); "Deng" 〈等〉 ("Waiting," 1944), translated into English as "Little Finger Up" (1961); and "Guihuazheng – A Xiao beiqiu" 〈桂花蒸——阿小悲秋〉 ("Steamed Osmanthus: Ah Xiao's Unhappy Autumn," 1944), translated into English as "Shame, Amah" (1962). These works provide examples of her strategies of re-evaluating and re-contextualizing her earlier stories to create new versions seen from different critical perspectives.

Seeking more literary inspiration and job opportunities, Chang went to Taiwan and Hong Kong briefly in 1961. She later wrote "A Return to the Frontiers" (1963), which she translated into Chinese as "Chongfang biancheng" 〈重訪邊城〉 ("Revisiting the Frontier," 1967). During her travels in Taiwan, she also planned to interview Zhang Xueliang 張學良 (Peter Hsueh Chang, 1901–2001), General of the National Revolutionary Army of the Republic of China. Due to political struggles, however, Zhang Xueliang was under house arrest and could

---

2 Though Eileen Chang wrote the English version of *The Rice-Sprout Song* before her Chinese translation *Yangge*, the Chinese version was published first.

3 Chang could not find a publisher to publish *Pink Tears* and later rewrote it into the Chinese novel *Yuannü*.

INTRODUCTION 9

not accept any interview at that time. Nevertheless, Chang did partially finish *The Young Marshal,* which was posthumously published in 2014.[4]

In 1966, Chang became a writer-in-residence at Miami University in Oxford, Ohio. Two years later, she became a scholar at the Bunting Institute of Radcliffe College in Cambridge, Massachusetts, where she translated Han Bangqing's 韓邦慶 (1856–1894) *Haishanghua liezhuan* 《海上花列傳》 (*Flowers of Shanghai,* 1892) from Wu dialect into English; she produced this work between 1967 and 1975, but lost it while moving and then found it again in 1997; in 1981, she also translated it into Mandarin Chinese. She also revised her earlier novel, *Shibachun* 《十八春》 (*Eighteen Springs*), which was serialized in the Chinese newspaper *Yibao* 亦報 in 1950–1951 in Shanghai, into *Banshengyuan* 《半生緣》 (*Half a Lifelong Romance*), published in Taiwan in 1968 with its pro-communist message removed from the end of the earlier version.

From 1969 to 1972, Chang worked at the University of California, Berkeley, translating Communist idioms from official documents published in mainland China. Her speeches on "Chinese Translation" given between 1966 and 1969 at various American universities, including Miami University, Radcliffe Institute for independent Study, and the State University of New York, Albany (C. Lee 2017, 68–70), were posthumously published under the title "Chinese Translation: A Vehicle of Cultural Influence," a reflection of her unique perspectives on Chinese translation and global modernity. She spent more than twenty years writing the Chinese short story "Se, Jie" 〈色，戒〉 ("Lust, Caution," 1977). Her English version of the story titled, "The Spyring/Ch'ing k'ê! Ch'ing k'ê!" (2008), was published posthumously. These and other self-translations produced during the Cold War period present, and represent, her significant role as a cultural translator between China and the West.

Chang is regarded as one of the best-known Chinese writers and public intellectuals of the twentieth century. Her earlier works were enjoyed by many in the Shanghai International Settlement of the 1940s (Gunn 200–231), and most of them were published in the periodicals of the *Yuanyang hudie pai* 鴛鴦蝴蝶派 (Mandarin Ducks and Butterflies School),[5] which offered an alternative

---

4 See Chang's "Letter to Mae Fong Soong" dated October 2, 1961 (*To My Beloved Friends* 1.102).

5 According to Lu Xun's 魯迅 (Zhou Shuren 周樹人, 1881–1936) article "Suowei guoxue" 〈所謂國學〉 ("The So-called Scholar," 1922), the Mandarin Ducks and Butterflies School flourished in Shanghai in the late Qing Dynasty and became popular in the 1920s and 1930s. The classical works of this school describe tragic love stories of intellectual men and beautiful women. Representative authors of this movement include Xu Zhenya 徐枕亞, Chen Diexian 陳蝶仙, and Li Dingyi 李定夷; some of their publications include *Minquansu* 《民權素》 (*Rights of Citizens*), *Xiaoshuo congbao* 《小說叢報》 (*Fiction's Serial Paper*), *Xiaoshuo*

narrative to the revolutionary literature that dominated the literary scene in China during the May Fourth Movement.[6] Chang's works are famous for their effective use of symbolism, their characters' psychological and moral sophistication, their depictions of relationships between women and men, their sense of desolation, their detailed depictions of the daily lives of the bourgeoisie in Shanghai and in Hong Kong against a backdrop of wars, the downfall of an aristocratic family as well as of the country, and the incorporation and transgression of Western and Chinese literary and cultural norms. Some of these themes and literary techniques, however, do not truly belong to the Mandarin Ducks and Butterflies School, and Chang was invested in the May Fourth Movement in her own critical and affective way.

Chang's literary reputation faded drastically after the Sino-Japanese War ended in 1945, as she was criticized for her relationship with her first husband Hu Lancheng, a famous writer and collaborator in the Japanese-occupied territory. The establishment of the Communist regime in 1949 became an additional obstacle to her pursuit of a writing career because of her aristocratic background. She and her works were not mentioned in the official literary histories of the People's Republic of China in the following decades, mainly due to the anti-Communist stance present in her novels *The Rice-Spout Song* and *Naked Earth*. In the early 1960s, Chinese American literary scholar Hsia Chih-tsing 夏志清 (1921–2013) reasserted her significance and positioned her in the modern Chinese literary canon; subsequently, her work regained popularity in Taiwan, Hong Kong, and Chinese diaspora communities. With the re-evaluation of Chinese literary history in the post-Mao era and the efforts to rediscover the cultural history of Shanghai and remake it into an international city, Chang's works became popular again in mainland China. Her writings have had an enormous impact on contemporary Chinese writers; for instance, young women writers formed an "Eileen Chang school" in Taiwan and Hong Kong in the 1970s, and in the PRC in the 1980s and 1990s. David Der-wei Wang 王德威 (b. 1969), a scholar of modern Chinese literature, even crowned her

---

xinbao 《小說新報》 (*Fiction's New Paper*), *Libailiu* 《禮拜六》 (*Saturday*), and *Xiaoshuo shijie* 《小說世界》 (*Fiction's World*). Among these publications, *Libailiu* was produced in vernacular language and enjoyed the largest readership, earning the school the alternative name of the Saturday School.

6   The May Fourth Movement was a national salvation movement characterized by anti-imperialism and anti-feudalism. The movement took place in Beijing in 1919, with thousands of students protesting in Tiananmen Square against the foreign presence in China. It was connected to the New Cultural Movement that started in 1916, and was characterized by revolution and Westernization in Chinese culture and literature.

INTRODUCTION

with the title of *zushi nainai* 祖師奶奶 [grand mistress] (see "Zhang Ailing Became Grand Mistress").

2 Translation History in China

Translation activities in China provided the geopolitical and transcultural backgrounds for Eileen Chang's self-translation. Translation has been part of Chinese literary history, particularly along its border, for at least three thousand years. It is an index to China's evolving relationship with the world, crossing linguistic, cultural, geographical, and national boundaries. In this study, I argue that translation is also part of China's global modernity, as a means by which it is opening to the world. During the process of cultural importation, core values of individual, familial, cultural, social, and national identities are challenged and transformed, thus leading to both cultural encroachment and enrichment. Translation manifests itself in the historical transition from dynastic to nationalist rule, in the "break" of modernity, which has turned out not to be a definite break at all, but a certain experience of time to which Chang would return again and again.

The beginning of the long and prolific history of Chinese translation can be traced to the translation of Buddhist Sutras from Sanskrit into Chinese by Indian, Central Asian, and Chinese monks during the Eastern Han Dynasty (AD 25–AD 220). These Buddhist Sutra translations have enriched Chinese literature in terms of literary topics, themes, plot stories, structure, devices, and vocabulary. Approaches to the preaching of Buddhist scriptures in the Tang Dynasty (618–907) inspired mixtures of poetry and essays that have had profound influences on classic works such as *Xiyouji* 《西遊記》 (*Journey to the West*, 1592) and *Hongloumeng* 《紅樓夢》 (*Dream of the Red Chamber*, 1791).

The earliest translations of the Bible into Chinese may have been made as early as AD 300, though the first written record of one dates to AD 635, in the Tang Dynasty, when a missionary from the Nestorian branch of Christianity visited Chang An 長安, the capital of the Tang Empire. There have been many Chinese versions of the Bible since the Tang Dynasty, in classical and vernacular Chinese and mixtures of these, Han Chinese, ethnic Chinese languages, Romanized Chinese, and Guoyu Chinese. The *Shengjing heheben* 《聖經和合本》 (*Chinese Union Version Bible*, 1919) is a foundational work in both the reading and interpretation of translations in the Chinese-speaking world (Xie, *A Brief History* 72–73).

Translations of foreign science and technology texts into Chinese began at the end of the Eastern Han Dynasty. Along with the translations of Buddhist

Sutras came translations of ancient medicine, astronomy, and mathematics texts from India. In AD 632, during the Tang Dynasty, Arabic medical science texts were translated, while translations of works of Western science and technology flourished during the Ming Dynasty (1368–1644). Italian Jesuit missionary Matteo Ricci (1552–1610) introduced the "Shanhai yudi quantu" 〈山海輿地全圖〉 ("Complete Terrestrial Map," 1584), a world map engraved in Nanking, and collaborated with Xu Guangqi 徐光啓 (1562–1633) to translate Euclid's *Stoicheia* (c. 300 BC) into Chinese as *Jihe yuanben* 《幾何原本》 (*The Origin of Geometry*, 1607), a foundation of modern mathematics. In the late Qing Dynasty and the early Republican years, Chinese intellectuals such as Lin Zexu 林則徐 (1785–1850), Wei Yuan 魏源 (1794–1856), Liang Qichao 梁啓超 (1873–1929), Kang Youwei 康有爲 (1858–1927), and Tan Sitong 譚嗣同 (1865–1898) advocated the adoption of science and technology for national salvation (Xie, *A Brief History* 109–124).

The translation of Western knowledge in China, beginning in the sixteenth century, marked a significant cultural movement. Jesuit missionaries who collaborated with the Chinese played important and catalytic roles in translating and promoting Western learning. In the face of both external aggression and internal turmoil, translation activities in the mid-nineteenth and early twentieth centuries were, to a great extent, politically motivated. Apart from Western encroachment, the late Qing era experienced internal uprisings, corrupt bureaucracy, a worsening economy, military deficiency, and social problems that eventually led to its collapse. Chinese intellectuals' responses changed "from reacting to the 'aggressive West' to reacting to the 'progressive West,' yet during this very same period the West had become more aggressive" (Hung 94–95; Wong 111).

In early modern China, translation played a crucial role in politics, with a critical change of attitudes from understanding the barbaric West as a reaction to their aggression, to learning from their advanced skills in order to suppress them. For instance, shortly before the Opium War, Lin Zexu 林則徐 (1785–1850), the commissioner of Guangzhou, authorized translations in order to learn more about the Western powers; one of these was Emerich de Vatel's (1714–1767) *Le Droit des Gens* (*The Law of Nations*, 1758). Though only three paragraphs were completed, the translation introduced the concept of international law to China. In his negotiation with the British regarding their activities on Chinese soil, Lin applied the concepts he learnt from the translation to justify his confiscation of opium. After the end of the Opium War, some Chinese intellectuals began to consider the West a progressive force that could be employed to contain its aggression towards China. Wei Yuan 魏源 (1794–1857), for example, advocated the idea of *shiyi changji yi zhiyi* 師夷長技以

制夷 [learning the superior skills of the barbarians to control the barbarians] in his work *Haiguo tuzhi* 《海國圖志》 (*An Illustrated Gazetteer of the Maritime Countries*, 1844, 1847, 1852) (Wong 113).

After their defeat in the second Anglo-Chinese War (1858–1860), many Chinese intellectuals considered conciliation with the Western powers as a strategy to gain time for self-strengthening and modernization. Hošoi Gungnecuke Cin Wang 和碩恭親王 (Prince Gong), posthumously known as Aisin Gioro Yixin 愛新覺羅奕訢 (1833–1898), initiated a number of modernization programs, including the establishment of the *Tongwen Guan* 同文館 [School of Interpreters/Common Learning], the first Western-language school in China. Tongwen Guan trained translators, interpreters, and government officers in Western languages in order to equip them to deal with foreign affairs. In the 1860s, the *ziqiang yundong* 自強運動 [Self-Strengthening Movement], also known as *yangwu yundong* 洋務運動 [Westernization movement], was implemented, with the aim of modernizing China by acquiring Western knowledge. Many translation activities were launched during this time (Hung 96; Wong 114–118).

Following the first Sino-Japanese War (1895), Kang Youwei 康有爲 (1858–1927) and his disciple Liang Qichao 梁啓超 (1873–1929) advocated the vigorous Hundred-Day Reforms (1898), which were granted by Emperor Guangxu 光緒 (1875–1908). However, a coup d'état authorized by the Empress Dowager Cixi Taihou 慈禧太后 (1835–1908) ended this reform abruptly, since she regarded the reform program as taking power away from her. The Empress Dowager then accepted Zhang Zhidong's 張之洞 (1837–1909) mild reforms that promoted the idea of *zhongxue weiti, xixue weiyong* 中學爲體, 西學爲用 [Chinese learning as principles, Western learning for application]. In modern China, conservatives welcomed Zhang's moderate proposals because Chinese cultural identity could be maintained; however, progressive intellectuals such as Yan Fu 嚴復 (1854–1921) criticized the inadequacy of these reforms (Yan, "Yu waijiaobao zhurenshu" 558–559).

During the early modern period, Chinese intellectuals became more inclined toward Westernization, inspiring many significant Chinese translators and increasing the readership of translations. One such translation, which had a profound effect on its readers, was Yan Fu's *Tianyanlun* 《天演論》 (*On Evolution*, 1898), a partial translation of Thomas H. Huxley's *Evolution and Ethics* (1891). In this translation, Yan introduced Social Darwinism into China and recommended the necessity of adaptation to the changes in the world in order to avoid the possibility of "racial distinctions." Yan's work provided his Chinese readers with possible solutions to the crisis they were experiencing. In order to tackle this national crisis, Liang Qichao called for literary translation to help reform the population. Liang claimed that fiction was the most effective genre for modernization because of its entertaining and far-reaching characteristics. He introduced political novels to educate the public about current affairs, science fiction to encourage scientific thinking, and detective stories to promote law and order.

The most influential fiction translator in the Late Qing period was Lin Shu 林紓 (1852–1924). While other scholars orally interpreted and translated foreign works into vernacular Chinese for him, Lin rendered the oral translation into *wenyanwen* 文言文 [written classical Chinese]. Working in collaboration, Lin translated 163 works by 98 writers from 11 countries. Most of these were works of patriotic fiction in which political elements were highlighted or even added. For example, he translated Harriet Beecher Stowe's (1811–1896) *Uncle Tom's Cabin* (1852) as *Heinu yutian lu* 《黑奴籲天錄》(*The Record of Negro Slave Calls Upon Heaven,* 1901). In his famous preface to this work, Lin compared the suffering inflicted on black slaves to the hardships endured by Chinese workers in the United States, so as to warn the Chinese that the possibility of their defeat by the West might lead to China's partition and enslavement (Wong 124–125).

In the early Chinese Republican era (1920s–1930s), a new generation of intellectuals yearned for a more thorough reform of *quanpan xihua* 全盤西化 [wholesale Westernization], a term formally coined by Hu Shi 胡適 (1891–1962) in 1929 (Wong 128). Translations of Western works were carried out on a large scale in the modern period, and Eileen Chang pointed out that

> Tolstoy, Marx, Bertrand Russell and the philosopher John Dewey were translated in the *New Youth* from 1915 on, with a special issue on Ibsen because Dr. Hu Shih, the leading figure in the May Fourth, believed that a wholesome individualism would be a corrective for the excesses of the familial system that, under neo-Confucianism, took away many fundamental human rights.
>
> "Chinese Translation" 492

In the sociohistorical context of Western learning as self-strengthening, Chinese writers were motivated to acquire proficiency in the English language and cultural knowledge, particularly by studying or working aboard. For instance, Lin Yutang 林語堂 (1895–1976), a prominent Chinese-English bilingual writer and self-translator, enjoyed an international literary reputation and became a role model for Eileen Chang's engagements in self-translation.

Eileen Chang contributed much to the modern Chinese history of translation. Her practice of self-translation is distinctive among Chinese writers and

INTRODUCTION

translators because she continued this practice throughout her literary career, translating not only other writers' works but also her own from Chinese into English and vice versa. She translated and constructed her evolving selves from childhood to adolescence, and into adulthood and old age, in her memoirs, semi-autobiographical novels, short stories, poems, essays, works of fiction, and family photo albums. She continuously interpreted and translated the world in which she was situated, including Shanghai, Tianjin, Hong Kong, Wenzhou, Taiwan, Japan, Toronto, and many cities and towns in the United States, in her work, spanning significant Chinese and global political events such as the Republican years (1912–1949), the second Sino-Japanese war (1937–1945), the Chinese civil war (1927–1949), the establishment of the Chinese Communist regime (1949), the Cold War (1947–1991), and the post-Cold War era.

3   Theories of Self-Translation

Self-translation activities often flourish during the birth of a political state, as self-translators embrace both domestic and foreign literature to address readers with different linguistic and cultural backgrounds in order to elevate the position of the translators' own literature and culture in the world. Under systems of imperialism or colonialism, writers may be mandated to write in governing languages. In anti-imperialist or postcolonial periods, these writers may self-translate their own works in their mother tongue. Writers who are engaged in voluntary or involuntary exile in foreign countries due to political turmoil, economic depression, or religious oppression at home may write and self-translate their works in both their native language and their adopted country's language. Globalization has also played a key role in more recent decades in enhancing resettlements and voyages, as writers with transcultural and translingual abilities may self-translate their works for readers in different parts of the world. Some representative self-translators include Nicole Oresme (1325–1382), Charles d'Orléans (1394–1465), Rémy Belleau (1528–1577), John Donne (1571–1631), Sor Juana Inés de la Cruz (1648–1695), Carlo Goldoni (1707–1793), Rabindranath Tagore (1861–1941), Giuseppe Ungaretti (1888–1970), Vladimir Nabokov (1899–1977), Samuel Beckett (1906–1989), Stefan George (1927–1933), and Rosario Ferré (1938–2016) (see Hokenson and Munson).

Self-translations in both Chinese and English have blossomed since the beginning of the twentieth century. Chinese scholars and intellectuals in the newly established Republic of China (1919–1949) launched a national salvation project that incorporated extensive translations of foreign literature, culture, science, and technology into Chinese, which nurtured Chinese writers with transcultural perspectives. Political unrest at home, economic advancement abroad, and/or personal lived experiences prompted some Chinese bilingual writers to migrate, exile, or travel to foreign countries. Many of these writers self-translated their works in order to reach readers of different markets, while some Chinese self-translators published their works in both Chinese and English simply to establish world literary fame. For example, modern Chinese writers such as Dai Wangshu 戴望舒 (1905–1950), Hsiung Shih-I 熊式一 (Xiong Shiyi, 1901–1991), Liang Zongdai 梁宗岱 (1903–1983), Bian Zhilin 卞之琳 (1910–2000), Lin Yutang 林語堂 (1895–1976), and Ling Shuhua 凌叔華 (Su-hua Ling Chen, 1900–1990) practiced self-translation while or after living abroad. Bilingual writers and self-translators such as Yip Wai-lim 葉維廉 (b. 1937), Kenneth Hsien-yung Pai 白先勇 (b. 1937), and Yu Kwang-chung 余光中 (1928–2017) were born in mainland China, educated in Taiwan, and spent a prolonged period of time in the United States. Self-translators with Chinese and other linguistic and cultural heritages, such as Amis, Khmer, Manchu, Mongolian, Thai, Tibetan, Vietnamese, and Uyghur, are perhaps beyond the scope of this book, but are worthy of further investigation.

Among contemporary theories of translation, self-translation has received insufficient attention, and the transcultural features of self-translation have thus not been adequately examined. For this reason, I shall attempt here to define several major theoretical innovations that can more precisely describe the specific characteristics of self-translation. This section investigates self-translation as a reconstruction of the self, the paradoxical relationship between a "former text/version" and a translation, the difference between self-translation and translation done by others, and the performativity of self-translation. In this discussion, I prefer the terms "former text/version" and "source text" to "original text," because the term "original text" denotes and connotes authenticity and influence, while the former names avoid such hierarchical connotations. Moreover, the "former text" or "source text" may be a translation itself or an adaptation of an earlier text, and its originality can be difficult to trace. Though it comes afterwards, the translation is not necessarily a second-rate production that is "influenced" by the "original" text. I will use the terms *Chinese text/version*, *English text/version*, or the title of the work in question directly, depending on the circumstances.

Modern Chinese translation theory focuses on translation criteria and on the debate between faithful translation and free translation. In the late nineteenth century, Yan Fu's (1854–1921) triple translation criteria of *xin* 信 [faithfulness], *da* 達 [fluency], and *ya* 雅 [elegance], stated in the Preface to *Tianyanlun* ("Tianyanlun yi liyan" 1–2), became the most influential theory of modern Chinese translation. Shortly before the publication of Yan Fu's theory,

INTRODUCTION

the lesser-known grammarian Ma Jianzhong 馬建忠 (1845–1900) outlined three translation requirements in *Nishe fanyi shuyuan yi* 《擬設翻譯書院議》 (*On Establishing a Translation Institution,* 1894).[7] Ma argues that a translator should be fluent in two languages, fully understand the source texts, and ensure there is no discrepancy between the source text and the translation, prioritizing fidelity to the source text. Similarly, based on Yan Fu's theory, Lin Yutang (1895–1976) ranks fidelity as the first criterion of a good translation, coherence as the second, and elegance the third.

The May Fourth Movement promoted the introduction of foreign literature to China. Lu Xun 魯迅 (Zhou Shuren 周樹人, 1881–1926), one of the most important writers in modern China, translated more than two hundred literary works from fourteen countries. In his famous essay "Yingyi" 〈硬譯〉 ("Strict Translation," 1930), he argues that faithfulness is the most significant element of a translation. According to Lu Xun, translation is a creative work, but one that is different from other works of literature, and his translations were intended to introduce foreign cultures and literary styles to China for the sake of national salvation. Applying his theory into practice, he and his younger brother Zhou Zuoren 周作人 (1885–1967) published *Yuwai xiaoshuo ji* 《域外小說記》 (*Foreign Fiction Reader,* 1906–1909), a collection of translated works from Russia and Eastern Europe.

In his correspondence with Lu Xun, leftist writer and translator Qu Qiubai 瞿秋白 (1899–1935) expresses a similar view on translation: he agrees that translators should prioritize fidelity to the meaning, syntactic structure, and writing style of the source text. He also claims that faithfulness and intelligibility are equally important to a translation, and that new words and expressions from foreign languages can be appropriated to enrich the Chinese language. Although Qu regarded Yan Fu's notion of elegance as an obstacle to the faithfulness and fluency of the translation (Qu 4), he seems to have overlooked Yan's idea that elegance can be used in the service of faithfulness. In the 1890s, when the majority of Chinese intellectuals still used the classical form of the language in their works, Yan's promotion of elegance in translation was aimed

---

7   Ma Jianzhong's and Yan Fu's translation theories coincide with that of Alexander Fraser Tyler (1747–1814). Tyler read an essay on "Translation" in the Royal Society in Edinburgh in 1790, and published the book *Essay on the Principles of Translation* in 1791. Tyler argues that a good translation should incorporate the meanings, style, and readability of the original work: "I) That the Translation should give a complete transcript of the ideas of the original work. II) That the style and manner of writing should be of the same character with that of the original. III) That the Translation should have all the ease of original composition" (29). See https://bibdig.biblioteca.unesp.br/bitstream/handle/10/6622/essay-on-the-principles-of -translation.pdf?sequence=3&isAllowed=y.

at gaining the support of more traditional intellectuals for literary and cultural reform (Wong 105–106).

Yan Fu's translation theory of *xin, da, ya* continues to assert its influence on Chinese translation theory, though the original theory has since been enhanced with new terminology and new interpretations. For example, Fu Lei 傅雷 (1908–1966), a famous translator of French literature in Modern China, advocated what he called *shengsi* 神似 [the imitation of the spirit] of the source text. In his preface to the second edition of *Gaolaotou* 《高老頭》 (*Old Man Gao*, 1950), a translation of Honoré de Balzac's *Le Père Goriot*, Fu argues that "In terms of effect, translation is like painting a picture. What is more important is the resemblance of the spirit rather than the form" (68), in which the "spirit" of the source text consists of its ideas, emotions, and style. In a similar vein, Qian Zhongshu 錢鐘書 (1910–1998), a well-known modern Chinese writer, established his "transmigration theory" in his discussion of Lin Shu's literary translation (Qian 302). "Transmigration" is a concept borrowed from Buddhism, which in this context refers to the transfer of the soul from the source text to the translation.

Based on Yan Fu's translation model of faithfulness, fluency, and elegance, Lu Xun and Zhou Zuoren favour fidelity to the syntactic structure and writing styles of foreign works, whereas Fu Lei and Qian Zhongshu prefer fidelity to the source texts' meaning, spirit, or soul. Although these scholars seem to be adhering to the notion of accuracy or faithfulness, they are also creating larger models that also admit, if unwittingly, the difficulty of faithfulness as such: being faithful to meaning, spirit, or soul would excuse them from not being entirely faithful to form, and vice versa. Nevertheless, fidelity remains the common principle in the practice of translation, though translators may disagree on whether fidelity to meaning or to form is more important. To join the debate, I argue that first of all, being absolutely faithful to either meaning or form would be almost unachievable, if not impossible, because all languages have their own unique linguistic systems and carry their cultural meanings in specific historical contexts. Faithfulness to meaning and/or to form, however, are not necessarily mutually exclusive. When such a dilemma occurs, the translator can decide case by case, depending on the genres of the source texts. For example, whereas poetry and verse might require more emphasis on form, essays and documents might demand more accuracy of meaning.

Western translation theories from antiquity to the late nineteenth century provoked similar debates on language and culture in the areas of rhetoric and linguistics. A rough survey of Western translation theories will be helpful for further discussion. In early antiquity, some influential Roman orators, such as Cicero, Pliny the Younger, and Quintilian, regarded translation as a pedagogical

INTRODUCTION 19

exercise in favour of sense-for-sense translation. For instance, Cicero argues, "I did not hold it necessary to render word for word, but preserved the general style and force of the language" (365; qtd. in Venuti, *The Translation Studies Reader* 13). Moreover, Horace's *Ars Poetica* (*The Art of Poetry*, c. 18 BC) advocated free translation of Greek texts that might inspire Latin poets. On the other hand, the grammarian or "interpreter" rendered "word-for-word" translation in terms of linguistic and textual analysis for academic purpose.

In late antiquity, Aurelius Augustine Hipponensis's *De doctrina Christiana* (AD 428) urged for the authoritative adherence of the Greek version of the Bible to the Hebrew Scriptures written in the third century, though the translation was mainly divinely inspired (Venuti, *The Translation Studies Reader* 14–15). Jerome's *Letter to Pammachius* (AD 395) also asserts sense-for-sense translation: "Indeed, I not only admit, but freely proclaim that in translation (interpretation) from the Greek – except in the case of Sacred Scripture, where the very order of words is a mystery – I render not word for word, but sense for sense" (23). From the Middle Ages to the Renaissance, as translations into vernacular languages became more prevalent, most commentators followed the style of rhetorical sense-for-sense translation. During the sixteenth and seventeenth centuries, French translators such as Nicolas Perrot d'Ablancourt popularized the domestication of foreign texts for receiving linguistic and cultural readerships, a trend that further influenced English commentaries on translation in the eighteenth and nineteenth centuries.

In contrast to the developments in French and English translation, German translators in the eighteenth century preferred a foreignizing approach to translation. For instance, in his 1813 lecture to the Berlin Academy of Sciences, Friedrich Schleiermacher argues, "Whatever, therefore, strikes the judicious reader of the original in this respect as characteristic, as intentional, as having an influence on tone and feeling, as decisive for the mimetic or musical accompaniment of speech: all these things our translator must render" (52). Schleiermacher considered foreignizing translation a nationalistic strategy to strengthen the German language and literature and counteract French political domination over German-speaking regions. Lu Xun's ideas of asserting violence on the receiving language and culture through foreignizing translation bear some resemblance to Schleiermacher's approach. The German tradition was, however, criticized by philosophers such as Johann Wolfgang von Goethe and Friedrich Nietzsche, who were concerned about the inevitable appropriation of foreign texts in translation to serve German cultural and political agendas.

Western translation studies in the twentieth and twenty-first centuries have engaged with an enormous variety of theories and methodologies that have reflected and influenced developments in linguistics, such as pragmatics, critical discourse analysis, and computerized corpora, and have themselves inspired linguistic studies of the process and outcomes of translation. For instance, Basil Hatim and Ian Mason conducted nuanced examinations of the style, genre, discourse, and pragmatics of translation, while Catford applied Hallidayan linguistic theory to investigate word and sentence in translation (Venuti, *The Translation Studies Reader* 273). Literary and cultural theories such as poststructuralism, postcolonialism, feminism, Marxism, and globalization have been increasingly intertwined with translation studies, and these interconnections have demonstrated the factors that influence the social construction of identities, such as ideologies, gender, sexuality, ethnicity, race, class, and nation.

Gayatri Spivak, for instance, argues that "Tracking commonality through responsible translation can lead us into areas of difference and different differentiations" (323); furthermore, she suggests that translation should respect the linguistic, cultural, and geopolitical terrains of the source text. In the twenty-first century, translation studies has continued to grow as an academic discipline with more acute divisions between linguistics-oriented approaches in pragmatic translator training programs in various institutions, and literary and cultural approaches to theoretical concepts and research methodologies in translation research. The growth of translation studies has also brought re-evaluations of critical points such as the agency of the translators and other parties involved in the translation process and the impact of globalization on the world literary and translation hierarchical system.

Self-translation, specifically, can be considered the translation of one's self from the mind to words, as well as from one's self to others, in a broad and general sense; and the author's translation of their own work from one language into another in a specific sense and common usage. In *On Translation,* Paul Ricœur argues that there are three levels of translation: the first level is a mental translation as a revealing of the inner self to the outer self, from the unconsciousness mind to the consciousness mind, and from the private domain to the public domain (Kearney xv). In Ricœur's words, "This is about much more than a simple internalization of the relationship to the foreign, in accordance with Plato's adage that thought is a dialogue of the soul with itself – an internalisation that would transform internal translation into a simple appendix to external translation" (24). Thus, he argues the articulation of the mind in self-translation.

The second level of self-translation refers to translating meanings from oneself to the other; as Ricœur contends, "There is something foreign in every other. It is as several people that we define, that we formulate, that we explain, that we try to say the same thing in another way" (25). According to Ricœur, self-understanding is achieved through the negotiation of signs, symbols, and texts. The self is discovered after it is translated to the other and returned to itself in a modified way, "soi-même comme un autre." Where the first and second levels of translation involves the internal and external translation of the self, the third level of translation adheres to the linguistic paradigm of translation, as it encompasses the translation of meaning from one language to another in contemporary usage.

Based on, but different from, Ricœur's explication of different levels and paradigms of translation, I further argue that rather than simply revealing the true self, self-translation functions as a performative act: the author/translator's self-identity is constructed through the process of self-translation. The idea of performativity was formulated by the English philosopher John Langshaw Austin in the 1950s. In the William James Lectures series delivered at Harvard University in 1955, Austin proclaimed his theory of speech acts, in which an utterance does not describe a situation but is an event or an action itself: "to utter the sentence (in, of course, the appropriate circumstances) is not to *describe* my doing or to state that I am doing it: it is to do it" (6; qtd. in Loxley 8). Jacques Derrida further explored Austin's speech act theory in his engagement with theories of deconstruction, which questions the presumptive boundary between "real" and "fictional" utterances. Feminists and queer theorists such as Judith Butler and Eve Kosofsky Sedgwick applied these constitutive and derivative characteristics of language in cultural politics and claimed that identities of sex, gender, and sexuality were socially and culturally constructed rather than biologically determined (Loxley 1–3).

In regard to Ricœur's translation theory and Austin's theory of speech acts, I propose that the meaning-making characteristics of language give rise to the power of self-translation in the construction of self-identity. Self-translators form their identity by articulating themselves from the inner self to the outer self, from the unconscious to the conscious, and from the private to the public. Moreover, self-translators make this declaration by announcing their identity to the other and also into other linguistic and cultural systems. During this journey, new experiences and perspectives are created as, travelling around and through various domains of minds, languages, and cultures, the self-translator establishes and presents new representations of their identity and their relation to other people and the world. It is through self-translation that the author/translator's identity is performatively constructed.

The relationship between a source text and its self-translation can be situated in the Chinese and Western debates on translation studies with regard to the spectra of faithful to free translation and of domestication to foreignization, and to the entanglement of translation with linguistic, literary, and cultural theories. I contend that any translation exists as a paradox: it "represents" the source text in its rendition of plots and characters, but cannot "reproduce" it completely, as it inevitably presents the source text using semiotic, semantic, and discursive strategies from another linguistic and cultural system. In "The Task of the Translator: An Introduction to the Translation of Baudelaire's Tableaux Parisiens," Walter Benjamin argues that a translation adds meaning to the source text over time, and thus contributes to its "afterlife," provoking new interpretations in "the age of its fame" (17). He further points out that "the language of a translation can – in fact, must – let itself go, so that it gives voice to the *intentio* of the original not as reproduction but as harmony, as a supplement to the language in which it expresses itself, as its own kind of *intentio*" (21). Benjamin recognizes that the language of a translation will transform the meaning of the source text, and for that reason, he sees the translation not as "repetition" but as "harmony" and as a "supplement" to the earlier text, offering it additional meaning. I further argue, however, that the language of a translation carries different connotations, ones in which the hierarchy of political, ethical, and social values may differ and, therefore, might actually subvert those of the source text. Accordingly, even as the translation may be in harmony with the source text, it may also be a challenge to that text.

As a practice, translation is neither totally new nor completely dependent on the source text as a product. Some translation scholars grant translation an independent status; for instance, as Brian T. Fitch notes of another famous self-translator, Samuel Beckett: "we have two distinct and indeed autonomous textual systems, each of which has to be studied in its own right. Thus interdependence of the two texts, posited earlier, initially has to be placed within parentheses: interdependence now gives way to independence" (33). In my opinion, although translation transforms the source text, it cannot, by definition, ever be independent because the same writer is responsible for both, and the translation renders the content and styles of the source text.

Focusing on the specific practice of self-translation, I argue that a self-translation can only partially destabilize the discourse of the source text because it still uses the forms of representation and structure of the earlier text, and from a position of proximity that an outside translator cannot attain. Its paradoxical nature, nevertheless, allows it to preserve the source text and potentially challenge it with the same tools. Supplementary meaning is, therefore, inevitably generated for the source text because the translation uses a different language, with its own cultural connotations, and the self-translator is thus situated in temporal and spatial distances from their position as author.

INTRODUCTION   23

The zone between faithfulness towards and betrayal of the author's own source text is the space of self-translation; as Jacques Derrida argues, "any given translation, whether the best or the worst, actually stands between the two, between absolute relevance, the most appropriate, adequate, univocal transparency, and the most aberrant and opaque irrelevance" ("What Is a 'Relevant' Translation?" 427). Self-translations oscillate between established discourses embedded in the source texts and counter-discourses constructed in translations. Cultural difference cannot be transcended when additional meaning is created without resolving these conflicting discourses, thus producing a state of in-betweenness. This is a notion of bridging the gap between author and self-translator, source text and self-translation, author and reader. Such breaking down of the boundaries and hierarchies between various dichotomies allows us to perceive multiple cultural views, as the transcultural elements of Eileen Chang's self-translations demonstrate.

The major feature distinguishing self-translation from translation done by others is that the author as the translator is in a more powerful and liberated position: the self-translator knows better what they intend to convey in the source text, while other translators are, in varying degrees, denied access to authorial intention; for instance, a close friend of the author in collaboration would have a greater sense of their intention than someone several generations removed from the author's lifetime and culture. Neither, of course, would know exactly what the author meant by the source text, but someone who knew the author well, with communication, would be in a good position to determine at least some of what they intended, while a translator from a future generation and culture would rely more on conjecture based on what they knew of the author, their other works, and their historical contexts.

Authorial intention "presupposes the preexistence of the fictive universe, subsequently realized by the text, in some nonlinguistic form antedating the actual writing of the work of which the two merged universes would somehow provide a more adequate representation than either one of them alone" (Fitch 28). Although intention cannot be totally neglected when discussing self-translation, the role, if any, of intention has long been highly controversial as a criterion of judgement in literary criticism. Opposition to the critical consideration of authorial intention has been articulated and theorized in various schools of criticism, such as New Criticism, poststructuralism, and New Pragmatism. For instance, W. K. Wimsatt and Monroe C. Beardsley's 1946 essay "The Intentional Fallacy," a formative work of New Criticism, argues that meaning exists on the level of the achieved text and the author's intention is insignificant when determining that meaning.

In his 1968 essay "The Death of the Author," Roland Barthes investigates the institutional force applied to upholding given readings of an author's work, and argues that what we call "the author" is really a "product of society" (4) at a given time, emerging from the Middle Ages and flourishing with the rise of individualism. He concludes his essay with the famous statement "the birth of the reader must be at the cost of the death of the Author" (7). In my view, however, the reader does not have to come into prominence at the cost of the author, and they can both co-exist. In "What Is an Author?" Michel Foucault, much like Barthes, contends that "the author is an ideological product" (22), and analyzes the characteristic traits of the "author function." This function is connected to the institutional system, i.e. the form of ownership, does not affect all discourses universally, is constructed rather than naturally acquired, and does not refer to a real individual who is a complex human being with multiple and contradictory selves (Foucault 14–18). Both Barthes and Foucault challenge the author's claim to sole authority, and both note that consideration of the author and of authorial intention hinders the free circulation, interpretation, and reproduction of a text instead of aiding in the proliferating of its meaning. Similarly, Steven Knapp and Walter Benn Michaels' "Against Theory" (1982), a representative text of New Pragmatism, argues that everything the text means cannot exactly be what the author meant. All these positions assert, in short, that it is worthless to enquire into an author's intention.

Jacques Derrida expressed a more ambiguous attitude toward authorial intention. For example, in *Of Grammatology* (1967), he argues:

> The writer writes in a language and in a logic whose proper system, laws, and life his discourse by definition cannot dominate absolutely. He uses them only by letting himself, after a fashion and up to a point, be governed by the system. In addition, the reading must always aim at a certain relationship, unperceived by the writer, between what he commands and what he does not command of the patterns of the language that he uses.
> 158

On one level, Derrida recognizes the significance of authorial intention, though he acknowledges that it does not control the entire meaning of a text. On another level, he points out the possibility of discrepancy between what the writer intends to convey and what the text ends up saying. In "Signature, Event, Context" (1977), Derrida resurrected, in a sense, the voice of the author: "the category of intention will not disappear; it will have its place, but from that place it will no longer be able to govern the entire scene and system of utterance" (192). According to Derrida, authorial intention cannot be dismissed, but

INTRODUCTION   25

rather is located within structures of signification. Nonetheless, its domination over textual interpretation is rejected.

Authorial intention not only should be recognized, but can be seen in a positive light in terms of interpretation. Instead of a tyrannical power hindering the proliferation of the meanings of a text, authorial intention can serve as yet another guide in the exploration of textual meaning, as "more a way of guiding the reader through a particular experience than a sovereign claim upon the textual center" (Burke 200). The affirmation of authorship is particularly important for literary theories that are intertwined with political agendas, such as feminism and postcolonialism. To recognize authorial intention is, in a way, to acknowledge the diversified identities and subjectivity of women authors, the subaltern, and the Other in general, all of whom are situated in specific sociohistorical contexts (Burke 202–203).

In response to Foucault's question, "What difference does it make who is speaking?" a feminist critic answers: "the difference it makes, in terms of the voices I can persuade you are speaking, occupies a crucial position in the ongoing discussion of difference itself" (Walker 157). I argue here that consideration of authorial intention is vital for self-translation, because it is what gives the self-translator the right to interpret the text produced by the author, who occupies the very same specific gender, class, and ethnic position in a particular sociohistorical period, and also to reconstruct it in a different language and cultural context; such a key is denied to other translators.

Within the Romantic individualistic concept of authorship in the West, authorship is assumed to be reserved for the source text, while the translation is considered a "secondary" representation (Venuti, *The Translation Studies Reader* 50–51). However, this may not be the case in terms of quality, rather than temporality; i.e., the translation comes after the source text. This is, indeed, a stereotype that I attempt to break down in this study. According to this concept of authorship, "the author freely expresses personal thoughts and feelings in the work, which is thus viewed as an original and transparent self-representation, unmediated by transindividual determinants (linguistic, cultural, social) that might complicate authorial identity and originality" (Venuti, *The Translation Studies Reader* 50). This concept is materialized as the *droit moral,* or right of personality. Copyright was developed in the French, German, and Scandinavian legal systems during the nineteenth century and received international recognition with the Rome Revision (1928) of the Berne Convention for the Protection of Literary and Artistic Works (Venuti, *The Translation Studies Reader* 51). The *droit moral* considers the author's personality embodied in the work and grants the author the right "to be identified as author," "to control the first publication," and "to object to a distorted treatment of the work which may damage the author's reputation" (Venuti, *The Translation Studies Reader* 52).

International jurisdiction, in principle, empowers the author to assert an economic right of property over not only the source text, but also the translation; thus, in effect, such jurisdiction denies the authorship of the translator. The self-translator both has the copyright on their own work and is correspondingly free in terms of moral responsibility to the author; therefore, they enjoy much more aesthetic freedom in the translations of their own work than any other translator who would be bound by copyright or even by concerns of loyalty to the source texts. Above all, however, a self-translation is not a mere repetition of the translated work, nor is it simply another interpretation of the earlier work; instead, it articulates the writer's very own re-interpretation and reconstruction of their work (Fitch 31). In the process of translating their own work, the author can follow or freely adapt their earlier representations. The author, rather than the translator, has the final say when the two are not the same person.

Self-translators can interpret their own works by extending, reducing, and even subverting their earlier depictions so as to highlight or rearticulate key issues. A greater space of in-betweenness is produced between the source text and the self-translation because self-translators enjoy the flexibility to travel freely in the liminal space between the two texts. The source text and the self-translation form an interdependent relationship. Self-translation both derives its meaning from and adds value to the source text, while the source text not only gives meaning to but also reveals the significance of the self-translation's changes. The two works cannot be substitutes for one another, thus making the significance of the two texts combined greater than that of either of them alone (Fitch 32). I further argue that self-translation is not a mere work of literary study, but also a condition of in-betweenness interwoven with different languages, cultural discourses, historical events, political ideologies, and entities.

Benjamin has articulated the notion of complementarity between the source text and the translation in "The Task of the Translator": "all suprahistorical kinship of languages rests in the intention underlying each language as a whole – an intention, however, which no single language can attain by itself but which is realized only by the totality of their intentions supplementing each other: pure language" (18). According to Benjamin, pure language binds the source text and the translation to a realm of co-existence. In "Des Tours de Babel," Derrida reworks Benjamin's idea of pure language by noting that "[t]hese languages relate to one another in translation according to an unheard-of-mode. They complete each other, says Benjamin; but no other completeness in the world can represent this one, or that symbolic complementarity" ("Des

INTRODUCTION

Tours de Babel" 201). This interdependency destabilizes hierarchies and breaks through the usual divisions set up between the source text and the translation, as well as between the author and the translator. The chronological order of the source text and translation is also effectively questioned in the case of self-translation. Self-translations, therefore, suggest a non-linear process of translation from one text to another into a different cultural and linguistic system, as well as a more pluralistic and non-hierarchical structure for the process of translation.

Eileen Chang's perspectives on translation can be glimpsed from her speech "Chinese Translation: A Vehicle of Cultural Influence" (1966–1969). Focusing on the significance of translation in modern Chinese literature and culture, Chang highlights the values of translation in terms of cultural exchange. She calls attention to Western cultural biases towards China and attempts to rectify such fallacies by offering her expertise on Chinese literary and cultural development as a vivid reader, literary critic, and cultural historian. For instance, she laments that William Somerset Maugham (1874–1965) despised Song Chunfang 宋春舫 (1892–1938), who advocated European drama, and applauded Gu Hungming 辜鴻銘 (1857–1928), who stubbornly defended Chinese traditions after their brief rendezvous during his visit to China (1919–1920).

Rather than engaging with linguistic characteristics, Chang identifies the intricate relationship between translation and geopolitics. She argues that the West's deep-seated misinterpretations of China resulted in an inability to appreciate modern Chinese literature. Conversely, she notes that while mainland China exhibited xenophobic anti-imperialism during the Cultural Revolution (1966–1976), Taiwan became increasingly commercialized. Her analysis shows the limitation of translation. Catering to her target readers and to her sociopolitical environment, she adjusted the languages, genres, literary styles, topics, tones, and cultural and historical background information of her writing, showing the adaptability, fluidity, and performative characteristics of her self-translation. Her life-long practice of self-translation, nevertheless, demonstrates her concept of translation in general and self-translation in particular, and its complex relationship with culture, history, and geopolitics.

4   Summary of Each Chapter

This book is divided into four parts: (1) translating the self; (2) paradoxical in-betweenness; (3) cultural translation; and (4) political ambivalence. Each part focuses on one significant aspect of Eileen Chang's self-translation. Part One, consisting of three chapters, examines how Chang constructs her identities in her memoirs, semi-autobiographical novels, and family photo album. Chapter One concentrates on her memoirs, as Chang depicts her individual, familial, and social identities while living in China in her essays mostly written in the 1940s, such as "Tiancaimeng" 〈天才夢〉 ("Dream of Genius," 1940), "Gongyu shenghuo jiqu" 〈公寓生活寄趣〉 ("Notes on Apartment Life," 1943), "Tongyan wuji" 〈童言無忌〉 ("From the Mouths of Babes," 1944), and "Siyu" 〈私語〉 ("Whispers," 1944), "Jinyulu" 〈燼餘錄〉 ("From the Ashes," 1944), "Ziji de wenzhang" 〈自己的文章〉 ("Writing of One's Own," 1944), and "Wo kan Su Qing" 〈我看蘇青〉 ("My View on Su Qing," 1945). Her essays and travelogues written in the 1950s and onwards, such as "Yi Hu Shizhi" 〈憶胡適之〉 ("Remembering Hu Shizhi," 1968), "Yijiubaba zhi – ?" 〈一九八八至——?〉 ("1988 to – ?", 1995), and "New England ... China" (2000) illustrate her diasporic identities during her time living in the United States. Chapter Two explores how Chang constructs and develops the multiple and dynamic identities of the characters in her posthumously-published semi-autobiographical novels *Xiaotuanyuan*, *The Fall of the Pagoda*, and *The Book of Change*. Chapter Three analyzes *Duizhaoji – kan lao zhaoxiangbu*, which enigmatically showcases photographs of herself from childhood to adulthood, along with her family members and friends, with captions providing autobiographical anecdotes. Chang produces a legendary self-image in her memoirs, novels, and family photo album as a way to overcome trauma, loss, and nostalgia and to articulate her diasporic experience, and in so doing constructs multiple and dynamic identities, rather than a single essential and static identity.

Part Two includes five chapters that discuss the paradoxical in-betweenness in Chang's short stories and novels. Chapter Four analyzes the multiple revisions and translations of the tale "Jinsuoji," *The Rouge of the North, Yuannü*, and "The Golden Cangue." In this chapter I explore the revisions of the representations of female agency in the four versions of the story, as well as the reasons for their transformations, and their significance. Chapter Five deals with the idea of authorship, with reference to Chang's "Guihuazheng: A Xiao beiqiu," her self-translation into English as "Shame, Amah," and Simon Patton's English translation "Steamed Osmanthus Flower: Ah Xiao's Unhappy Autumn." While Chapter Six examines the re-evaluation of Chinese patriarchal concubinage system in Chang's "Deng" and her English self-translation "Little Finger Up," Chapter Seven analyzes the recontextualization of "Stale Mates: A Short Story Set in the Time When Love Came to China" and her self-translation into Chinese as "Wusi yishi – Luo Wentao sanmei tuanyuan." Chapter Eight examines the relationship among Chang's newly discovered English manuscript "She Said Smiling" (2017), her Chinese short story "Xiangjianhuan" 〈相見歡〉 ("A Joyful Rendezvous") first published in *Huangguan zazi* 《皇冠雜誌》 (*Crown*

INTRODUCTION   29

Magazine) in Taiwan in 1978, her metacommentary essay "Biaoyi xiyi ji qita"
〈表姨細姨及其他〉 (*Biao Aunt, Little Aunt, and Other Issues*, 1979), and
a revised version of "Xiangjianhuan" published in her collection *Wangranji*
《惘然記》 (*A Record of Bewilderment*, 1983), with references to other critics'
commentaries on these works.

Part Three consists of three chapters that examine cultural translation in
terms of interpretation, distanciation, and transformation in Chang's essays
and self-translation. Chapter Nine analyzes Chang's interpretation of Chinese
religions and customs in "Demons and Fairies" and her own translation of this
work into Chinese as "Zhongguoren de zongjiao." Chapter Ten investigates how
Chang adopts foreign perspectives to study Peking Operas in "Still Alive" and
"Yangren kan jingxi ji qita." Chapter Eleven discusses Chang's essay "Chinese
Life and Fashions" and its self-translation into Chinese as "Gengyiji." In this
section I argue that Chang depicts the cultural negotiation in modern Chinese
women's fashion of the early twentieth century, which simultaneously
embraced traditional and modern Chinese cultural elements as well as
Chinese and Western clothing styles, in her essays and drawings.

Part Four features four chapters that investigate how Chang depicts her
transcultural imaginary homelands to deconstruct the literary polarization
of the Cold War, thus manifesting her political ambivalence. Chapter Twelve
examines the ideological ambiguity in *The Rice-Sprout Song* and *Yangge* as
a reconsideration of the novels' authenticity. Chapter Thirteen studies the
postmodern intertextuality in *Chidi zhi lian* and *Naked Earth*, with a focus on
the questions of plot pre-determination and certain publication issues, but
it centres on self-destruction as political protest. Chapter Fourteen focuses
on Chang's travelogue "A Return to the Frontier" and her own translation
and rewriting of this essay into Chinese as "*Chongfang biancheng,*" and discusses how she transgresses geopolitical, cultural, linguistics and personal
frontiers. Chapter Fourteen analyzes her short stories "The Spyring" and "Se,
Jie," and argues that she blurs the boundaries of history and fiction, performance and performativity, and personal and poetic memories in these two
works.

The Conclusion examines the power of performativity of all these interlo-
cutions and adds a vital discussion to the final section of this book. Above all,
it highlights the significance of Chang's life-long practice of self-translation:
she produces a "transcultural hospitality" that fosters a sense of hope and
cross-cultural understanding, and ultimately reconstructs her revolving identities. She depicts the linguistic and cultural negotiation between Shanghai,
Hong Kong, Taiwan, and the United States; between Mandarin, Cantonese, Wu
dialect, Taiwanese, English, and Japanese; between tradition and modernity;

between women and women; and between women and men. She adopts the literary techniques of equivocal contrast, symbolism, intertextuality, and linguistic and cultural hybridity to present the complexity of individual desires, family relations, and the contradictory yearning for both human attachment and reclusiveness at the same time. Most of all, she constructs the identities and agency of her characters and public personas who dare to redefine their roles in twentieth-century Chinese global modernity.

PART 1

Translating the Self

∵

CHAPTER 1

Rewriting the Self in Memoirs

In a broad sense of translation, as explained in the Introduction, authors/ self-translators adopt a performative act of utterance as a medium of translating themselves from the inner unconscious to the outer conscious and from private thoughts to public articulation, and of translating themselves to others, as well as a way of interpretation, as Paul Ricœur points out:

> After Babel, 'to understand is to translate.' This is about much more than a simple internalisation that would transform internal translation into a simple appendix to external translation. This is really about approaching the mysteries of a language that is full of life, and at the same time, giving an account of the phenomenon of misunderstanding, of misinterpretation which, according to Schleiermacher, gives rise to interpretation, the theory of which hermeneutics wants to develop.
>
> *On Translation* 24–25

Based on Ricœur's ideas, I further argue that authors/self-translators, by translating their evolving selves, carry on a dialogue with themselves, bring forth their subjectivity into light in the world, and (re)construct their identities in their writing. Authors/self-translators narrate their lived experience to establish their self-concept and (re)create their identities through language in their writing, which is hitherto considered an act of self-translation.

Self-translation engenders the author/self-translator's self-representation and identity formation, as language constitutes a reality that shapes human consciousness and generates memories. This broad notion of self-translation as the conception of the self can be viewed, by extension, as an alternative form of life writing, a genre that focuses on the lives of individuals. Life writing includes both verbal and visual portraitures in a variety of genres, such as memoirs, essays, letters, short stories, poems, novels, and family photo albums. Either a specific protagonist in the first person, an unspecific literary voice in the third person, or multiple narrators with shifting perspectives convey both the narrator's inner feelings and thoughts and their everyday existence to the readers. When the narrative is presented in a language different from the author/self-translator's first language, some meanings of cultural values and memories are lost, but other meanings are added by critical distance. The portrayal of different characters in the self-narration, nonetheless, manifests

© JESSICA TSUI-YAN LI, 2025 | DOI:10.1163/9789004730052_003

different worldviews of the author/self-translator and proclaims their multiple selves. The representation of the self in self-translation is continuously constituted and reconstituted in the process of life writing, rather than discovered from any essentialist pre-existing conditions. The act of self-translation is the author/self-translator's creative endeavour to construct and transform their self-concept and to produce plural and fluid identities. Such production demonstrates its power of performativity.

Life writing in Chinese literary history has enjoyed long and rich traditions, exhibited in various genres such as biography, autobiography, memoirs, essays, autofiction, and other texts that depict the life experiences, the conception of the self, and the identity construction of characters. Some representative examples include the Han dynasty (206 BC–220 AD) historian Sima Qian's 司馬遷 (c. 145 BC–c. 86 BC) autobiographical narrative "Tai shigong zixu" 〈太史公自序〉 ("Autobiographical Afterword of the Grand Historian," c. 91 BC); Tao Yuanming's 陶淵明 (365–427) self-written epitaph "Zijiwen" 〈自祭文〉 ("A Requiem for My Soul") (427); Lu Yu's 陸羽 (733–804) autobiographical essay "Lu wenxue zizhuan" 〈陸文學自傳〉 ("Autobiography of Imperial Instructor Lu") (761); Yu Dafu's 郁達夫 (1896–1945) autobiographical novella *Chenlun* 《沉淪》 (*Sinking*, 1921); Xie Bingying's 謝冰瑩 (1906–2000) autobiographical novel *Yige nübing de zizhuan* 《一個女兵的自傳》 (*A Woman Soldier's Own Story*, 1936), and Pu Yi's 溥儀 (1906–1967) autobiography *Wo de qian bansheng* 《我的前半生》 (*The First Half of My Life*, also known as *From Emperor to Citizen*, 1960), ghostwritten by Pu Yi's brother Pu Jie 溥傑 (1907–1994). Marjorie Dryburgh and Sarah Dauncey have pointed out the characteristics of the development of life writing in Chinese literary history: "Whereas once, it was possible to understand Chinese auto/biography as overwhelmingly 'Confucian,' didactic, state-centred and masculine, more recent work departures from that apparent norm" (21). Both inheriting and departing from Chinese literary conventions, Eileen Chang's life writing embraces both Chinese and Western precepts and practices, and sometimes even challenges hegemonic values of both cultures, so as to convey individual ideas and to promote personal reputation.

Life writing offers a window to the conception of self that is characterized by and fashioned within various historical and cultural spectra, including gender, class, race, ethnicity, religion, and sexual orientation. The conception of self generally refers to one's individual perception of who they are as a person physically, emotionally, spiritually, and socially, encompassing one's thoughts and feelings about their behaviours, activities, and unique personality traits. One's self-concept develops throughout one's life, influenced by experience, self-reflection and others' responses. It tends to be more pliable during childhood and adolescence, and becomes more solid but continues to develop over time as a person ages (see Rosenberg and Kaplan xi–xv). The self can be further categorized into the individual self, the relational self, and the collective self. The individual self consists of distinctive characteristics that distinguish one from others, the relational self delineates one's relationships with significant others, and the collective self specifies one's means of belonging in social communities (see Sedikides and Brewer). Humanist psychologist Carl Rogers further explicates the conception of self in terms of self-image, self-esteem, and the ideal self (see Rogers).

The traditional Chinese conception of self is relatively relational, and has, to a large extent, been directly or indirectly influenced by Confucianism, with its focus on role fulfillment and ethical practices such as self-cultivation, regulation of the family, serving the nation, and making peace in the world. The Chinese cosmic hierarchy of yin/yang natural order and the unity of Heaven, human, and earth have been extended to human social hierarchy, in which "the self is seen as a process of realizing the different roles a person has at different stages of life" (Tam, "Introduction" xi). In the early twentieth century, however, the Confucian notion of self, regulated by relational, familial, and social roles and obligations, encountered challenges in the form of the importation of European Romantic concepts of self, especially in literary translation. Modern Chinese writers such as Lu Xun 魯迅 (1881–1936), Guo Moruo 郭沫若 (1892–1978), Tian Han 田漢 (1898–1968), Ba Jin 巴金 (1904–2005), Ding Ling 丁玲 (1904–1986), and Xie Bingying 謝冰瑩 (1906–2000), to name but a few, explore and promote a modern Chinese self in their works, which "demonstrate the transformation of the Chinese self from a traditional Confucian relational model to a more Westernized image characterized by Romantic individualism. The Chinese female self is often noted for its transcultural orientation, characterized by the writers' treatments of female subjectivity, and gender politics" (Yip 276).

The concept of identity, on the other hand, "provides an important way for individuals to conceptualize their sense of self and their relationships with history, social communities, and cultures. It reflects cultural ideologies that affect individuals' and communities' self-projection and self-perception" (Li, "Introduction" 6). Social and cultural factors such as sex, gender, sexual orientation, class, education level, race, ethnicity, or religion contribute to how individuals express and position themselves in the world both individually and collectively. Identity is socially and culturally constructed through historical circumstances, ideologies, social structures, and cultural practices. Individual and collective identities are not static, but undergo continuous and diverse transformations through personal experience and public history. The fluidity and plurality of identity open up spaces for individuals to reconstruct their self-perceptions and worldviews. The concept of identity is characterized not only by the aforementioned diversity and fluidity, but also by performativity.

Eileen Chang's self-translation is her own making of self and identities. Chang employs her lived experience and translates her inner feelings and thinking into her creative writing. This section examines how Chang translates her self-concept in the genre of self-translation as an alternative form of life writing through an (inter-)textual analysis of her memoirs, semi-autobiographical novels, and family photo albums. Chang articulates her own experience from childhood to young adulthood in Tianjin, Shanghai, and Hong Kong from the 1920s to the mid-1950s in her early memoirs, which were mainly written and published in Shanghai and Hong Kong. She also depicts her diasporic experiences in different places in the United States, including her sense of displacement, her constant financial and cultural struggles in her early immigration years, her contemplation of her own past and modern Chinese history, and her Chinese American lifestyle in her old age, in her essays written between the mid-1950s and the 1990s. While her memoirs explicitly present her subjectivity with references to real life events, her semi-autobiographical novels, written in both Chinese and English, suggest more nuanced transcultural connotations in the remaking of her identities. Her family photo album further self-consciously displays the highlights of her personal life, with captions and reflections that engage in dialogues with her early writing. These dialogues help to reveal her inscription of the self as well as her identity formation, and to showcase her constant performative self-becoming.

As a genre of life writing, memoir is the narration of lived experience, written from the perspectives of the author about an important part of their life, focusing on a particular aspect of the self. Memoir differs from autobiography in that the latter tends to present a fuller account of the author/subject's life than the former. Although based on the author's lived experience, memoir is nevertheless, to a large extent, a literary creation because the events, characters, dialogues, and emotions presented in the memoir are selectively narrated, and stylistically and rhetorically edited, by the author with conscious and unconscious emphasis, negligence, and exaggeration. In terms of the ethics of memoir, G. Thomas Couser identifies a "paradox at the heart of memoir: the genre demands a fidelity to truth that may overtax its source and conflict with its aspirations as art" (80). Couser is concerned about a balance between the memoir's adherence to truth and its aesthetic values. I argue here that Eileen Chang translates her evolving self in her memoirs by oscillating between truth and fiction through a literary record of her experiences growing up in Tianjin, Shanghai, and Hong Kong, both to overcome trauma, loss, and nostalgia, and to articulate her diasporic experience in the United States In so doing, she constructs individual, relational, and collective identities that are multiple and dynamic rather than essential and static. This analysis of her memoirs reveals the multifaceted identities and public personas she creates through continuous negotiations between personal experiences, family sagas, and public history amid transcultural hybridization in the twentieth century.

Chang's translations of her childhood and adolescent selves are at the heart of her self-representation. Her memoirs trace her family relations, events, and history, some of which she did not witness with her own eyes but she creatively reconstructs in words. The referential truth in her autobiographical essays, and its role as literary testimonial, is ambiguous and paradoxical. On the one hand, she recaptures her experiences growing up and her intense feelings of lost time in language and images to unlock buried memories. On the other hand, she rewrites her memories of her childhood and youthful development from her current perspectives during different stages of her adulthood, so as to reconcile with her childhood and adolescent past and to reconstitute it as part of her multiple and fluid self. Thomas Couser notes that "I think it's helpful to think of memoir as subjective life writing, whether about the author, about someone known to the author, or about the relationship between them" (20). Chang's memoirs demonstrate this subjectivity as, based on her reminiscences and her imagination, she reconstructs her relational familial and social identities in her memoirs by tracing the genealogy of her family history, which is largely shaped by transcultural and social forces in the historical transitional period from the late Qing dynasty (1644–1912) to the May Fourth Movement (1919) and its aftermath.

Chang adopts a literary technique that she calls *cenci duizhao* 參差對照 [equivocal contrast] to portray her love-hate relationship with her family members. In "Ziji de wenzhang" 〈自己的文章〉 ("Writing of One's Own," 1944), she clarifies her writing styles and themes as responses to Fu Lei's 傅雷 (1908–1966) criticism of the weakness of her storytelling (see Xun) and its divergences from the doctrines of realism and idealism advocated during the May Fourth Movement. She claims that she likes desolation because it is an equivocal contrast, like light green with pink, rather than a striking contrast such as that of dark green with bright red: 「我喜歡參差對照的寫法，因爲它是較近事實的。」 ["I like writing by way of equivocal contrast because it is relatively true to life" (Chang, "Ziji de wenzhang" 115; Jones 19)]. According to Chang, the notions of simplicity and stability will lead to eternity, which forms the basis of good literary works. Her analogy between the low contrast of colours and a sense of desolation in reality serves as an illustration of her philosophy of not committing to moral judgements of specific strong ideals in her writing. The ambiguity and fluidity of ideas presented in her works could be attributed to her transcultural education and dynamic family background, combining Chinese heritage with Western cultural exposure, situated in a transitional historical period between tradition and modernity. Her characters are, therefore, often ambiguous, with no absolute moral clarity, especially during the social and political transformations of early modern China: virtuous people may harbour petty thoughts, and villains may show empathy toward others. Her works feature psychologically sophisticated characters whose daily interactions and mundane lifestyles demonstrate the wisdom of ordinary people.

In her memoir "Siyu" 〈私語〉 ("Whispers," 1944), Chang uses equivocal contrast in contemplating her feelings about her father, Zhang Zhiyi 張志沂 (Zhang Tingzhong 張廷重 1898–1953), whom she sees as both loving and detesting. For example, her father bought a copy of George Bernard Shaw's *Heartbreak House* (1919) and inscribed his name, address, and date in English on a blank flyleaf. She claims that she likes those few lines, which resemble the air of spring days passing leisurely, just like their home in Tianjin ("Whispers" 144). The title of the book, *Heartbreak House*, however, may also symbolize her sorrowful feelings for her home. On the one hand, she looks down upon everything in her father's house, such as opium, chapter novels, and the senior private tutor who teaches her younger brother *Han Gaozulun*《漢高祖論》 (*On Emperor Gaozu of Han*). On the other hand, she likes the misty clouds of opium, the foggy sunshine, and the cluttered tabloids in the room, which provide a sense of familiarity ("Whispers" 150). These examples of impressions of her home and family demonstrate how Chang re-creates her relationship with her father, from a distance and from a young adult perspective, by presenting that relationship from both positive and negative angles.

Most of all, "Whispers" provides a testimony of the trauma Chang experienced during her adolescence, translating her psychic journey into the depth of her youthful self. She recalls staying at her mother's home for two weeks due to the bombing noise at night during the Battle of Shanghai in 1937. When she returned home, her stepmother slapped her for not notifying her about it, and accused Chang of hitting her instead. Chang's father then beat her and locked her up in the basement, during which she almost died from dysentery ("Whispers" 153–154). Adopting the literary devices of unfamiliarity and metaphor, she expresses her broken heart at the threshold of madness: 「我暫時被監禁在空房裏，我生在裏面的這座房屋忽然變成生疏的了，像月光底下的，黑影中現出青白的粉牆，片面的，癲狂的。」 ("Whispers" 153). Andrew F. Jones translates this passage as follows: "I was locked for the time being inside the empty room downstairs, and my existence in the house where I was born suddenly became strange and unfamiliar, like a wall in the moonlight whose whiteness only stands out against the blackest of shadows, its contours flattened and demented" (Jones 170). Her once-familiar house now becomes a prison for her, producing a sense of strangeness represented by the frivolous whiteness of the wall. Her translation of her feelings of imprisonment delves into the abyss of the wounded psychic of her youthful self.

With a similar use of equivocal contrast, Chang describes her mother, Huang Yifan 黃逸梵 (1898–1957), as both romantic and realistic, and familiar yet remote, in a manner that is different from, but somewhat similar to, her perception of her father. Chang's romantic, idealized, and mysterious portrait of her mother stems in part from her mother having left her when she was four years old. She remembers feeling both excitement and unfamiliarity when her mother held her hand while they were crossing a road ("From the Mouths of Babes" 124), and this combination of emotions paradoxically captures their emotional distance despite their physical proximity. She loves everything in the house associated with her mother, such as the piano, blue chair covers, and rose-patterned carpet ("Whispers" 148). Furthermore, Chang envisions her mother as a brave and independent woman, reminding her of Nora from Henrik Ibsen's *A Doll's House,* in the transitional period of modern China. Though her mother had once had her feet bound and then unbound when binding was no longer the fashion, her aunt, with her natural feet, claimed that her mother was a better skier than she was (*Mutual Reflections* 22).

Chang's depiction of her mother, despite its positive and almost mystical tone as noted above, is not without sorrow, as "Whispers" presents a spatially and emotionally distant relationship between mother and daughter. For example, she recalls not perceiving any defects in her home life without her mother, because her mother had been gone for a long time ("Whispers" 146). When she lived temporarily with her mother, she saw that her mother had sacrificed much for the family and wondered whether that was worth it or not ("Whispers" 155). According to her younger brother Zhang Zijing 張子靜 (1921–1997), Chang here discreetly refers to their mother having had a boyfriend at that time but feeling bound by her responsibilities as a parent (Z. Zhang 109). Her most distressing moments with her mother are her attempts to request an allowance from her mother, who herself was experiencing financial constraints that slowly eroded the relationship between the two ("From the Mouths of Babes" 125). Examples of both happy and sad memories, such as those outlined above, demonstrate Chang's ongoing processes of deciphering meanings from those memories. Her perception of her mother and the relationship between them, an important formative factor in the development of her childhood and adolescent self, is a fluid concept rather than a fixed one.

Chang similarly re-creates her childhood memories of her younger brother in her memoirs while reconstructing her relational self as an older sibling in her childhood and teenage years. In "From the Mouths of Babes," she recounts imagining a story of "Jinjiazhuang" 「金家莊」 ("Homestead of the Jin") and enacting the play with her brother:

> 一同玩的時候，總是我出主意。我們是「金家莊」上能征慣戰的兩員驍將 … … 沒等他說完，我已經笑倒了，在他腮上吻一下，把他當個小玩意。
>
> "From the Mouths of Babes" 132

> When we played together, I was always the one who set the agenda. We are two stalwart and valiant warriors of "Jun Family Village" … But before he could even finish, I would collapse into laughter and kiss his little cheeks, as if he were merely a plaything.
>
> Jones 14

Her account of their pleasurable play-acting creates the persona of a young girl engaging in childhood fantasies and developing a sense of dominance in terms of both intelligence and emotion in the position of the elder sister.

Chang also describes more intense moments with her brother in an endeavour to repair her broken ties with him. She recalls that once she went home from her high school dormitory and found her younger brother, tall and thin, wearing filthy clothes, a striking reminder of her family's neglect of his welfare. She also scolds him severely for his lack of self-discipline and ambitions in life ("From the Mouths of Babes" 131–132). However, her fierce reactions to and "disapproval" of his behaviour are motivated by love and care for him, which Chang translates in her memoir. The most disturbing such moment comes when her father suddenly slaps her brother's face for a minor issue at the dinner table. The account that follows is narrated like a close-up in a movie: she looks at the tears running down her face in front of a bathroom mirror and says, 「我要報仇。有一天我要報仇。」 [I want revenge. One day, I shall have my revenge ("From the Mouths of Babes" 132; Jones 17)]. The theatricality of this self-conscious performative act translates her passionate and determined youthful self.

During the transitional period of modernization in China in the early twentieth century, Chang's parents were both, on the one hand, trapped by various customs and expectations of traditional Chinese culture, such as patriarchy, recitations of Chinese classics, foot-binding, arranged marriage, concubinage, and opium smoking; and, on the other hand, exposed to new ideas and practices, such as individualism, feminism, Western art and culture, unbound feet,

REWRITING THE SELF IN MEMOIRS

freedom of love, and modern health science. The effects of these clashes of different ideologies and social practices were enormous, not only on Chinese society but on individuals and families within that society. Her parents' irresolvable conflicts were deeply intertwined in these social and cultural transformations, which in turn affected her brother and herself as they grew up in their troubled and traumatized family.

In "Whispers," Chang expresses a sense of desolation and reflects on her concept of home: 「亂世的人，得過且過，沒有真的家。」 [People living in chaotic times get by however they can, without a real home to call their own (143; Jones 156)]. Upon returning to Shanghai from Hong Kong after narrowly escaping from the war in 1942, she lived with her aunt Zhang Maoyuan 張茂淵 (1902–1991) in flat 62, Eddington House, now known as Changde Apartment 常德公寓, 195 Changde Street 常德公路, in Shanghai.[1] Her recollections of her aunt's home call forth feelings of both belonging and alienation, though she also claims feelings of permanence and completeness, since her mother and aunt had lived together for many years. However, once when she broke a glass, she compensated her aunt by paying six hundred dollars to replace it, despite her financial troubles at the time. Another time when she had broken a glass on the balcony door, her aunt looked at her mild wound and then immediately interrogated her about the broken glass ("Whispers" 143). In both of these anecdotes, the broken glass symbolizes the fragility of her relationship with her aunt and calls her position in her aunt's home into question. These incidents demonstrate what Robert Tally points out in *Spatiality*: "space is not merely a backdrop or setting for events, an empty container to be filled with actions or movements," but "both a product and productive" (119–120). In this sense, her aunt's home can be interpreted not merely a dwelling place for her, but also as her imagined family unit that she yearns for but which ultimately disappoints her and contributes to her melancholy and disengaging familial self.

In "Whispers," Chang makes a nostalgic but ambivalent return to her earliest memory in the care of servants, of whom He Gan 何干 was the one she was closest to:

> 只記得被傭人抱來抱去，用手去揪她頸項上鬆的皮——她年紀逐漸大起來，頸上的皮逐漸下垂；探手到她頷下漸漸有不同的感覺了。」
>
> "Whispers" 144

---

1   Eileen Chang lived with her aunt Zhang Maoyuan in flat 51, Eddington House, in Shanghai in 1939 before she left for Hong Kong to study. See Chunzi 淳子, *Zhang Ailing Ditu* 《張愛玲地圖》 [*Eileen Chang Map*] (42).

FIGURE 2 Changde apartment sign, Shanghai (Photo taken in August 2013)
PHOTO CREDIT: JESSICA TSUI-YAN LI

FIGURE 3 Changde apartment, Shanghai (Photo taken in August 2013)
PHOTO CREDIT: JESSICA TSUI-YAN LI

> All I remember of that time is being carried hither and thither by a servant [He Gan] as I held on to the loose skin around her neck with my hand. As she grew older, the skin gradually began to sag, and it felt different each time I reached my hand under her chin.
>
> JONES 157

The "loose skin" around He Gan's neck symbolizes Chang's tangible attachment to her nanny, which gradually subsides as she grows up and her feelings about He Gan's droopy skin change over time. After she was beaten by her father, He Gan asked her, 「你怎麼會弄到這樣的呢？」 [How could you have let things come to such a pass? ("Whispers" 152–153; Jones 169)]. It was only then that she realized her own feelings of anger and injustice, leading to a burst of crying. In the face of parental negligence, she perceives He Gan as her anchor of affection, but only finds out that He Gan has turned 「冷而硬」 [cold and hard hearted ("Whispers" 153; Jones 169)] towards her for fearing her father's revenge. Those intimate and heartbreaking experiences of her childhood and youthful years are recaptured and reconstructed in her early adulthood, accompanied by ambiguous feelings of both longing and remorse.

Chang's interaction with her household servants demonstrates the early development of her gender consciousness as an important influence on her mind and character. In "Whispers," she recalls that Zhang Gan 張干, her younger brother's nanny, always gained an upper hand over He Gan because Zhang Gan was in charge of a boy rather than a girl. She is particularly infuriated by Zhang Gan's prediction that she would be married far away from home and even her younger brother would not want to see her again. Zhang Gan's idea pertains to the Chinese patriarchal idiom, 「嫁出去的女兒，潑出去的水。」 [Daughters who have been married off are equivalent to water that has been splashed]. She further elaborates, 「張干使我很早地想到男女平等的問題，我要銳意圖強，務必要勝過我弟弟。」 [From very early on, Zhang Gan made me aware of the inequality between men and women, and because of that awareness, I was determined to sharpen my wits and surpass my little brother ("Whispers" 145; Jones 160)]. Her narrative of Zhang Gan's chauvinism underscores the connections between her childhood experience and the Chinese patriarchal and patrilineal social and familial structures, echoing the popular slogan of the feminist movements of the 1960s and 1970s in the US, where she moved in 1955, "the personal is political." Chang's translation in her memoir of her self-determination and her desire to surpass her brother highlights her growth towards maturity and exhibits her vigorously performative self-translation.

Chang's memoirs also recall her relationship with her friend Yanying 炎櫻 (Fatima Mohideen, Modai 莫黛, Modai 獏黛, Momeng 獏夢) (1920–1997),[2] whom she met at the University of Hong Kong. Yanying's mother was Chinese, from Tianjin, and her father was an Arabic Muslim from Ceylon (now Sri Lanka) who owned a Mohideen jewelry store in Shanghai. Chang devoted a number of essays, such as "Yanying yulu" 〈炎櫻語錄〉 ("The Sayings of Yanying," 1944), "Shuangsheng" 〈雙聲〉 ("Double Voices," 1945), "Qiduan qingchang ji qita" 〈氣短情長及其他〉 ("Short of Ambition, Everlasting Love, and Others," 1945), "Yanying yipu" 〈炎櫻衣譜〉 ("The Spectrum of Yanying's Clothes," 1945), and "Jili" 〈吉利〉 ("Auspicious"), to their friendship. In these essays, Chang and Yanying discuss various subjects and share their perspectives and worldviews with each other and with the reader. For example, in "Double Voices," when Yanying expresses a sense that her passion for Japanese culture is gone, Chang resonates with her. While Yanying claims that she once loved the childish charm in Japanese culture, Chang favours its subtlety, resembling the delicacy of ancient China ("Double Voices" 256). Through her dialogues with Yanying, Chang reconfigures her relational self from both her inside and outside voices, which are sometimes reflected to her in Yanying's perspectives.

Of her contemporary women writers, Chang particularly appreciates Su Qing 蘇青:「只有和蘇青相提並論我是心甘情願的。」 [I am only willing to be compared with Su Qing ("My View on Su Qing" 271)]. In her essay "Wo kan Su Qing" 〈我看蘇青〉 ("My View on Su Qing," 1945), she constructs her relational self by narrating her understanding of Su Qing in personal anecdotes. For example, in recalling Su Qing's depression on the night of the air raid in Shanghai, she remembers the uncertainty in her own life amid this chaotic historical period. Having studied at the University of Hong Kong and achieved the highest scores ever according to her professors, she laments that her academic records, the evidence of her hard work and her achievements, were lost in the Battle of Hong Kong.[3] In a similar vein, she expresses her worries that her writing career might decline in the future no matter how hard she works in the present:「我於是想到我自己 …… 想到從前，想到現在，近兩年來孜孜忙著的，是不是也注定了要被打翻的——我應當有數。」 [So I thought about myself, the past, and the present. I should have counted

---

2 Yanying's original English name was Fatima Mohideen, and her Chinese name was Modai 莫黛. Eileen Chang renamed her Yanying in Chinese. After she learned that a dream-eating beast in Japanese mythology was named Mo 獏, Yanying changed her name to Modai 獏黛. Since she did not like the sound of the name Modai, she changed her name again, this time to Momeng 獏夢 (see Chang, "Double Voices" 260).

3 Eileen Chang's academic transcripts were retrieved and archived in "Eileen Chang at the University of Hong Kong: An Online Presentation of Images and Documents from the Archives."

whether what I have been busy with in the past two years is also doomed to be overturned ("My View on Qu Qing" 276)]. Her narratives embody a virtual return to the Hong Kong she experienced earlier, and the critical decision she made in her teenage years with an opaque sense of nostalgia and a vague future direction. Her experiences of family trauma and wartime struggles ceaselessly shape her present self-concept and contribute to her anxious view of the future.

Social and psychological theories of self-concept are useful in exploring how Chang presents her thoughts, feelings, and behaviours in her memoirs, and how these are influenced by experiences, ideologies, institutions, and social norms. For instance, Chad Gordon's model of the four subjective senses of self is a particularly fruitful approach to one's sense of autonomy and self-esteem. Extending Talcott Parsons' action theory of goal-attainment, pattern maintenance, adaptation, and integration (631–638), Gordon correspondingly develops a systematic framework of the configuration of self-conception, consisting of self-determination, moral worth, competence, and unity. According to Gordon, the sense of self-determination refers to a person's self-motivated "tendency to optimize gratification through selecting goals and instrumental steps for their attainment" (18). To obtain self-gratification, a person will take the initiative to make decisions and commitments in order to achieve their high-priority goals. The sense of moral worth refers to a person's "adherence to a valued code of moral standards" (Gordon 17) to evaluate their attributes and actions in particular social situations. Where the sense of competence conceptualizes a person's ability to adapt and thereby develop self-esteem (Gordon 19–20), the sense of unity theorizes a person's "internal harmony of the constituent elements" (Gordon 18), which is crucial to developing ego identity.

Applying Chad Gordon's social psychological framework, this section examines how Chang has vividly exhibited her conception of self in terms of self-determination, moral worth, competence, and unity in "Tiancaimeng" 〈天才夢〉 ("Dream of Genius," 1940), an essay she submitted to the Shanghai magazine *Xifeng* 《西風》 (*West Wind*) for a competition when she started her studies at the University of Hong Kong in 1939. The essay was first published in *West Wind* number 48, in August 1940, and it presents Chang's sense of individual self with prominence and clarity. Regarding her sense of self-determination, she claims in the essay that she had been perceived as a genius since she was a child; therefore, developing her talent was her highest goal in life. In her road to attain this goal, she learned to recite Tang poetry at age three and she wrote two novels at age seven ("Dream of Genius" 8). Her gratification was achieved when she received the news from *West Wind* that her essay won the first prize, only to be dashed when she was notified that her essay had received only an "honorable mention" instead ("Yi Xifeng" 〈憶西風〉 ("Recalling West Wind" 96). During her late teenage years, when her emotions were particularly heightened, her disappointment over not winning the first prize felt like a "dead decayed tooth" ("Recalling West Wind" 98). Her sense of self-worth also shows through in her plan at age eight to write a novel, *Kuaile cun* 《快樂村》 (*Happy Village*), which describes a tribe of highlanders living in China as a self-sustained and self-governed big family clan isolated from the outside world ("Dream of Genius" 8), an ideal society in an imagined world, blessed with peace and happiness.

"Dream of Genius" demonstrates Chang's positive sense of self-determination and moral worth, but also shows how her sense of competence is challenged, as she struggles with daily chores and with interactions with others. For example, her mother tried very hard for two years to teach her to cook, do the laundry, pay attention to her walking postures, and read people's minds, but all of this was in vain. Her inadequate adaptation to her environment affected her self-esteem, and deterred her from interacting effectively with other people. The discrepancy between her high-level senses of self-determination and moral worth and her low-level sense of competence leads to her ambivalent sense of unity: 「生命是一襲華美的袍，爬滿了蝨子。」 [Life is a splendid gown, crawling with fleas ("Dream of Genius" 10)]. The metaphor suggests both her understanding of life as glamorous and her annoyance about trivial matters. "Dream of Genius" presents a significant milestone of her self-concept as both confident and uneasy in her late adolescence, forming the basis of her ego identity to further "experience intimacy and achieve a meaningful connection between self and a small, unitary set of occupational, professional, ideological, membership, family, and interpersonal roles" (Gordon 19). Chang's contradictory conception of self leads to her challenges with teenage identity crisis and interpersonal relationships on the one hand, and her determination to achieve her goals on the other.

Chang reconstructs an important phrase of her challenges growing up, and her transition of self-concept from adolescence to young adulthood, in her memoir "Jinyulu" 〈燼餘錄〉 ("From the Ashes," 1944). The Battle of Hong Kong between December 8 and 25, 1941, and the Japanese occupation that followed prompted dramatic changes in her self-conception. Having left Hong Kong for Shanghai for two years, she has adopted a retrospective perspective from which to re-examine her thoughts and feelings during her struggle for survival in Hong Kong amid the Second World War, as recounted in "From the Ashes." Based on her observations of her classmates' behaviours, she conjectures their personality traits and attitudes and makes inferences about their naiveté at the beginning of the war:

至於我們大多數的學生，我們對於戰爭所抱的態度，可以打個
譬喻，是像一個人坐在硬板凳上打瞌睡，雖然不舒服，而且沒
結沒完的抱怨著，到底還是睡著了。

"From the Ashes" 66

For most of us students, however, our attitude toward the war could be
summed up by a simile: we were like someone sitting on a hard plank
bench, trying to take a nap. Although in terrible discomfort and ceaselessly complaining of it, we managed to fall asleep all the same.

Jones 46

Her characterization of the majority of the people she observes as sleeping
during wartime echoes Lu Xun's metaphor in *Call to Arms* of the "Iron House"
in which most people had long fallen asleep. Chang's wartime observation and
contemplation inspire her to formulate her philosophy of life that appears in
her subsequent writings: even though people have suffered from hunger, fear,
and imminent death during the war, the majority of them have not been awak-
ened to become heroes or heroines ("Writing of One's Own" 115).

In a similar vein, in "From the Ashes," Chang also narrates her observations
of her own behaviours as though an outsider, and makes inferences about her
own attitudes. As Daryl Bem argues in his self-perception theory, "To the extent
that internal cues are weak, ambiguous, or uninterpretable, the individual is
functionally in the same position as an outside observer, an observer who must
necessarily rely upon those same external cues to infer the individual's inner
states" (5). Through a "meta-cognitive" process of self-perception, Chang condemns herself as selfish and irresponsible. For instance, when working in a
temporary university hospital, she and other nurses cold-heartedly rejoice over
the death of an annoying patient: 「我們這些自私的人若無其事的活下
去了。」 [Selfish people such as ourselves went nonchalantly on with living
("From the Ashes" 73; Jones 56)]. She further reflects on the concern of many
people including herself with basic instinctual desires such as eating, appearance, and sex, as an example of the egotism of human nature even in wartime.
However, she does lament the death of her beloved professor during the war,
whom she might have based on her history professor Norman Hoole France
(1904–1941) (Huang, *Hong Kong Connections*; 47–49). In this essay, she largely
constructs her specific female bourgeoise identity by providing an alternative
voice for middle- and upper-class university students' endurance of the war, in
contrast to the patriarchal nationalistic narratives of Lu Xun 魯迅 (1881–1936),
Ba Jin 巴金 (1904–2005), and Mao Dun 茅盾 (1896–1981). With its narration of
her loss of innocence and exposure to stark human nature, "From the Ashes"

can be seen as Chang closing the book on her adolescence and opening a new page on a journey to her early adulthood.

In "Gongyu shenghuo jiqu" 〈公寓生活寄趣〉 ("Notes on Apartment Life," 1943), Chang constructs an urban identity in her depiction of her life in Eddington House in Shanghai in the early 1940s. Adopting a first-person narrative, she recalls the vitality of urban life, her friendship, and the fame of her early writing career. She admits that she has become more sensitive to the urbanity of Shanghai after having sojourned on the hilly campus of the University of Hong Kong for several years:

> 我喜歡聽市聲。比我較有詩意的人在枕上聽松濤，聽海嘯，我是非得聽見電車響才睡得著覺的。在香港的山上，只有冬季裏，北風徹夜吹著常青樹，還有一點電車的韻味。長年住在鬧市裏的人大約得出了城之後才知道他離不了一些什麼。
>
> "Notes on Apartment Life" 36

> I like to listen to city sounds. People more poetic than I listen from their pillows to the sound of rustling pines or the roar of ocean waves, while I can't fall asleep until I hear the sound of streetcars. On the hills in Hong Kong, it was only in the winter when the north wind blew all night long through the evergreens that I was reminded of the charming cadence of a streetcar. People who have lived their entire lives amid the bustle of the city do not realize what they cannot do without until they have left.
>
> Jones 28

Chang's lived experience in an apartment building greatly affected her perspectives towards the urban Shanghai of the time. As Nicole Huang points out, "Here private space is constantly intruded upon by external forces, and Chang's animated world of images, sounds, and objects brings to mind themes of unemployment, social unrest, and economic instability" ("Afterword" 242). I argue here that Chang's testimonial presents both a visualized temporal and spatial return to her alma mater in Hong Kong and an appreciation of her current apartment in the vibrant metropolitan environment of Shanghai as a professional writer. Her introspection demonstrates her individual self's dialogue with itself and suggests the shaping of her mind and character as she moves towards maturity and thriving in the world, a signal of her independent identity construction.

Recollecting her observation of the outside world from the private space of her apartment, Chang exhibits her rhetorical ways of seeing Shanghai's urban culture in "Notes on Apartment Life." With her delicate sensibility and playful imagination, she perceives Shanghai's cityscape from a high angle in her quiet comfort zone and comments that 「公寓是最合理想的逃世地方。」[An apartment is an ideal retreat from the world outside ("Notes on Apartment Life" 39; Jones 32)]. Compared with the tight-knit communities in the countryside in which the villagers share all their secrets, apartment life protects the residents' privacy. However, the tenants usually open their doors to get fresh air in the summer, and therefore can peek into each other's everyday lives, such as telephone conversations, piano practices, and cooking (39). The apparently detached but genuinely gregarious neighbourhood spontaneously fosters a sense of community in the apartment building. From her early adult perspective, her depiction of apartment life in Shanghai resonates with the Chinese field and garden poet Tao Yuanming's 陶淵明 (365–427) famous portrayal of the "Taohuayuanji" 〈桃花源記〉 "Peach Blossoms Spring" (421) in the classical Chinese poetic imaginary that she enjoys.

During the Second Sino-Japanese War (1937–1945), Chang ruled out any collaboration with the Japanese, although she had shown admiration towards Japanese culture and made acquaintances with Japanese people in Shanghai. In her essay "You jiju hua tong duzhe shuo" 〈有幾句話同讀者說〉 ("Have a Few Words with the Readers," 1946), she defends herself against the accusation of being a *wenhua hanjian* 文化漢奸 [cultural traitor], as she had never published any works about politics, nor received any financial support from the Japanese. She mentions that the Third Greater East Asia Literary Conference had once invited her and published her name as a participant in a newspaper. Though she wrote a letter to the conference to decline the invitation, her name was not removed ("Have a Few Words with the Readers" 294). By openly denouncing her alleged association with the Japanese institutions, she constructs a cultural and historical public identity devoid of accusations of treachery.

In her early years in the United States, Chang recalls her collective self as closely related to modern China. Narrating her encounters with Hu Shi 胡適 (1891–1962) in "Yi Hu Shizhi" 〈憶胡適之〉 ("Remembering Hu Shizhi," 1968), she reaffirms her ongoing transfiguration of self-concept, which is intimately entwined with her personal, familial, and collective memory. Her personal connection with Hu begins with several mail exchanges (1954–1955) in which she receives positive comments on her novel *Yangge* 《秧歌》 (*The Rice-Spout Song*, 1955) and inspiration for her later translation of Han Bangqing's 韓邦慶 (1856–1894) *Hai shang hai liezhuan* 《海上花列傳》 (*The Sing-Song Girls of Shanghai*, 1894) from Wu dialect into Mandarin and English. Their first meeting triggers an intense feeling of misplaced familiarity on Chang's part. Though his apartment building in New York reminds her of Hong Kong, Hu's long gown and his wife's Anhui 安徽 accent make her feel at home. Her *déjà vu* brings back a familial memory associated with Hu: her aunt, Zhang Maoyuan, and her mother were close to Hu, and they had once played Mahjong games together. Hu told her that his father knew her grandfather, who seemed to have offered them some help ("Remembering Hu Shizhi" 12–19). All these recollections point to their friendly intergenerational relationship. In their farewell at the doorstep, she feels 「一陣悲風，隔著十萬八千里從時代的深處吹出來，吹得眼睛都睜不開」 [a gust of grief blown out from the depths of times across a hundred and eight thousand miles, making her not able to open her eyes ("Remembering Hu Shizhi" 22)]. The "gust of grief" symbolizes her lament for the social and political upheavals and transformations in modern China that, in her memory, are so remarkably connected to her and her family and serve as continuations of the pre-modern period. Her strong feelings of the shifting of time and space further point to her sense of desolation in her diasporic life in the United States.

Travelling from the cosmopolitan cities of Shanghai, Hong Kong, and New York to a small town in New England in 1956, Chang articulates her multifaceted diasporic experiences of cultural interaction and exchange in her posthumously published essay "New England ... China" (2000). Upon her arrival, she is fascinated by the integrity of the townspeople, which she compares to the virtue of Confucius (511 BC–479 BC) in ancient China. For example, through enquiries with the bus driver, she is astonished to find out that she could leave her luggage in the middle of the street without being stolen ("New England ... China" 270). Her juxtaposition of small-town New England with the utopia she imagines in ancient China produces a self-reflection that resonates with not only the ideal society she depicted in her early novel *Happy Village* that she wrote at the age of eight, but also with her new perspectives on life. Though there are vicissitudes in life everywhere in the world, as depicted, for instance, in the American soap opera *Peyton Place* (1964) and the eponymous New England town in which it is set, people's attitudes and worldviews depend on their mindset and life purposes ("New England ... China" 271). Her self-retrospection asserts the significance of spiritual civilization, albeit recognizing that materiality is essential to human survival.

The manuscript of this essay also projects Chang's positive relational self with her second husband, American playwright Ferdinand Reyher. The typewritten manuscript features both typewritten and handwritten changes made by Chang in darker ink, and different handwritten changes made by Reyher in lighter ink. Reyher mainly suggests reorganizing the material in the last paragraph in order to emphasize the similarities between rural New England and Confucian China (Kingsbury, "About 'New England ... China'" 273–275). Though it is unknown whether she accepted his changes and suggestions, the notes do demonstrate their collaborative work as a couple. In fact, Chang had never published any works about or photographs of Reyher, or her first husband Hu Lancheng, during her lifetime; only some of her posthumously-published novels, essays, and personal letters refer to Hu and Reyher. The absence of Hu and Reyher from Chang's published works remains an enigma, leaving a blank page of her own private life stories for readers to ponder, and illustrating the point Roland Barthes makes in "The Death of the Author," that "[t]his evictive state naturally corresponds to a plenitude of virtualities: it is an absence of meaning full of all the meaning" (42).

In her posthumously-published essay "Yijiubaba zhi – ?" 〈一九八八一至 —— ? 〉 ("1988 to – ?" 1995), Chang uses imagery derived from nature and the environment to express her situation and feelings about her old age in Los Angeles. Adopting the literary device of *xing* 興 [evocation], widely used in *Shijing* 《詩經》 (*The Book of Songs* or *The Classics of Poetry*) (11 BC–7 BC), she describes her surrounding scenery of blue skies, green mountains, bridges, and boutiques as an inspiration, while waiting for a bus in suburban Los Angeles. On the back of a bench at the bus stop, the words "Wee and Dee 1988 – ?" come to her attention ("1988 to – ?" 106). From the romanization of the names, she speculates that the writers are members of the Chinese diaspora, probably from Southeast Asia. In her imagination, Wee and Dee are impatient waiting for the bus, despite the beautiful scenery. The mundane mood manifested in her pondering those few words on the bench can be read as a self-reflection on her old age and the diasporic life she had lived since the 1970s. In her letter to Hsia Chih-tsing 夏志清 (1921–2013) dated April 6, 1988, she admits to having been troubled by excessive skin sensitivity and toothache and to being exhausted by everyday movement over the past few years (340–341). David Der-wei Wang argues in his essay "Xin de lunlixue" 〈信的倫理學〉 ("The Ethics of Letters") that her ailments may be psychosomatic symptoms, a trial of her body as a battlefield to attain an aesthetics of both cruelty and perseverance (397). Using the graffiti as inspiration, Chang contends that people who meet their fellow countrypeople in foreign lands in chaotic times will need to wait for the future to unfold ("1988 to – ?" 107). Meditating on the meaning of fate, she conjectures the unpredictability of the future, that all depends on individual disposition and circumstances, an insight she conveys in her old age. Chang's reflections on the natural scenery, the Chinese diaspora, and fate destabilize the dichotomy between the sublime objectivity of nature and the more mundane subjectivity of human society, and in so doing sheds light on not only her self-representation, but also her perspectives on life itself.

CHAPTER 2

Reimagining the Self in Eileen Chang's Semi-Autobiographical Novels: *Xiaotuanyuan* 《小團圓》 (*Little Reunions*), *The Fall of the Pagoda*, and *The Book of Change*

In addition to the self-translation present in her memoirs, Eileen Chang also translates her conception of the self in her semi-autobiographical novels, which demonstrate an aesthetic imaginary approach to autobiography. By presenting multifarious perspectives on characters or their selves and their circumstances, Chang opens up infinite possibilities for interpreting the multiplicities of selves in her semi-autobiographical fiction. Mikhail Bakhtin argues that "[t]o a greater or lesser extent, every novel is a dialogized system made up of the images of 'languages,' styles and consciousness that are concrete and inseparable from language" (*The Dialogic Imagination* 49); in a novel, different voices of the author, with different worldviews, engage in dialogue or dispute that exposes their complex, compounded, and contradictory characteristics. Translating her own semi-autobiographical novels from one language into another, Chang further recreates new divided and composite selves in translingual and transcultural space, producing a multicultural self-dialogue with plural consciousness. By retelling factual or fictitious stories of her life in autobiographical fiction in both Chinese and English, Chang remakes her conception of the self in a constantly changing manner, which demonstrates the performative quality of writing, public persona, and identity.

This chapter discusses how Eileen Chang translates her conception of the self in her posthumously published autobiographical novels *Xiaotuanyuan* 《小團圓》 (*Little Reunions*, 2009; hereafter cited as *LR*), *The Fall of the Pagoda* (2010; hereafter cited as *FOP*), and *The Book of Change* (2010; hereafter cited as *BOC*) by portraying the multiple and dynamic selves of the characters. The chapter begins with an examination of how Chang depicts the childhood and youthful development of Jiuli 九莉 and Lute, her respective alter egos in the Chinese and English versions, to recreate their journeying selves in both productive and subversive dialogues with each other in the genre of *Bildungsroman*. It also investigates the paradoxical significance of privacy in these works. By using fictional disguises, Chang's semi-autobiographical novels, on the one hand, seem to protect the identities and privacy of her families and

© JESSICA TSUI-YAN LI, 2025 | DOI:10.1163/9789004730052_004

friends and herself. On the other hand, a breach of privacy appears when private family matters are on display, albeit mediated by rhetoric, thus challenging familial and cultural taboos. Moreover, this chapter discusses the notions of performance and playacting that lead to performative acts in life narratives.

In her semi-autobiographical novels, largely written in her middle age, Chang re-evaluates and reconstructs her experiences from a distance in time and space. She began writing the English version in 1957 in the United States (Chang, *To My Beloved Friends* 1.70), and gave it the title *The Book of Change* in 1961. (Chang, *To My Beloved Friends* 1.99). In 1963, she decided to separate her long work into two novels: *The Fall of the Pagoda* and *The Book of Change*. *The Fall of the Pagoda* chronologically narrates Lute's childhood from age four to her anticipation to study abroad, and *The Book of Change* starts with her university life in Hong Kong and ends with her return to Shanghai after the Japanese occupation of the British colonial city. In her correspondence with her acquaintances, Chang notes that she had written half of *Little Reunions*, a Chinese counterpart, in 1975, and finished a draft of the entire novel in 1976 (*To My Beloved Friends* 1.292), but promised in 1993 to keep revising it afterwards (*LR* 16). *Little Reunions* begins with Jiuli's imminent examination at university in Hong Kong, which coincides with the start of the Battle of Hong Kong in December 1941. In flashbacks, the reader sees her childhood and adolescent experiences in Tianjin and Shanghai. *Little Reunions* further explores Jiuli's early adulthood as a prominent writer who has an infamous love affair with a Japanese collaborator in Shanghai.

Chang's fictional re-creations of her middle- and late-life retrospectives correspond to various significant life events she retells in her autobiographical essays, memoirs, and family photo albums. Such correspondence breaks down the boundaries between self and other, fact and fiction, and autobiography and autobiographical fiction, as Paul Ricœur points out in *Time and Narrative*: "The story of a life continues to be refigured by all the truthful or fictive stories a subject tells about himself or herself. This refiguration makes life a cloth woven of stories told" (246). Ricœur points out the interconnectedness of true and fiction in the narration of a life story. Similarly, Linda Hutcheon notes that "we now query these boundaries between the literary and the traditionally extraliterary, between fiction and non-fiction, and ultimately, between art and life. We can interrogate these borders, though, only because we still posit them" (*A Poetics of Postmodernism* 225). Where Hutcheon underscores the destabilization of genre boundaries, I argue that in her semi-autobiographical novels, Chang portrays the making of her protagonists' selves from various perspectives, by tracing the childhood and youthful development of Juili and Lute, analyzing their minds and personalities as they grow towards maturity and assert themselves in the world, and celebrating everyday life in translingual and transcultural dimensions.

Chang's recollection of her traumatic experience of being wrongly accused by her stepmother and then cruelly beaten and trapped by her father in her adolescence is at the core of her *Bildungsroman*, as demonstrated in her response in "Whispers" to being questioned by her nanny He Gan: 「這時候才覺得滿腔冤屈，氣湧如山地哭起來抱著她哭了許久。」 [It was only then that I felt the resentment and injustice of it all bubble up inside me, and I burst into a wail. I sobbed in He Gan's arms for a long time ("Whispers" 153; Jones 169)]. From the vantage point of early adulthood, she pours out her grievances against her youthful maltreatment, and her feeling of entrapment informs her novels *Shibachun* 《十八春》 (*Eighteenth Spring*, 1950–1951) and its revised version, *Banshengyuan* 《半生緣》 (*Half a Lifelong Romance*, 1968). The female protagonist of these novels, Gu Manzhen 顧曼楨, is locked up in a room in her sister Gu Manlu's 顧曼璐 house, after having been raped by her brother-in-law Zhu Hongcai 祝鴻才. Manzhen's desperation and futile hope for her lover Shen Shijun 沈世鈞 coming to rescue her has turned her into a mad woman in the attic, with her inner feelings manifested in her outer behaviours, and in her self-consciousness of her wounded psyche:

> 她說她被人陷害，把她關了起來了，還說了許許多多話，自己都不知道說了些什麼，連那尖銳的聲音聽著也不像自己的聲音。這樣大哭大喊，砰砰砰槌著門，不簡直像個瘋子嗎？
>
> *Half a Lifelong Romance* 224

> She said she'd been cruelly mistreated, had fallen into a trap, then been locked up. She went on and on, she no longer knew what she was saying, till even she did not recognize her own raspy, cracked voice, screaming and crying like this, pounding on the door with her fists – wasn't that exactly what mad people did?
>
> KINGSBURY 235

The intense emotion of youthful trauma gradually fades in Chang's subsequent self-reconstruction, as she presents a conception of the self as a constantly evolving entity over time. She similarly revisits her traumatic experience of imprisonment in *The Fall of the Pagoda*, written in her middle age. Instead of hysterical sensation, she depicts Lute's restrained feelings as "[s]he looked in the mirror. Tears ran down her swollen red-striped cheeks" (*FOP* 237), emphasizing her suffering all alone. By contrast, in *Little Reunions*, mostly written in her sixties, she presents Jiuli as rather calm: 「一住下來就放心了些，那兩場亂夢顛倒似的風暴倒已經去遠了。」 [As soon as she settled in, Julie felt a little better. The two nightmarish storms that had just turned her life upside down were now fading away (*LR* 129; Pan and Merz 120)]. Her retelling of this story in *Mutual Reflections* in her old age shows that she had already let go of her feelings of agony and pain by simply saying: 「我終於逃出來投奔我母親。」[I finally escaped and went to my mother (*Mutual Reflections* 48)]. The rewriting of this traumatic experience in her memoir, fiction, autobiographical essays, and novels, in a fluid interchange between memory, events, and imagination, demonstrates her life-long self-healing process, her production of literary testimony, and her assertion of freedom in the end.

In her semi-autobiographical novels, Chang focuses more on her ambivalent relationship with her mother than she does with her traumatic experiences with her father. She reimagines episodes of her life narratives to produce a promiscuous and mysterious mother-figure in her fiction. For instance, in *The Book of Change*, after having visited Lute at the university's dormitory in Hong Kong, "Well, I have to be on my way," Dew said and mumbled. 'A car is waiting below,' in a way that stopped the others where they were instead of following her to the bottom steps and having to be introduced to whoever was in the car" (*BOC* 80). In the English version, Dew takes the initiative to stop others from prying into her privacy by hinting at a man waiting for her in the car. In *Little Reunions*, this scene is reinvented as a dialogue:

> 「你怎麼來的？」亨利嬤嬤搭訕著說。
> 「朋友的車子送我來的，」蕊秋說得很快，聲音又輕，眼睛望到別處去，是撇過一邊不提的口吻。亨利嬤嬤一聽，就站住了腳，沒再往下送。
> > *LR* 29

"How did you come here?" Sister Henri asked to break the awkward silence.

"In a friend's automobile," Rachel answered. Looking away, she spoke rapidly in a soft voice, as though she did not want to discuss the topic further.

As soon as Sister Henri heard that she stopped in her tracks and did not continue down the path to see the visitor off.

> PAN AND MERZ 16

In the Chinese version, Ruiqiu replies passively to Sister Henry's question. Her facial expressions and gestures are also described in more detail, and these indirectly suggest her uneasiness and embarrassment in the awkward situation of being associated with an unknown man, which is not considered honourable in Chinese society. Where the English version directly spells out

Dew's intention in a low context conveyed to Anglophone readers, the Chinese version discreetly portrays Ruiqiu's sophisticated psychological state in a high context presented to Sinophone readers.

Chang further negotiates between private experience and public representation by breaking taboos of revealing family secrets and challenging moral boundaries of the time in imagined narratives, as shown in the following passage from *The Book of Change*:

> Lute was so put out she watched the rest of the scene with no comprehension at first, her mother wading, an impersonal figure now that could be anybody, and a waist-length man rearing up from the water or coming forward to meet her. Lute had missed seeing which it was. A sense of taboo switched her eyes away instantly as in reflex action. She had only had time to see it was foreigner with wet brown hair matted over his forehead, a youngish face, rather long jutting chin and hefty white torso.
>
> BOC 98

Lute is shocked and ashamed as she describes the scene she witnessed of Dew, in a bathing suit, walking into the water to meet a foreign young man who is unknown to her. Ruiqiu's licentious behaviour is ahead of her time in Republican China, while Lute's reaction demonstrates her moral values and uneasiness due to her coincidental intrusion of Dew's privacy.

This scene is translated/rewritten as follows in *Little Reunions*:

> 水裏突然湧起一個人來，映在那青灰色黃昏的海面上，一瞥間清晰異常，崛起半截身子像匹白馬，一撮黑頭髮黏貼在眉心，有些白馬額前拖著一撮黑鬃毛，有穢褻感，也許因為太使人聯想到陰毛。他一揚手向這邊招呼了一聲，蕊秋便站起身來向九莉道：「好，你回去吧。」。
>
> LR 43

> Suddenly a man surged forth out of the water. Against the backdrop of the ash-gray sea at dusk, the image was in that instant exceptionally clear: his torso rose from the water like a pure white stallion, a lock of dark hair clinging to the space between his eyebrows like a tuft of black on a white horse's mane. It was a slightly licentious image, perhaps because it triggered on association with pubic hair. The man raised his hand high and called out a greeting. Rachel stood up, turned to Julie, and said, "Very well, then. You may go now."
>
> PAN AND MERZ 30

REIMAGINING THE SELF 57

Chang rewrites Ruiqiu's passive reaction to the young man's calling in the Chinese version, in contrast to Dew's initiative in the English version. The Chinese novel also stresses the sexual quality of the rendezvous with its use of the word "obscenity" to describe the young white man's outward appearance and, by extension, the private sexual encounter between Ruiqiu and the half-naked foreign man on a public beach. The Chinese novel translates Lute's strong negative feelings about the man, and about Dew's behaviour toward him, which was not normal for Chinese society at the time the story takes place.

Little Reunions provides another example of Chang's rewriting and mediation of private family concerns in her fiction and memoirs, as Jiuli speculates that Ruiqiu's lover is in Singapore: 「正因爲她提起過要找歸宿的話，就像是聽見風就是雨，就要她去實行。勞以德彷彿說在新加坡。」 [Rachel had only recently announced she intended to find a "place" for herself and now it appeared she was racing to put her words into action. Julie recalled hearing that Lloyd was in Singapore (*LR* 45; Pan and Merz 32–33)]. Jiuli is used to respecting her mother's privacy by not asking her questions, a sign of their distant relationship. Chang might have attempted to protect the privacy of her mother, who is ambiguously fictionalized in the novel, but nonetheless inevitably reveals some traces of her private life in her semi-autobiographical novels. Chang's younger brother Zhang Zijing 張子靜 (1921–1997), however, explicitly exposes their family's matters in his memoir:

> 另外我表哥還透露，我母親那次回上海，帶了一個美國男朋友同行。他是個生意人，四十多歲，長的英挺俊美，名字好像叫魏葛斯托夫。 … 一九四一年底新加坡淪陷，我母親的男友死於砲火。
>
> Z. ZHANG, *LR* 108–109

> In addition, my cousin also revealed that when my mother returned to Shanghai, she brought an American boyfriend with her. He was a businessman, in his forties, very handsome, and his name seemed to be Wagstaff. ... At the end of 1941, Singapore fell, and my mother's boyfriend was killed by artillery fire.

Zhang states that his cousin told him about his mother's boyfriend who had once lived in Singapore, a piece of publicly revealed family gossip that matches Chang's fictionalization of Dew's private life story. Zhang Zijing's memoir serves as a doubled and paradoxical echo of Chang's novel, which simultaneously claims to disclose part of their mother's privacy and to mediate her story through his perspective and memory.

More details about the lover can be found in news reports and archives. For instance, *The Singapore Free Press and Mercantile Advertiser* reported that "Miss Yvonne Whang did not shade her electric lights sufficiently in her house in Lincoln Road on Dec. 16 about 7.45pm" and was "arrested and locked up for the night during a brown-out" (Dec 30, 1941). It is believed that Chang's mother, Huang Yifan, was the Yvonne Whang reported in the newspaper. The address was allegedly Lincoln Road 35, Singapore, which was an official address of W. W. Wagstaff. Thus, Huang Yifan's boyfriend is speculated to be W. W. Wagstaff's younger son Alec Wagstaff, a British sculptor and businessman who was conscripted to join the Straits Settlements Voluntary Force (SSVF) in Singapore before December 16, 1941. He was then kidnapped by the Japanese military force on February 15, 1942 with the number WO 345/53, and was forced to build the railway road connecting Thailand and Yangon, Myanmar. After enduring severe working and living conditions, he died at age thirty-six in the construction camp on June 22, 1943 (*Lianhe Zaobao* Feb 21, 2021). Chang's fictional portrayal, Zhang Zijing's retellings of family anecdotes, newspaper reports, and scholarly discussions all represent parts of Huang Yifan's romantic love story from different angles, whether true or not. These various narratives form a palimpscst, an ongoing after-life recreation that blurs the boundaries of autobiography, memoir, fiction, news reports, and scholarly discussion.

In her novels, Chang interprets her mother's thoughts and behaviours by translating her roots, culture, and family, which she both preserves and rebels against. In *The Fall of the Pagoda* and *The Book of Change*, young Lute adores her mother, Dew. However, as she grows up, her admiration of Dew goes sour. The turning point in their relationship comes when Lute makes a great effort to earn a private scholarship of eight hundred dollars from her university teacher but receives only contempt from Dew. Lute interprets her mother's thought as "So her mother thought she had given herself to her history teacher for eight hundred dollars and she could perhaps tell by looking" (*BOC* 104). Here Lute directly points out Dew's assumption that Lute had prostituted herself to her teacher, an immoral act in a culture that values chastity, for her scholarship. In *Little Reunions*, however, the direct speculation becomes a dialogue of indirect implication:

> 蕊秋很用心的看了信，不好意思的笑著說：這怎麼能拿人家的錢？要還給他。
> 九莉著急起來。不是，安竹斯先生不是那樣的人。還他要生氣的，回頭還當我 …… 當我誤會啦，她囁嚅著說。又道：除了上課根本沒有來往。他也不喜歡我。
> *LR* 31

REIMAGINING THE SELF

> Rachel read the letter carefully. "How can we possibly accept someone else's money?" she said with an embarrassed smile. 'It must be returned to him."
>
> "No, Mr. Andrews is not that sort of person," Julie muttered anxiously. "He'd be offended if the money were returned. He'd think ... I'd misunderstood his intentions." She paused, then added, "We have no contact out of class. He doesn't even like me."
>
> PAN AND MERZ 18

The topic of sex is taboo in traditional Chinese culture, and therefore cannot be openly spelled out in conversations between mother and daughter. Ruiqiu's discreet suggestion of Jiuli's sexual transaction with her teacher is, nonetheless, clearly explicated in the Chinese version. Where the English version presents Lute's interpretation of Dew's thoughts in a stark manner that helps Anglophone readers understand the Chinese story more clearly, the Chinese version depicts the dialogue between Jiuli and Ruiqiu with subtle hints about sexual immorality that Sinophone readers would more tacitly comprehend. In both cases, Lute and Jiuli defend their innocence in the face of Dew and Ruiqiu's respective false accusations.

In traditional Chinese culture, daughters are expected to show filial piety to their mothers in tangible ways; in Chang's novels, such piety is violently replaced with monetary compensation. The daughter becomes upset and protests strongly against the notion of dutiful respect when her mother casually loses her scholarship, a reward for her hard work and an embodiment of her self-worth, at the mah-jong table. In *The Book of Change*, Lute attempts to repay her familial debt to Dew by returning her two gold bars as a medium of exchange for the filial devotion expected in Chinese society. Dew misunderstands Lute's ungrateful attitude as though it is her own promiscuity that turns Lute against her, leading Lute to ponder, "But now am I to tell her that it isn't this at all. Then what is it? I just don't like her? No, it's better to let her think it's this. Being Chinese she will think it's only right that I should feel this way. She'll be resigned. There is a beauty and dignity in seeing one's self as a sinner" (*BOC* 108). With her Anglophone readers in mind, Chang emphasizes the importance of filial piety and women's chastity in traditional Chinese culture, while translating her mother's cultural context from a critical distance.

Lute's self-contemplation and emphasis on filial piety and women's chastity is, however, omitted in the Chinese version. Instead, in *Little Reunions*, Jiuli tells her aunt Chudi how she feels about Dew after the scholarship incident: 「『自從那回，我不知道怎麼，簡直就不管了。』她夾著個英文字。」["After that, I don't know why, but I simply didn't care anymore." This part she relayed in English (*LR* 32; Pan and Merz 20)]. In the Chinese novel, though Chang does not explicitly identify which word is spoken in English, it is implied to be "care," the verb that touches Jiuli's heart. This passage demonstrates the notion that "[n]ot only writers, then, but also fictional characters start to behave more independently in a second language. Maybe they would not be able to speak otherwise of the secret, of the forbidden, of that which cannot be said? Might not one find fragments of memories which would have remained hidden from view in the safety of one's first language?" (Evangelista 183). In *Little Reunions*, when she finds it too difficult or impossible to articulate her thoughts and feelings in her mother tongue, Jiuli expresses those feelings in English, her second language, which creates an alienation effect that allows her to let go of them. The dialogue further demonstrates how confused she is about her ambivalent feelings toward her mother.

The estranged mother-daughter relationship is further elaborated in *Little Reunions*. For instance, when she attends the funeral of her cousin Chun, who died of osteoarthritis, Jiuli expresses indifference: 「除了輕微的恐怖之外，九莉也毫無感覺。」 [Apart from a slight eeriness, Julie felt nothing (*LR* 93; Pan and Merz 82)]. Ruiqiu then says of Jiuli: 「『那樣喜歡純姐姐，一點也不什麼，』她回家後聽見蕊秋對楚娣說，顯然覺得寒心。」 ["She used to be so fond of Miss Purity," Julie overheard Rachel saying to Judy on the way home from the funeral, "but she showed no emotion at all." Rachel was obviously disappointed by Julie's lack of compassion (*LR* 93; Pan and Merz 82)]. Though the story itself is told by an omniscient third-person narrator, this particular episode focuses on Jiuli's point of view. Analyzing the critical implications of Ruiqiu's words and feelings, Jiuli projects her own perception of her mother, who is petrified because of her lack of empathy. Ruiqiu seems to be bitterly disappointed because she is nervous about Jiuli's coldness towards her own death in the future which have come true many years later (*LR* 291). This fictional episode can be traced to an experience from Chang's own life: she claimed in a letter to her friends Mae and Stephen Soong, dated October 24, 1957, that she was disturbed about her mother's illness but was unable to visit her mother on her deathbed in England (*To My Beloved Friends* 1.73), which could be plausibly related to her financial constraints at the time.

In her short story "Huadiao" 〈花凋〉 ("Withering Flower," 1944), Chang told the story of another young woman, Zheng Chuanchang 鄭川嫦, who dies of osteoarthritis. However, instead of the mother-daughter relationship, the fragility of romantic/parental love is at the heart of this story. Chuanchang, who grew up with many siblings in a declining aristocratic family in Shanghai, is not her parents' favourite. Her brother introduces her to a doctor, Zhang Yunfan 章雲藩, who is an overseas returnee from Vienna. Soon after beginning her relationship with Yunfan, she contracts tuberculosis, which gradually worsens into osteoarthritis. After six months of her illness, Yunfan says to her, 「我總是等著你的。」 [I am always waiting for you ("Withering Flower" 106)]. However, he cannot fulfill his promise because his passion for her does not last in the face of her illness; two years later, her parents tell her that he has a new girlfriend. In addition, her parents refuse to spend money on her medicine, as her father admits to her mother: 「我花錢可得花個高興，苦著臉子花在醫藥上，夠多冤！」 [I would spend money in a happy way, and spend it on medicine with a bitter face, so wronged! ("Withering Flower" 109)]. Her mother is not willing to buy her medicine either, saying, 「若是自己拿錢給她買，那是證實了自己有私房錢存著。」 [If I buy it for her with my own money, it proves that I have private money saved ("Withering Flower" 109)]. Parental love is severely tested, and found wanting, by financial burden. Ironically, her parents do spend money on a marble angel for her tomb, complete with a loving eulogy, but all this proves their concern for her reputation after her death, rather than for her well-being while she was alive.

The tale of "Withering Flower" can be traced to the real-life story of Chang's relatives, and it demonstrates how she blends the realms of autobiography and fiction by incorporating details of her life and those of her family members into her creative works. According to Chang's younger brother Zhang Zijing, the story's female protagonist, Zheng Chuanchang, was inspired by their cousin Huang Jiayi 黃家漪 (Z. Zhang 258); Chuanchang's father Mr. Zheng is based on their mother's younger twin brother Huang Dingchu 黃定柱 (Z. Zhang 258); and her fiancé Zhang Yunfan is based on Huang Jiayi's fiancé Tang Ouzhou 唐歐洲 (Z. Zhang 262). Chang describes Mr. Zheng as follows: 「鄭先生是個遺少，因爲不承認民國，自從民國紀元起他就沒長過歲數。雖然也知道醇酒婦人和鴉片，心還是孩子的心。他是酒精缸裏泡著的孩屍。」 [Mr. Zheng is a young remainder [of the bygone dynasty], since he does not recognize the Republic of China. Although he also knows good wine, women, and opium, his heart is still the heart of a child. He is the corpse of a child soaked in an alcohol tank ("Withering Flower" 93)]. Zhang Zijing indicates in his memoir that their uncle Huang Dingzhu was displeased with Chang's depiction of him, and with the disclosure of private family issues, in "Withering Flower": 「可是看了花凋，舅舅很不高興。我的表妹黃家瑞回憶說，她爸爸讀完花凋大發脾氣，對我舅媽說：『她問我什麼，我都告訴她，現在她反倒在文章裡罵起我來了！』」 [But having read "The Withering Flower," my uncle was very unhappy. My cousin Huang Jiarui recalled that her father lost his temper after reading "The Withering Flower," and said to my aunt: "I told her whatever she asked me, but now she scolded me in the story instead" (Z. Zhang 258)]. Huang's response to Chang's story was not only prompted by breach of confidentiality, but also by her exaggeration of his personal traits for public literary consumption.

Even as she depicts various characters in her novels in both Chinese and English, Chang translates her multiple selves and reinvents many identities of the self in two linguistic and cultural contexts. Anthony Cordingley notes that "the self-translator is the intermediary of and for an 'original' text and, in some interpretations of the term, also for his or her own 'self'" (*Self-Translation* 1). As part of her self-reflection, she represents not only her own traumatic experiences but those of her brother Zhang Zijing. Money is a major factor in the mistreatment of Hill or Jiulin 九林, the alter ego of Chang's younger brother, in the novels. For example, Hill picks up a check from a wastebasket and signs his name to it. Honor Pearl provokes Elm Brook to slap and accuse him of signing his own name on Elm Brook's checks. Lute is shocked by this incident, and her "tears [pour] down her face in a hot sheet .... She stood crying in her own room, her anger heaving up like a new mountain pushing up out of the earth" (*FOP* 209). She swears revenge against her father and stepmother, echoing Chang's similar sentiments as presented in her life-narrative "Tongyan wu ji" 〈童言 無忌〉 ("From the Mouths of Babes") (132). However, in contrast to his more dispassionate portrayal in *The Fall of the Pagoda, Little Reunions* depicts a more sorrowful Hill, driven by anger and sadness: 「他突然憤怒的睜大了眼睛， 眼淚汪汪起來。」 [Suddenly he glared at Julie, and tears welled up in his eyes (*LR* 114; Pan and Merz 105)]. Both Hill and Jiulin are forced to endure daily beatings; the fatal blow to Hill comes when Honor Pearl regularly offers him drinks of tonic from her cup, so that he contracts tuberculosis from her, from which he ultimately dies (*FOP* 280). As David Der-wei Wang points out, "this imagined loss is where Chang asserts her power as a fiction writer. She must have concluded that she could not spell out the demonic magnitude of her own trauma without seeing the death of hill, Lute's only sibling and the last male descendant of her family" ("Introduction to *FOP*" XI). I further argue that Hill's death also symbolizes Chang's perception of part of her childhood self as dead, due to the prolonged psychological and physical abuse of her brother by her father and stepmother.

During the process of self-translation, Chang produces hermeneutic representations of the multiple selves of her characters. For example, in *The Fall of the Pagoda*, when Dew asks Hill about his weight, Hill mumbles "like a mosquito's hum." Then Lute translates for him to Dew in a louder voice. In addition to speaking for Hill, Lute also outlines his goals in life: "to marry a pretty girl, have a little money and live like a grown-up" (*FOP* 282). In *The Book of Change*, Chang elaborates on Lute's perception of Hill and her responsibility

REIMAGINING THE SELF

for his suffering: Lute blames herself for not being able to "pull him out and remake him" (*BOC* 84). Lute's contemplation of Hill's life goals in *The Fall of the Pagoda* and her self-accusation in *The Book of Change* transition from internal reflection in English into external dialogues between Jiuli and Jiulin in *Little Reunions* in Chinese: 「『你有沒有女朋友？』她隨口問了聲。他略有點囁嚅的笑道：「沒有。我想最好是自己有職業的。』」 ["Do you have a girlfriend?" Julie asked causally. "No," Julian stammered," I think it'd be best to find one who has a job" (*LR* 312; Pan and Merz 310)]. The dialogues between the siblings in their mother tongue underscore their familial bond, an intimate kinship with the warmth of being at home.

Employing the rhetoric of the uncanny, Chang creatively rewrites her brother's life experience into her short story "Moli xiangpian" 〈茉莉香片〉 ("Jasmine Tea," 1943), whose protagonist, Nie Chuanqing 聶傳慶, experiences doubling, a castration complex, and repetition-compulsion, all of which are signs of his familial, affective, and sociocultural disengagement. Chuangqing admires his Chinese professor Yan Ziye 言子夜, whom Chang might have based on her Chinese professor Xu Dishan 許地山 (1893–1941) at the University of Hong Kong (Huang, *Hong Kong Connections*; 135). Suffering from physical and psychological abuse from his father and stepmother, Chuangqing identifies with Yan Danzhu 言丹朱, whose father, Professor Yan Ziye, is his biological mother's ex-lover, as his sister/the Other. Danzhu, however, perceives him as a girl, which damages his sense of masculinity and exposes his hidden anxiety of castration. Chuanqing sees his biological mother as 「銹在屏風上的鳥」 [a bird embroidered onto a screen] and himself as an addition, 「打死他也不能飛下屏風去。他跟著他父親二十年，已經給製造成了一個精神上的殘廢，即使給了他自由，他也跑不了。」 [no matter how much he's beaten, he can't fly away. Twenty years with his father had crippled his spirit. Even if he did receive his freedom, escape was impossible for him (Kingsbury, "Jasmine Tea" 92)]. The repetition-compulsion of the fate of Chuanqing and his mother gives rise to Chuanqing's lifelong sense of melancholy. "Jasmine tea," after which the story is named, is characterized by its sweet smell but bitter taste, a symbol of the discrepancy between Chuangqing's fantasy of growing up in a happy and healthy family in order to develop a vigorously masculine personality, and the cruel reality of his unfulfilled wishes. The emotional despondency that Chuanqing suffers resembles not only Chang's brother's feelings, but also Chang's own reclusiveness and perhaps her yearning for familial and social bonds throughout her life. On the one hand, she revisits the life experience and suffering of herself and her brother in her writing, a therapeutic exercise that allows her to come to terms with her feelings. On the other hand, her urge to retell her traumatic life stories and repressed feelings is an instance of uncanny narration.[1]

The protagonists' wartime experiences in Hong Kong are very much drawn from Chang's own experience. In *The Book of Change*, while studying in Hong Kong, Lute experiences the Japanese invasion and occupation, and Chang incorporates Cantonese words and cultural practices into the story, such as: "Mow dey! Mow dey! Touch the ground! Touch the ground!" cried a pugnacious looking black-browed young man in an open-collared shirt. There was one like this in almost any Cantonese gathering" (*BOC* 180). The Cantonese words *mau dai* 踎低 mean "squat down," a command that may well have been used in an emergency situation in a Cantonese gathering such as the one described in the novel. However, Chang (mis)translates the words into Mandarin as the similar-sounding *mo di* 摸地, which means "touch the ground." She had previously used the Mandarin phrase in her autobiographical essay "Jinyulu" 〈燼餘錄〉 ("From the Ashes," 1944): 「『摸地！摸地！』哪兒有空隙讓人蹲下地來呢？」 (68); ["Hit the deck! Hit the deck!" How could one possibly find a place to hit the deck surrounded by such a lot of people? (Jones 48)]. Chang's juxtaposition of the utterance of "*mo di*" 摸地 [touch the ground] and the following question about squatting down suggests that Chang may have confused the Cantonese colloquial words "*mau dai*" with the Mandarin Chinese words "*mo di*." The inclusion and (mis)translation of Cantonese in an English novel do not simply remind Anglophone readers of different co-existing linguistic and cultural systems, but also create a heterotopia in which Lute constantly navigates back and forth during the war.

These novels also feature coming-of-age stories and rites of passage for their young protagonists. In *The Book of Change*, after having studied at university in Hong Kong for a couple of years and having also escaped the war, Lute has become more self-assertive and developed new perspectives towards her family members. Chang tells the heroic story of Lute who courageously and strategically blackmails Dr. Mok, head of students' relief at university, about his smuggling of food from Japanese army stores and about the death of the Number Four patient involved. Having successfully achieved her plan, Lute purchases one tourist-class boat ticket for herself and seven steerage boat tickets for her friends to Shanghai (*BOC* 285). She describes her new insight near the end of the novel as follows: "Back after three years and still no money to send her [He Gan]. But it seemed enough if both were to hear that the other

---

1 As David Der-wei Wang argues in his introduction to *The Fall of the Pagoda*, "One can discern in Chang's rewritings a Freudian impulse to overcome her childhood trauma by explaining away" (VII).

FIGURE 4   University of Hong Kong Fung Ping Shan Library, Hong Kong (Photo taken in July 2023)
PHOTO CREDIT: JESSICA TSUI-YAN LI

still lived. She also yearned to see her aunt and would not even mind to come face to face with her father and stepmother again with nothing to show. She had learned things in the war and forgotten much too" (*BOC* 293). Lute looks forward to reconnecting with her formerly estranged family members as she yearns for human attachment, which, following the war, has become all the more precious to her. The enlightenment she achieves during the war marks a milestone of her growing up experience.

These dramatic episodes and forgiving reflections are, however, removed in *Little Reunions*. In the Chinese version, Jiuli's inquiry about the boat ticket from Hong Kong to Shanghai is reduced to a few matter-of-fact sentences: 「項八小姐與畢先生來看過她，帶了一包腐竹給她。她重托了他們打聽船票的消息。」[Miss Hsiang and Mr. Pi came to visit Julie, bringing a packet of dried bean-curd skin for her. She in turn implored them to ask on behalf for any news of boat tickets (*LR* 71; Pan and Merz 60)]. There is no elaboration as to how Jiuli manages to get the boat tickets in *Little Reunions*. Perhaps the scene in the Chinese version of the blackmail of several high-ranking officials in Hong Kong could potentially have exposed the identities of those officials, or could have been interpreted as mocking and/or criticism of certain real people, especially for readers who are more familiar with Chinese history and political figures. Therefore, writing during the Cold War period, Chang chose to self-censor the Chinese text in order to avoid controversy. The English version, on the contrary, allows more room for Chang to imagine Lute's possibilities and potentials, or simply to capitalize on the exotic adventurous elements of corruption and blackmail, to improve the novel's mesmerizing power.

Autobiographical experiences may spill out into the spiritual world of fictional characters, as authors lay bare the characters,' and their own, fears and desires, in ambiguously metaphorical self-revelations. In 1906, Stephen Reynolds coined the term *autobiografiction*, which he defined as a "record of real spiritual experiences strung on a credible but more or less fictitious autobiographical narrative" (28). Max Saunders further notes that "Autobiografiction detaches the narrator from the actual writer, using autobiographical form to attach the story securely to the fictional narrator – the actual writer thereby hoping both to tell a good story and to be able to express himself or herself better than might be possible directly" (770). Chang rhetorically translates her self-concept in her stories of the intimate love experiences of Jiuli, her alter ego, in *Little Reunions*:

> 九莉無法再坐下去，只好站起來往外擠，十分惋惜沒看到私訂終身，考中一拼迎娶，二美三美團圓。」
>
> LR 265

> Julie couldn't linger any longer. She stood up and jostled her way to the back of the theater, deeply regretting not being able to witness the unveiling of the lovers' secret pledge to marry without parental permission, the scholar returning a licentiate and marrying both girls, the joyful reunion with the two beauties (or maybe even three).
>
> PAN AND MERZ 262

Jiuli cannot bear watching the ending of the folk performance that embodies the cultural heritage of the Chinese traditional concubinage system, in which she performatively acts out a role. The unseen scene of the protagonist's reunion with the three beauties also underscores the irony of the title *Little Reunions* – Jiuli's lover Zhiyong's patriarchal dream that cannot come true because she decides to walk away from it. This episode corresponds to Chang's actual experience with her first husband Hu Lancheng, who maintained intimate relationships with several other women, before Chang divorced him in 1947.

REIMAGINING THE SELF 67

Even as Jiuli shows her acting self in her conscious decision to walk away from the play, her private self is unconsciously displayed in the dream she has at the end of *Little Reunions*:

有好幾個小孩在松林中出沒，都是她的。之雍出現了，微笑著把她往木屋裏拉。非常可笑，她忽然羞澀起來，兩人的手臂拉成一條直線，就在這時候醒了。 她醒來快樂了很久很久。

LR 325

Some children emerged from the pine forest, and they all belonged to her. Then Chih-yung appeared – elated, beaming – and took her hand to lead her back to the cabin. A comical scene. She blushed as their arms stretched out horizontally in a line, at which point she woke up.

PAN AND MERZ 323

Though in her waking life Jiuli breaks up with Zhiyong due to his adultery and his betrayal of her, she dreams about a harmonious family life with him in a monogamous relationship, and feels happy when she wakes up. Could Jiuli's unfulfilled wish also be Chang's unconscious desire, as she had once experienced some happy moments with her own first love, Hu Lancheng? Or, is Jiuli's dream an impossible one that in reality was already doomed to fail?

Private pain and redemption are transcended in the depiction of Jiuli's bodily experience in *Little Reunions*: 「十幾年後她在紐約，那天破例下午洗澡。在等打胎的來，先洗個澡，正如有些西方主婦在女傭來上工之前先忙著打掃一番。」 [Over a decade later in New York, she made an exception to her usual practiced and bathed in the afternoon. Bathing while waiting for the abortionist to come was like those housewives in the West tidying up the house before the maid arrived (LR 177; Pan and Merz 171)]. The narration of Jiuli's love for and sexual relationship with Zhiyong is interspersed with flashbacks of her abortion of the fetus she conceived with Rudi, a man much older than she is, in New York more than a decade later. This interlude suggests that the emotional and physical pain Jiuli experiences with both Zhiyong and then Rudi, more than ten years apart, is of a similar, if not greater, intensity. The innocent male fetus becomes a sacrifice to the desolation of the human world:

夜間她在浴室燈下看見抽水馬桶裏的男胎，在她驚恐的眼睛裏足有十吋長，畢直的欹立在白磁壁與水中，肌肉上一層淡淡的血水，成爲新刨的木頭的淡橙色。

LR 180

> That night, under the bathroom light, she saw a male fetus in the toilet bowl. In her terrified eyes it was at least ten inches long, leaning upright against the white porcelain, partly submerged in the water. The thin smear of bloody liquid on its skin was the light orange color of newly planed wood.
>
> PAN AND MERZ 173

Jiuli's "terrified eyes" demonstrate her horror at witnessing the death of a human being. However, she compares the fetus' bloody colour with the pale orange of a modified object, showing her emotional detachment from this flesh that came out of her body. Jiuli's abortion experience can be traced to an incident in Chang's life: according to Sima Xin 司馬新, Chang had been pregnant by her second husband Ferdinand Reyher, and may have had an abortion while she was living in New York (104–107). If this were true, Chang may have released her private pain over this alleged event via the fictional utterance she gives to Jiuli. Chang's close friend Stephen Soong convinced her not to publish *Little Reunions* in the 1970s because of its daring content and stark self-revelation. His son Roland Soong then facilitated the publication of this novel in 2009, after most of the key figures represented therein were already dead. *Little Reunions* has enjoyed a growing popularity among Chang's fans, especially in Chinese communities, showing a paradigm shift of moral values regarding the cultural taboos about sex and abortion, which are no longer as unspeakable as they had once been.

CHAPTER 3

Self-Translation as a Performative Act: *Duizhaoji – kan lao zhaoxiangbu* 《對照記——看老照相簿》 (*Mutual Reflections – Looking at Old Photo Albums*)

Though they seem on the surface to project reality, photographs are inevitably mediated by the apparatus and perspectives of the photographer and framed by captions. W.T. Mitchell says of the performative significance of photographs that "[p]erhaps the redemption of the imagination lies in accepting the fact that we create much of our world out of the dialogue between verbal and pictorial representations, and that our task is not to renounce this dialogue in favor of a direct assault on nature but to see that nature already informs both sides of the conversation" ("Image and Word"). This chapter discusses Eileen Chang's *Duizhaoji – kan lao zhaoxiangbu* 《對照記——看老照相簿》 (*Mutual Reflections – Looking at Old Photo Albums*, 1994; hereafter cited as *MR*), which was published shortly before her death, following her reclusive existence in the United States for more than twenty years. In this photo album, Chang enigmatically showcases photographs of herself from childhood to adulthood, along with those of her family members and friends, accompanied by captions that present autobiographical anecdotes. Chang's self-arranged family photo album and captions serve as a critical form of autobiography, in which she reconstructs her public personas and life stories in her own terms.

The first image Chang presents in *Mutual Reflections* is a photograph of herself in the middle, with her aunt Zhang Maoyuan 張茂淵 (1902–1991) on the left and her paternal niece Niuer 妞兒 on the right (*MR* 7), rather than a conventional nuclear family photograph of her father Zhang Zhiyi 張志沂 (Zhang Tingzhong 張廷重 1898–1953), her mother Huang Suqiong 黃素瓊 (Huang Yifan 黃逸梵 1893–1957), her brother Zhang Zijing 張子靜 (1921–1997), and herself. Indeed, there are no such family photographs in the book at all, signifying the fragmented nature of her family and her relationship with them since her childhood. She states that she was probably three or four years old in the photograph because her aunt had left China for Europe when she was four (*MR* 6). Her aunt was a representative of new women in modern China. Influenced by the idea of women's rights and independence advocated during the May Fourth Movement, her aunt and her mother went to England and France to study art and culture. Unlike her mother, who spent most of her life abroad, her aunt accompanied her throughout her turbulent years of childhood, youth,

© JESSICA TSUI-YAN LI, 2025 | DOI:10.1163/9789004730052_005

FIGURE 5
Zhang Maoyuan, Eileen Chang, and Niuer
PHOTO CREDIT: USC DIGITAL LIBRARY. AILING ZHANG (EILEEN CHANG) PAPERS COLLECTION

and early adulthood. The positioning of this photograph at the beginning of the album implicitly discloses how important Chang's aunt was to her, even as she re-creates her family relationships in her old age.

The caption that accompanies this first photograph explicitly translates Chang's individual and relational selves through her kinship and her self-representation. She explains that her paternal niece, Niu'er 妞兒, who looks like a teenager, and much older than her, in the photo, belongs to a younger generation of their family because her paternal niece's grandfather Zhang Renjun 張人駿 (1846–1927) is the paternal nephew of her grandfather Zhang Peilun 張佩綸 (1848–1903). Xiaojue Wang points out that "[a]lthough no single photograph of Zhang Renjun is available in Chang's volume, she nevertheless vividly conveys a prose picture of him by means of a 'visual narrative'" ("Memory" 193). The paradoxical discrepancy in age and generation between Chang and her paternal niece points to her aristocratic family's complex hierarchical system of multiple generations and their corresponding status in the clan. Both her aunt and her paternal niece also display a transcultural outlook in their choice of round eyeglasses, a fashion introduced to China from the West in the early twentieth century. Regarding her own image, she interprets her facial expression as somewhat 「來意不善」 [coming with malevolent intention (*MR* 6)], perhaps a deliberate effort to toughen herself up so as not to be pushed around easily. In this textual image, she constructs a hard-bitten public persona that is intricately intertwined with her fragmented family relationships and her transcultural intermingling.

Chang's depiction of her parents, who had a significant impact on her childhood and adolescent life, is central to the translation of her relational self in her self-fashioned family photo album. A photograph in *Mutual Reflections* features a family gathering of her father, mother, aunt, and two paternal nephews, Niu'er's brothers, sitting at a picnic table in the garden of a Western-style house in Tianjin, where she lived from age two to eight (*MR* 11). Where her father and one paternal nephew wore Chinese long gowns, the other paternal nephew wore a Western-style suit, and her mother and aunt seemed to be wearing blouses with trumpet-styled sleeves and long skirts, adhering to women's fashion in China in the 1910s and 1920s (*MR* 293). This picture represents and translates a transcultural modern lifestyle of an upper-class family in China of the time. Her parents are sitting apart from each other with her paternal nephew standing in the middle; everyone is looking at the camera, except her mother, who is pouring a drink into her glass. This is the only photograph in the book that shows both of her parents together, but it does not reveal any sort of intimate relationship between them.

FIGURE 6   Nephew, Zhang Zhiyi, Nephew, Huang Suqiong, Zhang Maoyuan, Tianjin
PHOTO CREDIT: USC DIGITAL LIBRARY. AILING ZHANG (EILEEN CHANG) PAPERS COLLECTION

The caption reveals the memory of Chang's parents sparked by this image, as she recalls a photo of her father that she found among her mother's belongings. Unfortunately, she had since lost it, but she remembers that her father had written a *qijue* 七絕, a four-line classical Chinese poem with seven characters in each line with rigid tonal and rhyme schemes, on the back. She speculates that her father probably sent it to her mother during the Zhili-Fengtian battles in the northeastern part of China between 1922 and 1924. Though this artefact did not survive the passage to the US and her existence in diaspora, its representation of her parents' mutual affection for each other provided a fond memory that lasted into her old age. She reveals that her father took a concubine and smoked opium, and her parents eventually divorced. However, her mother always asked her not to blame her father (*MR* 10), showing her mother's concern for her relationship with her father and, perhaps, to a certain extent, her mother's understanding of her father's having been nurtured in Chinese patriarchal culture. This family photograph and the poem help to bridge the distance between Chang and her parents, serving as a melancholic and elegiac reconstruction of her family from a distance of many years.

Chang then expands on her thoughts of her adolescent traumatic experience, recounting the story of the day before she sat for the university entrance exam, when she told her father that she would stay at her aunt's home for two days. He permitted her to do so because he knew that her mother and aunt were living together and he 「舊情未斷」 [still had affection towards her mother (*MR* 48)]. This additional information leavens her retrospective reinterpretation of this traumatic incident with a slight sympathy for her parents' ambivalent relationship, even as her testimony of this experience revisits her loss of innocence in her transition from adolescence into adulthood. Her rewriting serves as a prolonged healing process throughout her life, offering the possibility of a positive self-reconstitution.

The photographs of Chang's mother and brother included in *Mutual Reflections* similarly allow her to reconstruct her perceptions of them in word and image and thereby establish her relational self in her own voice. She includes nine portraits of her mother taken in Nanjing, Tianjin, Beijing, London, West Lake in Hangzhou, France, and on a boat, spanning the time from the 1910s to the end of the 1930s. Her selection of these images showcases her admiration for her mother's assertion of autonomy as well as her feelings of unattainability toward her mother's idealized image. Her mother's transcultural taste and diasporic lifestyle have left a deep imprint in her memory, shaping her childhood and teenage self and her appreciation of Western culture. She also includes three photographs of her younger brother and herself in their early childhood: one in which they are holding toys sent from England, one taken at a French

SELF-TRANSLATION AS A PERFORMATIVE ACT

FIGURE 7   Huang Suqiong, London, 1926
PHOTO CREDIT: USC DIGITAL LIBRARY. AILING ZHANG (EILEEN CHANG) PAPERS COLLECTION

FIGURE 8   Eileen Chang and Zhang Zijing, West Lake, Hangzhou
PHOTO CREDIT: USC DIGITAL LIBRARY. AILING ZHANG (EILEEN CHANG) PAPERS COLLECTION

Park in Tianjin, and one from Hangzhou's West Lake (*MR* 16–20). These textual images help her reconstruct her memory of her younger brother as her childhood companion, growing up in a transcultural environment of lost time.

Looking at her family history through family photographs and anecdotes, Chang recreates her ancestors' life stories from the past to assert her sense of self in the present. A portrait of her maternal grandmother in her twenties, staring at the camera with a blank facial expression, is accompanied by a caption telling the story of her grandmother as a farmer's daughter who married a Xiang naval warfare officer's son as a concubine. Her maternal grandmother probably lived close to her maternal grandfather's hometown, Changsha 長沙 in Hunan 湖南 Province. Both of her maternal grandparents passed away in their twenties, so her mother was raised by her step-grandmother. The photograph of her maternal grandmother not only heightens the visual effect of her maternal family history, reminding her of the family member who had been absent since before her birth, but also recreates her grandmother's life story and its effects on her mother's experience that Chang did not see with her own eyes, thus embarking on a journey and, to a certain extent, making up rather than tracking down her family roots.

FIGURE 9
Eileen Chang's maternal grandmother, Changsha, Hunan
PHOTO CREDIT: USC DIGITAL LIBRARY. AILING ZHANG (EILEEN CHANG) PAPERS COLLECTION

Through dynamic oscillation between family history, portraits, memories, and fiction, Chang rewrites her life story and translates a multiple and fluid childhood and youthful self. She finds traces of her paternal family history in the historical novel *Niehaihua* 《孽海花》 (*A Flower in a Sinful Sea*, 1930), written by Zeng Pu 曾樸 (1871–1935) and Jin Songcen 金松岑 (1873–1947). When she visited the house of her great-aunt, Chang noticed that beside their telephone was a list of frequently-used phone numbers, the first of which belonged to Zeng Xubai 曾虛白 (1895–1994), whose father was Zeng Pu. Since Zeng Pu was a close family member, Chang considers Zheng's fictionalized story of her great grandparents and grandparents in *Niehaihua* reliable, even though literary devices are involved: 「《孽海花》裏這一段情節想必可靠，除了小說例有渲染。」 [This part of the plot in *Nie Haihua* must be reliable, except for some renderings (Chang, *MR* 35)]. Negotiating between history and fiction, Chang regards her family history as undetermined rather than absolute, and as subject to her imagination and interpretation.

Producing an intelligible family history based on dynamic points of view, Chang translates her relational self from both individual imagination and collective memory. *Niehaihua* depicts Zhuang Lunqiao 莊崙樵, the literary persona of her grandfather Zhang Peilun, as a righteous late Qing official who impeached other officials, including Li Gong 李公, the literary persona of her great grandfather Li Hongzhang 李鴻章 (1823–1901), leading to their demotion

SELF-TRANSLATION AS A PERFORMATIVE ACT 75

or downfall. The novel implies that since Zhang Peilun advocated for defending his country from foreign invasion rather than compromising its interests, he was assigned to fight against the French military but lost the battle: 「李鴻章愛才不念舊惡。」 [Li Hongzhang loved talents and forgave and forgot grievances of the past (*MR* 34)]. Putting their past behind them, Li Hongzhang admires Zhang Peilun's talents and recruits him to his office. In revisiting this episode from her family history, Chang establishes her public persona by reflecting on her great- grandfather's and grandfather's virtue and competence as told in fictional sources that she considers reliable, albeit mediated by her perspectives, and thus contributing to the building of her self-esteem.

The truth of the account of Chang's grandparents' romantic relationship is, however, controversial. *Niehaihua* fictionalizes the story of how Zhang Peilun met Li Hongzhang's daughter, Li Juou 李菊藕 (1866–1912) in a signing office and later happened to read her *qilü* 七律, an eight-line poem with seven characters to a line and strict tonal and rhyme schemes, titled "Jilong" 〈雞籠〉 ("Chicken Coop"). Li Hongzhang then invited Zhang Peilun to propose to Li Juou (*Niehaihua* 143–144). Her grandparents' coincidental encounter and the existence of the poem "Jilong" described in *Neihaihua*, however, were denied by her father, who could not have witnessed the events himself; Chang notes that 「他一味闢謠，說根本不可能在簽押房撞見奶奶。那首詩也是捏造的。」 [He just refuted the rumour, saying that it was basically impossible [for grandpa] to meet grandma in the signing room. That poem was also fabricated (*MR* 34)]. Chang's fictional portrayal of her grandparents' romantic engagement and her father's personal speculation are both reciprocal and contradictory: though both stories provide conflicting perspectives, they supplement each other in the discourse of family history that is always indeterminate.

Chang's grandparents' love story is upheld by family memory and bound by words, as she uses her artistic freedom to recreate her own imagined intimate world of her family history. In *Mutual Reflections*, she republishes the portrait of her grandmother taken at home and the portrait of her grandfather taken in a photo studio, with similar backgrounds, side by side, so that they appear as a photograph of a couple, put together by her aunt Zhang Maoyuan. According to her aunt, her grandparents collaborated on a collection of poetry, a cookbook, and a martial arts novel, *Zixiaoji* 《紫綃記》 (*The Legend of Purple Hairpin*). Since her grandfather was more than twenty years older than her grandmother, her aunt speculated that her grandmother was not willing to marry her grandfather in the first place, to which Chang then confesses: 「我太羅曼蒂克，這話簡直聽不進去。」 [I am too romantic to bear hearing that (*MR* 40)]. Her reflexive metacommentary on her grandparents' images and anecdotes given by her aunt adds to the indeterminate framework of her family history, a prior text that becomes part of the formation of her early relational self.

FIGURE 10 Li Juou, Eileen Chang's paternal grandmother
PHOTO CREDIT: USC DIGITAL LIBRARY. AILING ZHANG (EILEEN CHANG) PAPERS COLLECTION

FIGURE 11 Zhang Peilun, Eileen Chang's paternal grandfather
PHOTO CREDIT: USC DIGITAL LIBRARY. AILING ZHANG (EILEEN CHANG) PAPERS COLLECTION

Garnering both objective evidence and subjective opinion, Chang accumulates different perspectives from which to approach buried family memories of her grandfather. The photograph of her grandfather she includes in *Mutual Reflections* is yellowish, creating a visual sense of nostalgia. With admiration, she recalls that the portrait of her grandfather in the oil painting hanging during ceremonies of ancestor worship looks 「比較英俊」 [more handsome (*MR* 36)]. Though her father was very stingy, he paid to publish her grandfather's collection of poetry, showing his appreciation and love for his works. Many years later, she heard from others about her grandfather's poetic talent, and she is willing to believe it. Referring to *Niehaihua*, she writes about her grandfather's indulgence in alcoholism due to his job dissatisfaction, leading to his death in his fifties (*MR* 36–38). Through recounting her grandfather's ups and downs in his life from historical, fictional, and personal points of view, she translates her relational self with nostalgic fascination in her own terms to overcome her loss of family connections and rebuild relationships in her visual and textual recreations.

SELF-TRANSLATION AS A PERFORMATIVE ACT

As with her narration of her grandfather's story, Chang embraces other people's perspectives from which to observe her grandmother's life stories, and reconstructs them with her commentary, thus empowering herself to attain a new vision of her relational self. Her aunt Zhang Maoyuan remembers that she loved to touch the small red moles on her grandmother's fair skin and considered them beautiful, showing their intimate mother-daughter bond. Her aunt also says that her grandmother hated the French who invaded China and the Fujianese who blamed her grandfather for losing the battle, which subtly discloses her grandmother's love and defence for her grandfather. Her grandmother's maid He Gan similarly claimed that 「老太太那張總是想方（法）省草紙。」[The old lady always finds a way to save toilet paper (*MR* 44)]. In her commentary, Chang sympathizes with her grandmother's anxiety over financial constraints and her efforts, as a widow, to resolve these constraints.

What strikes Chang most is her grandmother's meticulous and unconventional ways of raising her father and her aunt. Chang's grandmother strictly trained her father to fluently recite Chinese classical literary and historical texts, the pertinent skill set for the Chinese Imperial Examination (587–1905), which only made Chang feel sad because those skills were no longer useful in early modern China. Her grandmother also made her father wear old-fashioned colourful clothes in order to detain him at home, preventing him from getting into trouble. Conversely, her grandmother dressed up her aunt in men's clothes and required the others to address her as "master" and "uncle" instead of "mistress" and "aunt" (*MR* 44–46). In her commentary, Chang considers her grandmother's masculinization of her aunt a peculiar instance of feminism in hopes of ensuring that her aunt would have autonomy in her marriage. Her narration of and reflection on her grandmother's stories present the dialectics between her roles as author and critical reader, adding her own points of view to her self-(re)construction in her old age.

Through narrating the life stories of her great grandparents and grandparents, Chang finds her own voice to re-establish her relationship with her family members. She claims that she was not born early enough to have met her great grandparents and grandparents. However, they quietly provide her with unconditional support, which may seem futile but is what she needs the most: 「他們只靜靜地躺在我的血液裏，等我死的時候再死一次。我愛他們。」[They simply silently lie inside my blood. When I die, they will die again. I love them (*MR* 47)]. Embracing her ancestors' history from different perspectives provides her with a means of translating her relational self from inside and outside. Her pondering of their stories metaphorically revitalizes their lives, which will wither away when she is gone. In this way, she has established her self-concept in the centre of her life writing by recreating her ancestors' after-life stories. Through reconstructing her family sagas in her own words, she comforts her nostalgia for the past family lives she has not experienced first-hand. Her encounter with her family history is indeed a process of her self-becoming.

Chang documents some of her happy moments with her best friend at university, Yanying 炎櫻 (1920–1997), when they returned to Shanghai from Hong Kong in 1942 and lived with Chang's aunt Zhang Maoyuan. Many of the photos in *Mutual Reflections* that feature Yanying were taken on the rooftop of the Eddington House; one of these shows a full body shot of Chang and Yanying, dressed in blouses and skirts, standing on the rooftop of the apartment building (*MR* 52). The smiles on their youthful faces attest to their amiable friendship in the golden years of their early adulthood. Another image features a half-length shot of both of them looking up to the sky, as if envisioning their dreams of the future. The book also includes a close-up portrait of Chang, with artificial highlights and dramatic shadows of blue and orange painted by Yanying. In this image, Chang is wearing a piece of floral cloth as a makeshift shawl (*MR* 56). Her eyes are looking down, suggesting a narcissistic contemplation. Where the photos that depict both Chang and Yanying document their mutual affection, the image that features Chang by herself presents her self-image as a young and vigorous woman, seen from her friend's perspective.

FIGURE 12   Yanying and Eileen Chang, Shanghai, 1944
PHOTO CREDIT: USC DIGITAL LIBRARY. AILING ZHANG (EILEEN CHANG) PAPERS COLLECTION

SELF-TRANSLATION AS A PERFORMATIVE ACT 79

Chang also includes in *Mutual Reflections* a photo taken with the famous actress Li Xianglan 李香蘭 (Yamaguchi Yoshiko 山口淑子, 1920–2014) at a garden party in 1943, which epitomizes her aloof public persona. In this photograph, she sits on a chair with her body tilting to her right and her head to her left, while her eyes gaze at the ground with an indifferent and mocking expression. By contrast, Yamaguchi is smiling at the camera and properly standing aside. Chang explains the photo as follows: 「我太高，並立會相映成趣，有人找了張椅子來讓我坐下，只好委屈她侍立一旁。」 [I was too tall, and it would be interesting to stand side-by-side. Someone found a chair for me to sit on, so I had to make her stand aside (*MR* 60)]. The caption also indicates that Chang's dress was made from her grandmother's bed quilt cover decorated with traditional Chinese patterns of phoenixes, and its modern Western style was designed by Yanying. Her conceited facial expression, inattentive body posture, and transcultural costume combine to establish her individualistic and unconventional public image, especially when compared to Yamaguchi's adherence to conventions Figure 13.

Chang seems dissatisfied with her self-concept in her adolescence, as she recalls an unpleasant experience with her stepmother Sun Yongfan 孫用蕃 (1905–1986). Two photographs from this period appear in *Mutual Reflections*,

FIGURE 13
Eileen Chang and Li Xianglan, Shanghai, 1943
PHOTO CREDIT: USC DIGITAL LIBRARY. AILING ZHANG (EILEEN CHANG) PAPERS COLLECTION

one of which depicts Chang in old clothes that once belonged to her step-mother. Though her stepmother insisted that her old *qipao* dresses were very good quality, some of the collars were already broken. Chang was even more disappointed about having to wear her stepmother's second-hand clothes to St. Mary's Hall, the aristocratic Christian school she attended in Shanghai, especially when she compared her outfits to those of her wealthy and conservative classmates. The negative self-image that resulted was an important contributing factor to her self-characterization as 「衣服狂」 [clothes-crazy (*MR* 30)] later in her life. Her passion for and indulgence in idiosyncratic styles of clothes in her early adulthood can be seen as stemming from not only her low self-esteem at the time but also the discrepancy between her negative self-image and the positive ideal self she envisioned in her adolescence. Carl R. Rogers considers the ideal self "the term used to denote the self-concept which the individual would most like to possess, upon which [one] places the highest value for [oneself]" (200). In a sense, Chang's yearning for the way she wishes she could see herself is manifested in her attire, a factor that she can control when she achieves financial independence in her adulthood.

In depicting her visual and textual self-representation, Chang uses the self-fashioning images in *Mutual Reflections* to perform her acting self in constructing a legendary autobiography at each moment of the different stages of her life. For example, she includes two photographs of herself that were taken in 1944 at the peak of her writing career in Shanghai. In one, she is wearing an oversized robe with wide sleeves in the style of the Qing dynasty and a *qipao* underneath, in a standing pose with her head turning to the right and her left hand raising to touch the wall. In another, she is wearing a bathrobe over a *qipao* in a seated pose, with her left arm embracing her right one, while gazing at the floor with a contented smile (*MR* 62–63). Linda Haverty Rugg points out the significance of agency in photographs and autobiographies, noting that "photographs and autobiographies work together as signs to tell us something about the self's desire for self-determination, it will also be necessary to explore the ways in which these images and texts relate to the body that both constructs and is constructed by them" (9). Chang's idiosyncratic costumes and staged poses promote her glamorous status as a celebrity, as she translates her private self into her public self as a performative enactment.

By displaying her passport photographs in *Mutual Reflections*, Chang explores the conception of the self as the other. One of these, showing her with a slight smile on her face and looking at a distance away from the camera, was taken in 1950 or 1951 when she applied for a certificate, and includes a caption explaining that she was given two pieces of rationed cloth from which she

SELF-TRANSLATION AS A PERFORMATIVE ACT

made a Tang suit with trumpet-style sleeves and a pair of pants. A communist officer who saw her in this costume asked her if she was illiterate, not knowing that she was a famous writer in Shanghai. The other passport photograph was taken shortly before she left Shanghai for Hong Kong in 1952. She recalls that an immigration officer checked her gold-clad rattan bracelet and then praised her honest appearance, saying 「這位同志的臉相很誠實，她說是包金就是包金。」 [This comrade's face is very honest; she said that it was gild then it was gild (*MR* 69)]. While she is amazed by the communist officers' comments on her appearance as documented in the photographs, she sees herself as others see her, bringing to mind Roland Barthes' observation,

> When consideration (with the etymological sense of seeing the stars together as significant constellation) treats the image as a detached being, makes it the object of an immediate pleasure, it no longer has anything to do with the reflection, however oneiric, of an identity; it torments and enthralls itself with a vision which is not morphological (I never look like myself) but organic.
>
> *Roland Barthes* 71

In this sense, the mirrored and double relationship between Chang herself and her photographic images both alienates and blurs the boundary between the self and the other.

Chang compares two self-staged photographs taken in Hong Kong in the 1950s during her heyday. One was taken in a photo studio on Queen's Street in Hong Kong in 1954, and depicts her accompanied by Stephen Soong's wife Mae Fong Soong. She met the Soongs while working for the United States Information Services (USIS), and they became life-long friends. In this half-length snapshot, she is standing in a statuesque pose with her face tilting upward, gazing at a far distance, and her right hand is on her hip, showcasing her confidence in and pride of her public persona as a famous writer. When she found this photograph thirty years later in 1984 in Los Angeles, she lamented the passing of her golden era. Another photograph, taken in 1955, before she left Hong Kong for the United States, is a close-up of the side of her face, looking down in contemplation. She recounts that the immigration officer in Honolulu recorded her height as six feet and six and a half inches, and considers this misrepresentation the officer's Freudian slip for his perception of her height due to her slender stature (*MR* 71–73). In these two iconic photographs, she performs her highly esteemed public self, appearing in dignified costumes and poses, shaped by the act of lofty literary self-representation with nostalgia.

 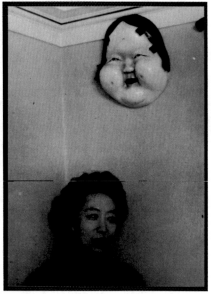

FIGURE 14 Eileen Chang, Hong Kong, 1954
PHOTO CREDIT: USC DIGITAL LIBRARY. AILING ZHANG (EILEEN CHANG) PAPERS COLLECTION

FIGURE 15 Eileen Chang, San Francisco, 1961
PHOTO CREDIT: USC DIGITAL LIBRARY. AILING ZHANG (EILEEN CHANG) PAPERS COLLECTION

Displaying her personal significant photographic self-portraits, Chang weaves a continuously coherent self that appears to be multifaceted. One image reprinted in *Mutual Reflections*, taken at home in San Francisco in 1961, shows her smiling face under a Japanese Otafuku Noh mask. *Otafuku* means *good fortune*, represented by a smiling Japanese woman who brings happiness to her husband. Her self-contented image and the stylized and codified facial expression conveyed by the mask are juxtaposed within the frame, establishing a profound association that stimulates the audience's imagination about her harmonious married life with her second husband, Ferdinand Reyher (1891–1967).

Figure 16 This image is followed by a passport photograph taken in a photo studio in San Francisco before she went to Hong Kong in 1962, as well as two close-up images. She looks straight at the camera with a grin in one of these, taken in 1966 before she left Washington, D.C., and she looks at a far distance with a beam of satisfaction in the other, taken in Boston in 1968 (*MR* 74–78). In her caption, she states that she publishes those photographs because she is afraid to lose them. She sketches a coherent and continuous, yet still chaotic and

SELF-TRANSLATION AS A PERFORMATIVE ACT 83

FIGURE 16
Eileen Chang, Washington, D.C., 1966
PHOTO CREDIT: USC DIGITAL LIBRARY.
AILING ZHANG (EILEEN CHANG) PAPERS
COLLECTION

scattered, 「自畫像」 [self-portrait (MR 79)]. In *The Russian Album,* Michael Ignatieff states, "For many families, photographs are often the only artefacts to survive the passage through exile, migration or the pawnshop" (4); Chang reconstructs her diasporic life experiences in San Francisco, Hong Kong, Washington, D.C., and Boston in this group of visual and textual self-portraits, which produce both penetrating and esoteric shaping effects on her public persona.

At the end of *Mutual Reflections*, Chang displays a photograph of herself holding a newspaper with a headline marking the passing of President Kim II-sung 金日成 (1912–1994) one day prior. She reflects on her feeling that 「天涯共此時」 [from afar we share this moment (MR 80)] as a way to prove that she was still alive on June 9, 1994. This Chinese phrase is quoted from Tang poet Zhang Jiuling's 張九齡 (AD 678–AD 740) poem "Wangyue huaiyuan" 〈望月懷遠〉 ("Longing for Loved Ones Afar while Looking at the Moon"), which might echo Chang's nostalgic feelings of her past, acquaintances, and imagined homeland at that moment. The image is followed by a poem in which she thanks time for treating her well so far, though she knows her life will end at any time, presenting her satisfactory but cynical view of life and death in her old age. This photograph illuminates her public persona amid the arcaneness of her life journey nearing its end, witnessing not only her own existence at that moment but also the passing of an era, the Cold War period (1947–1991), that had significantly affected her life and writing career, which will be discussed in more detail in Chapter Four. The revealing and concealing of both her acting self and her private self in her memoirs, semi-autobiographical fiction, and family photo album together constitute her multiple and dynamic self in her self-promotion as a legendary figure.

Chang's memoirs, semi-autobiographical novels, and family photo albums mainly focus on her childhood and adolescence, accompanied by sketches of her diasporic life experience in adulthood. She perceives her childhood as happy and mellow, but stumbles through her teenage years with the romance of her grandparents as a comfort, and then represents her adulthood with montages of visual and textual self-portraits. She translates her self-concept in her memoirs of her early adulthood, tracing the development and formation of her individual, relational, and collective identities. The construction of multiple selves in her semi-autobiographical novels exhibits not only their constitutive factors of her individual personalities, but also the power of the making of the self from her perspectives in her middle age. Her self-translations of *The Fall of the Pagoda* and *The Book of Change* into *Little Reunions* appear to be rather loose renditions with extensive changes of not only the language, but also the plots, characters' names, focuses, sensibilities, literary styles, and sentence structures. *Little Reunions* can be considered as a rewriting, rather than a narrowly defined translation, of the two English novels. She cautiously paid attention to her target audience, and, more importantly, she exercised her author as self-translator's liberty to recreate her own works at this mature writing stage. The photographs featured in her album show her changes in appearance through both time and space, with captions framing her self-representation from the vantage point of her old age. Her numerous recollections of her life stories are inevitably incomplete, just as the complexity of the self can never be truly known. The multiple selves and identities Chang constructs in various texts during the different stages of her life show not only her earnest quest for self-analysis and her urge to construct her identity in her own terms by communicating her experience and feelings to others, but also her family upbringing, and the sociohistorical impact of the May Fourth Movement, the Second World War, and the subsequent Cold War.

PART 2

Paradoxical In-Betweenness

∵

CHAPTER 4

Interdependence: "Jinsuoji" 《金鎖記》 ("The Golden Cangue"), *The Rouge of the North, Yuannü* 《怨女》 (*Embittered Woman*), and "The Golden Cangue"

This study of the relationship between Eileen Chang's fiction and self-translations focuses on her works' transcultural features, particularly on the state of in-betweenness that can more precisely describe the specifically transcultural characteristics of Chang's self-translations. As noted in the Introduction, Chang's self-translation is paradoxical: it 'represents' the source text in the rendition of plots and characters, but it cannot "reproduce" completely, as her translations present them with semiotic, semantic, and discursive strategies from another linguistic and cultural system. Moreover, the hierarchy of political, ethical, and social values in the language of a translation may differ from, and therefore subvert, those of the source text. Accordingly, the translation can be both in harmony with and a challenge to the source. Although Chang's self-translation transforms the source text, it cannot, in my view, be independent because a translation still employs the forms of representation and structure of the source text. In this sense, no translation, including self-translation, is completely new; any additional meaning is generated by the source text.

Chang's self-translations differ from translations of her works done by others. The most important factor is that she knows what ideas she intends to convey in her writing better than others do; therefore, in the process of translating her own works, she can follow and adapt her earlier representations. Other translators are denied access to her authorial intention, a fact that is controversial in literary criticism, but cannot be ignored. Through self-translation, Chang can interpret her own works by extending, sometimes even subverting, her earlier writings and highlighting and rearticulating key issues. The major feature of Chang's self-translations is that they are her very own interpretations and reconstructions of her works. Her translated work and the self-translation become interdependent. Her self-translation both extricates meaning from and adds value to the source text, while the source text not only gives meaning to but also exposes the significance of her self-translation. This interdependent relationship breaks through the boundaries between source texts and translations as well as between author and translator. Because the

© JESSICA TSUI-YAN LI, 2025 | DOI:10.1163/9789004730052_006

two works cannot be substituted for one another, the significance of both texts together is greater than that of each one seen in isolation.

Here I offer a new perspective on Chang's works as instances of what had previously seemed to be a unique case, but which is, in the globalized world of the future, becoming more common: writers with bilingual and bicultural backgrounds translating their own works. This study focuses on two aspects of her production. First, as a self-translator, Chang has the copyright on her own work and is thus free in terms of *droit moral*; therefore, she enjoys much more aesthetic freedom in translating her own work than any other translator, who would be bound by copyright and concerns of loyalty to the source texts. Second, in translation herself, Chang re-evaluates and re-contextualizes her own works by expanding and even undermining the formulations of her source texts, including depictions of the body – a significant theme in her work that is discussed in more detail below. These conversions between different linguistic and cultural systems are made in order to construct a transcultural aesthetics of the body.

The aesthetics of the body is a prominent theme in Chang's writing, particularly the three different perspectives on the beauty of the body and of bodily sensations in Chinese culture: first, the flesh or the corporeal body; second, the whole human being who unifies the corporeal body and the mind; third, the harmony of social relationships, an important virtue in Confucianism, that is regulated by the aesthetics of the body. In Western culture, the body and the mind are traditionally regarded as separate, and only relatively recently has the interaction between the two been investigated. Western theories concentrate on the social construction of the aesthetics of the body through materialization, commodification, and performance.

This section investigates the interdependent relationship between Chang's fiction and self-translations, the authorship of Chang as author and self-translator, the difference between Chang's self-translations and translations of her works done by others, and the re-evaluation and recontextualization of her works in a globalized context. The particular case studies in this section are her novella "Jinsuoji" 〈金鎖記〉 ("The Golden Cangue," 1943) and her multiple translations of this work as *The Rouge of the North* (1967), *Yuannü* 《怨女》 (*Embittered Woman*, 1966), and "The Golden Cangue" (1971); her Chinese short story "Guihuazheng: A Xiao beiqiu" 〈桂花蒸——阿小悲秋〉, 1944), her translation into English as "Shame Amah" (1962), and Simon Patton's English translation as "Steamed Osmanthus Flower: Ah Xiao's Unhappy Autumn" (2000); her Chinese short story "Deng" 〈等〉 ("Waiting," 1944) and her English translation "Little Finger Up" (1957 and 1961); her story "Stale Mates – A Short Story Set in the Time When Love Came to China" (1956) and her own

INTERDEPENDENCE

translation into Chinese as "Wusi yishi – luowentao sanmei tuanyuan" 〈五四遺事——羅文濤三美團圓〉 ("Regret after the May Fourth Movement – The Reunion of Luo Wentao and the Three Beauties," 1957); and her English short story "She Said Smiling" (2022) and its Chinese version "Xiangjianhuan" 〈相見歡〉 ("A Joyful Rendenzvous," 1978). All of these stories focus on the aesthetics of the body in both Chinese and Western contexts. This section aims to show the importance of the state of in-betweenness, seen as a notion of bridge-building across the space between author and self-translator, translated text and self-translation, author and reader, as well as the Chinese and Western representations of the female body. This breaking down of boundaries and hierarchies between various dichotomies allows us to perceive multiple cultural views of the female body that both perpetuate and transgress Chinese and Western perspectives.

The relationship between a source text and a self-translation is complementary and interdependent, as the author/self-translator creates and recreates their source text and self-translation that have implications for each work alone. Moreover, they might produce their source text and self-translation simultaneously, or make changes back and forth in the process. As Julio-César Santoyo argues, "This dynamic relationship is born especially when original and self-translation face each other during the writing process, and both become witnesses and protagonists of their common development, recreating and influencing each other as the author writes one text in parallel with the other" (Santoyo 30). Santoyo points out that the process of self-translation can be parallel and interactive rather than linear in a traditional sense. Analyzing the nuance of the languages, styles, tones, and content between the source text and self-translation will yield a better understanding of all the related texts together.

This chapter[1] examines Chang's "Jinsuoji" and her three rewritings/translations of it into *The Rouge of the North* (hereafter cited as *RON*), *Yuannü*, and "The Golden Cangue" (hereafter cited as "TGC"). In *Paratexts: Thresholds of Interpretation*, Gérard Genette refers to such multiple stories with similar plots as palimpsests, in which earlier versions leave traces for later ones, and the later versions transcend their predecessors but remain in between the invisible marks left behind by the earlier versions. I argue that "Jinsuoji" and its revisions/translations exemplify a state of in-betweenness, in which Chang both elaborates upon and undermines the representations of the female body

---

1   Part of this chapter has been based on the following previously published article: Li, Jessica Tsui- yan. "Self-Translation/Rewriting: The Female Body in Eileen Chang's 'Jinsuo ji', *The Rouge of the North, Yuannü* and 'The Golden Cangue.'" *Neohelicon* 37.2: 391–403. DOI 10.1007/s11059-009-0028-y

90   CHAPTER 4

in earlier versions. The female body, as constructed in these four versions of the story, illustrates simultaneously an imprisonment by and a resistance to both Chinese and Western aesthetic ideals. In what follows, I will investigate the multiple revisions and translations of this tale, the changes of title and focus, the beginnings and the endings, and the revisions of the representations of the female body, and will offer some possible reasons for their transformation and the significance of those transformations. All these versions form an interdependent relationship that provides a fuller meaning of both Chinese and Western aesthetics during the modernization period in China in the early twentieth century.

The novellas "Jinsuoji" and "The Golden Cangue" narrate the life of Ts'ao Ch'i-ch'iao (henceforth Ch'i-ch'iao); and the novels *The Rouge of the North* and *Yuannü* depict the life of Chai Yindi (henceforth Yindi). Both Ch'i-chi'iao's and Yindi's physical and psychological degenerations parallel the breakdown of their respective aristocratic families from the fall of the Qing dynasty to the end of the Sino-Japanese War. Using the beauty and youthfulness of their bodies as commodities, they attain wealth, at the expense of love and sexual desire, through arranged marriages with a blind and crippled husband, the Second Master, in Chinese aristocratic feudal households, called the Chiangs in the novellas and renamed the Yaos in the novels. Tormented by unsatisfied sexual drives, these two women seduce their respective brother-in-law, named Chi-tse in the novellas but referred to only as the Third Master in the novels. Where Ch'i-ch'iao is rejected by Chi-tse in her youth and becomes disillusioned by his deceptive affection in her middle age, Yindi surrenders to the Third Master's flirtation in a temple and attempts to commit suicide afterwards. Both Ch'i-ch'ao and Yindi then torture their children and daughters-in-law, and eventually die.

Chang wrote "Jinsuoji" based on the family anecdotes of Li Jingshu 李經述 (1864–1902), the second son of her great-grandfather Li Hongzhang 李鴻章 (1823–1901) (Z. Zhang 242–262). Working from the characters and plot of "Jinsuoji," Chang wrote *Pink Tears* during her stay at the MacDowell Colony between 1956 and 1958 (Sima 81, 98, 126); however, it was not accepted for publication. Chang then rewrote it as *The Rouge of the North*, but this was not published either (Q. Song, "Siyu Zhang Ailing" 41). She subsequently translated this version into Chinese as *Yuannü*, which was first serialized in *Xingdao wanbao* 《星島晚報》 (*Singdao Night Newspaper*) in Hong Kong (Tang 372) and *Huangguan* 《皇冠》 (*Crown*) in Taiwan in 1966. She then retranslated *Yuannü* into English, under the same English title as her earlier novel, *The Rouge of the North*. The revised English version was then published by the Cassell Company of London in 1967 and republished by the University of California Press in 1998. She revised *Yuannü* again after she thought its manuscript was lost in the mail when she sent it to Hong Kong in 1965, as she mentioned in a letter to Hsia Chih-tsing dated March 31, 1966 (Zitong and Yiqing 293). The Crown Publishing Company then republished the modified Chinese version in 1968. Later on, Chang translated her Chinese novella "Jinsuoji" into English as "The Golden Cangue," which was included in *Twentieth Century Chinese Stories,* published by Columbia University Press in 1971. In all, Chang rewrote this particular story at least seven times (Kao, *Zhang Ailing xue* 294–295). This section focuses on four widely circulated versions of the story: the Crown publications of "Jinsuoji" and *Yuannü*, the University of California Press's version of *The Rouge of the North*, and the Columbia University Press's version of "The Golden Cangue."

The Rouge of the North can be seen as both a rewriting and an English translation of "Jinsuoji." Chang used a Western language to recontextualize a culturally Chinese story in order to depict the alienation of women in Chinese feudal society in the early twentieth century by highlighting the traditional Chinese cultural codes that normalized gender behaviour. While writing *Yuannü*, Chang likely had both "Jinsuoji" and *The Rouge of the North* in mind. In *Yuannü*, she both extended and transformed her earlier depictions of the female body. This change can in turn be explained by Chang's familiarity with her mother tongue and its culture, and her consideration of the reception of *The Rouge of the North* by Anglophone readers. Most importantly, these texts allow her to foreground key issues in order to rearticulate a representation of the female body that is unique to her. The later versions of *The Rouge of the North* and "The Golden Cangue" complicate the entire writing and translation processes by referring to all their previous versions. Chang's rewriting/translation of the story breaks down the conventional linear process of translation from one language and cultural context to another, and suggests instead a multiple and non-hierarchical structure for the process of translation.

In his preface to *The Rouge of the North*, David Der-wei Wang has offered a detailed analysis of possible reasons why Eileen Chang rewrote and translated the same story several times. First of all, she may have wanted to establish herself as a distinguished writer of both Chinese and English fiction in China and in the United States. Her "Jinsuoji" was praised by Fu Lei 傅雷 (1908–1966), a renowned Chinese scholar and translator of French literature, as one of the best literary works of the time in China (Xun/Fu 121). In the pioneering *History of Modern Chinese Fiction* (1961), Hsia Chih-tsing calls the novella "the greatest novelette in the history of Chinese literature" (398). Since Chinese critics reviewed "Jinsuoji" positively, Chang may have attempted to win the same acclaim for its English revisions, *Pink Tears* and *The Rouge of the North*, in the United States, but in vain (Sima 81; Wang, "Foreword" IX–X). In addition, she might have wanted to recapture more than once her memories of her beloved city, Shanghai, in the early twentieth century. Moreover, the story of "Jinsuoji" might have reminded Chang of the saga of her own aristocratic family, and rewriting that story could have allowed her to overcome the trauma of her own family's decline in the late Qing period. Furthermore, in her English translation Chang was able to use a different language to explore the alienation of women in a feudal system (Wang, "Foreword" x–xii). I further argue that Chang explores the evolving aesthetics of the body in general, and the female body in particular, in Shanghai in the early twentieth century through the fictionalization of her family saga in "Jinsuoji" and her multiple self-translations/ rewritings of it in both Chinese and English over a span of twenty-four years. All these renditions form an interdependent relationship that epitomizes the ongoing transformation of Chinese traditions and the interaction of those traditions with Western values and practices, and it is this possibility that engages the representations of the female body, my specific concern in this chapter.

Chang's female protagonists' entanglement with the ongoing transformation of gender regulations can be studied in light of the dynamic gender politics operative in each version's specific sites of production in particular periods of time. Ch'i-ch'iao's observation, and slight transgression, of the Confucian doctrines of women's conduct can be traced to the gender politics in Shanghai in the early twentieth century. The story as narrated was probably set in Shanghai between the 1910s and the 1940s, with the time and place of the story both shaping the representation of Ch'i-ch'iao. The May Fourth Movement in 1919 advocated the emancipation of women from domestic roles in traditional families; similarly, Henrik Ibsen's (1828–1906) *A Doll's House* (1879) was popular among cultivated women who regarded its protagonist, Nora, as a symbolic figure of the new woman who leads an independent life. The leftist writer Lu Xun (1881–1936) gave a talk at the Peking Women's Normal College on December 26, 1923, titled *Nuola zouhou zenyang?* 〈娜拉走後怎樣？〉 (*What Happens After Nora Leaves Home?*). This speech explores the disastrous consequences of women's escape from Chinese traditional families and the lack of opportunities for women to earn a living in China in the early twentieth century. Eileen Chang's mother, Huang Yifan 黃逸梵 (1896–1957), was perhaps one of those few resourceful women who were able to leave their families and seek an independent life. Most women, by contrast, still remained in the domestic domain. The magazine *Liangyou huabao* 《良友畫報》 (*The Young Companion*) often included photos of young women in different styles of fashionable clothes, sometimes with children in newly furnished homes: as these "advertisements suggest, women's new roles are still to be found in the home, and it is a home-made anew by modern conveniences and interior design. The domestic space of the household is now fully open, 'published,' and as such becomes a public issue" (L.O. Lee 69). The availability of modern technology and luxuries in early twentieth-century Shanghai changed the lifestyles of bourgeois women, whose gender roles were still confined by Confucian teachings, while simultaneously evolving in a liberal manner. Such dynamic female consciousness serves as a background to "Jinsuoji" and its translation "The Golden Cangue," in which Ch'i-ch'iao plays her female roles prescribed by Confucian teachings in order to secure her position in the feudal family, though she slightly transgresses those boundaries, driven by her personal desire.

Chang's rather liberal portrayals of female subjectivity in *The Rouge of the North* and *Yuannü* can be traced to the gender politics in the United States in the 1960s, when both versions were published, during which time sex discrimination was being criticized and social norms were being challenged. Following the model of the civil rights movement, the feminist and gay and lesbian movements attempted to transform American society, and they were themselves being transformed in the process as well. Gender politics intertwined with racial politics as people from different ethnic backgrounds worked together to create a more integrated society (Breines 3–18). One such active American feminist was Rebecca Hourwich, the former wife of Eileen Chang's second husband Ferdinand Reyher (1891–1967). The more heterogeneous and fluid conceptualizing of the female body of Yindi in Chang's novels perhaps may well have been influenced by the social movements of the time, Chang's involvement with Hourwich's husband, and her personal lived experience.

The titles of "Jinsuoji" and "The Golden Cangue" highlight the cultures of the material and of consumption in the twentieth century, which, arguably, women have exploited and in turn been exploited by. The literal translation of the title "Jinsuoji" is "the record of the golden chain," with the word *suo* 鎖 [chain] referring to the connected metal links used to hold a prisoner. The word *cangue* in the English title is French, and its meaning can be traced to an old device used for corporal punishment and public humiliation, consisting of "a broad heavy wooden frame or board worn round the neck like a kind of portable pillory as a punishment in China" (Simpson and Weiner, *Oxford English Dictionary* 831). Both the golden chain and cangue paradoxically connote both, on the one hand, jewellery items such as rings, bracelets, and necklaces, which women wear to signify beauty and social status; and, on the other, the marital, economic, and social bondage to which women are subjected regardless of conscious or unconscious consent. Since the cangue offers a more severe association with punishment than the chain, the title of the translation makes the imprisonment of the female protagonist much more overt than in the Chinese text.

In both versions, the golden chain and cangue specifically symbolize the material imprisonment to which Ch'i-ch'iao confines herself. The golden cangue also represents her later perverted and malicious behaviour in abusing the people living around her, such as her son, daughter, and daughter-in-law:

三十年來她(七巧)戴著黃金的枷。她用那沉重的枷角劈殺了幾個人，沒死的也送了半條命。她知道她兒子女兒恨毒了她，她婆家的人恨她，她娘家的人恨她。

"JINSUOJI" 285

For thirty years now she [Ch'i-ch'iao] had worn a golden cangue. She had used its heavy edges to chop down several people; those that did not die were half killed. She knew that her son and daughter hated her to the death, that the relatives on her husband's side hated her, and that her own kinsfolk also hated her.

"TGC" 190

The colour, metal, and circular shape of the cangue all vividly symbolize the material and ethical confinement that Ch'i-ch'iao suffers and, in return, uses to exploit others. Chang uses the word 「恨毒」 [maliciously hate] to describe Ch'i-ch'iao's children's attitude towards her in the Chinese version, and the words *hated her to death* in the English version, with the word choice not only reflecting the different languages in which the texts are written but also strengthening the dramatic significance of the word "cangue" in the English title.

While the golden cangue metaphorically represents her socioeconomic confinement, Ch'i-ch'iao's corporeal body concretely shows her dreams, anguish, and hopes, with her jewellery embodying both her increasing wealth and her spiritual decline. When contemplating her life on the opium couch as she approaches her own death, she knows that her body has been significantly transformed:

她摸索著腕上的翠玉鐲子，徐徐將那鐲子順著骨瘦如柴的手臂往上推，一直推到腋下。她自己也不能相信她年青的時候有過滾圓的胳膊。就連出了嫁之後幾年，鐲子裏也只有塞得進一條洋縐手帕。

"JINSUOJI" 285

She groped for the green jade bracelet on her wrist and slowly pushed it up her bony arm as thin as firewood until it reached the armpit. She herself could not believe she'd had round arms when she was young. Even after she had been married several years the bracelet only left room enough for her to tuck in a handkerchief of imported crepe.

"TGC" 190

The 「翠玉鐲子」 [green jade bracelet] she has been wearing since she was married echoes the symbol of the golden cangue, and both the Chinese bracelet and the metaphorical cangue are tightly connected with the transformation of Ch'i-ch'iao's body. The change of her arm from 「滾圓」 [round] to 「骨瘦如柴」 [as thin as firewood] represents the difficulties she has undergone. The Chinese idiom 「骨瘦如柴」 [as thin as firewood] is literally translated in "The Golden Cangue," thus also translating the Chinese literary convention of the bony body into the English text.

The values and practices of consumption presented in "Jinsuoji" and "The Golden Cangue" highlight the material culture of Shanghai as a cosmopolitan metropolis in the early twentieth century. The international settlements in Shanghai brought various Western modern urban facilities to the city: banks (introduced in 1848), Western-style streets (1856), gaslights (1865), electricity (1882), telephones (1881), running water (1884), automobiles (1901), and trams (1908) (L.O. Lee 6). Infrastructure such as office buildings, hotels, churches, clubs, cinemas, coffeehouses, restaurants, deluxe apartments, and racecourses were also influenced by Western models of material modernity. Department stores sold both Chinese and foreign commodities as daily necessities and modern luxuries, advertised in newspapers, magazines, journals, and billboards lit up by neon lights, and all of this inspired an almost ritualistic approach to material consumption among Shanghai citizens (L.O. Lee 6, 16). All of these elements originating in both Chinese and foreign markets contribute to the cultural background of material consumption Chang depicts in "Jinsuoji" and her multiple revisions of this story.

Based on the aesthetics of the material and the ideology of consumption presented in "Jinsuoji" and "The Golden Cangue," *The Rouge of the North* and *Yuannü* further elaborate on representations of the female body, but this time as a means of provocation. The title of *The Rouge of the North* is derived from the epigraph of the book: "The face powder of southern dynasties, the rouge of northern lands." This epigraph is, however, absent in all other versions. The title, *The Rouge of the North*, introduces the motif of rouge and offers a more benign image than the tragic and fearful sense given in the novella. In *The Rouge of the North*, Yindi is marked by the colour of rouge, instead of by the golden cangue as Ch'i-ch'iao is in "Jinsuoji" and "The Golden Cangue." Compared to the novellas, the novel uses the details of Yindi putting on makeup more vividly and symbolically as representations of the aesthetic ideal: "She tore off a piece of crimson cotton wool, dipped it in the basin and rubbed it on her lower lip making a perfectly round red spot, the current abstract representation of the small cherry mouth" (*RON* 33). The "round red spot" and "small cherry mouth" are instances of the dominant aesthetic sensibilities of twentieth-century Shanghai to which Yindi seeks to conform, though the pressure she feels to use excessive face powder goes against Shanghai's traditional beauty norms:

> She had noticed that the women of the house used much more rouge than was customary and there were heavily painted middle-aged women among their relatives. They were northerners, countrified by Shanghai standards. Their clothes also – all the fashionable pale colours were forbidden – too like light mourning. Old Mistress would say, 'I'm not dead yet, no need to wear mourning.' Pale cheeks were also called funereal. Yindi steeled herself to smear both palms red and simply draw them down the sides of her face from eyelids down.
>
> *RON* 33

The discrepancy between the aesthetic ideals of the Yaos and those of most of Shanghai reflects the displacement of the family: they are northerners who came to Shanghai, an international settlement, during the downfall of the Qing dynasty. It also reflects the family's conservatism, since the bright colour of the rouge is meant to avoid the paleness that is associated with death, and is also a mark of the Old Mistress' control over the female family members' physical appearances. Having grown up in Shanghai, Yindi is obliged to cope with this inversion of values (because of cultural displacement) in the Yaos by conforming to their aesthetic standards. The amount of rouge signifies both the cultivated and popular ideals of beauty, as well as the dislocation of the family and Yindi's sense of being displaced in the household.

The title of *Yuannü* suggests similar but different motifs. The word *yuan* 怨 denotes an "embittered," "sullen," and "rancorous" state in a person, often associated with the feminine persona in *guiyuan shi* 閨怨詩 [Boudoir Lament Poetry], a category of classical Chinese poetry. Situated in an oppressive patriarchal system, women who are incapable of defending themselves from maltreatment develop feelings of frustration and bitterness. The word *nü* 女 refers to "women" in general. *Yuannü*, therefore, is not only the story of Yindi herself, but is also a story of the stereotypical representations of melancholy and vengeful women who have been denied independence in Chinese society (Wang, "Foreword" XXII). For instance, Yindi finds her own archetype in Peking Operas and classical Chinese literature:

> 臉上胭脂通紅的，直搽到眼皮上，簡直就是她自己在夢境中出現，看了有很多感觸。有些玩笑戲，尤其是講小家碧玉的，伶

牙俐齒，更使她想起自己當初 … … 像《紅樓夢》裏的老太太，跟前只要美人侍奉。就連他們自己家的老太太不也是這樣？娶媳婦一定要揀漂亮的，後來又只喜歡兒子的姨奶奶們，都是被男人擱在一邊的女人，組成一個小朝庭，在老太太跟前爭寵。

YUANNÜ 169

The women on the stage had rouged eyelids continuous with the deep pink cheeks just like she herself when she was young .... The comediennes wore the jacket and trousers fashionable about ten years ago, like hers, just flashier and embroidered all over, which looked right over the footlights. The resemblance was so haunting she was easily moved by the story .... Like the old lady in *A Dream in the Red Chamber* who likes to be surrounded by beauties and served only by them. Even their own Old Mistress here had had her court made up of her sons' wives and concubines, all chosen for their charms and then relegated to a manless life.

RON 157

Yindi finds herself resembling not only Peking opera singers in terms of makeup, costumes, and witty speech, but also those married beautiful women who are soon abandoned by their husbands and urged to please the old matriarch in *Hongloumeng*《紅樓夢》 (*Dream of the Red Chamber*, 1791). She thus herself becomes an emblematic figure of the melancholy lived experience of women in the traditional Chinese patriarchal society. In the Chinese version, Chang uses the word 「伶牙俐齒」 [eloquent] to describe 「小家碧玉」 [a beautiful young woman in a humble family], with the particular connotations that these words would have for Chinese readers in mind. In the English version, Chang only focuses on the singers' fashionable costumes without describing their characteristics, giving Anglophone readers an impression of stylish beautiful women.

The beginnings and endings of the novellas and the novels suggest a shift in Chang's representation of female subjectivity from rigid to dynamic. The novellas begin with descriptions of the moon: 「老年人回憶中的三十年前的月亮是歡愉的，比眼前的月亮大、圓、白；然而隔著三十年的辛苦路望回看，再好的月色也不免帶點淒涼。」 ("Jinsuoji" 238) [In old people's memory the moon of thirty years ago was gay, larger, rounder, and whiter than the moon now. But looked back on after thirty years on a rough road, the best of moons is apt to be tinged with sadness ("TGC" 138)]. The moon signifies the mixed feelings of desire, hope, happiness, frustration, and sorrow that Ch'i-ch'iao has experienced in her life. The story similarly ends with imagery of the moon, giving the reader the sense of both a lament and a repetition:

「三十年前的月亮早已沉下去，三十年前的人也死了，然而三十年前的故事還沒完——完不了。」("Jinsuoji" 286) [The moon of thirty years ago has gone down long since and the people of thirty years ago are dead but the story of thirty years ago is not yet ended—can have no ending ("TGC" 191)]. Though time has passed and Ch'i-ch'iao and several people around her have died, traditional patriarchal ideology remains and continues to haunt the people who are alive. The cycle of oppressors and oppressed, played by mother and daughter-in-law, enforces a rigid model of female subjectivity.

In contrast to the socially static mood produced in the novellas, the novels suggest the possibility of change. Both *Yuannü* and *The Rouge of the North* begin with a door being pounded at night: 「一句話提醒了自己，他轉過身來四面看了看，望回走過幾家門面，揀中一家，蓬蓬蓬拍門。『大姑娘！大姑娘！』」(*Yuannü* 4) [That reminded him. Turning around he looked about him and retraced his steps peering at all the familiar shopfronts until he came to the right one. He pounded loudly on the boards and shouted, "Miss! Miss!" (*RON* 2)]. The man who knocks on Yindi's door stands for all the men in her life she could choose for a husband; it is Yindi herself who chooses to marry the disabled man in the feudal family. The novels end with the memory of the same scene: 「『大姑娘！大姑娘！』在叫著她的名字。他在門外叫她。」["Miss! Miss!" Her name was being called. He was calling her outside the door (*Yuannü* 197; *RON* 185)]. The Chinese version depicts someone calling Yindi's name, and the English version uses "her name" as the subject that is called upon, subverting Yindi's subject and object positions. Upon her sickbed, Yindi rethinks her choices in life; as David Der-wei Wang points out, "Chang might have suggested that it bespeaks more emphatically the elusiveness of Meaning of any kind. Despite her eventful life, what happens to Yindi is really a repetition of her precursors' fate. The pounding at the beginning becomes an empty promise, with hollow echoes resounding throughout the narrative" (Wang, "Foreword" XXIV). I further argue that the pounding at the beginning and the end of the novels symbolizes both the challenges and the opportunities Yindi experienced in her prime, when she was young and beautiful and had the bargaining power to choose from different choices. It is this bloom of youth that Yindi recalls and yearns for in her old age. Though the novels mimic the bookended structure of the novellas, the novels diverge from the novellas' stern cycle of recurrences into a spiral movement that opens up infinite possibilities of choices for women, whatever the results, and suggests a comparatively fluid sense of female identity.

Both Ch'i-ch'iao and Yindi manifest examples of Chinese fashions of the female body, which includes not only women's corporeal bodies, but also their minds and their social relationships with other people and the world.

In "Jinsuoji" and "The Golden Cangue," Ch'i-ch'iao's physical appearance reflects her villainous personality: 「瘦骨臉兒，朱口細牙，三角眼，小山眉」 [On her thin face were a vermilion mouth, triangular eyes, and eyebrows curved like little hills ("Jinsuoji" 243; "TGC" 145)]. The Chinese version uses familiar and concise phrases, which contain more information than their English counterparts, to describe Ch'i-ch'iao's facial features. For example, the words 「瘦骨臉兒」 [thin bone face] and 「細牙」 [small teeth] are not translated in the English version; nevertheless, though they can be considered beautiful, "thin face," "vermilion mouth," "triangular eyes," and "curved eyebrows" have generally been associated in premodern Chinese literary discourse with cunning and vicious characters. Her bodily gestures also speak of her aggressiveness and arrogance; when her sisters-in-law give their seats to her, she ignores them and occupies more space by stretching her arms: 「那曹七巧且不坐下，一隻手撐著門，一隻手撐著腰」 ["With one hand on the doorway and the other on her waist, she first looked around" ("Jinsuoji" 243; "TGC" 144)]. She uses this gesture to mark her territory and to establish her legitimacy in the family; her actions are meant to imply a shrewish personality, even if they are in reaction to the Yaos' psychological exploitation of her because of her lower-class background.

The ferocity of Ch'i-ch'iao's bodily appearance is sharply contrasted with the vulnerability of her husband's body. When she smells pig's oil, she compares dead pigs' meat with his husband's flesh: 「朝祿從鉤子上摘下尺來寬的一片生豬油，重重的向肉案一拋，一陣溫風撲到她臉上，膩滯的死去的肉體的氣味 … … 她皺緊了眉毛。床上睡著的她的丈夫，那沒有生命的肉體 … … 」 [Ch'ao-lu plucked a piece of raw fat a foot wide off the hook and threw it down hard on the block, a warm odor rushing to her face, the smell of sticky dead flesh … she frowned. On the bed lay her husband, that lifeless body … ("Jinsuoji" 254; "TGC" 157)]. The juxtaposition of the pig's "dead flesh" and her husband's body rhetorically underlines the infirmity of the latter, and its ambiguous effects on Ch'i-ch'iao. His infirmity is what allows her to marry into a wealthy household. Though he is ailing, the Old Mistress pays a substantial dowry to Ch'i-ch'iao's family in order to "purchase" her body so she can give birth to his heirs, thus ensuring the continuation of his name and that of the feudal household. In Chinese traditional feudal society, marriage was usually arranged between two families of equal social status, as reflected in the Chinese saying *mendang hudui* 門當戶對 [the matching of doors and families]. Though she enjoys an affluent life, this woman occupies a low status in the family. In addition, since he is an invalid, she suffers from sexual frustration that leads to her entanglement with Chi-tse and the abuse of her children.

The descriptions of Yindi and her husband show a greater bodily contrast in the novels than those of Ch'i-ch'iao and her husband in the novellas. For instance, Yindi's face is described in gentler, almost religious, terms than Ch'i-ch'iao's: 「她向空中望著，金色的臉漠然，眉心一點紅，像個神像。」 [Gazing into the air, her golden face impassive with the red mark between the brows, like an idol (*Yuannü* 9; *RON* 9)]. Yindi is depicted as a surreal figure associated with the spirituality, harmony, and benevolence embodied by Chinese goddesses, such as *guanyin* 觀音 (the Goddess of Mercy). In sharp contrast to her holy appearance, Yindi's husband's body is secularly sickly, as illustrated in the wedding scene in which his body is described in detail through the eyes of her brother:

> 炳發這還是第一次看見他妹妹嫁的人，前雞胸後駝背，張著嘴，像有氣喘病，要不然也還五官端正，蒼白的長長的臉，不過人縮成一團，一張臉顯得太大。眼睛倒也看不大出，瞇著一雙弔梢眼，時而眨巴眨巴向上瞄著，可以瞥見兩眼空空，有點像洋人奇異的淺色眼睛。
> *YUANNÜ* 26

> Bingfa saw for the first time the man his sister had married, hunch-backed and pigeon breasted, panting as if he had asthma. The pale clean-cut face seemed too large for the bunched-up frame. The eyes were not too noticeable, tilted slits now closed, now squinting upward, empty.
> *RON* 24

Yindi's husband's body is more elaborately depicted than that of Ch'i-ch'iao's, even to being called "pigeon-breasted," an avian metaphor implying a lower natural form. His body parts are disproportionate and malformed. In *Yuannü*, his eyes, which do not have dark pupils, are even described as similar to 「洋人奇異的淺色眼睛」 [Westerners' strange light-coloured eyes (*Yuannü* 26)]. In Western culture, light-coloured eyes, especially bright blue-green, have long been considered the most beautiful of all, according to the *Etymologies* of Isidore of Seville, an influential text of Western aesthetics (Eco 113). The metaphor of Westerners' light-coloured eyes, here used to refer to Yindi's husband's abnormal eyes, reflects the estrangement of Western concepts of the body from the perspective of Chinese people. Here, at least in the Chinese version, Chang situates Chinese culture at the center with Western culture at the periphery. Yindi's husband's unappealing and ailing body is contrasted to her beautiful and healthy body, which is even compared to an image of a goddess. This juxtaposition ironically represents her tragic marriage – a mismatch of two incompatible bodies – that leads to her emotional and sexual frustration.

In "The Golden Cangue," the last version of the story, the two maids' gossip about Ch'i- ch'iao's background contains traditional Chinese phrases that are literally translated, thus producing a sense of Chineseness in the English version. For example, "*xiao dao*" 笑道 ("Jinsuoji") is translated as "said, smiling" repeatedly and deliberately, in order to preserve an echo of Chinese traditional literary style in the English texts: "Feng-hsiao *said, smiling*, as she buttoned it up, 'No, you've got to tell me.' 'My fault, I shouldn't have let it out,' Little Shuang *said, smiling*" ("TGC" 140; my emphasis). Hsia comments on Chang's use of this expression of reported speech in the footnotes of "The Golden Cangue":

> The repetition of the phrase 'said, smiling' (hsiao tao) may seem tiresome to the reader. However, this and similar phrases are routinely prefixed to reported speeches in traditional Chinese fiction, and Eileen Chang, a dedicated student of that fiction, has deliberately revived their use in her early stories. It is to be regretted that their English equivalents cannot be equally unobtrusive.
>
> QTD. IN CHANG, "TGC" 139

Though the phrase "said, smiling" is an instance of Chinese phraseology, it is inevitably transformed in English, as the literary conventions of classical Chinese fiction require explanation for English readers. Here, Chang makes a vital choice of text over context when deciding what to translate. The invisibility of the idiomatic expression in Chinese is lost in English, in which the expression instead stands out. Therefore, Chang is, in effect, calling attention to what is not meant to be attended to in Chinese. This changes the texture, and shifts the focus from the story itself to the representation of the Chinese literary style. By inserting the literal translation of a Chinese phrase for reported speech into her English rendition, Chang makes the Anglophone reader aware of the existence of the context of the Chinese traditional language and culture in the narrative, but through the translation. A terrain of "in-betweenness" is thus produced between the Chinese and English languages, between traditional Chinese and contemporary English literary styles.

In *Yuannü* and *The Rouge of the North*, Chang depicts in detail a kind of feminine beauty that commands public visual attention. For example, when Yindi rides to the Temple of the Bathing Buddha to celebrate the sixtieth birthday of the long-dead master of the house, her face and her costume are viewed by the public. Detailed descriptions of her outward appearance provide readers with crucial information about her, and about how her position and her make-up represent her social status: 「她們這浩浩蕩蕩的行列與她車上的嬰兒表出她的身分，那胭脂又一望而知是北方人，不會拿她誤認爲坐馬車上張園吃茶的倌人。」 [The cavalcade and the baby marked her high respectability and the rouge placed her as a northerner. There was no danger of her being mistaken for one of those singsong girls that drove to Chang Park for tea (*Yuannü* 77; *RON* 72)]. In *Yuannü*, Chang uses the word *guanren* 倌人 to refer to high-class prostitutes in contrast with Yindi's respectable social status. The word has multiple connotations; here, it refers to Shanghai courtesans between the late Qing dynasty and the early twentieth century, who were trained to sing and recite poetry, knew how to read and write, and were privileged to choose clients who were poetic and knowledgeable. *Guanren* were also called *xiangsheng* 先生, pronounced as /ɕi⁵⁵ sã²¹/ in Wu dialect, referring to female storytellers who became prostitutes. Anglophone people in Shanghai at that time misrecognized those words as "singsong" because of the words' phonetic similarities and the courtesans' musical talents, and therefore called the courtesans "singsong girls." In *The Rouge of the North*, Chang used the phrase "singsong girls," a common English translation for *guanren*, though "singsong girls" has a rather superficial connotation of girls who sing songs for a living. As high-class prostitutes, *guanren* may ride to the theatre in an extravagant manner that is similar to Yindi's ride to the temple, though for different reasons: the prostituted body being bought and gazed upon in contrast to the domestic married woman as a primarily reproductive tool becoming a spectacle in modern urban culture. Chang's rearticulating and recontextualizing of the story in Chinese both preserves and elaborates upon Yindi's physical appearance and its cultural connotations.

The theory of the male "gaze" is a paradoxical one: it objectifies the female body, but it also reveals female desire and power. In other words, the female body can be perceived as an object while still wielding power and influence over the perceiver. Gazing at a woman's body has usually, however, been interpreted in terms of objectifying the female body and sexuality. In *Ways of Seeing*, for instance, John Berger suggests that "men act and women appear. Men look at women. Women watch themselves being looked at" (47). Berger's argument is that men are constructed as subjects whose desire is manifested through the male gaze, and women as objects whose desire is socially and historically constructed, based on the taste of men in a patriarchal culture.

Yindi's objectification can be examined in light of Berger's idea, though that is only part of the story. From this perspective, Yindi is viewed as an object of desire, with her beauty, wealth and high social status on display in public: "Everybody turned to look" and was "startled" (*RON* 72). The public crowd may visually "possess" the extravagance and beauty of Yindi's body or narcissistically identify with her while watching her pass by. Gender relations are projected onto the traffic of gaze. Yindi's mother-in-law, personified as the agent of patriarchy, symbolically owns her body: 「老太太最得意的是親戚們都說她的三個媳婦最漂亮，至於哪一個最美，又爭論個不完。」 [Old Mistress was proud that all the relatives said she had the prettiest daughters-in-law and argued endlessly which was the most beautiful (*Yuannü* 77; *RON* 73)]. Chang uses the possessive pronoun 「她的」 [her] to indicate the relationship between the Old Mistress and the daughters-in-law in the Chinese version, and uses the possessive verb "had" to underscore the Old Mistress' ownership. Here domestic space intersects with social space, and the domesticated woman becomes a spectacle not unlike a courtesan. The mother-in-law is positioned as the possessor of her daughters-in-law because she exercises a power granted to her by the patriarchal society in which she exists.

While describing the public gazing at Yindi's body, the narrator becomes a member of the crowd – albeit one reporting from a critical distance. The narrator comments on this scene's "theatrical look" (*RON* 72), an observation that resonates with Judith Butler's argument in *Bodies that Matter* that 'sex' is materialized and practiced through time, thus producing and reinforcing ideal norms (1–2). Yindi's clothing is regulated precisely by Butler's concepts of materialization, reiteration, and performance, as they existed in the norms for women's fashion in Shanghai in the Late Qing dynasty. In her essay "Chinese Life and Fashions" (1943), later translated as "Gengyiji" (1943), Chang discussed Yindi's outfit as an example of fashion in Shanghai in the late 1920s: *yuanbaoling* 元寶領 [the old Sycee collar], which was "a tall, stiff collar reaching to the level of the nose. A long neck of swanlike grace was consequently much admired" (57).

Though women are both subjects and objects of the gaze, they are not absolutely denied subjectivity: they can reappropriate their bodies through self-sufficient sexuality, just as a theorist such as Joanna Frueh can assert herself as a carnal subject in *Erotic Faculties* (1996). Instead of being solely an object of desire, Yindi also performs as a subject showing her desire, though it has been socially and historically constructed, and even experiencing pleasure through its performance: 「她覺得她們是一個戲班子，珠翠滿頭，暴露在日光下，有一種突兀之感；扮著抬閣抬出來，在車馬的洪流上航行。她也在演戲，演得很高興，扮做一個為人尊敬愛護的人。」 [she felt they were a troupe of players incongruously out under the sun sailing along the traffic. She was acting too and enjoyed it, posing as the loved and admired one (*Yuannü* 77–78; *RON* 72)]. The Chinese version contains many more descriptive phrases, such as 「珠翠滿頭」 [her head full of jewelry], 「有一種突兀之感」 [there is a sense of awkwardness], and 「扮著抬閣抬

出來」 [pretending to be being carried for marriage], which are not present in the English version, perhaps due to Chang's better mastery of the Chinese language than of English. Yindi is self-consciously aware of her acting, and she is willing to perform in order to attain, or at least pose as, what she desires: beauty, wealth, social status, love, and admiration. Here is another instance of the paradoxical notion of both being seen and showing off, of both objectification and a certain empowerment. The power, therefore, lies in between the perceivers and Yindi as the perceived. She is objectified and fetishized as an object of desire in public. She, nevertheless, demonstrates her female desire and power through Chang's valuing of the female experience of her body.

In order to reclaim the female body as a site of both meaning and value, Yindi satisfies her desire by putting on make-up and a costume, posing in the fashion of her time, and displaying herself in public. In these episodes, the novels implicitly present a feminist discourse that challenges long-established patriarchal ideologies and practices regarding the female body, thus revealing opportunities for the possible reconstruction of these social norms. As Butler argues in *Gender Trouble*, rebellions against social norms create the possibility of change (141). When women reject conformity to patriarchal limits imposed on the female body, new meanings and values can be attributed to the female body.

In "Jinsuoji" and "The Golden Cangue," Ch'i-ch'iao's state of desolation is driven by her unsuccessful pursuit of love and sexual satisfaction, which can be seen in her desire for her brother-in-law Chi-tse, whose stout and healthy body forms a strong contrast to that of her ailing husband:

「季澤是個結實小伙子，偏於胖的一方面，腦後拖一根三股油鬆大辮，生得天圓地方，鮮紅的腮頰，往下墜著一點，青濕眉毛，水汪汪的黑眼睛裏永遠透著三分不耐煩」
"Jinsuoji" 246

A robust youth, tending toward plumpness, Chiang Chi-tse sported down his neck a big shiny three-strand pigtail loosely plaited. He had the classic domed forehead and squarish lower face, chubby bright red cheeks, glistening dark eyebrows, and moist black eyes where some impatience always shown through.
"TGC" 148

Chang Chi-tse's "plumpness" and "chubby bright red cheeks" suggest youthfulness and playfulness, and "moist black eyes" are considered sexually attractive in Chinese culture. Chang's use of these traits shows her prioritizing a faithful rendering of "authentic" Chinese aesthetic preferences over a cultural translation into equivalent beauty standards for the Anglophone world.

Ch'i-ch'iao slightly transgresses the boundaries of Confucian codes of conduct by sexually inviting Chi-tse through her bodily gestures; however, his rejection announces her deprivation of love and sexual fulfillment as a price she pays for her material status: 「她順著椅子溜下去，蹲在地上，臉枕著袖子，聽不見她哭，只看見髮髻上插的風涼針，針頭上的一粒鑽石的光，閃閃掣動著。」 [She slid down from the chair and squatted on the floor, weeping inaudibly with her face pillowed on her sleeve; the diamond on her hairpin flashed as it jerked back and forth ("Jinsuoji" 248; "TGC" 150)]. Her weeping and squatting implicitly entice Chi-tse to make physical contact with her. Not showing her face, she hides her emotions and intentions, while the diamond in her hairpin flashes out her sexual invitations.

In *Yuannü* and *The Rouge of the North*, Yindi shows her transgression of gender roles by pursuing the Third Master, who is depicted more abstractly than in the novellas. The Third Master is deprived of a name in the novels, and is given only a title that signals his position in the family. His identity, therefore, is generalized into simply the third son of the Old Mistress, with less room for individuality than if he were identified by name. Yindi chooses to transgress the conventions of feminine virtue by surrendering to her brother-in-law's seduction, this time at a Buddhist temple, when she is, ironically, looking at the iron incense pot on which are inscribed thousands of names of women who have led decent lives (Wang, "Foreword" XXVII). Yindi's flirtation with the Third Master also violates the traditional Chinese concepts of the permanence of marriage and of women's constancy in love and loyalty, presented as pretexts in patriarchal culture for binding a wife for life to one man. Yindi's violation of traditional Chinese ethics and expectations for women demonstrates her strong desire for love and sexual satisfaction that has been repressed by traditional Chinese gendered morality.

In the English version, Yindi whispers "enemy" (*RON* 82) during her sexual flirtation with the Third Master. In the Chinese version, Chang translates "enemy" as *yuanjia* 怨家, which, unlike the connotations of hostility in the English word "enemy," refers to a person whom one apparently hates but actually loves; someone who brings trouble but with whom one cannot break up. The word is usually used to refer to a lover, spouse, or children; Chang uses it to characterize Yindi's feelings of love and hate toward the Third Master and provide a fuller description of her psychological struggle with the dilemma of her sexual desire and the dangers of entanglement. Yindi's sexual encounter with the Third Master ends just after he has aroused her, leaving her with only frustration and shame. She tries to kill herself but is ironically rescued by her husband by whom she feels trapped (Wang, "Foreword" xxv). This unattainable love and unsatisfied sexual desire create a sense of desolation. Yindi's moving towards and away from both her husband and brother-in-law echoes *Yuannü*'s oscillation between faithfulness and betrayal in *The Rouge of the North*, which, as a result, positions both Yindi and her counterpart in *Yuannü* in that terrain of "in-betweenness."

Both Ch'i-ch'iao and Yindi are subjugated in the Chinese feudal system, but they appropriate the power granted in that patriarchal society to become oppressors themselves. The Chinese proverb 「三十年媳婦三十年婆，反正每一個女人都輪得到。」[Thirty years a daughter-in-law, thirty years a mother-in-law, every woman has her turn" (*Yuannü* 177; *RON* 164)] expresses the dual roles of women as both victims and victimizers. The Chinese version uses the conjunction 「反正」 [anyway] to connect the phrases together and demonstrate their explanatory relationship, which is unnecessary in the English sentence structure. Traditionally, men have held the role of oppressors, while women endure oppression in the domestic sphere, but obtain power and authority when they become mothers-in-law. In "Jinsuoji" and "The Golden Cangue," the tyranny of the mother-in-law passes from the Old Mistress of the Qiang family to Ch'i-ch'iao; in *The Rouge of the North* and *Yuannü*, though Yindi has power over her daughter-in-law, she loses control of her son's concubine, showing a sign of hope for the next generation. Both Ch'i-ch'iao and Yindi conventionally, and extremely, oppress their daughters-in-law; as a substitute, Ch'i-ch'iao selects a maid, named Miss Chüan, as Ch'ang-pai's concubine, who follows the same path as Chih-shou.

Yindi chooses a maid, Dungmei, to be Yensheng's concubine; Dungmei not only develops a husband-and-wife relationship with Yensheng, but also gives birth to many children, a reversal of Yindi's malicious intention of depriving them of love. The phrase "when she got on her nerves" is an English colloquial construction that not only provides a contemporary tone but also implicitly echoes the new situation of the power relations in Yindi's family. Yindi's loss of tyrannical control over her son's concubine and her own grandchildren signifies the possibility of change in the cycle of the roles of victims and victimizers, turning the mimesis of repetition of oppression into mimicry with a sign of hope.

The four versions of this story that both preserve and transcend Western and Chinese aesthetics of the female body form an interdependent relationship with one another. Where "Jinsuoji" and "The Golden Cangue" perpetuate a more transcultural aesthetics of the material and the Chinese Confucian doctrines of women's conduct, *The Rouge of the North* and *Yuannü* present more of a transcultural aesthetics of provocation and offer more possibilities for female transgression. A homogeneous and stable aesthetics of the female body gives way to a heterogeneous and dynamic one in the rewriting and translating of the tale. The gender politics in Shanghai between the 1910s and the 1940s and in the United States in the 1960s, as well as her lived experiences in these years, contribute to Chang's reconstitution of the female body as a terrain of significant and different meaning in-between preservation and transgression.

CHAPTER 5

Authorship: "Shame, Amah!" and "Guihuazheng – A Xiao beiqiu" 〈桂花蒸——阿小悲秋〉 ("Steamed Osmanthus Flower: Ah Xiao's Unhappy Autumn")

Self-translators, as authors of both the source text and the translation, enjoy the power of authorship that brings forth the freedom of revising and rewriting in the process of self-translation. As Anthony Cordingley argues, "Research to date has shown that self-translators bestow upon themselves liberties of which regular translators would never dream; self-translation typically produces another 'version' or new 'original' of a text. What is being negotiated is therefore not only an 'original' text, and perhaps the self which wrote it, but the vexatious notion of 'originality' itself" (2). The distinctive authorship status of self-translators, whose translations of their own work are derived from their own perspectives and sociohistorical backgrounds, thus separates them from translators of other authors' works.

The implications of the idea of authorship can be applied in an examination of Eileen Chang's Chinese short story 〈桂花蒸——阿小悲秋〉 "Guihuazheng: A Xiao beiqiu" (hereafter cited as "GHZ"), her self-translation into English, "Shame, Amah!" (hereafter cited as "SA"), and its English translation by Simon Patton, "Steamed Osmanthus Flower: Ah Xiao's Unhappy Autumn" (hereafter cited as "SOF"). This chapter begins with a look at the major difference between the two translations, before discussing Chang's "Shame, Amah!" as a re-interpretation and reconstruction of her prior work "Guihuazheng." It also explores the interdependent relationship between Chang's "Guihuazheng" and "Shame, Amah!"

The plot of all three versions of the story follows a typical day in which a Chinese maid works for her German master in an apartment in the international settlement of Shanghai during the second Sino-Japanese war in the early 1940s. The story unfolds when the Chinese maid climbs up ten floors with her adopted son to her master's apartment. While feeding her son before he goes to school, she performs housework and answers phone calls from her master's casual girl-friends. When the maid next door comes over to return some cutlery, she invites her to examine the foreign master's bedroom for novelty and complains about her housework. Two other maids and the woman's unofficial husband come to visit her during the day. At the end of the story, her plan to spend a night with her husband alone at home is cancelled because of a severe downpour.

© JESSICA TSUI-YAN LI, 2025 | DOI:10.1163/9789004730052_007

AUTHORSHIP   109

Chang, as the author of the story "Guihuazheng," is situated in a more liberated and authoritative position from which she prepares her self-translation "Shame, Amah!" than Patton as an external translator. Thanks to the Western individualist concept of authorship, Chang enjoys the legal and moral rights granted by the laws of ownership and copyright of *droit moral,* as discussed in the introduction to this book. Though Chang is acknowledged as the author of both versions, Patton as the translator is denied the authorship of his translation; Chang enjoys much more flexibility in the translation of her own work than Patton, who is bound by copyright and the need to be faithful to Chang's "Guihuazheng." In contrast to Chang, who can freely transform her earlier representations, Patton must strictly follow the content and syntax of Chang's work in his translation. The space of in-betweenness for Chang's "Guihuazheng" and "Shame, Amah!" is greater than for Chang's "Guihuazheng" and Patton's "Steamed Osmanthus Flower."

The major difference between Chang's and Patton's translations is signaled in each version's respective title. Patton's title is a word-for-word translation of "Guihuazheng: A Xiao beiqiu": "Guihua" 桂花 means "Osmanthus Flower"; "Zheng" 蒸 means "steamed." The Chinese title in Chang's source text resembles the style of *zhanghui xiaoshuo* 章回小說, classical Chinese fiction that uses poetic thematic titles for each chapter. The steaming of the Osmanthus Flower conveys the image of the hot and humid climate in autumn that makes Ah Xiao feel uncomfortable and annoyed. "Bei" 悲 signifies "lament" (verb) and "unhappy" (adjective), and "qiu" 秋 denotes "autumn." "A Xiao beiqiu" could mean "Ah Xiao laments about Autumn," as in the Chinese expression *shangchun beiqiu* 傷春悲秋, which refers to grieving over the passing of spring and lamenting the advent of autumn. Patton, however, translates "A Xiao beiqiu" as "Ah Xiao's Unhappy Autumn." He adds the English possessive's suffix after *Ah Xiao*, which is equivalent to Ah Xiao "de" in Chinese, and then interprets "bei" as an adjective describing "qiu" [autumn]. The Chinese title explicitly tells us the focus of the story: Ah Xiao is upset in autumn, a season that symbolizes her old age and brings her sorrow, as Eva Hung points out in the editor's note: "The fragrance of the flower is synonymous with autumn. 'Steamed' refers both to the heat and the humidity of an oppressive Indian summer. The title is also a metaphor for the heroine who is past her prime" ("SOF" 59; trans. Patton). The Chinese title conforms to the accepted literary conventions and needs no explanation for Chinese readers, but Patton's literal translation into English does not adequately convey the Chinese style and meaning on its own, requiring an editorial explanation.

Apart from attempting to translate every word in the title, Patton also retains the quotation from Fatima Mohideen, a girl of Indian descent whose

Chinese name is Yanying 炎櫻 (1920–1997) who became Chang's best friend when they met at the University of Hong Kong: 「秋是一個歌，但是『桂花蒸』的夜，像在廚裏吹的簫調，白天像小孩子唱的歌，又熱又熟又清又濕。——炎櫻」 [Autumn is a song. On nights of 'steamed osmanthus flower' it is like a flute melody played in a kitchen. In the daytime, it is a song sung by small children: ardent and familiar and clear and moist. – Yan Ying ("GHZ" 200; "SOF" 59)]. Chang's quotation of Mohideen gives the reader a hint of the story to come: a sense of the miserable, but passionate, "Indian" summer. Ah Xiao spends her later years in a melancholy state in her kitchen, like the sound of a flute, but she also displays energy and enthusiasm about her life. The joy and sorrow of her advancing years are depicted in metaphors within metaphors, such as the temperature and humidity of the seasons, the music of a flute, the songs of children, the smell of flowers, and the mood of familiarity. However, the absence of this quotation from "Shame, Amah!" suggests a different thematic focus than that of "Guihuazheng."

The change in title from "Guihuazheng" to "Shame, Amah!" signals a shift of focus in the story; such changes are not only obvious examples of Chang's legal and moral freedom in self-translation, but also evidence of her deliberate reinterpretation and reconstruction of her prior work. The title "Shame, Amah!" sounds simple and direct, conforming more to an English literary style than Patton's word-for-word translation of the title of "Steamed Osmanthus Flower." The phrase "Shame, Amah!" comes from Mr. Schacht's criticism of Ah Nee's poor work due to her deficiency in English: "'Shame, Amah!' wagging a finger at her. 'Never have the numbers right'" ("SA" 95). In response, her "thin, pretty face" ("SA" 93) turns red, accompanied by an apologetic smile and timid bodily gestures: "Ah Nee crimsoned and smiled ruefully, hands wrapped in the apron" ("SA" 95). The title thus recalls Ah Nee's embarrassment about her poor English-language skills, her low class and ethnic status, her shame about Miss Li's immorality, and even her pride in adopting a son. The story describes her life's bliss and grief, but also explores the manifestation of her feelings and thoughts in her blushing and shy bodily gestures, so that, once again, the representation of the female body is foremost.

Chang makes significant changes in her translation "Shame, Amah!" while Patton's "Steamed Osmanthus Flower" is, relatively speaking, a more word-for-word translation of Chang's "Guihuazheng." For example, in "Shame, Amah!" the Chinese maid Ding Ah Xiao 丁阿小 is now named Ah Nee. Her master's name is changed from Ge'erda xiansheng 哥兒達先生 to Mr. Schacht. However, in "Steamed Osmanthus Flower," Ding A Xiao's name remains the same but is spelled phonetically, while Ge'erda xiansheng becomes Mr. Garter, a transliteration of his Chinese name. Chang's choice for the maid's name, "Ah

AUTHORSHIP   111

Nee," is easier for English-language readers to pronounce than Patton's transliteration "Ding A Xiao." Conversely, the name "Mr. Schacht" would be more difficult for Chinese-language speakers to pronounce than "Mr. Garter," but the former matches better with the story, in which his new girlfriend cannot even say his name properly. Thus, the choice of name reflects the linguistic and cultural differences between Ge'erda and his sexual partners. Moreover, where Chang uses *zhuren* 主人 in "Guihuazheng" and translates this word as "master" in "Shame, Amah!", Patton chooses the word "employer" for his triangular translation, thus decontextualizing the story.

Chang has translated both *tian* 天 ("GHZ" 116, 135, 137) and *shangdi* 上帝 ("GHZ" 116) as "Heaven" (92, 112), while Patton translated *tian* as "sky" ("SOF" 59, 87) and *Shangdi* as "God" ("SOF" 59), both more basic and literal translation choices than Chang's use of "Heaven" in each case. As the author of "Guihuazheng," Chang has access to her own authorial intention and speaks from the position of a Chinese native who is familiar with Chinese literature and cosmology. The word *tian* in Chinese cosmology refers not only to the physical sky, but also to the metaphysical concept of "Heaven." For example, *ren* 人 [human beings] are located between *tian* 天 [Heaven] and *di* 地 [earth]; *tianrenheyi* 天人合一 [unity of Heaven and Human] signifies the harmony between nature and human beings. The emperors from the Zhou dynasty to the Qing dynasty, who were believed to be descended from the heavenly powers, were called *tianzi* 天子 [Sons of Heaven]. *Di* 帝 [emperor] exists both in Heaven and on earth, such as *yuhuangdadi* 玉皇大帝 [the Jade Emperor or the Supreme Deity of Taoism] and *huangdi* 皇帝 [emperor]; 上帝 *shangdi* connotes the figure who holds power in Heaven. By choosing to translate both *tian* and *shangdi* as "Heaven," Chang uses self-translation to present the Chinese cosmological concept of metaphysical power to Anglophone readers. Though Patton tends to translate "Guihuazheng" word-for-word into English, Chang's literal translation is in this case more "faithful" in cultural terms to the meaning intended in her source text.

Where Patton's "Steamed Osmanthus Flower" is generally a literal translation of Chang's "Guihuazheng," Chang deliberately elaborates on, and at times even undermines, her own earlier work "Shame, Amah!" For instance, she adds to Mr. Schacht's girlfriend Miss Li's intention to speak English on the phone, the comment "Miss Li had spoken to her in English under the illusion that it kept her anonymous" ("SA" 97). She attempts to use a foreign language to disguise her identity. However, her voice betrays her, as Ah Nee recognizes it right away and Mr. Schacht rejects her. Her vulnerability becomes more evident in the English version than in the Chinese version, in which her intention is not mentioned. Similarly, in the Chinese version, Ah Xiao's husband is described as 「阿小的男人抱著白布大包袱, 穿一身高領舊調長衫。」 ["Ah Xiao's husband wore an old silk gown with a high collar and carried a large white cloth bundle in his arms" ("GHZ" 128; "SOF" 78)]. Chang adds the phrase "the mark of his trade" as an explanatory detail in her description of Ah Xiao's husband's "high-collared old silk gown" with "a big white bundle" in her English self-translation ("SA" 105). His low status is explicitly articulated in his soiled, old-fashioned clothes, and the money-earning tools that he carries around. Overall, the story of "Shame, Amah!" is considerably simplified from its Chinese version; for instance, Chang omits the extravagance and arguments of the newlywed couple upstairs in order to focus more on Ah Xiao's story. The five short paragraphs describing the scenery of Shanghai viewed from Mr. Schacht's apartment, conveying a sense of desolation, are also omitted, providing "Shame, Amah!" with a more down-to-earth narrative that emphasizes gender and class, in a colonial setting, in contrast to the more philosophical and subtle narrative of "Guihuazheng."

The Chinese maid blushes on several occasions, indications of her traditional Chinese femininity. In addition to getting the numbers wrong, Ah Nee feels ashamed when Mr. Schacht suspects she has stolen his bread for her son: "Ah Nee blushed so that red welts rose on her cheeks as if she had been slapped. The amahs from Soochow were the most sensitive" ("SA" 96). Though Ah Nee has not committed a crime as Mr. Schacht suspects, her face signals that she has been insulted, even as she maintains her pride and dignity typical for those from Soochow. Mr. Schacht's staring and Ah Nee's blushing suggest the unequal economic and social power between master and servant. However, their relationship is not one-dimensional, but reciprocal, as Ah Nee sometimes shows sympathy and motherly love toward Mr. Schacht. For instance, when Miss Li offers to buy a new bed sheet for Mr. Schacht to replace his torn one, "Ah Nee said firmly, defending her master's face, 'but this bed came with the apartment; he was always going to buy a bigger one, then again the cover won't fit. I gave it a few stitches. It's not noticeable any more'" ("SA" 109). Similarly, when Mr. Schacht is short of flour, Ah Nee uses "some of her own rationed flour" ("SA" 111) to make pancakes for him and his new girlfriend. Ah Nee's protective attitude toward Mr. Schacht rhetorically breaks down the hierarchy and boundary between employer and employee, and creates a reciprocal, if paradoxical, relationship.

Ah Nee's relationship with Mr. Schacht can also be situated as part of an East/West dialogue. Ah Nee, as a Chinese maid, serves Mr. Schacht, a German master, who consistently searches for female sexual adventures in Shanghai, a site of severe tension between China and the West during the Second World War. Both versions of the story provide critiques of its colonial setting from the perspective of the colonized. On the surface, Mr. Schacht seems to be more highly positioned in the hierarchy of political, economic, and social power than Ah Nee. However, though she shows love and kindness toward Mr. Schacht, Ah Nee also exposes details of his private life: for instance, when Ning Mei, the maid next door, comes over, Ah Nee shows her "a silver bowl and silver chopsticks" ("SA" 99) that belong to Mr. Schacht, which are both love tokens given by Miss Li and emblems of Mr. Schacht's attractiveness. Ah Nee's perspective also invites the reader to peep into Mr. Schacht's bedroom: "There were Peking opera masks on the wall and a framed nude painting which had been a whiskey advertisement, Peking rugs, a wastebasket made out of a lantern, a nest of carved rosewood tables" ("SA" 99–100). Mr. Schacht's materialistic fetishization of the Oriental can be examined in light of the double-edged discourse of postcolonialism: "The fetish or stereotype gives access to an 'identity' which is predicated as much on mastery and pleasure as it is on anxiety and defence, for it is a form of multiple and contradictory belief in its recognition of difference and disavowal of it" (Bhabha 107). Mr. Schacht's sexual souvenirs and Chinese collections register his self-affirmation through the difference and the lack perceived in his Oriental trophies – the simultaneous interchange between "metaphor as substitution" and "metonymy," in Bhabha's terms. While Mr. Schacht gazes at Ah Nee's son's bread, Ah Nee and Ning Mei gaze at Mr. Schacht's bedroom, and the reader gazes toward Mr. Schacht's private self. The hierarchies and boundaries between servant and master, female and male, and China and the West, are thus destabilized and blurred.

Chang further destabilizes the hierarchies of master and maid, man and woman, and German and Chinese in a colonial international zone in Shanghai in the early 1940s by focusing on the Chinese maid's viewpoint and narrative voice and diminishing the role of the German master as a supporting character. In her analysis of the dynamic relationship between Eileen Chang's works and those of Somerset Maugham (1874–1965) in the context of East/West postcolonial studies, Hsiu-Chuang Deppman argues that the centering of the narrative voice of the Chinese maid provides a reverse counterpart to the absence of any Asian characters' perspectives in Maugham's South Seas narratives (1919–1931). Chang was an admirer of Maugham's writing, and she adapted some of his literary techniques and themes into her fiction published between 1942 and 1945. Where Maugham's works are mainly Eurocentric, Chang's works are, in principle, Sinocentric (Deppman 3).

Maugham's "The Letter" (1926), for example, tells the story of a British lawyer gazing at and questioning a Chinese woman whose body represents the mystery and materiality of the female in the British colony of Singapore:

Mr. Joyce looked at her. He had heard much about her since Hammond's death, but he had never seen her. She was a stoutest person, not very young, with a broad, phlegmatic face. She was powdered and rouged and her eyebrows were a thick black line, but she gave you the impression of a woman of character. She wore a pale blue jacket and a white skirt, her costume was not quite European nor quite Chinese, but on her feet were little Chinese silk slippers. She wore heavy gold chains round her neck, gold bangles on her wrists, gold earrings and elaborate gold pins in her black hair .... He said something to her and nodding she gave an incurious glance at the two white men.

"Has she got the letter?" asked Mr. Joyce.

"Yes, Sir."

"THE LETTER" 210–211

The body of the Chinese woman is described from the perspective of an authoritative professional white male, so that not only her body, but her very identity is judged from that perspective. Though she is seen, her voice is not heard because it is merely "represented."

Gayatri Chakravorty Spivak notes that, regarding the suppression of the female voice in colonialist discourse, "both as object of colonialist historiography and as subject of insurgency, the ideological construction of gender keeps the male dominant. If, in the context of colonial production, the subaltern has no history and cannot speak, the subaltern as female is even more deeply in shadow" (28). By contrast, Chang's "Guihuazheng" and "Shame, Amah!" openly present the Chinese maid's criticism of her employer's calculated pursuit of romance in Shanghai, and her comments on his sexual life and his physical body:

> 會得喜歡他！他一個男人，比十個女人還要小奸小壞 … … 看他現在越來越爛污，像今天這個女人，——怎麼能不生病？前兩個月就弄得滿頭滿臉瘭子似的東西，現在算好了，也不知道塌的什麼藥，被單上稀髒。
>
> "GHZ" 208–209

To think anyone would love him. A man more cunning than ten women … He's getting messier and messier. Like this woman today – how can he not get sick? Something like summer boils all over his head and face a few months ago. Gone now, I don't know what medicine he put on. It dirtied the sheets.

"SA" 99

AUTHORSHIP

Ah Xiao/Ah Nee's comments provide her point of view on Mr. Ge'erda/ Mr. Schacht's illusionary Orientalist romances and diseased body. Her voice and perspective dominate the story, establishing the presence and legitimacy of her position as a Chinese maid, in contrast to the absent (and implicitly illegitimate) voice and perspective of the Chinese woman in Maugham's "The Letter."

In addition to blushing under the Master's gaze, the Chinese maid Ah Xiao/ Ah Nee also flushes with embarrassment for Li Xiaojie 李小姐 [Miss Li] on behalf of all decent women. Miss Li, whom the Chinese maid suspects is the concubine of a wealthy man, consistently pursues her Master but in vain. The Chinese maid's blushing underscores her moral commitment to the virtue of chastity, part of the Confucian codes of conduct for women. Disregarding her dislike of Miss Li, she shows sympathy towards her in order to have a more harmonious relationship with her. For example, when Miss Li realizes that the Master refuses to answer her phone calls, Ah Xiao explains: 「今天他本來起 得晚了，來不及的趕了出去，後來在行裏間，恐怕又是忙，又是人 多，打電話也不方便 … … 」 ["He was up late today and had to rush out, [and] then in the *hong* [company] he was probably very busy" ("GHZ" 216; "SA" 108)]. Chang elaborates on Ah Nee's kind intention for her Anglophone readers in the English version: "Whether she believed it or not it would make it less embarrassing" ("SA" 108).

While speaking English, the Chinese maid shows signs of shyness. When she talks to a nameless yellow-haired woman who represents the West in general, she performs a persona that is as blissful as it is fictitious: 「阿小便也和她虛 情假意的，含羞帶笑，彷彿高攀不上似的。」 ["Ah Xiao then became hypocritical with her, smiling shyly, as if she could not match with her" ("GHZ" 206)]; "She acted up to the yellow-haired woman, shyly laughing, emitting in the foreign language the series of piercing chirps as happy and unreal as the world in advertisements" ("SA" 98). Patton translates this passage as "Ah Xiao's responses were similarly false. With her shy laughter she seemed unable to bridge the social gap between them" ("SOF" 67). Chang's Chinese version depicts the hierarchies between Ah Xiao and the Westerner in terms of language, culture, and social status, while her English version portrays the cheerful and illusory characteristics associated with the English language as a marker of the desirable political and cultural power of the West in the semi-colonial environment of 1930s–1940s Shanghai, as exemplified in the construction of a utopian world in advertisements. Patton's triangular translation highlights the social discrepancy between the master and the maid.

Language can be seen as a token of exchange and circulation in the political economy of the sign:

> The foreign quality (Fremdheit) of language describes a shared process of circulation in translation and in economic transaction, which produces meaning as it produces value when a verbal sign or a commodity is exchanged with something foreign to itself ... The English language of the late twentieth century would be the closest analogue to the gold of the preceding era.
>
> L.H. LIU 22

Extending the time period of the analogy that Lydia H. Liu cites, the English language of the early twentieth century is similar to the gold of the time. When speaking English to a Westerner, the Chinese maid feels her linguistic insufficiency associated with the political and cultural discrepancy between China and the West. However, when she yells "Hello!" in English to her Chinese husband on the phone, she positions herself on a higher cultural and social level than he, who timidly replies with "Wei?" 喂? [Hello?] in Chinese in response. In this Chinese and English bilingual conversation, Ah Xiao/Ah Nee as the bilingual speaker is the locus of the linguistic transaction; she strategically manipulates the English language and in so doing intimidates her husband. By partially transgressing the Confucian virtues of humility and obedience towards her husband, she demonstrates ambivalence towards Chinese feminine ideals.

The Chinese maid blushes not only when she is ashamed, but also when she is proud of herself. When "Elder Sister" asks her about her boy, Baishun, she behaves humbly, as 「[阿小]慢迴嬌眼，卻又臉紅紅的向朋友道歉似的說：『像個癟三哦？』」 ["She turned to her friend and said blushing apologetically, 'Doesn't he look like a tramp?'" ("GHZ" 210; "SA" 103)]. Patton translates this sentence as "Ah Xiao brawled at Baishun, blushing as she turned to her friends as if she owed them an apology: 'He looks like a little tramp, doesn't he?'" ("SOF" 74). Chang's Chinese version describes Ah Xiao's facial expression as 「慢迴嬌眼」 [slow motion with charming eyes], a distinctly feminine expression of contentment. This modifier is omitted in "Shame, Amah!" but Patton translates it as "brawled," with a sense of irritation. Despite the words of denigration, Ah Xiao/Ah Nee is pleased by the fact that she has a son. Rather than showing her pride, she blushes as a sign of humility, partly conforming to Chinese traditional femininity. In Chinese society, a capable woman without an heir would sometimes adopt a son, expecting him to take care of her in her old age. "Guihuazheng" and Patton's translation imply that Baishun is the maid's adopted son, whereas "Shame, Amah!" states this outright: "He was not her son, just as her husband was not her real husband. She had adopted him from an orphanage" ("SA" 104). Chang's self-translation further elaborates

AUTHORSHIP

that not only did Ah Nee adopt her son from an orphanage, but she also has a husband in Australia. As a working woman, Ah Nee supports herself, her son, and also her unofficial husband in Shanghai; her self-reliance and capability demonstrate the evolution of, and perhaps also away from, traditional Chinese ideals of womanhood.

Chang, as the author of "Guihuazheng," enjoys more flexibility and autonomy when translating/rewriting it into "Shame, Amah!" than Patton, who was bound to strictly follow the content and syntax of the Chinese source text, but would not always follow Chang's "authorial intention" as closely. Chang's "Guihuazheng" and "Shame, Amah!" thus exhibit both an in-betweenness and an interdependent relationship. "Shame, Amah!" preserves the plot and characters of "Guihuazheng" while also transforming its title, focus, language, and cultural meaning. "Guihuazheng" not only provides more background to Ah Nee's misery and enjoyment in her aging years than "Shame, Amah!" but also provides a comparison point for the latter's depiction of changing views on the representation of women in the Chinese context. The two works complement each other to produce a meaning greater than each one's alone.

CHAPTER 6

Re-Evaluation: "Deng" 〈等〉 ("Waiting") and "Little Finger Up"

Translation is a translingual and transcultural activity that can bring forth self-aggrandization, self-reflection, or self-criticism. Translation allows the translator to endorse or question ethnic cultural values and stereotypes by either assimilating to or resisting foreign values. Domestic cultural ethics may be lost, and foreign cultural beliefs may be added to the source text, thus producing a linguistically and culturally hybridized translation. As Lawrence Venuti argues in *The Scandals of Translation*, "The hybridity released by translation in colonial and postcolonial situations does indeed transgress hegemonic values, submitting them to a range of local variations" (178). Likewise, self-translation inevitably re-examines the translator/author's domestic cultural values, leading to subversion of well-established cultural hierarchies. The distinctive feature of self-translation is that the re-evaluation is conducted by the self-translator, who is also the author of the source text, from their very special sociohistorical position within the complexity of globalization.

Eileen Chang's Chinese short story "Deng" 〈等〉 ("Waiting") and her English self-translation "Little Finger Up" can be studied in this kind of globalized context. Chang first published "Deng" in the monthly magazine *Zazhi* 《雜誌》 (*Magazine*) in Shanghai in 1944. In her essay "You jijuhua tong duzhe shuo" 〈有幾句話同讀者說〉 ("A Few Words For Readers," 1946), Chang points out that she included "Deng," with modifications, in her newly edited volume of *Chuanqi* 《傳奇》 (*Romances*), published by Shanhe tushu gongsi 山河圖書公司 (Mountains and Rivers Books Company) in Shanghai in 1946. "Deng" was later collected in *Zhang Ailing Wenji* 《張愛玲文集》 (*Collected Works by Eileen Chang*), published by Anhui wenyi chubanshe 安徽文藝出版社 (Anhui Literature and Art Publisher) in 1992, appeared in *Zhang Ailing duanpian xiaoshuo ji* 《張愛玲短篇小說集》 (*Collected Short Stories by Eileen Chang*) by Xianggang tianfeng chubanshe 香港天風出版社 (Hong Kong Sky and Wind Publisher) in Hong Kong in 1954, and then republished in *Zhang Ailing quanji* 《張愛玲全集》 by Huangguan wenhua chuban youxian gongsi 皇冠文化出版有限公司 (Crown Publishing Co., Ltd.) in 1968. Chang translated "Deng" as "Little Finger Up," published it in the journal *Orient Review and Literary Digest,* edited by Alfred Schenkman and P. Lal, in Calcutta (now Kolkata, India) in 1957, and then revised and published it in *New Chinese*

© JESSICA TSUI-YAN LI, 2025 | DOI:10.1163/9789004730052_008

Stories: Twelve Short Stories by Contemporary Chinese Writers, edited by Lucian Wu, in Taipei, Taiwan in 1961[1] (Kao, *Zhang Ailing xue xupian* 30).

This discussion focuses mainly on the Chinese text "Deng," published by Crown Publishing in 2020, and the later English translation, "Little Finger Up," published in 1961, and compares them to the earlier Chinese and English texts. The Chinese versions are mostly the same except for instances of censorship of politicians' names. The two English versions are largely the same except that the later version displays a more polished English style and features instances of Cold War censorship upon publication. The Chinese story "Deng" is characterized by a strong sense of desolation over the inevitable process of waiting, while the English translation "Little Finger Up" re-evaluates the Chinese concubinage system for Anglophone readers. This chapter outlines the major differences between the Chinese and English versions in terms of titles, themes, plots, characters, and literary styles. It also explores Chang's re-evaluation of her culturally Chinese story in her translation of that story into the English language and context. Finally, it examines how both versions, taken together, provide a better picture of both Chinese and Western perspectives on gender relations in the twentieth century.

The tale mainly follows the circumstances of several patients waiting for traditional Chinese-style chiropractic massages in Mr. Pang Songling's 龐松齡/Mr. Peng's clinic. After Mr. Kao 高先生 has received the treatment, his concubine meticulously cares for him. Ah Fang 阿芳/Ah Mei, the masseur Mr. Pang/Mr. Peng's daughter, converses with a patient named Mrs. Xi 奚太太/Mrs. Yu, whose husband has taken a concubine in the interior of China. Another patient, named Mrs. Tong 童太太/Mrs. Ho, complains to Mrs. Xi/Mrs. Yu about her husband, who privileges his concubine and ignores her at home. Offended by Mrs. Pang/Mrs. Peng, who regards her as a poor patient, Mrs. Xi/Mrs. Yu allows her thoughts to turn to her husband, hoping that he will return to her once her lost hair grows back. The Chinese version also depicts the characters of Mrs. Wang 王太太, Mrs. Bao 包太太, a young man, and a little boy and his maid, all of which the English version omits in order to simplify its plot and refocus its theme.

As the author, Chang translated and reinterpreted "Deng" from her specific position as a Chinese female writer with an insider's knowledge of both Chinese and Western languages and cultures. Thanks to copyright laws, she had total aesthetic freedom in her self-translation. In her self-translation, Chang

---

1 In his book *Zhang Ailing laixin jianzhu* 《張愛玲來信箋註》 (*Notes on Eileen Chang's Letters*), Zhuang Xinzheng 莊信正 (b. 1935) notes that Chang would not let other people translate her works and insisted on translating/rewriting them on her own (151).

began by transforming the title of the Chinese text, "Deng," into "Little Finger Up," and subsequently made that phrase the new theme of the story. The title "Deng" means "waiting," with connotations on three levels. On the first level, the patients in the massage clinic are waiting for their turn at treatment to alleviate their bodily pain. On the second level, the title signifies not only their constant waiting for their massage treatment, but also their prolonged waiting for recovery from their illnesses. On the third level, the characters in the clinic are waiting for remedies for significant events in their lives, which give them hope to empower them move forward but are often beyond their personal control, thus conveying a strong sense of uncertainty and passivity in the face of miserable circumstances.

"Little Finger Up," the title of the English translation, however, indicates a shift in focus, as the editor Wu points out: "Holding up the little finger is a gesture commonly understood to refer to a concubine" ("LFU" 65 [1961]). The plot of the English version is simplified, with accents on the custom of concubinage, a legitimized traditional Chinese practice. The 1961 English version also adds a Chinese title, "Fuzheng" 扶正 ("Straighten Up"), referring to the rumour presented in the story, of allowing concubines to take up the proper positions of wives in interior China in wartime. In place of underscoring the philosophical meaning of life in "Deng," Chang spells out both Chinese and Western perceptions of gender relations in "Little Finger Up" through her deliberate re-evaluation, manifested in the space of in-betweenness regarding "Deng" and "Little Finger Up."

The story opens with the famous masseur Mr. Pang Songling 龐松齡, renamed Mr. Peng Yu-fung in the English translation, performing massage therapy for Mr. Kao while conversing with him about current affairs, thus setting up the story's sociohistorical background of Japanese-occupied Shanghai during the second Sino-Japanese war. The name Pang Songling means "giant" (pang), "pine" (song), and "age" (ling), a typical name for healing professionals that signifies longevity. Pang Songling's transliteration in English loses its meaning for Anglophone readers: the name Peng Yu-fung is associated with *ku fung* [martial arts] that cultivates healing power through resilience of body, mind, and spirit. Mr. Pang boasts that he has the privilege of riding in the pedicab of Mr. Zhu in "Deng," renamed Mr. Chow in "Little Finger Up," so that he does not need to pay the ten-dollar fee to the police while crossing a bridge. Mr. Chow may refer to Zhou Fohai 周佛海 (1897–1948) (Kao, *Zhang Ailing xue xupian* 36 1), Chinese politician and second-in-command of the Executive Yuan in Wang Jingwei's collaborationist Reorganized National Government of the Republic of China during the Second Sino-Japanese War. Chang names him Mr. Zhu in "Deng" in order to avoid political sensitivity among Chinese communities in

RE-EVALUATION   121

Shanghai in 1944 when Mr. Chow was still in power, but uses the name Mr. Chow in "Little Finger Up" to highlight the story's political elements for Anglophone markets when it was published in Calcutta in 1957 and then in Taipei in 1961, following Chow's death and the political changes in mainland China.

Other instances of political censorship appear in "Little Finger Up." For example, in the Chinese versions of "Deng," published in 1944, 1946, and 1992, Chang uses the name 「蔣先生」 [Mr. Chiang] to refer to the leader of the Republic of China (ROC). However, "Mr. Chiang" was replaced by "shangmian" 「上面」 [above] ("Deng" 227) or omitted entirely in the version published in Taiwan in 1968. In the English version of "Little Finger Up" published in Calcutta in 1957, Chang explicitly uses the name "Mr. Chiang" ("LFU" 45, 48 [1957]) with a footnote, "President Chiang Kai-Shek" ("LFU" 45 [1957]). However, when "Little Finger Up" was republished in Taipei in 1961, the name was replaced by the phrases "somebody inside there" ("LFU" 71 [1961]) and "[o]ur government there 'inside'" ("LFU" 79) to refer to Mr. Chiang and his government (Kao, *Zhang Ailing xue xupian* 34), when Mr. Chiang was president of the ROC in Taiwan. Whether the censorship was imposed by the journals' editors/publishers or self-imposed by Chang, political restrictions on the story's publication in Cold War-era Taiwan were inevitable. It was only when Chang published her English translation in Calcutta, out of reach of either side of the opposing political entities in China, that she could explicitly use the Nationalist leader's name, though she was still obliged to observe Anglo-American political censorship. However how apolitical she might have had claimed she and her stories were, she was still subject to the constraints of the greater political environment in which she wrote.

"Deng" presents various instances of the wartime hardships that everyday people experienced. For example, Mrs. Wang notices that the ladies waiting in the clinic's lounge have not bought new coats in a while. Therefore, when Mrs. Pang praises her coat that had been newly made in the previous year, she replies humbly by echoing everyone's concern that things are getting more expensive than ever. Mrs. Xi, who is wearing a woolen coat, strongly asserts, 「現在就是這樣呀，裝滿了一皮包的錢上街去還買不到稱心的東西——價錢還在其次！」 [That's the way it is now. When you go to the street with a bag full of money, you can't buy anything you like, and the price is second! ("Deng" 227)]. Mrs. Xi's opinion, as though she is defending her poor outfit, reflects the lack of supply and high inflation during the war. Immersed in her comparatively affluent and comfortable zone, Mrs. Wang smiles with 「小弄堂的平安」 [small alley's peacefulness ("Deng" 228)]. After a small quarrel with Mr. Pang, Mrs. Wang again is described as smiling with 「小弄堂的陰暗的和平」 [small alley's shady peace ("Deng" 229)]. The "shady peace" in Mrs. Wang's smile is an instance of seeking temporary refuge in a chaotic time, marking her as self-possessed, yet transient and doubtful.

Ordinary people's ambivalent feelings about the war are demonstrated in the characters' dialogue and expressions. For instance, while receiving his massage treatment, a nameless young man, who embodies youth in general, tells Mr. Pan about a war documentary he saw in the Russian club, and the cruelty depicted therein. Mr. Pan then replies, 「『殘忍真殘忍！打仗這樣東西，真要人的命的呢，不像我這推拿，也把人痛得嘰哩哇啦叫，我這是爲你好的呀！』他又笑又嘆息。」 ["Cruelty is cruel! Battle is such a thing that really kills people. Unlike my massage, which also makes people scream in pain, I'm doing this for your own good!" He laughed and sighed ("Deng" 235)]. Mr. Pang compares and contrasts killing in war to his massage therapy as sources of pain and suffering for different purposes. His inappropriate comparison of these very different things and his combination of laughing and sighing display, on the one hand, a sense of fleeting contentment in his comfort zone, but on the other, a malicious sense of superiority over the unfortunate victims of the war. When the young man offers to help him buy film tickets, Mrs. Pang replies, 「『要它人死得多一點的——』嗨嗨嗨嗨笑起來了。龐先生也陪她笑了兩聲。」 ("Deng" 236) ["Want it to die a little more –" hey hey hey hey, laughing. Mr. Pang also laughed twice with her]. Like her husband, Mrs. Pang exhibits numbness and insensitivity toward the brutality of war.

Other characters who appear in "Deng" are ordinary people waiting for the end of the war in hopes of a brighter future. For example, a domestic maid brings a five- or six-year-old boy to the clinic. When the boy cries upon his turn for massage treatment, Mr. Pang shouts loudly, ordering him not to cry, as he loves him. Then the maid echoes that Mr. Pang loves the boy and asks the boy to invite Mr. Pang to his future wedding banquet. Mr. Pang replies with a smile: 「對了！將來時局平定，你結婚的時候，不請我吃酒我要動氣的呵！」 [That's right! The situation will settle down in the future. When you get married, I will be angry if you don't invite me to your banquet! ("Deng" 234)]. Both the maid and Mr. Pang console the boy with his future happiness and the promise of a wedding banquet that can only happen in a peaceful time. However, the characters do not know of the civil war and political turmoil that will occur over the next few decades in China. Those promises and the hope generated during the process of waiting, however uncertain they might be, help the little boy cope with his suffering and pain at the moment. The characters waiting for the end of the war also serve as instances of ordinary people's lives being disturbed, and their resulting feelings of not being in control of their lives in the face of disruptive sociopolitical circumstances.

Ah Fang/Ah Mei's unsuccessful yearning for a boyfriend also illustrates the theme of waiting. Coming from a humble family with many siblings, she needs to wait for a suitor so that her parents will provide her with nice clothes to make herself look attractive. However, she falls into the trap of the unachievable prerequisite:

要想做兩件好衣裳總得等有了對象，沒有好衣裳又不會有對象。這樣循環地等下去，她總是杏眼含嗔的時候多。
"DENG" 224

The family wouldn't make nice clothes for her until she had a peng-yu, a friend; in this case a boy friend with serious intentions. But without nice clothes, the peng-yu would not materialize. The vicious circle had already been going on for years.
"LFU" 48 [1961]

Chang uses the word 「對象」 [object] to refer to Ah Fang's desired but unattainable boyfriend in "Deng," but she inserts the Chinese transliteration "peng-yu," followed by an English translation "a friend," to signify Ah Mei's future dating object in "Little Finger Up." In "Deng," however, Chang also adopts the Chinese idiom 「杏眼含嗔」 [almond eye with anguish], a familiar expression in Chinese literature, to describe Ah Fang's facial expression and psychological conditions. Her word choices demonstrate, on the one hand, the Chinese linguistic and cultural context in "LFU" and, on the other hand, her mastery of the Chinese language in "Deng."

Where the Chinese version emphasizes the theme of waiting, the English version focuses on the Chinese custom of concubinage. For example, Mr. Kao's "concubine of the old school" ("LFU" 69 [1961]) painstakingly takes care of him, and both the Chinese and English texts describe her appearance and mannerisms in negative terms. However, the English translation emphasizes her status as a concubine and thus as an object of derision, as epitomized in the dialogue added in "Little Finger Up": "After they were gone, a lady asked carefully, 'Was that Mrs. Kao?' Ah Mei held up a little finger significantly. 'I thought so,' said the lady. 'I certainly hope that the real Mrs. Kao wouldn't act so cheap'" ("LFU" 70 [1961]). The legitimacy of taking concubines, and their low status in Chinese society, are more implicitly depicted in "Deng," as the language carries the Chinese cultural codes that were well known to any reader from the same background. However, in "Little Finger Up," concubines are explicitly denounced through the gesture of the "little finger up," and the female characters' conversation further conveys their disapproval. The critical distance provided by the English language and culture similarly highlight the alienated positions of concubines and mistresses. "Little Finger Up" can thus be seen as a conscious re-evaluation of "Deng" through Chang's own re-interpretation and reconstruction.

The situation of Mrs. Xi/Mrs. Yu further underscores the major themes of waiting and concubinage in "Deng" and "Little Finger Up." The Chinese character Xi 奚 is a surname, but is also part of the word *xiluo* 奚落 [insult (Kao, *Zhang Ailing xue xupian* 44)]. Mrs. Xi is renamed Mrs. Yu in the English translation, perhaps because the latter name is easier for Anglophone readers to pronounce. When Mrs. Pang/Mrs. Peng spits her mouth-washing water into a spittoon at Mrs. Xi's/Mrs. Yu's feet, Mrs. Xi/Mrs. Yu waits for an apology but in vain:

> 奚太太也笑，但是龐太太只當没看見她，龐太太兩盞光明嬉笑的大眼睛像人家樓上的燈，與路人完全不相干。
> "DENG" 236

Mrs. Xi also laughed, but Mrs. Pang just pretended not to see her. Mrs. Pang's two big bright and laughing eyes were like lights upstairs, completely irrelevant to passers-by.

Chang parallels Mrs. Pang's eyes with the "lights upstairs" to implicitly depict her aloof and despicable attitude towards Mrs. Xi in "Deng." However, in "Little Finger Up," she replaces this metaphor with a more straightforward account of Mrs. Pang's perception of Mrs. Yu: "As she bent close to Mrs. Yu, the latter looked up smiling, half expecting that she would say something. But Mrs. Peng ignored her completely. Apparently she had been classified among the poorer patients" ("LFU" 82 [1961]). Mrs. Xi/Mrs. Yu has been abandoned by her husband, who moved to the interior of China two years earlier to work and has taken a concubine. Without a husband by her side, other people tend to bully her due to the patriarchal belief that a woman needs a man's support. Her situation also refers to the rumour that the government encouraged men to take concubines if their wives were not present, and that a concubine could take the proper place of a wife, thus hinting at the Chinese title "Straighten Up" in the 1961 English version. While she waits for her husband's return, neither too late nor too soon, just "before her hair had had a chance to grow back" ("LFU" 83 [1961]), the chances of her husband returning to her and her hair growing back by rubbing ginger slices on her scalp are, in fact, very low.

Mrs. Tong/Mrs. Ho's struggle to cope with her miserable marriage, in which her husband has taken a concubine, shows the inequitable gender relations present in the traditional concubinage system. Tong is a Chinese

RE-EVALUATION 125

surname that also means *children*, associated in Chinese culture with inno-cence, simplicity, and gullibility (Kao, *Zhang Ailing xue xupian* 44)]. How-ever, in "Little Finger Up," she is renamed Mrs. Ho, a name that lacks these connotations. Mrs. Tong/Mrs. Ho is described as 「矮腳大肚子，粉面桃腮，像百子圖裏古中國的男孩。」 ("Deng" 234) [Short-legged and pot-bellied and with her open face painted pink and white, she looked like a little boy in old Chinese paintings, any one of the hundred boys in the tra-ditional *pai tze tu*, the pictures of one hundred sons ("LFU" 81 [1961])]. Once again, Chang translates her work closely, with the transliteration of "*pai tze tu*" followed by an English explanation, reminding readers of how Mrs. Tong/Mrs. Ho's youthful, even boyish, appearance signals her ingenuous character.

When Mrs. Tong/Mrs. Ho complains that she has tried hard to rescue her hus-band from prison but cannot even receive his admiration or affection, Mrs. Xi/Mrs. Yu compliments her as follows: 「童太太你是女丈夫。」 ("Deng" 234) [Mrs. Ho, you are a *nü chang-fu*, a manly woman ("LFU" 77 [1961])]. "Nü chang-fu" 「女丈夫」 literally means "womanly husband," as opposed to Chang's translation of the phrase as "manly woman." Under a patriarchal ide-ology, women and men are socialized to enact and reproduce the hierarchi-cal gender order in which men are regarded as superior to women. Gender stereotypes are socially constructed; for instance, women are conventionally seen as passive, sentimental, and introverted, while men are expected to be active, rational, and extroverted. When Mrs. Tong/Mrs. Ho displays character-istics stereotyped as "masculine," such as capability and independence, she is dismissed as a woman but praised as a man in "Deng," adhering to assumptions about the perceived superiority of men and masculinity to women and femi-ninity. In "Little Finger Up," Chang re-evaluates Mrs. Tong/Mrs. Ho as "a manly woman"; in other words, a woman who is appreciated for showing otherwise masculine qualities. Her reversal of the meaning of the Chinese idiom from "womanly husband" to "manly woman" in her self-translation/rewriting is an effort to question the assumptions of gender norms and beliefs and propose new gender relations in place of the old ones.

Many Chinese cultural features prominent in "Deng" remain in Chinese *pin-yin* (phonetic signs) accompanied by explanations in English in "Little Finger Up." For instance, Mrs. Yu tells Miss Peng that her husband has probably taken "a hsiao, a small one" ("LFU" 71 [1961]), which refers to a concubine. However, Mrs. Yu will be "ta, the great one" ("LFU" 72 [1961]), which signifies the Mis-tress at home. Mrs. Ho is waiting to marry off her three "ta hsiao chieh, young daughters" ("LFU" 74 [1961]), after which she will "shang shan, go up a moun-tain" ("LFU" 74 [1961]). The English version provides an explanation of the Chi-nese customs and practices implied in the Chinese source text: "By going up a mountain, she meant retiring into a nunnery in some secluded spot" ("LFU" 74–75 [1961]). The relationship between concubines and mistresses and their way of life cannot be fully represented in the English text without explanation. Special terms, such as *hsiao* and *ta,* do remain in Chinese romanization in the English translation, as a reminder to Anglophone readers of their linguistic and cultural estrangement from the Chinese source text while simultaneously drawing the reader's attention to, and re-evaluating, the institution of concubinage.

The highlighting of concubinage here may be due to Wu's intention to give the anthology "a distinctly Chinese flavor, not only in surface detail but in the author's basic attitude toward the people he writes about and what happens to them" (VII). Nevertheless, it is not necessarily Chang's intention to conform to Wu's desire to sell stories with a "distinctly Chinese flavor" to Anglophone readers, but rather her re-evaluation of the story that motivates her emphasis on, and criticism of, the practice. Nevertheless, creating or drawing on the stereotypical identities of a foreign culture for a domestic market is perhaps inevitable in translations; as Lawrence Venuti argues in *The Scandals of Translation*: "Translation patterns that come to be fairly established fix stereotypes for foreign cultures, excluding values, debates, and conflicts that don't appear to serve domestic agendas" (67). On the other hand, it is often the publisher's decision to commission translations that produce and reinforce literary, cultural, and/or political values already held by the targeted readers: "To enable the foreign text to engage a mass readership, the best-selling translation must be intelligible within the various domestic identities that have been constructed for the foreign culture, often stereotypes that permit easy recognition" (Venuti, *The Scandals of Translation* 127). Chang employs a foreign language and perspectives to re-evaluate Chinese marriage and concubinage systems in "Little Finger Up," and Wu identifies this decision as a marketing strategy to give her self-translation a "distinctly Chinese flavor".

"Deng" focuses on life as a process of inescapable and fruitless waiting, while "Little Finger Up" emphasizes concubinage as a Chinese cultural practice. The characters' endless waiting underscores a major theme in most of Chang's stories: a sense of desolation. Near the end of the story, a cat that is black on top and white on the bottom passes by: 「一隻烏雲蓋雪的貓在屋頂上走過，只看見牠黑色的背，連著尾巴像一條蛇，徐徐波動。」("Deng" 236) [A cat walked over the roof, the kind of cat called *wu yun kai Hsueh,* a black cloud over snow. From a distance only its dark back and tail were visible, moving sinuously across the field of vision like a black snake ("LFU" 83 [1961])]. Chang's translation into English follows the Chinese source text closely, adding an English explanation to the imagery of the black-and-white cat as a symbol of the immanent and opposing domains of life. She ends "Deng" with the statement 「生命自顧自走過去了。」 [Life walked away by itself ("Deng" 237)], which becomes the simpler "Life walked by" in "Little Finger Up" ("LFU" 83 [1961]). The Chinese version of this sentence stresses the apathetic characteristics of "life" as endless suffering and endurance, as well as involuntary waiting and uncertainty. In "Little Finger Up," the legitimacy of concubinage is problematized and the relationships among concubines, mistresses, and husbands are re-evaluated through the English language and Western perspectives. The combination of both versions, therefore, presents a better picture of both Chinese and Western perspectives on gender relations and life philosophy in early twentieth-century China.

CHAPTER 7

Recontextualization: "Stale Mates – A Short Story Set in the Time When Love Came to China" and "Wusi yishi – Luo Wentao sanmei tuanyuan" 〈五四遺事——羅文濤三美團圓〉 ("Regret after the May Fourth Movement – The Reunion of Luo Wentao and the Three Beauties")

Associations of various literary images, historical figures and events, landscapes, values, and mentalities can help to recontextualize translations into new languages and cultures. In the process of translation, the source text will undergo transformations that may confirm or challenge its traditional cultural values. As Xie Tianzhen 謝天振 argues, 「文學翻譯的創造性性質是顯而易見的，它使一件作品在一個新的語言、民族、社會、歷史環境裏獲得了新的生命。然而，文學翻譯除了創造性一面外，另外還有叛逆性的一面。」 [The creative nature of literary translation is obvious; it gives a work a new life in a new language, nation, society and historical environment. However, alongside the creative side, literary translation also has a rebellious side (Xie, *New Perspectives in Translation Studies* 66)]. In a similar vein, self-translation is re-evaluated and re-contextualized in a different linguistic and cultural system; its distinctive feature is that the author/self-translator is simultaneously situated in both worlds and is constantly crossing the boundaries.

This chapter[1] focuses on the aesthetics of the body, the philosophical study of the beauty of the body, in Eileen Chang's English short story "Stale Mates – A Short Story Set in the Time When Love Came to China" (1956; hereafter cited as "SM") and her own translation of this story into Chinese under the title "Wusi yishi – Luo Wentao sanmei tuanyuan" 《五四遺事——羅文濤三美團圓》 ("Regret after the May Fourth Movement – The Reunion of Luo Wentao and the Three Beauties," 1957; hereafter cited as "Wusi yishi"). It argues that, as the author of the source text, Chang enjoys the aesthetic freedom to

---

1 Part of this chapter has been based on the following previously published article: Li, Jessica Tsui-yan. "The Politics of Self-Translation: Eileen Chang." *Perspectives: Studies in Translatology* 14.2: 99-106. http://www.tandfonline.com/doi/abs/10.1080/09076760608669023

© JESSICA TSUI-YAN LI, 2025 | DOI:10.1163/9789004730052_009

highlight and interpret cultural perceptions of men and women through the practice of self-translation, which is an example of oscillation between faithfulness toward and betrayal of the source text, as well as her presentation of the body in both Western and Chinese aesthetics. By making changes to the representations of the body in her self-translation "Wusi yishi," Chang both preserves and transforms her descriptions of physical beauty in "Stale Mates." Having implicitly re-evaluated and explicitly recontextualized "Stale Mates" in "Wusi yishi," Chang points to a transcultural aesthetics of the body that incorporates both Chinese and Western cultural influences.

Chang's story depicts a variety of related themes – beauty, costumes, sexual desire, love and loss – and their relations to the issues of gender, sexuality, and history. The plot revolves around a young man named Lo and a young woman named Miss Chou, who are fascinated by the concept of the freedom of love that was fashionable in early twentieth-century China. Because of his lack of faith in love, Lo ends up living with not only Miss Chou, but also two other women with whom he is in arranged marriages. Miss Chou carefully maintains her beauty and keeps up with fashion to please Lo, but eventually fails to keep abreast of it and therefore bores him. In her translation of the English story into Chinese, Chang rearticulates its gender relations in her own language with additional meanings and perspectives. In the Chinese version, Chang tells the story to readers who are familiar with Chinese culture, and uses more subtlety and irony; she also uses the Chinese language to subvert the Chinese patriarchal culture. The characters attempt to use Western concepts of love, fashion, and poetry to rebel against the Chinese practice of arranged marriages involving families and clans, as well as the Confucian codes that regulate gender relations, but their attempts are doomed to failure because they adopt Western practices without adapting Chinese cultural concepts. In order to reform the Chinese traditional patriarchal culture, they must revolutionize Chinese ideology by finding solutions that suit modern Chinese society.

The English and Chinese versions of Chang's story reflect the historical and cultural situation of China in the 1920s, when new values challenged old ones and Western ideas encountered Chinese traditions. The Western ideas that were imported into Chinese society, and their meanings, must be explained clearly in the English text, whereas the Chinese traditions undergoing transformations can be seen clearly in the Chinese text so that readers grasp their significance. Both versions together present a picture of Westernization in China after the May Fourth Movement that began in 1919. However, the implications are different for Chinese readers than they are for Anglophone readers. Therefore, interaction between these texts is necessary to understand the clash between Western ideas and Chinese traditions in the 1920s. The ideal readers would be bilingual Chinese/English speakers who know both languages and recognize the nuances of and differences between the two languages and cultures.

The different connotations of the English and Chinese titles indicate Chang's awareness of her readers' cultural backgrounds as well as her recontextualization of her text. The English title "Stale Mates" functions on two levels. First, it refers to the women who are not interesting because they are no longer beautiful and fashionable. Second, it implies that the characters are in a deadlock, as, although they comprehend the Western concept of love, they are incapable of dealing with it. The subtitle is straightforward: the story is set when love came to China. For the English reader, "love" refers to "love" in the Western sense, and the time is the beginning of the May Fourth Movement in 1919. For the benefit of Anglophone readers who may not be familiar with the story's Chinese historical background, Chang simply inserts the words "the Time" into the title. The Chinese title "Regret after the May Fourth Movement – The Reunion of Luo Wentao and the Three Beauties" is more subtle and ironic, and carries with it paradoxical implications: the story deals with a sad event after the May Fourth Movement that sought to introduce new ideas of freedom and love from the West. The subtitle alludes to the traditional patriarchal norm that entitles a man to have several wives, which, in theory, conflicts with the Western concept of monogamy, love between only one man and one woman. The more straightforward English title demonstrates Chang's awareness of her reading public's cultural backgrounds, while the Chinese title explicitly underscores the problematic romantic relationships between the characters, as she exposes the incompatibility between Western theories and practices of love in China at the time the story takes place.

In the 1920s, the Chinese regarded Westernization as a means of modernization. The story contains many references to "novelty," such as new women and men, styles, clothes, spectacles, and words, all modelled according to both modern Chinese and Western standards. Descriptions of female bodies focus on appearance: "'Missu Chou is very stylish today,' one of the men said. It was also stylish to address girls as "Miss" [『密斯周今天好時髦！』男子中的一個說。稱未嫁的女子爲『密斯』也是時髦。 ("SM" 249; "Wusi yishi" 249)]. The comment demonstrates the male assertion of power over female sexuality by gazing at and commenting upon Miss Chou's body, but Miss Chou also exercises her own power by commanding visual attention. The man uses the word "stylish," implying that he appreciates her up-to-date dress, which may become old-fashioned by the next day, and would thus make her into one of the "stale mates" of the English title.

Here, readers are told that addressing young women as "Miss" is also "stylish," so the man is also being "stylish" himself by using that word. In the English version, he pronounces "Miss" as "Missu," stressing the consonant "s" in "Miss" and pronouncing the word with a Chinese accent. In the Chinese version, "Miss" is phonetically translated as *misi* 密斯 instead of the lexical equivalent, *xiaojie* 小姐. The translation of the word "Miss" incorporating a confusion between two languages breaks away from conventional linear processes of translation, and implies a multiple and non-hierarchical translation.

Spectacles, which were invented in the West and imported into China, symbolize the translation of new Western languages and culture into Chinese during the modernization period in early twentieth-century China: "The year was 1924, when eyeglasses were fashionable. Society girls wore them. Even streetwalkers affected glasses in order to look like girl students" [這是一九二四年，眼鏡正入時。交際明星戴眼鏡，新嫁娘戴藍眼鏡，連鹹肉莊上的妓女都戴眼鏡，冒充女學生。 ("SM" 250; "Wusi yishi" 249)]. Chang hints that it is stylish to wear spectacles, and sarcastically adds in the Chinese version that even new brides wear blue eyeglasses to highlight the popularity of this fashion trend. Similarly, "Miss Chou glared at him through her new spectacles" [密斯周從她新配的眼鏡後面恨恨的白了他一眼。 ("SM" 249; "Wusi yishi" 249)], indicating her adoption of new Western perspectives on things in her life, as well as her commanding of visual attention. While gazing symbolizes action and power, being gazed upon is, paradoxically, both objectification and empowerment. In addition to becoming an object of desire, Miss Chou is also a subject showing her own desire, though this desire has been socially and historically constructed, and she is pleased with it. The power is therefore shared between the perceived, Miss Chou, and the perceiver, the man.

The women's clothes demonstrate the transcultural aesthetics of the female body in different ways. Miss Chou and Miss Fan follow Western fashions, but their clothes also combine styles of traditional Chinese dresses. For example, "[Miss Fan] wore little make-up and no ornaments except a gold fountain pen tucked in her light mauve tunic. Her trumpet sleeves ended flaring just under the elbow" ("SM" 250). In the Chinese version, readers are given more details about her clothes:

薄施脂粉，一條黑華絲葛裙子繫得高高的，細腰喇叭袖黑水鑽狗牙邊雪青綢夾襖，脖子上圍著一條白絲巾。周身毫無插戴，只腕上一隻金錶，襟上一支金自來水筆。
"WUSI YISHI" 250

She wore little make-up in a black skirt tied up high on her slender waist and a light mauve silk wool jacket with trumpet sleeves decorated by black rhinestones and zigzag edges. There are no bodily ornaments, only a gold watch on the wrist, and a gold fountain pen on the lapel.

132   CHAPTER 7

These details provide vivid examples of the transcultural nature of fashion in modern China; for instance, the "gold fountain pen" and "gold watch" symbolize the Western culture that Miss Fan has embraced, whereas the "trumpet sleeves ended flaring just under the elbow" are reminiscent of Chinese theatrical costumes. This blending of Western and Chinese styles situates Miss Fan in a position of "in-betweenness," but she does not totally duplicate either style. In addition, Chang's mastery of the Chinese language, and most importantly, her practice of self-translation, not only give rise to such elaborate descriptions but also position her, like her character, in the realm of "in-betweenness." Miss Fan's appearance also embodies the paradox of objectification and empowerment noted above, as her modern style of dress reveals her bodyline and arouses male desire.

The two female protagonists are appreciated not only for their outward appearance but also for their inner qualities:

> The girls were around twenty – young for high school in those days when progressive women of all ages flocked to the primary schools. Miss Chou was much admired for her vivacity and boldness as being typical of the New Woman, while Miss Fan's was the beauty of a still life.
>
> "SM" 250

> 兩個女郎年紀約在二十左右，在當時的女校高材生裏要算是年輕的了。那時候的前進婦女正是紛紛的大批湧進初小、高小。密斯周的活潑豪放，是大家佩服的，認爲能夠代表新女性。密斯范則是靜物的美。
>
> "WUSI YISHI" 250

The women's pursuit of knowledge at school and their adoption of personality traits, such as "vivacity" and "boldness," that are associated with modern Chinese women, as well as "the beauty of a still life," or traditional Chinese femininity, all contribute to their charm. Their appeal to others also serves as a reminder that the Chinese concept of the body encompasses not only the flesh but also the mind, as well as human and social relationships.

In the English version of her text, Chang re-evaluates and recontextualizes Chinese social codes that regulate women; in the Chinese version, she subtly presents those codes. Harmonious human and social relationships are crucial virtues in Chinese aesthetics concerning women. Confucius, for instance, outlines *sancong side* 三從四德 [three obediences and four virtues] in *Yili* 《儀禮》 (*The Book of Etiquette and Ceremonial*) and *Zhouli* 《周禮》 (*The Rites of Zhou*), and discusses women's education in *Liji* 《禮記》 (*The Book of Rites*); these ethics are the cultural basis of Chang's story. In setting moral rules for the female body, the "three obediences" establish that a woman is expected to obey her father before marriage, her husband during marriage, and her son after the death of her husband; the "four virtues" are being virtuous, discreet in speech, tidy, and diligent in work.

In "Wusi yishi," Chang merely names these Confucian codes, which are familiar to Chinese readers, without further explanation. When Lo declares that he will divorce his first wife, Wang, he is asked which of *qichu zhi tiao* 七出之條 [the Seven Out Rules] she has violated. The Seven Out Rules are prescribed in *Liji*: "First, disobey parents; second, bear no sons; third, adultery; fourth, envy; fifth, serious illness; sixth, garrulous; seventh, theft" (Chapter 12). In "Stale Mates," Chang explains these in terms of the Chinese cultural context: "Ancient scholars had named the seven conditions under which a wife might justifiably be evicted from her husband's house" ("SM" 255). Through recontextualization, the English version exposes the Confucian doctrine that regulates gender relations and prompts readers to contemplate the unequal relationship of a husband and wife under this patriarchal and patrilineal family system, whereas these Confucian rules are familiar to Chinese readers and are consequently omitted.

Descriptions of the male characters' clothing in the story also reveal their personalities and talents. In "Stale Mates," for instance, we are told that "Lo was tall and thin. His pale turquoise long gown hung well on him in a more literal sense than when the phrase was applied to [the] westerner's clothes" (251). Lo is wearing the typical outfit of learned Chinese poets, which Chang describes with the phrase "a literal sense" in order to convey the cultural significance of the "long gown" to Anglophone readers. In "Wusi yishi," Lo is also described as long and thin, but with a 「長長的臉」 [long face]. A "long face" in English may signify unhappiness, which does not convey the "literal sense" of the bodily figure; therefore, this expression is not used in the English version. The transformation highlights Lo's inner qualities. In the Chinese version, readers are told that 「一件湖色熟羅長衫在他身上掛下來，自有一種漂然的姿致。」 [a pale turquoise long gown hung well on his body, showing his carefree posture ("Wusi yishi" 251)]. In ancient China, scholars and middle- and upper-class people wear long gowns, while lower-class people wear short gowns. Lo's long gown and "carefree posture" thus mark his learned and poetic character and upper-class social status in a Chinese context. Here the translation, therefore, also oscillates between faithfulness to and betrayal of the source text.

The story makes more references to men's social status and professions than to those of women, showing the different social expectations imposed on men and women as well as their lived experiences at the time the story takes place; for instance, "[Lo] taught in the same school as Wen.[2] They both owned land in their home village and taught school in Hangchow merely as an excuse to live by the West Lake, where every scenic spot was associated with the memory of some poet or reigning beauty" ("SM" 251). Both Lo and Wen, being intellectually and financially secure, "cultivate their bodies" by living in a historical and poetic environment that constructs their educated and upper-class identity. In "Wusi yishi," Chang elaborates further upon their poetic inclinations:

兩人志同道合，又都對新詩感到興趣，曾經合印過一本詩集，因此常常用半開玩笑的口吻自稱「湖上詩人」，以威治威斯與柯列利治自況。

[Lo and Wen] had common interests. Both of them were interested in new poetry. Since they had published a collection of poetry together, they always half-jokingly addressed themselves as "poets on the lake," associating themselves with Wordsworth and Coleridge.

"WUSI YISHI" 251

The Chinese version makes note of Lo and Wen's cultivation of their bodies and minds through their indulgence in Romantic poetry, which was introduced to China in the 1920s. Although Romanticism and the Western concept of love both hold individuality in high esteem, individuality is not valued in China; due to social taboos, couples date in groups of four or six people. Even on a boat, one person sits on one side and the other sits on the other side, so as to maintain the balance that symbolizes the virtue of harmonious Confucian relationships.

Thanks to her right as the author and her practice of self-translation, Eileen Chang enjoys more aesthetic freedom than "ordinary" translators of her works would have. She can highlight and manipulate cultural perceptions of men and

---

2 In "Wusi yishi," Wen becomes Guo, because, according to Chang, "Wen" is easy for Anglophones speakers to pronounce. When translated into Chinese, *Wen* can be written as the words for *literary* or *mild*, which may be associated with scholars. *Wen* can also be translated as *hearing*. As Chinese has no capital letters, names are not identified by capital initials, and the word "wen" would be easily misinterpreted as 'hearing' (Lin Yiliang, "Cong Zhang Ailing de 'Wusi yishi' Shuoqi" 49).

women by introducing different features in "Wusi yishi" and in "Stale Mates." Having explicitly re-contextualized the source text in the translation, Chang points to a transcultural aesthetics of the body that incorporates both Chinese and Western styles and is produced by materialization and performance. In her rendition of her own work, she establishes a terrain of in-betweenness, the space of her self-translation. Both versions formulate an interdependent relationship that allows the bilingual reader who understands both English and Chinese languages and cultures to grasp a greater significance.

CHAPTER 8

Metacommentary on "Xiangjianhuan" 〈相見歡〉 ("A Joyful Rendezvous") and "She Said Smiling"

Eileen Chang's Chinese short story "Xiangjianhuan" 〈相見歡〉 ("A Joyful Rendezvous") was first published in *Huangguan zazi* 《皇冠雜誌》 (*Crown Magazine*) in Taiwan in 1978. This short story has inspired various critical commentaries, including Chang's own metacommentary essay "Biaoyi xiyi ji qita" 〈表姨細姨及其他〉 ("Biao Aunt, Little Aunt, and Other Issues," 1979) and a revised version of "Xiangjianhuan" published in her collection *Wangranji* 《惘然記》 (*A Record of Bewilderment*, 1983). A newly discovered manuscript of Chang's English version of "Xiangjianhuan," titled "She Said Smiling" (2022), prompts a revisiting of the "afterlife" of these aforementioned works. This chapter discusses the relationship between Chang's English manuscript "She Said Smiling," her Chinese short story "Xiangjianhuan," and her metacommentary essay "Biaoyi xiyi ji qita," with reference to other critical responses to these works. Some discussion in this chapter also focuses on the female body and sensibilities. The analysis presented here demonstrates how Chang's writing, self-translation, and metacommentary establish an interdependent relationship and generate a dialogue of in-betweenness with each other.

The term *commentary* generally refers to the interpretive activity of a critic, who translates the textual and subtextual meanings of a work into a form that is accessible to readers. *Metacommentary* refers to authors' self-reflexive analysis of elements present in their own work, such as language, syntax, structure, plot, characters, literary techniques, and themes. Fredric Jameson defines the main purpose of metacommentary as authors' illuminating the underlying meaning of their texts in a forbidden discourse: "Metacommentary [...] aims at tracing the logic of censorship itself and of the situation from which it springs: a language that hides what it displays beneath its own reality as language, a glance that designates, through the very process of avoiding, the object forbidden" (17). Jameson's notion of metacommentary focuses on a condition of censorship imposed on an object in the fictional reality that the author unearths in the social reality beyond the literary world.

This chapter elaborates on Jameson's idea on metacommentary in light of John Langshaw Austin's performative speech act model. Austin suggests two distinctive forms of speech acts: constative utterances, which make factual

© JESSICA TSUI-YAN LI, 2025 | DOI:10.1163/9789004730052_010

METACOMMENTARY ON "XIANGJIANHUAN" 〈相見歡〉

statements; and performative utterances, which create actions. Performative utterances do not simply describe or reflect a reality, but also induce activities that transform the reality they depict in highly conventionalized contexts. I argue here that, like the performative speech act, metacommentary does not merely refer to authors' own clarification of the meaning of their writing under censorship within the literary world, but also generates insights that shape readers' interpretation of their texts and invite further commentary in social reality. Self-translation, not unlike metacommentary, produces meaning that complements or even subverts those given in the source texts by the author and self-translator themselves within and beyond the literary world.

The English manuscript of Eileen Chang's short story "Xiangjianhuan" was discovered in 2017, in her papers in the Special Collections at the University of Southern California (USC) Libraries, by a patron. This manuscript contains twenty-two typewritten pages that were formerly considered part of her English translation of Han Bangqing's 韓邦慶 (1856–1894) *Haishanghua liezhuan* 《海上花列傳》 (*The Sing-Song Girls of Shanghai*, 1894). Li Junguo 李俊國 and Zhou Yi 周易 argue that this newly discovered manuscript is one version of Chang's unpublished short story "She Said Smiling," an English counterpart of "Xiangjianhuan" (152). They point out that Chang's agent Marie Rodell mentions "She Said Smiling" in a letter dated April 29, 1964 (155), and examine the similarities of plot, characters, and structure between "She Said Smiling" and "Xiangjianhuan" (158). They also identify nine instances of the phrase "she said smiling" in the manuscript (157), further supporting the identity of the manuscript as the story "She Said Smiling."

This manuscript displays signs of the multiple revision processes of Chang's writing. The pages are typewritten in black, with some words overridden by the typed characters "xxxx" to signify deletions, and some others crossed out by hand in blue ink. Above some of these deletions are replacements, either typed in black or handwritten in blue. Some sentences also feature handwritten symbols to indicate reversals of word order. Handwritten lines, crossing out several paragraphs, can also be seen alongside the typed and written changes. On the top right-hand corner of this manuscript are either typed or handwritten page numbers. Some of the typed page numbers have been crossed out and replaced by handwritten page numbers, while others are purely handwritten with either a whole number or a whole and a half number, such as 10 ½, 11 ½, and 13 ½, to suggest inserted pages. The manuscript starts with page 2, while the last page has a typed number 20 that was replaced by a handwritten number 16. The first page is missing, and it is not known whether the last page in the manuscript as discovered is the last page of the entire manuscript.

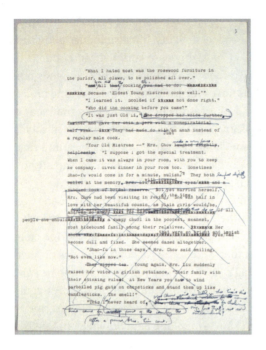

FIGURE 17

Chang, Eileen. "She Said Smiling" unpublished manuscript
PHOTO CREDIT: USC DIGITAL LIBRARY. AILING ZHANG (EILEEN CHANG) PAPERS COLLECTION

The newly discovered manuscript of "She Said Smiling" and the two published versions of "Xiangjianhuan" feature similar plots and characters, but display slight differences. Both stories focus on the conversations between two middle-aged cousins, who are named Mrs. Chow and Mrs. Liu in the English version but Mrs. Wu and Mrs. Xun in the Chinese version. They discuss various mundane topics such as hairstyles, house chores, the loss of old photos, Mrs. Liu's/Mrs. Xun's husband Shao-fu lending money to relatives, the future of Mrs. Liu/Mrs. Xun when Shao-fu passes away, and clothes. Shao-fu joins the dialogues after dinner but falls asleep when his wife Mrs. Liu/Mrs. Xun talks about her experience of being stalked by a young man in Peking many years ago. The English manuscript, as noted above, starts on page two with the words "Mrs. Chow" and a period, suggesting that the first page is missing. The story starts on the second page with the cousins talking about their children, and the last page ends with a paragraph in which Shao-fu/Mr. Liu takes a nap on the couch, though this paragraph was crossed out with blue handwritten lines. The English manuscript's major difference from the Chinese versions is the presence in the latter of Yuanmei 苑梅, Mrs. Wu's married daughter, who listens to and reflects on the conversation between her mother and her aunt and sometimes jumps into their dialogues.

Whether Chang wrote the English version before the Chinese version of these stories, or vice versa, is uncertain. In her letter to Stephen Soong dated

January 4, 1983, she wrote: 「『色戒』等三篇全部都是先用英文寫的，但是既未發表，又都大改過，也就不用提了。」 [The three stories including "Lust, Caution" were all written in English first, but they have not yet been published, and they have all been largely revised, so there is no need to mention them (*To My Beloved Friends* 2.120)]. The other two stories Chang mentions in the letter may be "Xiangjianhuan" and "Fuhua langrui" 〈浮花浪蕊〉 ("Floating Flowers and Wavy Pistils," 1978). The Chinese version of "Se, Jie" was published in Taiwan in 1977, and "Xiangjianhuan" and "Fuhua langrui" were published in Taiwan in 1978, while their English counterparts had not been published in her lifetime.

Chang gives more hints about the writing process of these three stories in "Wangranji" 〈惘然記〉 (A Record of Bewilderment, 1983), the preface to her collection *Wangranji*:

> 這小説集裏三篇近作其實都是一九五零年間寫的，不過此後屢經撤底改寫，『相見歡』與『色，戒』發表後又還添改多處。『浮花浪蕊』最後一次大改，才參用社會小説做法，題材比近代短篇小説散漫，是一個實驗。
>
> 4

The three recent works in this collection were actually written in the 1950s, but they have been extensively rewritten many times since then, and many additions and changes have been made after "Joyful Rendez-vous" and "Lust, Caution" were published. The last major revision of "Floating Flowers and Wavy Pistils" employs the method of social novels. The subject matter is more loose than contemporary short stories. It is an experiment.

The discussion of these three stories in the preface to *Wangranji* is a further suggestion that these are the same stories to which Chang refers in her 1983 letter to Stephen Soong.

Based on the aforementioned letter and the preface to *Wangranji,* Li and Zhou argue that the English manuscript should be the *yuangao* 原稿 [original text] of this story. They also point out that some of the corrections made in the English manuscript seem to be closer to their counterparts in the Chinese version. However, since all these texts had been revised over a period of about thirty years, it is difficult to determine which text was written before the others (157). Li and Zhou make logical speculations about the order in which Chang wrote those texts, based in part on her reference to having written three stories in English first, which might include "Xiangjianhuan." I further argue that which one is the "original" text is unclear, because Chang might have used her lived experience and other literary and historical materials as her sources. She might have also had written an earlier version than the English manuscript that was recently discovered. It is also possible that Chang wrote both the English and Chinese versions simultaneously or revised all these versions back and forth. Her practices of writing and self-translation, therefore, can be considered multiple rather than linear processes.

A further indication of Chang's multiple revision process is the number of different titles for the story. Roland Soong claims that he has Chang's unpublished manuscript "Visiting," which may possibly be the English version of "Xiangjianhuan" (*The Legend of Soong Qi* 280). There is also the mentioning of the English title "She Said Smiling," discussed in Chang's agent Marie Rodell's letter dated April 29, 1964 (Li and Zhou 155). For the Chinese title, Chang indicates in her letter to Stephen Soong dated October 31, 1977, that she has considered "Wangshi zhi duoshao" 〈往事知多少〉 ("How Much Do You Know About the Past?"), "Huajiuji" 〈話舊記〉 ("Recounting Old Stories"), and "Qingzhiweiwu" 〈情之爲物〉 ("Love as a Thing") as working titles for the story. The only published title is "Xiangjianhuan," published in *Crown Magazine* in 1978 and in Chang's anthology *Wangranji* in 1983.

The Chinese title "Xiangjianhuan" can be traced to the name of a *cipai* 詞牌, *cige* 詞歌, and *cidiao* 詞調, which is the title of a set of tunes, rhythms, rhymes, and tempos, written to accompany the singing of *ci* 詞, also called *changduanju* 長短句 (lines of irregular lengths), and *shiyu* 詩餘 (poetry aside from *shi*). *Cipai* can be written to suit particular lyrics and vice versa. The same *cipai* can accommodate several *ci*; therefore, *cipai* might have no relationship with its content. The most representative *cipai* with "Xiangjianhuan" as its title is the *ci* poem written by Li Yu 李煜, also known as Li Houzhu 李後主 (937–978), the last ruler of the Southern Tang state during the Five Dynasties and Ten Kingdoms period (907–979). He reigned between 961 and 976, when he was captured by Song dynasty (960–1279) military troops that annexed his kingdom. He wrote this poem, which expresses nostalgia for his extravagant past, lamentation for the loss of his kingdom, and frustration over his imprisonment, during his house arrest in the Song capital of Kaifeng.

The title "Xiangjianhuan" evokes classical Chinese *ci* poetry, particularly those of Li Yu, and also calls back to the historical contexts of Li and his poetry. Thus, the allusions inherent in the title help to create a sense of nostalgia in Chinese readers, which Chang recontextualizes in her work. The story's protagonists, Mrs. Chow/Mrs. Wu and Mrs. Liu/Mrs. Xun, move from Beijing to Shanghai, and their family members live in Hong Kong or the US, separated from them by the war between the Communist Party and the Nationalist

METACOMMENTARY ON "XIANGJIANHUAN" 〈相見歡〉 141

Party. The characters' feelings of isolation, unsettlement, and uncertainty are chanted softly and shared with readers through poetic and fictional expressions. Chang's use of the title "Xiangjianhuan" invites her readers to make associations with Li Yu's poem, sensibilities, and historical events, thus drawing her readers closer to the past and enriching the imaginary world of her writings. She also revisits and recreates Chinese *ci* poetry by giving it an "afterlife" in her vernacular Chinese short stories, rendering it between English and Chinese, between Beijing and Shanghai with reference to Hong Kong and the United States, and between different political parties.

The sisterhood of Mrs. Chow/Mrs. Wu and Mrs. Liu/Mrs. Xun is a striking instance of the story's portrayal of the interpersonal relationships of members of bourgeois families in 1940s Shanghai. The handwritten corrections in blue and typed corrections in black show how Chang developed this relationship in the process of writing the story:

> The geopolitical separation/was (is) a convenience to blind marriages which did (do) not turn out well. xxxx a(A)s xxxxxx it (As with) had been Chungking and / (the) occupied areas during the war, now it was (is) Hong Kong or Taiwan and the mainland. (Mrs. Chow wrote regularly but Mrs. Liu would not ask after him unless Mrs. Chow volunteered info).
>
> 2

This addition underscores Mrs. Chow's affection for Mr. Chow, who is currently residing in Hong Kong; Mrs. Liu considers Mrs. Chow's feelings by not asking her about him unless she offers any information. The words underneath "xxxx" are indecipherable; here, I use words being crossed out and words in brackets to represent Chang's handwritten editorial notes. In this example, some of the changes pertain to grammatical and stylistic issues, such as turning the past tense of "was" into "is" and "did" into "do," adding the article "the" to modify "occupied areas," and changing the beginning of the sentence into "As with." She also adds a handwritten sentence, "Mrs. Chow wrote regularly but Mrs. Liu would not ask after him unless Mrs. Chow volunteered info" (2), to the paragraph.

The revised Chinese version of "Xiangjianhuan," published in 1983, displays slight changes in its reference to Mr. Wu's marital situation:

> 政治地緣的分居，對於舊式婚姻夫婦不睦的是一種便利，正如戰時重慶與淪陷區。他帶了別的女人去的——是他的女秘書，跟了他了，兒子都有了——荀太太就沒提起他。
>
> 69 [1983]

Geopolitical separation is a convenience for incongruous couples in old-fashioned marriages, just like Chongqing and the enemy-occupied areas during the war. He brought another woman – she was his secretary who followed him and had a son – Mrs. Xun did not mention him.

This Chinese version adds more details about Mr. Wu's extramarital affair to justify why Mrs. Xun does not mention him in front of Mrs. Wu. With this explanation, readers understand that Mrs. Xun, being a close friend of Mrs. Wu, does not talk about Mr. Wu for the sake of Mrs. Wu's feelings. The Chinese version, however, is different from the English manuscript. In the latter, Mrs. Chow stays behind in Shanghai to guard her family house, not talking about Mr. Chow's betrayal at all, and thus demonstrating Mrs. Liu's affection and care for her cousin and best friend, Mrs. Chow.

Chang's story also depicts harmonious relationships between husbands and wives, as, even though Mrs. Chow/Mrs. Wu is separated from her husband, they maintain a polite relationship with each other. The Chinese version notes that Mr. Wu has a concubine in Hong Kong but still regularly sends remittance to his wife, and they also send what Mrs. Wu considers "love letters" to each other; Mrs. Liu/Mrs. Xun and Shao-fu are also depicted as similarly mutually caring and cordial. In her metacommentary essay "Biaoyi xiyi ji qita," Chang explains that Mr. Xun loves his wife despite occasionally misunderstanding her as men often do toward their wives. For instance, he shows interest in his wife's clothes and speaks with her in a particular soft voice. If blind marriage is a lottery, he considers himself the first prize winner. Though the couple has passed middle age, he still has sexual desire for her (20). The following conversation between Mr. and Mrs. Liu demonstrates Chang's use of dialogue, action, and opinions to reveal her characters' personalities and perspectives:

> "You found the soup?" Mrs. Liu asked conversationally. "I hid it in the drawer in case the cat comes in."
> "Yes, I heated the soup and fried the rice with the left-over shredded pork." When he answered his voice was muted, almost tender, husky from the sudden change of key and he had to clear his slightly. Without lifting his eyes to her his tired lumpy face had turned a shade (still) darker as if the lights had gone down in the room.
> 13 ½

Mrs. Liu casually asks if Shao-fu has found the soup that she thoughtfully saved in a drawer for him, a kind gesture that shows her concern for his well-being. Shao-fu replies with a tender voice that is different from his usual tone.

METACOMMENTARY ON "XIANGJIANHUAN"〈相見歡〉

The dialogue between them, as well as Shao-fu's voice and actions, helps to illustrate their attentive and warm relationship, as Chang points out in her metacommentary essay. In the manuscript, the word "tired" is crossed out in handwritten blue ink, to let the description of "lumpy face" carry the imagery of fatigue. The words "a shade" are also crossed out, and the word "still" is added, both handwritten in blue ink, as grammatical corrections.

Chang's Chinese version closely resembles her English manuscript except for some additions that heighten Shao-fu's feelings:

> 你找到湯沒有？我藏在抽屜裏，怕貓進來。」荀太太似乎是找出話來講。
> 「嗯，我熱了湯，把剩下的肉絲炒了飯。」他回答的時候聲音低沉，幾乎是溫柔的。由於突然改變音調，有點沙啞，需要微嗽一聲，打掃喉嚨。他並沒有抬起眼睛來看她，而臉一紅，看上去更黑了些，彷彿房間裏燈光更暗了。
>
> 90 [1983]

"Did you find the soup? I hid it in the drawer, lest the cat come in." Mrs. Xun seemed to find something to say. "Well, I heated up the soup and fried the remaining shredded pork." He replied in a low voice, almost gentle. Due to the sudden change in pitch, he was a little hoarse and needed to clear his throat with a slight cough. Instead of raising his eyes to look at her, he blushed and looked darker, as if the lights in the room had been dimmed.

In this Chinese version, Chang adds the phrase 「而臉一紅」 [but his face turned red / but he blushed], to describe Shao-fu's expression and to indicate his fondness, and perhaps also his sexual desire, for his wife. The editing enriches the portrayals of the characters' personalities in accordance with Chang's rationale of Shao-fu's love for his wife, which she outlines in her essay "Biaoyi, xiyi ji qita." The addition also shows that this part of the Chinese version is a revised version of the recently-discovered English manuscript.

The traditional vicious cycle of the relationship between a mother-in-law and daughter-in-law is depicted, but transformed, in this story. Mrs. Liu/Mrs. Xun suffers from her mother-in-law's tyranny in both versions of the story, but diplomatically maintains a good relationship with her. Moreover, Mrs. Liu/Mrs. Xun's younger sisters-in-law openly rebel against their mothers-in-law, and in so doing challenge the authority of the matriarch who embodies the Chinese patriarchal culture: "She had been quite a match for her mother-in-law in her own way, never answering back, while the younger daughters/in-law lacked such finesse. It was/(would be) galling that in the end the old lady preferred her to the others" ("She Said Smiling" 6). The word "daughters-in-law" was corrected as "daughter-in-law," handwritten in blue ink. In addition, the word "was" was crossed out and replaced by the handwritten words "would be," another grammatical correction. The paragraph is circled, with an arrow indicating where it should be moved.

Chang's "Xiangjianhuan" contains the above paragraph in Chinese in the same position as in the edited English manuscript:

> 荀太太對付她婆婆也有一手,儘管從來不還嘴。他們二少奶奶三少奶奶就不管,受不了就公然頂撞起來。其實她們也比她年輕不了多少,不過時代不同了。相形之下,老太太還是情願她。
> 80 [1983]

> Mrs. Xun has her own way to deal with her mother-in-law, although she never fights back. Their second and third young daughters-in-law did not care, and openly talked back when they could not bear it. In fact, they were not much younger than her, but times were different. In comparison, the old lady still prefers her.

Chang's Chinese version provides more details than the English manuscript about the rebellious attitudes and behaviour of the younger daughters-in-law, as opposed to Mrs. Xun's more tactful behaviour, illustrating the generational changes in the transitional period of modern China.

Mrs. Liu/Mrs. Xun is determined to change her traditional role as mother-in-law by refusing to live with her sons after they are married. Confucian ethics expect women to abide by the maxim of *sancong* 三從 (three obediences): daughters to their fathers, wives to their husbands, and widowed mothers to their sons. The idea of a mother regarding her son as refuge in her old age is challenged in the story:

> "I was thinking, if shao-fu dies I'm not going back either." She meant back to his xxxx family in Peking. "And I'm not going to live with the boys."
> "The boys are good. Tze-fan is going to be an engineer soon.
> She did not wish to point out that he / (was bound to) would be married. / (before / too long, ? from repeated [potentially?].)"I'm not going to live with them. (,)" she said brightly / (then mumbled).
> 7

A four-letter word was crossed out with typed "xxxx"; the original word is illegible. The words "wish to" were crossed out with a handwritten blue line, while the word "would" was replaced by the handwritten phrase "was bound to." The words "before too long from repeated [potentially?]" were also written in, but the last word of this sentence is illegible and is thus a guess. The words "she said brightly" were similarly replaced with the hand-written phrase "then mumbled." In this passage, Mrs. Liu declares that she will no longer play the role of an obedient daughter-in-law living under the roof of Shao-fu's family after he dies, nor will she play the role of a tyrannical mother-in-law living with her sons after they are married. By audaciously declaring her plan to reject conventional feminine roles, Mrs. Liu challenges the confining relationship between mothers-in-law and daughters-in-law in traditional Chinese culture.

Chang (re)writes/translates a similar episode regarding Mrs. Wu's future plans, but inserts Mrs. Wu's interpretation of what Mrs. Xun said in "Xiangjianhuan":

> 「我在想著，要是紹甫死了，我也不回去。我也不跟祖志他們住。」
> 她不用加解釋，伍太太自然知道她是説：兒子遲早總要結婚的。前車之鑑，她不願意跟他們住。
> 80 [1983]

"I was thinking, if Shao-fu died, I would not go back. I will not live with Zuzhi and the others either." She did not need to explain. Mrs. Wu naturally knew what she meant: her son will get married sooner or later. Lesson learned; she does not want to live with them.

The Chinese version specifies Mrs. Xun's son's name, Zhuzhi 祖志, which literally means "aspirations of ancestors," symbolizing his position as an esteemed descendant. The transliteration of the name in English would lose its cultural significance, as it is a reference to Chinese views of filial piety. Chang also adds the perspective of Mrs. Wu, who points out the reasons behind Mrs. Xun's decision as if Mrs. Wu can read Mrs. Xun's mind. The Chinese version corresponds to the edited version of the English manuscript, with handwritten corrections and additions in blue ink which indicate that the typewritten English manuscript is a rough draft, the handwritten edits are improvements to the text, and the Chinese version is refined from the drafts.

The major difference between the English manuscript and the Chinese versions is the addition to the latter of Mrs. Wu's daughter Yuanmei 苑梅, whose mother shows great care and concern for her:

> 幾個孩子就是爲苑梅嘔氣最多。這次回來可憐，老姊妹們説話，虧她也有這耐性一直坐在這兒旁聽——出了嫁倒反而離不開媽了。
> 82 [1983]

[Mrs. Wu] gets frustrated with Yuanmei the most among her few children. [Yuanmei] is pitiful when she came back this time. The old sisters are talking, but thinks that she has the patience to sit here and listen – after getting married, on the contrary, she cannot live without her mother.

Mrs. Wu worries about Yuanmei the most among her children because of Yuanmei's uncertain relationship with her husband and unstable living conditions.

Yuanmei, for her part, does reciprocate the care and concern her mother shows for her. When Yuanmei listens to Mrs. Xun's repeated recount of her story about being stalked by a young man in Beijing, she is shocked that Mrs. Xun has forgotten having already told that story, and Mrs. Wu forgets that she had heard it not long ago. Yuanmei believes that her mother is not that forgetful, but she may dislike this story and is thus choosing to ignore it. Nevertheless, she decides not to discuss this situation with her mother:

> 苑梅恨不得大叫一聲，又差點笑出聲來。媽記性又不壞，怎麼會一個忘了説過，一個忘了聽見過？但是她知道等他們走了，她不會笑著告訴媽：「表姑忘了説過釘梢的事，又講了一遍。」不是實在憎惡這故事，媽也不會這麼快就忘了——排斥在意識外——還又要去提它？
> 93 [1983]

Yuanmei could not wait to yell, and almost laughed again. Mom's memory is not bad, so how could one forget about having mentioned it and the other forget about having heard it? But she knew that when they were gone, she would not tell Mom with a smile, "Biao Aunt forgot that she had told you about the stalking tale, and she told it again." If it was not because Mom really hated the story, and Mom would not forget it so quickly – repelled it from consciousness – why would I mention it again?

METACOMMENTARY ON "XIANGJIANHUAN" 〈相見歡〉

Yuanmei's shocking moment provides an emotional climax. She seems unable to understand why people would tell, or listen to, the same story again, and so claims that her mother dislikes the story too much to forget it at all. She also shows compassion for her mother, enough not to talk about something she finds unpleasant. Mrs. Xun's story is, nevertheless, a reminiscence of her younger days when she felt beautiful and attractive, and Mrs. Wu's reaction to the story demonstrates her kindness about Mrs. Xun's desire to relive her youth.

"She Said Smiling" traces Mrs. Xun's evolving sense of independence and self-identity, as demonstrated in the following passage: "'I'/ was thinking I'd find something / (to do)," she (I don't know what,) mumbled, "anything at all. / (I don't care) I'd manage myself somehow," she ended louder, her voice unnaturally / (drawn out) broadened and (a bit) hoarse" (7). In this manuscript, the words "she mumbled" were crossed out and replaced by the handwritten words "I don't know what"; the words "I don't care" were crossed out and the words "drawn out" and "a bit" were written in. The edited version shows Mrs. Xun's determination to remain self-reliant even in an uncertain future, though the unnatural and rough sound of her voice betrays her nervousness.

Chang (re)writes/self-translates this episode in "Xiangjianhuan":

「我想著，我不管什麼地方，反正自己找個地方去，不管什麼都行。自己顧自己，我想總可以。」說到末了，比較大聲，但是聲調很不自然，粗嘎起來。
　　　80 [1983]

"I am thinking, I don't care where I am; I'll find a place to go anyway, no matter what. I'll take care of myself; I think it'll be all right somehow." At the end, her voice was a bit louder, but the tone was unnatural and rough.

The English manuscript emphasizes Mrs. Xun's desire to find a job so that she can financially support herself, while the Chinese version simply mentions her intention to live on her own and look after herself independently. Chang further elaborates in the Chinese version that Mrs. Xun has difficulty earning a living: she cannot work in an office due to her limited skills; she cannot work as a cook for fear of her son losing face; and she cannot open a restaurant due to lack of money. All of these explanations provide readers with more background information about Mrs. Xun's willingness to become independent even though she lacks the skills and resources that will allow her to do so.

The above passage shows evidence of multiple edits to a rough draft, intended to improve the grammar and clarity so that readers would more easily understand the ideas Chang sought to convey. The edited version of the English manuscript also features omissions, additions, and reversals of sentence structures and paragraph orders, some of which are present in the Chinese text. The Chinese text includes further additions that enhance the story's plot and characterizations. The question of the order in which these versions were written cannot satisfactorily be answered, because Chang often alternated between her English and Chinese texts during the processes of writing, rewriting, and self-translation, but the various texts do demonstrate the constant evolution of these processes. Chang translated these English and Chinese versions of the story closely in general, while making the aforementioned changes to improve and elaborate on her work.

The Chinese version of "Xiangjianhuan" that was first published in 1978 inspired further discussion. Lin Peifen's 林佩芬 essay "Kan Zhang – "Xiangjianhuan" de tantao" 〈看張——〈相見歡〉的探討〉 (Reading Chang – Discussion on "Joyful Rendezvous") was published in the second issue of the magazine *Shuping shumu* 《書評書目》 (*Taiwan Review of Books*) in 1979. In this essay, Lin argues that Yuanmei should address Mrs. Xun as *biaoyi* 表姨, the title of an aunt referring to one's mother's cousin, rather than *biaogu* 表姑, the title of an aunt referring to one's father's cousin, neither of which has an equivalent translation in English. She speculates that Yuanmei addresses Mrs. Xun as *biaogu* because Mrs. Xun is also a relative on Yuanmei's father's side. She also describes the characters in the story as 「槁木死灰」 [haggard wood and dead ashes] and 「麻木到近於無感覺」 [numbed to the point of no feeling]. Moreover, she points out that the story's generally omniscient narrative point of view is occasionally interrupted by authorial comments on the characters. Lin's comments show her careful reading of and interest in Chang's story. Her assumption also suggests the complex hierarchy of the Chinese familial structures and titles.

In response to Lin, Chang wrote a metacommentary essay, "Biaoyi xiyi ji qita," published in *Wangranji* in 1979, in which she clarifies the relationship between Mrs. Wu and Mrs. Xun in "Xiangjianhuan" by explaining that they are cousins; Yuanmei, strictly speaking, should therefore address Mrs. Xun as *biaoyi*. Chang uses *biaogu* in the story because the word *yi* is included in the phrase *yi taitai* 姨太太 [concubine], and was therefore considered taboo in many linguistic and geographical regions in mainland China at the time. Chang also defends the vitality and passion of her characters, who all display desires, frustrations, and hopes, no matter how insignificant those may seem. She explains that the narrative point of view is indeed an omniscient one, and that Lin is referring specifically to Mrs. Wu's contemplations; Mrs. Wu is educated and knows the English idiom 「死亡使人平等。」 [In death we are all equal (91)]. Chang omits the words "she thinks" when referring to Mrs. Wu's ideas because those reflections follow right after Mrs. Wu's saying. This discussion is an instance of Chang providing readers with a self-reflexive analysis of the word choices, narrative modes, and characterizations present in "Xiangjianhuan."

Chang's metacommentary essay also performatively generates revisions of the story that was published in *Wangranji* in 1983. In "Biaoyi xiyi ji qita," Chang admits that she wrote that Mrs. Wu has 「一肚子才學」 (32) [a belly full of talents and knowledge] but did not clarify that Mrs. Wu knows much about both Chinese and Western cultures. She also claims that Yuanmei has her own reasons for regretting not able to follow her husband abroad; at the end of the essay, she declares: 「以後要把這一點補寫進去，非常感謝林女士提醒我。」 (32) [I will add this point in the future; thank you very much, Ms. Lin, for reminding me]. Chang's metacommentary not only outlines her authorial intentions and provides guidelines for her readers, but also demonstrates a capacity for performativity, as the promises she makes in the essay come to fruition in the revised version of the story that was published five years later.

Chang made several changes in the revised version of "Xiangjianhuan" published in *Wangranji* in 1983. For instance, she adds Yuanmei's reflection on her own marriage after seeing an extra bed in the bedroom of Shao-fu and Mrs. Xun. Her contemplation of the inconvenience of the couple's sex life implies her yearning for her husband, whom she cannot follow abroad due to financial constraints. Yuanmei then remembers her parents, who went abroad together when they were young. Her mother, Mrs. Wu, is not good at cooking or socializing, and despite her rather plain physical appearance, she is confident that she can charm her husband with her youthful body. Mr. Wu is faithful to his wife when they are abroad, but has extramarital affairs when he becomes successful and prosperous in China. In the revised version, Yuanmei also thinks about her indifference to reputation and social status while listening to what Mrs. Xun say about Shao-fu who lends money to relatives. Yuanmei speculates that Mrs. Xun thinks she may look down on Mrs. Xun's poorer financial situation. A further addition to the revised story is Mr. Wu's use of an ancient Suzhou temple bell as a dinner bell, an indication of indulgence in power, which, as with the aforementioned additional details of the familial and social backgrounds of the other characters, helps to elaborate on and foreshadow his and their developments in the story.

The short story "Xiangjianhuan" has also inspired other comments and responses since its first publication. For example, in the essay "Yuedu Zhang Ailing xinzuo yougan" 〈閱讀張愛玲新作有感〉 ("Feelings after Reading

Eileen Chang's New Work") in *Mingbao zhoukan* 《明報周刊》 (*Ming Pao Weekly*) in 1979, Isabel Nee Yeh-su 倪亦舒 (a.k.a. Yi Shu 亦舒, b. 1946) criticizes "Xiangjianhuan" for having no discernable storyline and for its setting not being interesting enough for readers under the age of thirty. She even concludes that 「由此可知，復出是萬萬不可的，要不寫它一輩子，認了命。」. [It can be seen from this that she [Eileen Chang] absolutely ought not make a comeback, or she will write it for a lifetime and accept her fate]. However, in 1976, Yi Shu published a critique of Chang's ex-husband Hu Lancheng, titled "Hu Lancheng de xiazuo" 〈胡蘭成的下作〉 ("Hu Lancheng's Despicableness"), in *Mingbao zhoukan* 《明報周刊》 (*Ming Pao Weekly*), which condemned him for using Chang's name for self-advertising in his memoir *Jinsheng jinshi* 《今生今世》 (*This Life, These Times*, 1958):

> 張愛玲出了名，馬上就是他老婆，書中滿滿的愛玲，肉麻下作不堪，這種感覺是讀者的感覺，張愛玲或是瀟灑的女性，與眾不同，不介意有人拿她當宣傳。

> Eileen Chang became famous, and right away she became his wife. The book is full of Eileen, which is absolutely disgusting. This feeling is the reader's feeling. Eileen Chang is a chic woman, different from the majority, and does not mind if someone uses her as publicity.

As these essays show, Yi Shu began as an admirer of Chang, defending her from maltreatment by Hu Lancheng, but then changed her position in order to dismiss Chang's recently published work as inappropriate.

Chang's lifelong friend Stephen Soong sent both of Yi Shu's essays to her for reference. He sent her the earlier essay on December 6, 1976, to which she replied in a letter dated December 15: 「阿妹[亦舒]罵胡蘭成的一篇真痛快。」 (*To My Beloved Friends* 1.344) [Little sister's (Yi Shu's) article scolding Hu Lancheng is really delightful]. Soong then sent Chang a critical essay written by Yi Shu along with a letter dated August 19, 1979, in which he laments that Chinese readers remain in the stage of melodrama and complains that Yi Shu calls him 「老先生」 [an old man]. Chang replied to Soong in a letter dated September 4, 1979:

> 亦舒罵〈相見歡〉，其實水晶已經屢次來信批評〈浮花浪蕊〉〈相見歡〉〈表姨細姨及其他〉，雖然措辭較客氣，也是恨不得我快點死掉，免得破壞 image [形象]。這些人是我的一些老本，也是個包袱，只好揹着，不過這次帶累 Stephen。中國人對老的觀念太落後，尤其是想取而代之的後輩文人。

> *TO MY BELOVED FRIENDS* 1.420

Yi Shu rebuked "Joyful Rendezvous." In fact, Shui Jing had written me many times to criticize "Floating Flowers and Wavy Pistils," "Joyful Rendezvous," and "Biao Aunt, Little Aunt and other Issues." Although the wording is more polite, they wish I would die soon, so as not to ruin my own image. These people are some of my assets, and they are also a burden, so I must carry them on my back, but this time I drag in Stephen. The Chinese people's concept of the old is too outdated, especially the younger generation of literati who want to replace the older generation.

Both Soong and Chang appreciated Yi Shu's critical essay on Hu Lancheng, but they disagreed about her dismissal of "Xiangjianhuan" and her suggestion that Chang needed to stop writing. Although Chang did not reply publicly to these articles, she did generously accept them as her fan's opinion.

Other critics have contributed to the afterlife of "Xiangjianhuan" by responding to the story as well as to each other. For instance, in 2010, in his column "Ke shehui zhuanlan" 〈克社會專欄〉 ("Ke Society Column") in *Pingguo ribao* 《蘋果日報》 (*Apple Daily*), Mai Ke 邁克 published several articles defending Chang from Yi Shu's criticism. He argues that Chang tended to intentionally revolutionize her writing styles and points out that the setting of the story was recent at the time. He also praises "Xianjianhuan" for its depictions of human relationships and interactions. I further argue that "Xiangjianhuan" cannot be dismissed simply because it does not contain a conventional plot with a beginning, a middle, and an end. The characters' dialogues delve deeply into their psychological sophistication and their dynamic and intricate relationships, and reveal much about 1940s Shanghai middle-class people's ways of thinking and interacting. Moreover, Chang had been writing, translating, and publishing throughout her life, and her works have changed and evolved over time in terms of topics, genres, styles, sentiments, setting, and meaning.

Yan Zeya 顏擇雅 provides an interpretation of "Xiangjianhuan" in her article 〈張愛玲一題三寫——析〈留情〉、〈相見歡〉、〈同學少年都不賤〉〉 ("Eileen Chang Writing One Topic in Three Works – Analysis of 'Traces of Love,' 'Joyful Rendezvous,' and 'Classmates when Adolescence Was Not Despicable'"), published in *Jing Bao* 《晶報》 on February 7, 2013. She argues that these three stories are all about lesbian love, pointing out that Mrs. Wu enjoys listening to Mrs. Xun's accounts of being followed in Peking twice (41). Roland Soong, however, disagrees with Yan's reading of Mrs. Wu's response to Mrs. Xun's story of being stalked; in his essay "'Xiangjianhuan' jiujing xiang shuo shenme?" 〈〈相見歡〉究竟想說什麼？〉 ("What Exactly Does 'Xiangjianhuan' Want to Say?", 2014), he argues that 「伍太太是每一次聽都覺得反感，以致『排斥在意識外』，跟顏擇雅所謂『伍太太卻聽兩遍依然津津有味』剛好相反。」 [Mrs. Wu feels disgusted every time she listens to it, so that she "repels it out of consciousness," which is exactly the opposite of what Yan Zeya says about how "Mrs. Wu listened to it twice and still enjoys it"]. He also suggests that Mrs. Xun has told her old stories many times, and concludes that both she and Mrs. Wu are in a 「絕望處境」 [desperate situation].

In his article, Roland Soong also discusses Chang's letter to Stephen and Mae Soong dated October 31, 1977, which includes a metacommentary on "Xiang-jianhuan" revealing that the story's original title was "Wangshi zhi duoshao" 〈往事知多少〉 ("How Much Do You Know About the Past?"). Chang claims in the letter that the story was inspired by her own experience listening to two close friends chatting when she was in mainland China. One woman regarded her friend's marriage as beneath her, like a phoenix following a crow, and though she would like to see her friend having an extramarital affair, she disliked hearing her friend talk about being stalked. Several months later, her friend told her the same story again, and just as the speaker forgot having told the story before, the listener forgot having heard it: 「我在旁幾乎不能相信我的耳朵」 (*To My Beloved Friends* 1.368) [I can hardly believe my ears by the side]. She then further explains that Mrs. Wu detests this story so much that she forgets about it twice, thus demonstrating her alienation from others, and concludes: 「我非常震動。」 [I was very shocked] (*To My Beloved Friends* 1.368).

Chang's letter provides readers with another metacommentary on "Xiang-jianhuan." However, this commentary was not offered to the public, but to her close friends. Furthermore, it was not published during her lifetime, and was only published posthumously following controversial reader responses to the story. In the letter, Chang reveals that the source of the story was a real lived experience that made an impression on her. She suggests that she is a listener to, and observer of, the conversation of two close friends, and contemplates the loneliness of human beings who seem to be companions. She also presents her impressions of the thoughts and feelings behind her characters' interactions with each other. Although the authorial intention Chang explains in her letter may not be the last word on readers' interpretations of the story, she does provide her readers with some guidance toward understanding it. Nevertheless, as her story has had an afterlife of its own since its first publication, readers exercise their freedom of response to her story according to their cultural backgrounds and their temporal and spatial contexts. Chang's writing, rewriting, self-translation, and metacommentary interweave to produce greater meaning than each can provide on its own, and all of these generate new insights on the story, on ways of thinking and feeling, and on human relationships and life in general.

The relationship between Chang's fiction and self-translations is paradoxical. Her self-translations are neither completely new nor entirely dependent on the prior texts. Instead, the two versions form an interdependent relationship, producing meaning greater than either one of them enjoys alone. The major difference between Chang's self-translations and those made by other translators is that other translators are denied access to her authorial intention; her self-translations are her own re-interpretations from her specific ethnic, gender, class, and cultural perspectives. Moreover, the Romantic individualist concept of authorship manifested in copyright law and intellectual ownership grant Chang more legal and moral freedom in her self-translation than other translators would possess, thus situating her in a freer position to re-interpret her works. Both her Chinese and English texts display Chinese cultural features and Western imported values, interacting, and contracting, with one another. The above discussions of Chang's "Jinsuoji," "The Golden Cangue," *The Rouge of the North, Yuannü*, "Guihuazheng," "Shame Amah," "Deng," "Little Finger Up," "Stale Mates," "Wusi yishi," "She Said Smiling," and "Xiangjianhuan" demonstrate a state of in-betweenness existing between Chang as the author and as the self-translator, between her fiction and self-translations, between Chang and the reader, between Chang and the editor and publisher, between Chinese and Western representations of the female body, and between commentary and metacommentary, thus breaking down a whole series of hierarchies and boundaries.

Regarding her self-translation styles of these short stories and novels, Chang tends to translate her own writing from English into Chinese, or vice versa, principally based on her plots and characters, with slight transformations that cater to the linguistic and cultural backgrounds of her target audiences. In the larger context, Chang commands interest because, although she mastered Chinese better than English, she also deliberately took heed, in her narrative, of the background knowledge of her various audiences. She accomplishes this in her Chinese writings by drawing on the audience's familiarity with traditional Chinese codes, norms, and patterns of behaviour, and in her English works by explicating features that might otherwise strike her Anglophone readers as strange. She approaches foreign languages in her own ways, and some of her works may inspire other bilingual writers in the infinitely more globalized twenty-first century to cross linguistic and cultural barriers.

PART 3

Cultural Translation

∵

CHAPTER 9

Interpretation: "Demons and Fairies" and "Zhongguoren de zongjiao" 〈中國人的宗教〉 ("The Religion of the Chinese")

Cultural translation is an interlingual and intercultural activity that interprets the meaning of the source text and produces knowledge in the translation, particularly in the spheres of cultural convention and expression, catering to the sociohistorical background of the target audience. As Susan Bassnett argues, "Beyond the notion stressed by the narrowly linguistic approach, that translation involves the transfer of 'meaning' contained in one set of language signs into another set of language signs through competent use of the dictionary and grammar, the process involves a whole set of extra-linguistic criteria also" (*Translation Studies* 24). Self-translators, in particular, interpret the cultural connotations of one language into another language with understanding produced from their own experiences of gender, education, religion, family, and society. Linguistic and cultural distances between the source text and the self-translation offer further creative insights and literary expressions. Contested beliefs of cultural values and gestures are, however, underscored and transformed in a self-translation, especially when the author/self-translator is addressing ways of thinking and lifestyles, such as gender relations, political viewpoints, and religious thoughts, manifested in dress, literature, art, performance, and other cultural practices.

Eileen Chang deliberately performs the role of a cultural translator translating Chinese modernity in flux in the early twentieth century. She published three English essays, "Chinese Life and Fashions," "Still Alive," and "Demons and Fairies," in an Anglophone magazine, *The XXth Century*, in Shanghai between January and December 1943, and translated them into Chinese under the titles "Gengyiji" 〈更衣記〉 ("A Chronicle of Changing Clothes"), "Yangren kan jingxi ji qita" 〈洋人看京戲及其他〉 ("Westerners Watching Peking Operas and Other Issues"), and "Zhongguoren de zongjiao" 〈中國人的宗教〉 ("The Religion of the Chinese"), respectively, in 1943 and 1944. *The XXth Century* was an English-language magazine published in Shanghai and funded by the German foreign ministry. Klaus Mehnert, a Russian émigré to Germany, served as the editor between 1941 and 1945, and mainly wrote intellectual analyses of Soviet politics and Fascist propaganda for

© JESSICA TSUI-YAN LI, 2025 | DOI:10.1163/9789004730052_011

158   CHAPTER 9

the magazine.[1] The magazine was aimed at Anglophone residents in foreign concessions in Shanghai in the early 1940s.

This section examines the cultural translation of these three English essays and their corresponding Chinese translations, all of them written by Eileen Chang in Shanghai in the early 1940s. I argue here that Chang does not merely adopt a mimetic strategy to reflect Chinese fashion, Peking Opera, and religion in modern China, but also produces meaning in her essays and self-translation through interpretation, distanciation, and transformation, as she wrote her English essays with Anglophone readers in Shanghai of the time as her target audience. Interpreting Chinese culture from comparative perspectives, she addresses both commonalities and differences between Chinese and Western cultural practices and provides elaborate sociohistorical backgrounds in her English essays for her Anglophone readers. Rewriting her English essays into Chinese, she critically examines Chinese cultures from a spatial and emotional distance, and presents re-evaluations of deep-seated Chinese ethical values in both ironic and colourful ways. Her comprehensive and systematic analysis of the theological and cosmic worldview, literature and stage performance, and Chinese vestural trends in modern China delivers her very own penetrating interpretations of Chinese sociohistorical and cultural values, and in so doing paints a vivid picture of Chinese modernity at the turn of the twentieth century.

Translation involves the translator's interpretation of the source text by investigating the author's biography, the text, and its sociohistorical background, and acting as a go-between to bridge the text's languages, cultures, and beliefs with those of the target readers. Indeed, the word *hermeneutics* comes from the Greek verb *hermeneuin,* which means *to interpret* or *to translate,* Like Hermes, the mythical Greek messenger of the gods, translators interpret the meaning of the source text in the translation for target readers. As Anthony Cordingley argues, "The 'cultural turn' in Translation Studies has encouraged researchers to expand their field of investigation beyond the movement of texts from one language to another, and to chart and analyse the movement of cultural products, ideas, bodies and selves between different linguistic communities" (4). Likewise mediating between different linguistic and cultural worlds, self-translators especially bring forth their own self-understanding in comparative perspectives to convey messages in both their source texts and

---

1   For background information about Klaus Mehnert and the journal, see Michael Kohlstruck, "Klaus Mehnert und die Zeitschrift *The xxth Century.*"

INTERPRETATION   159

their self-translations in various cultural capacities, such as ways of life, dressing styles and codes, gender relation, religion, literature, and art.

This chapter examines Eileen Chang's English essay "Demons and Fairies," first published in the magazine *The xxth Century* in December 1943 in Shanghai, and her self-translation into Chinese as "Zhongguoren de zongjiao" 〈中國人的宗教〉 ("The Religion of the Chinese"), first published in the Chinese magazine *Tiandi* 《天地》 (*Heaven and Earth*) between August and October 1944 in Shanghai, with reference to David Pollard's translation of Chang's "Zhongguoren de zongjiao" from Chinese into English, "The Religion of the Chinese," in his edited volume *The Chinese Essay*, in 2000. I argue here that in "Demons and Fairies," Chang reflectively offers her own interpretations of Chinese psychological and philosophical thoughts in the form of their spiritual beliefs, cultural practices, and representations in Chinese literature and art for her Anglophone readers in Shanghai in the early 1940s. Translating her own essay from English into Chinese, she re-evaluates Chinese spiritual and secular thoughts and customs from comparative points of view for modern Chinese readers in "Zhongguoren de zongjiao." David Pollard's translation, however, focuses on the introduction of Chinese religion to readers. This chapter discusses Chang's comparison of Chinese religious values with Christian (both Protestant and Catholic) and Egyptian theology, and her outlining of the similarities and differences of the beliefs of Chinese intellectuals and less-educated Chinese people. It also examines her explanation of the transformation of Chinese familial relationships from Confucian traditional models to modern revolutionary ideas. The essays demonstrate Chang's roles as cultural translator and commentator for both Anglophone and Sinophone readers through her interpretations of Chinese thoughts, beliefs, and customs in her writing and self-translation.

Klaus Mehnert, editor of *The xxth Century*, provides a foreword to "Demons and Fairies" that guides the readers to interpret this essay's meaning. Mehnert argues that Chang focuses more on the Chinese mentality in general rather than superstition or religion:

> China has a vast, richly populated borderland, the borderland of the beyond, the borderland between superstition and religion. In her whimsical meanderings in these realms, the authoress does not attempt to answer religious or ethical questions. But in her own amusing way she succeeds in conveying to us a great deal of information on the mentality of the Chinese masses.
>
> 421

According to Mehnert, Chang has successfully played the role of cultural translator with insider knowledge of Chinese mindsets and behaviours that allows her to explain these to her readers, instead of delving into religious discussion as a marketing strategy to attract the general readers of the magazine. Mehnert's introduction serves as an allographic peritext, a subcategory of Gérard Genette's concept of paratextuality under the larger scheme of transtextuality (*Paratexts* 5). Joshua Ratner maintains that both authors and publishers frequently negotiated allographic peritext in the nineteenth century, and the peritext "might still be influenced by or actually composed by the author, while the authorially driven peritexts (dedications, prefaces, footnotes, epigraphs) might also have considerable input from publishers" (734). Whether Mehnert and Chang discussed this foreword would not be surprising. Nevertheless, Mehnert's remarks serve to provide commentary on Chang's "Demons and Fairies," which divert the attention of the readers to his comprehension and shape the significance of this essay to a certain extent.

At the beginning of her essays "Demons and Fairies" and "Zhongguoren de zongjiao," Chang paradoxically declares the apparent nonexistence of Chinese religion to stimulate readers' thinking. She opens her essays with the striking statement:

> A rough survey of current Chinese thought would force us to the conclusion that there is no such thing as the Chinese religion. The Chinese intelligentsia has always been staunchly atheistic.
>
> "DEMONS" 421

> 表面上中國人是沒有宗教可言的。中國知識階級這許多年來一直是無神論者。
>
> "ZHONGGUO" 179

> On the surface the Chinese have no religion to speak of. The intellectual class of Chinese have for many years been atheists.
>
> POLLARD 283

Understanding Chang's observation requires tracing Chinese religious and philosophical belief systems to ancestral rites and divination rituals dating to the Shang (1600 BC–1045 BC) and Zhou (1046 BC–256 BC) Dynasties. Chinese folk religion includes deities of the natural environment, cultural heroes, and moralities of ancestral and civil society that have been depicted in Chinese history and literature. Confucianism, Taoism, and Buddhism intertwine with

INTERPRETATION   161

each other as well as with Chinese folk religion, and all of these together have traditionally shaped Chinese religious and philosophical culture. However, the majority of Chinese people, in general, may not necessarily consider their philosophical and spiritual beliefs as any sort of institutional religion, for, as Confucius notes in the *Analects,*「未知生，焉知死。」(《論語》11:12) [If you have not understood life yet, how can you understand death?]. Confucius' teachings have had a profound influence on generations of Chinese intellectuals and have contributed in part to their seemingly atheistic worldview; conversely, however, in the early twentieth century the leaders of the New Cultural Movement (1916–23) accused Confucianism and other traditions of obstructing the development of modern China.

Adapting her essay for her Chinese readers, Chang made several changes in her Chinese self-translation. In "Zhongguoren de zongjiao," she adds an apologetic explanation to her introduction:「這篇東西本是寫給外國人看的，所以非常粗淺，但是我想，有時候也應該當像初級教科書一樣地頭腦簡單一下，把事情弄明白些。」(179) [This essay was originally written for foreigners, so it is very superficial, but I think sometimes it should be as simple as an elementary school textbook to make things clearer]. In these opening remarks, she admits the simplicity of her analysis of Chinese religious beliefs and practices, but also insists on its significance. Apart from adding the opening sentences, she also combines the sections of "Bohemian Fairies," "Earth Fairies," and "Love of Repetition" in the English essay into one section, "Unnecessary Heaven," in her Chinese self-translation. She also adds the entire section "The 'Bad' of the Chinese" and most of "Foreign Religion in China," and removes three sentences from "Mental Haziness a Virtue" and three paragraphs from "The Chinese in Despair." Near the ending, she combines the sections "Mental Haziness a Virtue," "The Ultimate Test," and "The Chinese in Despair" from the English essay into one large section, "The Unfathomable Heart of China," in her Chinese self-translation. All these changes are meant for the benefit of Chinese readers who already know about Chinese metaphysical beliefs and social practices.

In contrast to Mehnert's foreword and Chang's own introductions to her essays, Pollard interprets "Demons and Fairies" as Chang's effort to introduce Chinese religion to Anglophone readers. In his commentary, Pollard argues that Chang's essay "on Chinese religion was originally written for foreigners." In order to justify his abridged translation, he also claims that her Chinese essay is too long and fragmented: "The Chinese text is at seventeen pages too long to translate in its entirety, but as it is not very cohesive, excerptation does no great injury" (283). Based on his understanding, he removes Chang's introduction to "Zhongguoren de zongjiao" and also eliminates all sub-headings, the entire sections "Why Such Interest in the Coffin," "Natural and Unnatural Death," "Subhuman Swindlers," "The 'Bad' of the Chinese," and "The Unfathomable Heart of China," three paragraphs of the section "The Unnecessary Heaven," and seven paragraphs from the section "Foreign Religion in China." All of these omissions are related to Chang's analysis of Chinese thoughts and customs regarding both worldly and otherworldly values. His translation is, therefore, an abbreviated version of Chang's Chinese essay tailored to what he deems the theme of educating Anglophone readers on Chinese religion.

In her essays on Chinese religions, Chang often compares Chinese spiritual beliefs and social customs with those of Christianity. For instance, in "Zhongguoren de zongjiao," Chang adds a section titled "Foreign Religion in China," in which she suggests that a possible reason for the unpopularity of Catholicism in China is the common depiction of Saint Mary with blonde hair, a physical trait that is unusual among Chinese people. Moreover, she claims that the unfamiliar names, backgrounds, character traits, and events in the lives of Catholic saints make it difficult for Chinese people to comprehend them, let alone to replace the numerous gods of their own tradition. Protestant Christianity, with its focus on one God, however, seems to have gained more approval in China. She points out a significant difference between the relationship between God and His disciples in Christianity and in Chinese religious culture: 「基督教的神與信徒發生個人關係，而且是愛的關係。中國的神向來公事公辦，談不到愛。」(192) [The God of Christianity has a personal relationship with disciples, and it is a love relationship. Gods in China have always been business-like, having not reached to the level of love]. Chang here compares the god/disciple relationship within Christianity to the more human-like relationships present in Chinese religion: where the Christian God offers unconditional love to His disciples, the Chinese gods resemble governors ruling over their subjects with various regulations.

In "Zhongguoren de zongjiao," Chang discusses the origin of the universe, further distinguishing Christian faith from Chinese cosmic beliefs:

基督教感謝上帝在七天之內（或是經過億萬年的進化程序）爲我們創造了宇宙。中國人則説是盤古開天闢地，但這沒有多大關係——中國人僅僅上溯到第五代，五代之上的先人在祭祖的筵席上就沒有他們的份。

194

Christianity thanks God for creating the universe for us in seven days (or eons of evolutionary progression). The Chinese say that it was Pan Gu who created the world, but it does not matter much – the Chinese only

INTERPRETATION   163

trace back to the fifth generation, and predecessors above the fifth generation have no place in the feast of ancestor worship.

In contrast to the Christian scheme of the origin of the universe over eons
of development, Chang introduces the Chinese legend of Pan Gu creating the
universe, and more importantly, also emphasizes the notion of filial piety to
ancestors but only up to the fifth generation. This comparison showcases the
Chinese valuation of kinship and affinity, based on the proximity of relationship, with the most respect paid to close senior family members and the least
to those who are more distantly affiliated. This explanation of Chinese moral
principles is absent in the English essay "Demons and Fairies," as well as in
Pollard's translation. Chang's addition in her Chinese self-translation elaborates on her understanding of Chinese religion as a reflection of Chinese ethical
relationship, while Pollard's omission of this information serves to underscore
his reading of her essay and his translation's sole focus on Chinese religion.

In her discussion of Heaven, Chang compares Chinese perspectives of
the Christian and Taoist concepts. According to her interpretation, Chinese
people are generally apathetic to either the Christian Heaven for its eternal
peace ("Zhongguoren de zongjiao" 195) or the Taoist Heaven due to its lack
of the "vital concerns of humanity" ("Demons" 425 [1943]) that the Chinese
treasure. In the Chinese imagination, unceasingly playing golden harps in an
old-fashioned Christian church is unappealing ("Zhongguoren de zongjiao"
195), and likewise the Taoist "palaces of jade and jasper, [in which] prevails
an atmosphere of clean white emptiness, symbolic of the 'Do Nothing' policy
of Lao-tse" ("Demons" 425 [1943]) are equally undesirable. She points out that
the Chinese have adopted the strategy of free interpretation in their envisioning of Heaven: "if the Chinese never take heaven literally they can induce in
themselves a state of faith whenever it suits their purpose" ("Demons" 425).
In "Demons and Fairies," Chang contends that the Chinese do not take heaven
seriously and instead imagine it according to their interests. She then elaborates on these ideas in "Zhongguoren de zongjiao": 「可是即使中國人不拿
天堂當回事，他們能夠隨時的愛相信就相信，他們的幻想力委實強
韌得可驚。」 [But even though Chinese people put no store by heaven, they
can believe in it whenever it suits them. Their faculty of idealization is amazingly sturdy (187; Pollard 288)]. Chang adds that the Chinese have an aston-
ishingly immersive imagination; Pollard, however, translates 「幻想力」
[imagination] as "idealization" based on his interpretation of the Chinese religious belief in romanticizing and glorifying heaven in a more eulogizing tone.

When she describes the lifestyles of the celestial immortals in Chinese religious belief, Chang uses a Europeanized Chinese sentence structure, a popular

tactic in the early twentieth century for translations of English into Chinese, in "Zhongguoren de zongjiao": 「生活有絕對保障的仙人以沖淡的享樂，如下棋、飲酒、旅行，來消磨時間。」 (190) [Immortals with absolute security of life engage in watered-down pleasures, such as playing chess, drinking, and traveling, to pass the time]. The phrase "such as," which introduces a list of examples of pleasure, is inserted between the clauses "engage in watered-down pleasures" and "to pass the time," a conventional English sentence structure that is unusual in Chinese syntax. It is an example of the Westernization of Chinese vocabulary, grammar, syntax, lexicon, and phonology that was widespread in the early twentieth century, especially in the practice of translations of European languages in general and English in particular into Chinese. This Europeanization coincided with the gradual replacement of literary Chinese with *baihua* 白話 [vernacular Chinese]. Fu Ssu-nien 傅斯年 (1896–1950), an intellectual leader of the May Fourth Movement, advocated the Europeanization of Chinese written language in his essay "Zenyang zuo baihua wen" 〈怎样做白話文〉 ("How to Write Baihua Texts," 1919), as Leo Tak-hung Chan notes:

> [L]ooming in the background were concerns about the creation of a new Chinese vernacular to replace the old classical language, the confrontation of foreign languages with the indigenous tongue, the implementation of language reforms and, above all, the deeply-felt need to modernize the nation on the political, cultural and linguistic levels—to, in other words, realize the grand "May Fourth Project."
>
> 198

Deeply immersed in this sociohistorical context of Chinese language transformation in the early twentieth century, Chang experimented with foreignized stylistic language innovations in her Chinese writing, thanks to her proficiency in both Chinese and English, supported by her informal and formal bilingual education in Shanghai and Hong Kong.

Aside from comparing Chinese perspectives on the Christian and Taoist concepts of Heaven, Chang also juxtaposes the characteristics of the Christian and Buddhist concepts of Hell in "Demons and Fairies," with some further elaboration in her self-translation "Zhongguoren de zongjiao." In "Demons and Fairies," for instance, she notes: "The Chinese have a Taoist heaven and a Buddhist hell. All souls depart to hell after death to be judged there, so that it is not simply the abode of the damned in the Christian sense" (422). The passage is translated as follows in "Zhongguoren de zongjiao": 「中國人有一個道教的天堂與佛教的地獄，死後一切靈魂都到地獄裏去受審判，所以

不像基督教的地底火山，單只惡人在裏面受罪的，我們的地府是比較空氣流通的地方。」(181), while Pollard translates this passage as: "The Chinese have a Taoist heaven and a Buddhist hell. On death all souls go to hell to receive judgement, so in contrast to the Christian subterranean fiery pits, where only bad people go to suffer for their sins, our underworld is a comparatively well ventilated place" (285). The comparison points out the relatively neutral nature of the Buddhist hell, which every soul enters after death for judgement, in contrast to the more terrifying imagery of the Christian hell as the realm of the condemned. In her Chinese self-translation, Chang further adds the imagery of "subterranean fiery pits" for the Christian hell and "a comparatively well ventilated place" for its Buddhist counterpart.

In "Demons and Fairies," Chang notes that, much like the Chinese conception of heaven, the Buddhist conception of hell is subject to boundless interpretations: "Not being stereotyped, the administration of justice in the underworld leaves much room for conjecture and free interpretation" (423). She translates this passage in "Zhongguoren de zongjiao" as 「既然沒有一定，陰司的行政可以由得我們加以種種猜度解釋。」 [Because of its lack of constancy, the administration of underworld justice allows latitude for much guesswork and interpretation (183; Pollard 286)]. Buddhism spread to China from India as early as the Han Dynasty (202 BC–AD 220) and was integrated with Taoism and traditional Chinese folk religion. Many works of Chinese literature, opera, music, and popular culture have presented various imaginings of the Buddhist hell and its association with Chinese mythical figures. The predestined relationship in the infinite continuity of human life appears frequently in Chinese literature and art, such as the novel *Autumn Quince* and its adaptation into "a stage play, a Shao-shing Opera, a farce, a long ballad in the Shanghai dialect; and the identical audience will faithfully go to see it in every possible form" ("Demons" 427).

Chang credits the loose interpretation of heaven and hell with the popularity and endurance of Chinese folk religion, as she points out in "Demons and Fairies":

> Thus against the high-pressure missionary enterprises of the different forms of Christianity the native creed is able to hold its own, without any counterattack, unsupported by large capital, without any spokesman, propaganda literature, any consciously created atmosphere of peace and beauty, or even any classics to fall back on (Buddhist classics, never popularized, are as good as nonexistent).
>
> 427–428

According to Chang, Chinese folk religion, compared to Christianity, does not have a comprehensive canon. However, its flexibility, which has allowed it to integrate with Taoism, Buddhism, Confucianism, and local mythological tales, has produced its own organic network manifested in literature, performance, and art, and implemented in daily cultural practices and ancestral rituals, cannot be measured by standards of other cultures.

In "Zhongguoren de zongjiao," Chang translates the above passage as「所以本土的傳說，對抗著新舊耶教的高壓傳教，還是站得住腳，雖然它沒有反攻，沒有大量資本的支持，沒有宣傳文學，優美和平的佈景，連一本經書都沒有——佛經極少人懂，等於不存在。」(195). She uses the phrase "different forms of Christianity" in her English version because Western readers in general have a better understanding of the genealogy and complexity of the historical development and variations of Christianity than Chinese readers do. In her Chinese self-translation, she reworks this phrase as「新舊耶教」(new and old Christianity) to introduce two general categories of Christianity to her Chinese readers who are not as familiar with Christianity, and further elaboration is unnecessary in this context. Pollard's version reinterprets Chang's notion of new and old Christianity:

> so our native folklore can still stand up to the high-pressure proselytizing of Roman Catholic and Protestant Christianity, though it has not counter-attacked, though it hasn't the support of big capital, has no propaganda literature, no splendid peaceful sets, not even a bible – for since almost nobody understands the Buddhist sutras, it is as if they do not exist.
>
> 292

His translation, however, clarifies the phrase as referring to Roman Catholic and Protestant Christianity, based on his interpretation of Chang's Chinese essay.

In addition to her comparison of Chinese folk religion with Christianity, Chang also compares Chinese folk religion and Egyptian doctrines about the relationship between the soul and the body in order to explain the significance of the coffin in Chinese religion: "Since transmigration ensures the independence of the soul from the body, which is only transitory, the corpse plays no part in Chinese theology as it does in Egyptian theology" ("Demons" 423). By pointing out the Chinese belief in the independence of the soul from the body, Chang arouses her readers' curiosity about how filial piety for one's ancestors, preparation for imminent death, and serving wandering souls all establish the symbolism of the coffin. She translates this passage into Chinese in "Zhongguoren de zongjiao" as 「死後既可另行投胎，可見靈魂之於身體是有獨立性的，軀殼不過是暫時的，所以中國神學與埃及神學不同，不那麼注重屍首。」(183). In the English version, Chang uses the verb "ensures" to indicate certainty, while in the Chinese translation, she uses the verbs 「可見」[can be seen] to indicate possibility. The English sentence uses the phrase "plays no parts," providing an absolute sense, while the Chinese sentence uses the phrase 「不那麼注重」[does not emphasize too much], avoiding bluntness by adopting euphemism. Chang takes a direct and assured tone in her English essay, and an indirect and tacit manner in her Chinese translation, and these tonal variations demonstrate the different authorial personas she takes when addressing Anglophone and Chinese readers. Pollard omits all of these phrasal and tonal nuances, however, to simplify Chang's discussion of Chinese religion.

Alongside comparing Chinese folk religion to both Christianity and Egyptian theology, Chang also examines the differences in spiritual beliefs among various classes of the Chinese people themselves, particularly those of varying levels of education. According to Chang, many Chinese intellectuals, influenced by Confucianism, generally follow an atheistic worldview, while less educated or lower-class Chinese people are immersed in Buddhism or Taoism, and may also be attracted to fragmentary superstitions such as fortune telling, ghosts, spirits, fairies, vegetarianism, or meditation. In "Demons and Fairies" Chang stresses the interpretive principle of such superstitious cultures as parts of a philosophical understanding of the world: "The superstitions, then, are not superstitions, since they are intelligently related to a philosophical interpretation of the universe" (422). In "Zhongguoren de zongjiao," this passage reads, 「下層階級的迷信既然是有系統觀的一部份，就不是迷信。」["Since the lower-class superstitions are a part of a systematic world view, they do not qualify as superstitions" (180; Pollard 284)]. In her English essay, Chang first repudiates the nature of superstitions and then explains them in terms of intellectual and philosophical interpretations of the universe. In her Chinese self-translation, she provides first the reason and then her argument, but reduces the rationale of intellectual and philosophical interpretation to merely 「有系統觀的一部份」["a part of a systematic view" (180; Pollard 284)]. The elegant and grand tone in the English essay becomes a humble and constrained tone in her Chinese self-translation, in keeping with the preferences of each version's respective target readership.

When discussing whether Chinese folk belief systems can be classified as a religion, Chang suggests examining the sincerity of its followers. She explores the discrepancy between faith and confession among intellectuals and lower-class people in traditional Chinese society in "Demons and Fairies": "The only difference in its effect upon the learned and the vulgar is that the former believe more than they profess and the latter profess more than they believe" (421). The Chinese version in "Zhongguoren de zongjiao" reads 「讀書人和愚民唯一的不同之點是：讀書人有點相信而不大肯承認；愚民承認而不大肯相信。」 ["The only difference is that educated people are tempted to believe in it but won't confess it, while ignorant people confess it but don't much believe in it" (180; Pollard 284)]. Chang points out the paradoxical attitudes and behaviours of more and less educated people, and shows the diversity of religious values among Chinese people of different social backgrounds. In her English version, she uses the phrase "the vulgar" to refer to less educated and lower-class people, with the connotations of coarseness and lack of sophistication betraying her dismissive perspective of them. In her Chinese self-translation, she uses 「愚民」 [ignorant people], two Chinese compound words usually used to refer to the uneducated masses, which alleviates the degree of impropriety implied in their qualities. Pollard, however, chooses the less offensive "ignorant."

To differentiate between the religious beliefs of more educated people and those of less educated people, Chang discusses each social group's interpretation of ghosts. According to Chang, intellectuals see ghosts from a rather scientific point of view as the last condensed gaseous breath expelled from a dead person's body, appearing as grey or black silhouettes. Such vaporous haze is easily dispersed in the air, giving rise to the Chinese saying that new ghosts are bigger than the old ones. As pointed out in "Demons and Fairies," everyday people have a different view of ghosts: "However, popular imagination tends to make the ghost a realistic parody of the deceased" (422). In "Zhongguoren de zongjiao" this passage reads: 「但是群眾的理想總偏於照相式，因此一般的鬼現形起來總與死者一模一樣。」 ["But in the imagination of the masses ghosts incline to the photographic model, so when a ghost reveals itself it is always the dead spit of the dead person" (181; Pollard 285)]. In her English essay, Chang uses the word "imagination" to signify everyday people's fantasies about ghosts, while in her Chinese self-translation, she uses 「理想」 [ideal] to express their desire, or fear, to see images of the dead person again, albeit in a different form. Similarly, the English phrase "a realistic parody," a literary technique to denote the reproduction of the deceased, is translated into Chinese as 「照相式」 [photographic], a metaphor that allows the reader to visualize the image of the action of reproduction. In his translation, Pollard repeats the word "dead" twice in the short phrase "the dead spirit of the dead person," which emphasizes the ghost being the same entity as the deceased.

Despite some differences in religious beliefs and behaviours between more and less educated Chinese people, Chang concludes in "Demons and Fairies" that both groups highly regard ancestral worship: "The only idea which seems to be shared by the educated and uneducated alike is ancestor worship, and on the part of the intelligentsia this is pure sentimentality untinged by any religious significance, in other words, the mere extension of filial duties beyond the grave" (421 [1943]). The passage is translated in "Zhongguoren de zongjiao" as:

上等人與下等人所共有的觀念似乎只有一個祖先崇拜，而這對於知識階級不過是純粹的感情作用，對亡人盡孝而已，沒有任何宗教上的意義。

180

Ancestor worship appears to be the only concept that upper and lower class people have in common, albeit that to intellectuals it serves a purely emotional function, showing reverence for the dead, without any religious significance.

POLLARD 284

Chang identifies ancestral worship as the common cultural practice of the Chinese above and beyond educational backgrounds and social classes, and filial piety as the heart of this ritual shared among Chinese communities. In her self-translation, Chang uses the phrase 「上等人與下等人」 [upper- and lower-class people] for "the educated and uneducated," assuming that more educated people belong to the upper class and less educated people to the lower class. However, this assumption runs the risk of overgeneralization, as there is no absolute correlation between a person's class and his/her level of education. In his translation, Pollard uses the English phrase "showing reverence for the dead" to translate the Chinese phrase 「對亡人盡孝」 (paying filial duty to the dead [ancestor]), which conveys the idea of respect but disregards filial piety, the most important aspect of Confucian ethics.

The significance of Confucian ethical values, including filial piety, has been challenged in modern China. In "Zhongguoren de zongjiao," Chang discusses different perspectives towards human relationships, especially kinship and friendship, in ancient and modern China. She contends that in ancient China, human relationships were at the root of many recognized virtues, as Confucian rules aim to provide enough food and safety for people to ensure harmonious relationships can persist. Such ideals, however, have been highly contested in modern China:

近代的中國人突然悟到家庭是封建餘孽，父親是專制魔王，母親是好意的傻子，時髦的妻是玩物，鄉氣的妻是祭桌上的肉。

193

> In recent history the Chinese suddenly came to see that the family was the dregs of feudalism, fathers were diabolical tyrants, mothers were good-natured fools, fashionable wives were playthings, rustic wives were live offerings on a sacrificial altar.
>
> POLLARD 291

Chang's depictions of negative familial relationships in modern China are partially true, especially keeping in mind that many May Fourth intellectuals, such as Chen Duxiu 陳獨秀 (1879–1942), Yi Baisha 易白沙 (1886–1921), Lu Xun 魯迅 (1881–1936), Wu Yu 吳虞 (1872–1949), and Ba Jin 巴金 (1904–2005), regarded Confucianism as an obstacle to the modernization of China. For instance, Lu Xun's "Kuangren riji" 〈狂人日記〉 ("Diary of a Madman," 1918), one of the most influential literary works written in vernacular Chinese and published on the eve of the May Fourth Movement, perceives "cannibalism" in his family, village, and in the Confucian classics. Similarly, Ba Jin's semi-autobiographical *Jiliu sanbu qu* 《激流三部曲》 (*Trilogy of Turbulent Stream*), consisting of *Jia* 《家》 (*The Family*, 1933), *Chun* 《春》 (*Spring*, 1938), and Qiu 《秋》 (*Autumn*, 1940), chronicles intergenerational conflicts between traditional Confucian patriarchy and new youth's progressive thinking in an upper-class family in the city of Chengdu between 1919 and 1924. These May Fourth writers depict dysfunctional family relationships as calls for change aligned with their patriotic agenda; however, the families they describe are extreme cases that do not represent the majority of early-twentieth-century Chinese families. Chang does not mention the details in her English texts in order to avoid stereotypes and misunderstandings, but in her Chinese texts she is self-critical of and ironic about her countryfolk.

According to Chang's interpretation, the Chinese have not shown serious interest in either the source or the end of life, but they are passionate about their own existence. Though some people may be curious about the spiritual world, they will refrain from delving into those thoughts for fear of supernatural beings intruding into their lives and causing damage. In the conclusion of "Demons and Fairies," she, nevertheless, strongly confirms that "the Chinese religion is no less a religion because it has effect only within the scope outside which we find nothing but a vague comprehensive sadness" (429). Her reckoning of the Chinese religion tends to focus on what people can comprehend within their limited capacity of living and outside which uncertainty and ubiquitous sorrow is looming. At the end of her essays, she concludes, "All is vanity or, as the singsong girl phrased it in the Peking Opera "The Courtyard of the Black Dragon": I wash my hands and clean my nails, / To sew shoes to be trodden in the mud" (429) [「什麼都是空的，像閻惜姣所說：『洗手淨指甲，做鞋泥裏踏。』」 ("Demons" 429; "Zhongguo" 197)]. Though Chang published the English essay first, her English quotation is in fact a translation of the Peking Opera song from Chinese into English. This quotation conveys a religious sense of vanity, as people seek achievements in their lives that only lead to destruction in the end.

From her superficial observation that there is no religion in Chinese culture to her confirmation of the solid status of Chinese religion, Chang demystifies several stereotypes and biases of Chinese culture and, most importantly, offers her thoughtful interpretations of Chinese philosophical and supernatural thoughts and cultural practices throughout "Demons and Fairies" and "Zhongguoren de zongjiao." She takes a comparative perspective on the characteristics of Chinese religion that have been integrated with Confucianism, Buddhism, Taoism, and folklore and fairy tales, all of which are connected to the worldly concerns of everyday Chinese people's lives. The differences in religious belief among people with varying levels of education showcase the diversity of religious thoughts among the Chinese, and their common practice of ancestral worship points to filial piety as their core ethical value. The transformation of the Chinese people's attitudes toward human relationships in modern China reflects the fluidity of their religious culture over time and place. Chang's additions, omissions, word choices, syntax, and tones demonstrate her mastery of both Chinese and English and her consideration of the cultural and sociohistorical contexts of her readers in both languages.

CHAPTER 10

Distanciation: "Still Alive" and "Yangren kan jingxi ji qita" 〈洋人看京戲及其他〉 ("Westerners Watching Peking Opera and Other Issues")

Authors as self-translators complicate the notion of distanciation, particularly when authors produce self-translations in different times and places, and at different stages in their lives, from those in which the earlier work was created. The distanciation between the source text and the translation can be explained in terms of the semantic autonomy of a text that creates multiple meanings in its afterlife reception. The sociohistorical context of the text's production is different from that of its reception, as Paul Ricœur points out: "What we call the semantic autonomy of the text means that the text unfolds a history distinct from that of its author. The ambiguity of the notion of signification reflects this situation. To signify can mean what the text signifies or what the author meant to signify" (*Hermeneutics* 12–13; original emphasis). The distanciation of time and space between the text's production and reception opens up infinite possibilities for interpretation. In addition, the ambiguity of the text's implications for readers largely results from the inability of readers to access the author's intention directly. However, as the Introduction of this book notes, authorial intention still occupies a place in the composite meaning of the text, though it is not the absolute arbiter of meaning. The author's biographical, social, and historical contexts, and the socioeconomic and cultural milieux in which the text was produced, are also important factors in the reader's understanding of the text. Authors as self-translators, nonetheless, have the privilege of access to their own authorial intention and enjoy the freedom of copyright to rewrite their source texts.

With their target readers in mind, authors as self-translators very often serve as cultural translators who incorporate their respective cultural values in the process of their self-translation. The distanciation between the author, the text, and the reader is noticeably created when a text is translated from one language to another. Self-translators will inevitably produce an alienation effect because of the different cultural connotations between the source language and the target language, as Elin-Maria Evangelista argues:

> The distance – sometimes geographical – that a second language and subsequent translation creates, can also give life to new narratives.

© JESSICA TSUI-YAN LI, 2025 | DOI:10.1163/9789004730052_012

DISTANCIATION 173

> Writing from this distance, a writer might find that not only do perspectives and characters shift but also the ability to create narratives which might not otherwise have found an expression.
>
> EVANGELISTA 184

The linguistic and cultural distance generated by self-translation will produce new concepts and expressions, while the elaboration of social meanings in the source text underscores its traditional peculiarities. Furthermore, a language in the source text might have heterogeneous qualities that demonstrate both the intimate linguistic characteristics of the author/self-translator and the standard varieties of a language. Such linguistic hybridity leads to creative styles as well as ambivalent signification, thus generating multiple interpretations for readers in various times, places, and cultures. In the process of self-translation, the self-translator might have adopted a self-imposed alienated position, embracing foreign cultural values, and/or a cultural translator's standpoint with insightful knowledge that allows them to examine their traditional ethos and philosophy, which produces in-betweenness in the spheres of languages, literary styles, and cultural values.

This chapter examines Eileen Chang's English essay "Still Alive," initially printed in the Anglophone magazine *The xxth Century*, published in Shanghai in June 1943, and her Chinese translation "Yangren kan jingxi ji qita" 〈洋人看京戲及其他〉 ("Westerners Watching Peking Opera and Other Issues") (hereafter cited as "Yangren," first published in the Chinese magazine *Gujin* 《古今》 (*From Ancient to Present*) in Shanghai in November 1943, with reference to Andrew Jones' translation of "Yangren kan jingxi ji qita" from Chinese into English as "Peking Opera Through Foreign Eyes" (2005). In the English and Chinese versions of her essay, Chang adopts what she perceives as the respective perspectives of Westerners and amateurs to investigate why Peking Operas, with their long Chinese cultural history, were still popular in modern China in the early 1940s. "Still Alive" is Chang's work, and also can be considered an English translation of this Chinese cultural theatre form and its practices, while its Chinese translation is her reinterpretation and rewriting in her mother tongue of her understanding of Peking Opera; both are written from a critical distance. In these essays, Chang interprets the recollection of Chinese history, the reconstruction of Chinese people's memory of the past in the present, and the recreation of new memories for the future through distanciation in terms of languages, cultural perspectives, time, and space. This chapter discusses Chang's analysis of Peking Operas with regard to the genre's use of quotation conventions, blending of classical and colloquial speeches, her use of communal sentiments in the process of self-translation, and how all of these demonstrate the collective memory and creativity of artists and audiences.

The Chinese cultural tradition of quoting in and across various genres such as poetry, prose, plays, operas, and novels replicates common themes and sensibilities presented in earlier literary and cultural sources, but from a critical distance, by transforming and transgressing the meanings of the earlier works in the newer ones. This practice can be illuminated by the theory of adaptation. Linda Hutcheon argues that, unlike translations,

> adaptations are to a different medium, they are re-mediations, that is, specifically translations in the form of intersemiotic transpositions from one sign system (for example, words) to another (for example, images). This is translation but in a very specific sense: as transmutation or transcoding, that is, as necessarily a recoding into a new set of conventions as well as signs.
>
> *A THEORY OF ADAPTATION* 16

With Hutcheon's adaptation theory in mind, I maintain that the connotation of the quotation has been changed in a new literary and cultural work in different socio-historical contexts.

To illustrate the significance of quotations in Chinese culture, Eileen Chang uses the most memorable line in *Chiuhaitang* 《秋海棠》 (*Autumn Quince*), a popular play in Shanghai in the early 1940s, which is a quotation from a Peking Opera that itself quotes from a Chinese classical poem, as an example: 「酒逢知己千杯少，話不投機半句多。」 [Wine partaken with a true friend – a thousand cups are not enough; Conversation, when disagreeable – half a sentence is too much ("Still Alive" 432)]. The quotation underscores the importance and relevance of *Chiuhaitang* by connecting it to Peking Opera and classical poetry and by instilling a sense of nostalgia. It therefore shortens the distance between the modern play and Peking Opera by capturing the heart of the character Autumn Quince with revived sentiments, as well as between the actors and the audience by moving the audience to tears based on its connection to their respective circumstances.

The custom of quotation brings together Chinese sentiments, philosophy, and history in the past, present, and future, thus providing coherent narratives in Chinese people's collective memories. Chang contends that quotations function as reconstructions of the past: "Picturesque phrases, words of wisdom, jokes two thousand years old, freely circulate in everyday speech. These are the tissues of a living past" ("Still Alive" 433). She translates this passage into Chinese as 「美麗的，驚警的斷句，兩千年前的老笑話，混在日常談

吐裏自由使用著。這些看不見的纖維，組成了我們活生生的過去。」
[Lovely bons mots, words of wisdom and cautionary phrases, two-thousand-year-old jokes – all circulate freely in everyday speech. These invisible tissues constitute a living past ("Yangren" 14; Jones 115)]. In "Yangren kan jingxi ji qita," Chang inserts the adjective「看不見」 [invisible] to modify "tissues," thus adding a more abstract and intricate layer to the custom of quotation. Chinese people's knowledge of the past shapes how they refashion those materials into quotations recalling and resembling past events and feelings. Moreover, the past episodes, rituals, and emotions embodied in quotations are always renewed in the present through their constant usage, and this renewal of the past in the present creates fresh memories for the future.

Peking Opera musically accommodates both classical Chinese language and vernacular colloquial speech. Classical or literary Chinese, or *wenyan* 文言, which encompasses philosophy, ideas, and feelings associated with Chinese history, narratives, poetry, drama, and prose over thousands of years in a very concise format, is revived through recontextualization. Chang values the quoting style, noting that "With the aid of these phrases the classical language is able to convey the most complex feelings in an amazingly short sentence" ("Still Alive" 435). The classical Chinese language has endured, even since the beginning of the Vernacular Language Movement in the 1890s, because it, paradoxically, both preserves the past and generates a critical distance. Meanwhile, colloquial speech became popular in modern Chinese literature and culture. The English phrase *vernacular language* is equivalent to *baihua* 白話, the standard written language based on northern regional varieties of the Chinese language, now usually called Mandarin or Mandarin Chinese in English, *putonghua* 普通話 in mainland China, *guoyu* 國語 in Taiwan, and *huayu* 華語 in Singapore. Peking Opera in the early 1940s used a hybrid modern Chinese language that fuses classical Chinese and colloquial speech: "Nowhere else are the two co-existing languages so harmoniously blended as in Peking Opera" ("Still Alive" 435). The music of Peking Opera binds two very different styles of speech together and promotes a new development of linguistic and cultural hybridity.

The mixture of classical and colloquial Chinese speech in Peking Opera manifests the notion of in-betweenness in the linguistic, cultural, and historical domains. Linguistically speaking, the dialogue in Peking Opera embraces elements typical for oral expressions of colloquialism juxtaposed with the habitual usage of archaisms, reflecting the in-betweenness of Chinese speech in the early twentieth century. Moreover, classical Chinese and colloquial speech carry specific cultural connotations that embody the speakers' in-betweenness in their particular sociohistorical positions. Linguistic hybridity in Peking Opera is, therefore, not only a medium of oral expression, but also an object of representation, showcasing the singers' heterogeneously cultural qualities. The creative blending of classical and colloquial Chinese in Peking Opera, on the one hand, underscores the characteristics of modern China in the transitional period of modernization. On the other hand, the linguistic and cultural hybridity presented in Peking Opera in turn performatively contributes to shape the properties of this art form as well as the historical epoch in which it is performed, thus indicating a state of in-betweenness in terms of languages, culture, and discourses in early 1940s China.

Though Chang wrote "Still Alive" in English first and then translated it into Chinese, her English essay is in fact an English translation of Peking Opera, a distinctively culturally Chinese genre. With her target Anglophone readers in mind, she provides an introductory background of the stories told in these works. In "Still Alive," she estimates that one-third of the content of Peking Operas are war plays adapted from *Sanguo yanyi* 《三國演義》 (*The Tales of the Three Kingdoms*, c. 1522) and *Shuihu zhuan* 《水滸傳》 (*Water Margins*, c. 1524). According to Chang, "The Chinese are not a warlike race, but the life of a military man, full of the swiftest changes, excitement and ups and downs, provides much material for analogy to the official or business career" ("Still Alive" 437). Here, Chang positions herself as a Chinese cultural translator who uses her inside knowledge to explain the reasons for the popularity of war-related themes in Peking Opera. In "Yangren kan jingxi ji qita," however, she removes this section and adds some new insightful observation in her mother tongue: 「最流行的幾十齣京戲，每一齣都供給了我們一個沒有時間性質的，標準的形勢。」 [Each of the scores of popular plays that make up the bulk of the operatic repertoire provides us with standardized and timeless narrative molds (15; Jones 116)]. Chang's Chinese translation/rewriting re-evaluates the universal features of the most well-received Peking Operas for Chinese readers who are already familiar with the art form. From a critical distance, she examines the major themes of Peking Opera in English and Chinese, one in translation and one in reinterpretation.

To illuminate several characteristic motifs of Peking Opera, Chang discusses one of its most popular examples, *Hongzong liema* 《紅鬃烈馬》 (*Red-Maned Horse*), or *Lady Precious Stream* in English, which "portrays the exquisite self-ishness of men" ("Still Alive" 437); or, in Chinese, 「無微不至地描寫了男性的自私。」 [presents the selfishness of men in exquisite detail ("Yangren" 15; Jones 116)]. She further describes the protagonist's cruelty towards his wife: "It is characteristic of the male temperament that the hero pursues his career for eighteen years with never a thought of the wife back home" ("Still Alive" 437); or, in Chinese: 「薛平貴致力於他的事業十八年，泰然地將他的夫

人擱在寒窖裏像冰箱裏的一尾魚。」 [Xue Pinggui devotes himself to his career for eighteen years, cavalierly leaving his wife in cold storage, like a fish in an icebox ("Yangren" 15; Jones 116)]. "Yangren kan jingxi ji qita" spells out the name of the historical figure and visualizes the scenario with a vivid metaphor, while also criticizing Chinese patriarchal culture. While men occupy the public sphere and experience adventures, success, and glory, women stay in the domestic sphere and endure boredom and loneliness. Such male-dominated practice has been taken for granted in traditional Chinese literature and culture; therefore, in order to point out the unfair treatment of Xue's wife, Chang parallels the wife's undesirable situation to "a fish in an icebox" in her Chinese translation. She concludes, however, that the play does portray Xue as a decent hero who is beloved by the Chinese audience, illuminating the play's sympathetic attitude toward an otherwise unlikeable character.

In "Still Alive," Chang adopts the in-between position of a cultural translator to introduce the philosophy, social practices, and intimate feelings of the Chinese through the cultural form of Peking Opera. Klaus Mehnert claims that Chang "is a Chinese who, in contrast to most of her countrymen, does not simply take China for granted. It is her deep curiosity about her own people which enables her to interpret the Chinese to the foreigner" ("Still Alive" 432). Taking the perspectives of both Chinese and Westerners, Chang translates Chinese culture from her position of cultural translator, explaining the Chinese psychology of the crowd as "Like French monarchs of old, the Chinese are born in a crowd and die in a crowd" ("Still Alive" 433–434), translated into Chinese as 「中國人是在一大群人之間呱呱墜地的，也在一大群人之間死去——有如十七八世紀的法國君王。」 [Chinese people are born in a crowd and die in a crowd, not unlike the French monarchs of the seventeenth and eighteenth centuries ("Yangren" 18; Jones 120)]. She uses the phrase 「呱呱墜地」 "creakingly fell to the ground" in "Yangren" to translate the verb "born" in "Still Alive." Her account of how upper-class women are expected to open their bedroom doors for public inspection is a striking instance of the lack of privacy in Chinese life, a custom that is colourfully presented in Peking Opera. Chang's comparative perspectives, on the one hand, distance herself from Chinese conventional thoughts and feelings in order to explain Chinese culture through the characteristics of the Peking Opera from fresh points of view. On the other hand, she illuminates the nuances of Chinese ways of life by speaking from an insider's standpoint for her Anglophone readership.

Chang's Chinese translation of "Still Alive," likewise, adopts a distanced viewpoint, as signaled in its title, "Yangren kan jingxi ji qita" 〈洋人看京戲及其他〉 ("Westerners Watching Peking Operas and Other Issues"). The new title shifts the essay's focus from investigating the reasons for the continuing popularity of Peking Opera in China to interpreting Peking Opera from what she perceives as a Western perspective. Jones translates the title from Chinese into English as "Peking Opera Through Foreign Eyes," Though the word "foreign" may be a better usage of English, such a word choice, nevertheless, diminishes the orientalist undertones in Chang's source text for readers. Chang begins the essay with the statement 「用洋人看京戲的眼光來觀光一番罷。有了驚訝與眩異，才有明瞭，才有靠得住的愛。」 [To see China through the eyes with which foreigners watch Peking opera would be an exercise not entirely lacking in significance ("Yangren" 13; Jones 113)], suggesting that the fresh perspectives of Westerners who might have no or little knowledge of Chinese history and culture will provide a new understanding of the traditions of Peking Opera. Readers from other cultural backgrounds will not take Chinese cultural particulars for granted and, therefore, will comprehend the culture differently from those who are familiar with Chinese culture. The idea of viewing the familiar from the outside occurs in the classical Chinese poem "Ti Xilinbi" 《題西林壁》 ("Written on the Wall at West Forest Temple," 1084) written by Su Shi 蘇軾 (1037–1101) during the Song Dynasty (960–1279): 「不識廬山真面目，只緣身在此山中。」 [One could not know the true face of Mount Lu only because once is standing in this mountain]. Chang uses this idea of critical distancing to problematize the interpretation of Peking Opera and demand a critical reception that may lead to conflicting understandings of the subject.

In "Yangren kan jingxi ji qita," Chang admits to knowing relatively little about Peking Opera, and to appreciating it as an enthusiastic amateur:

> 因爲我對於京戲是個感到濃厚興趣的外行。對於人生，誰都是個一知半解的外行罷？我單揀了京戲來說，就爲了這適當的態度。」
>
> "YANGREN" 13

> Because I am an enthusiastic lover of Peking opera but also a layperson when it comes to its many intricacies. Who isn't a dilettante or a dabbler when it comes to life? I single out Peking Opera here because it lends itself so well to such an approach.
>
> JONES 113

By interpreting Peking Opera from her specific position, Chang generates new meanings that might diverge from the intentions of the playwrights and actors who produce the stage performance in different contexts from hers as an observer. The distanciation of her innovative perspectives on Peking Opera from conventional interpretation speaks to the complexity of hermeneutics in the task of reading, as she observes in her comment on the significance of unorthodox approaches: 「外行的意見是可貴的。門外漢的議論比較新鮮戇拙，不無可取之點。」 [the thoughts of laypeople can be unusually fresh and candid and are valuable for exactly that reason ("Yangren" 13; Jones 114)]. Amateurs' understanding of Peking Opera contributes to the rich meaning of this art form, thanks to the divergence of insight from its professional conception. New interpretations of Peking Opera in turn vitalize and transform its theatrical characteristics in the ongoing adaptation process, thus leading to a convergence of meaning in terms of production and reception.

In "Still Alive," Chang points out the strong presence of the past in the present of Chinese people's daily lives: "Perhaps nowhere else in the world does the past play so active a role in common everyday life – the past in the sense of elucidated experience, communal memories analyzed by the historical viewpoint" (433); in Chinese, 「只有在中國，歷史仍於日常生活中維持活躍的演出。（歷史在這裏是籠統地代表著公眾的回憶。）」 [Only in China does history perform itself so persistently in everyday life. (History here represents the sum of our collective memory) ("Yangren" 15; Jones 115)]. Though she emphasizes the role of historical analysis of the past, in "Yangren kan jingxi ji qita" she ensures the position of history as a representation of communal memories. She highlights the significance of the past in Chinese culture, which is reconstructed in the present through rhetorical language, narratives, and performances, in order to meet the needs and desires of Chinese people based on their current interests and concerns. Chinese people who share similar social experiences recollect and reiterate their knowledge of past events, social practices, and customs in their collective memories, which continuously influence their lives in the present. Collective memories, as suggested by Maurice Halbwachs, capture the memories of a group of people who share social experiences, which in turn shape individual memories (42). Our understanding of the past of our family, community, and culture, in this sense, is recreated in our collective memories that have structured our perspectives in seeing ourselves and our lives. Our collective memories are, therefore, important not only to our thinking, feeling, and behaviour in the present, but also to what we will become in the future.

The popularity of Peking Opera can be attributed to its preservation and representation of the collective memories of Chinese people: "If we see the quotations in this light, the relation of Peking Opera to the world of today is also in the nature of a quotation" ("Still Alive" 433). Chang translates this sentence into Chinese as 「假使我們從這個觀點去檢討我們的口頭禪，京戲和今日社會的關係也就帶著口頭禪的性質。」 [If we see our use of quotations in this light, the relation of Peking opera to the society of today also takes on an epigrammatic quality ("Yangren" 15; Jones 115)]. Chang uses the formal verb 「檢討」 [review] to translate the English word "see," thus providing her self-translation with a more determined tone than its source text. The quotations that Chinese people use in their daily lives carry the stories of historical events and their thoughts and sentiments dating back thousands of years, in much the same way that Peking Opera embodies the memories of past social experiences, cultural practices, social customs, and conventional sayings of Chinese people from time immemorial. All these collective memories are refashioned in current plays in the present, thus influencing the audience's memories of the past, shaping their present behaviours, and creating new memories for the future. The narratives and stage performances of Peking Opera have, therefore, transmitted and structured how Chinese people interpret their lives through a sociocultural lens. To a certain extent, Peking Opera has contributed to the construction of Chinese social and individual identities through the tales, chronicles, linguistic and facial expressions, costumes, music, lighting, and, most of all, the intimate thoughts and feelings that the performers convey on stage.

Peking Opera presents both real and imagined memories, as Chang notes in "Still Alive": "The world of Peking Opera bears a very thin resemblance to the Chinese world in any given stage of our evolution, and yet the public has at the back of its mind the impression that the Peking Opera world, with its tidy ethics, its beauty and finish, is a faithful representation of the old order" (433). She reiterates and elaborates on this idea in Chinese:

> 京戲裏的世界既不是目前的中國，也不是古中國在它的過程中的任何一階段。它的美，它的陝小整潔道德系統，都是離現實很遠的。
>
> "YANGREN" 18

> The world within Peking opera is not contemporary China, and neither does it bear much resemblance to ancient China in any stage of its development. Its beauty and its narrowly tidy ethical system are worlds away from reality.
>
> JONES 119

Though in the Chinese text, Chang does not regard the narratives of Peking Opera as true reflections of China and its history, in the English text she does acknowledge the audience's belief in the performance as representation even if it is not historically accurate. Peking Opera reconstructs collective memories

DISTANCIATION

by reinterpreting historical episodes while also creating new stories that suit the tastes of the audience in the present. The audience then uses their knowledge to reassemble what they perceive the past should look like. As Barbie Zelizer argues, "collective memory presumes activities of sharing, discussion, negotiation, and often contestation" (214). The collective memory presented in Peking Opera is subject to change over distances in time and place. The constant reinterpretation of collective memories in Peking Opera points to the characteristics of Chinese people's identities that are fluid rather than static.

The continuous transformation of Peking Opera showcases the collective creative effort of both the artists and the audience, as demonstrated by a case study Chang discusses in her English text: "A revolutionary actor, Wang Kwei-fung, experimentally combined the Anhwei Opera with the drama brought by the Manchus. The result was a great success, especially among royalty and officials, so that the center of theatrical activity shifted to the capital" ("Still Alive" 435). This example points out the combination of various ethnic and cultural elements in Peking Opera, and highlights its heterogeneous and dynamic qualities, themselves influenced by the audience members' informal conversations, current fashions, cultural practices, and worldviews. Chang further argues in "Still Alive" that "the sophisticated upper classes are receptive to such as product is a tremendous tribute, not so much to Peking Opera, as to its new audience" (435). On the one hand, performers experiment with incorporating diverse cultural and dramatic properties into the making of Peking Opera that influence, and are influenced by, the collective memories and reconstructed individual memories of the audience. On the other hand, audience reception contributes to revitalize this art form and enhance its performative aspects. This discussion, however, is removed in "Yangren" for the sake of reducing the account of the historical background of Peking Opera.

It is this performative aspect of Peking Opera that contributes to its regenerative nature, as Chang notes in "Still Alive": "Chinese men of taste are unanimous in pronouncing Peking Opera vulgar, lowbrow, but its childlike vigor appears to the primitive in us which the Chinese civilization has been too sloppy to root out. Somewhere about there lies our secret of eternal youth" (435). This passage appears in the Chinese text as

新興的京戲裏有一種孩子氣的力量，合了我們內在的需要。中國人的原始性沒有被根除，想必我們的文化過於隨隨便便之故。就在這一點上，我們不難找到中國人的永久的青春的秘密。」

"YANGREN" 20

182   CHAPTER 10

> the newly emergent Peking opera has a childish vigor that ministers to
> our inner needs. The primitive in us has yet to be rooted out, perhaps
> because we are too tolerant as a civilization. And herein may lie the
> secret of our eternal youth.
>
> JONES 122–123

In "Still Alive," Chang notes that Chinese elites consider Peking Opera "vulgar" and "lowbrow," but this cynical view is omitted from "Yangren kan jingxi ji qita" addressed to her fellow Chinese readers. Nevertheless, she contends that Peking Opera contains the childlike spirits of primitive curiosity, passion, and energy, which rejuvenates both the genre itself and its audience. Lin Yutang had earlier pointed out Chinese culture's favourable attitude toward primitivism in Chinese culture: "It would seem, therefore, that the Chinese, as a people, avoided the dangers of civic deterioration by a natural distrust of civilization and by keeping close to primitive habits of life" (*My Country and My People* 37). Both Chang and Lin contend that Chinese people adhere to vigorous primitive traits and lifestyles rather than fall into civil degeneration, so as to constantly revitalize their culture to achieve "eternal youth."

One typical example of the creativity of both artists and audience can be found in the Peking Opera *The Cotton Weaver*. Chang remarks about the interaction between performers and audience in "Still Alive":

> Dressed in the latest style instead of a Peking Opera costume, the Cotton
> Weaver sings while she works, mimicking the mannerisms of the Four
> Great Female Impersonators and other celebrities, and backchats with
> the audience, which has a voice in the choice of their subjects. An atmo-
> sphere of cheery informality prevails, a tremendous relief from the rigid
> conventions of Peking Opera.
>
> 438

The Chinese translation of this passage reads, 「《新紡綿花》之叫座固然是爲了時裝登台，同時也因爲主角任意唱兩支南腔北調的時候，觀眾偶然也可以插嘴進來點戲，台上台下打成一片，愉快的，非正式的空氣近於學校的遊藝餘興。」("Yangren" 16), which Jones retranslates into English as:

> The reasons *Xin Fangmianhua* sells so many tickets are that the actors
> are dressed in the latest styles instead of traditional Peking opera cos-
> tumes and that when the cotton-weaving girl breaks into folk songs and

DISTANCIATION 183

other ditties, the audience can join in the play and sing along, breaking down the barrier between on- and offstage and fostering an atmosphere of lively informality not unlike a performance in a school auditorium.

JONES 117–118

The performers of *The Cotton Weaver* present a modernized style of spontaneous singing and dancing that breaks down the rigid conventions of the play. What makes it extremely appealing is the participation of the audience, who have the opportunity to interact with the performers through conversation and suggestion of songs. The audience, therefore, is permitted a voice in the performance, which democratizes the longstanding tradition of authoritative presentation by challenging the well-established strict conventions of Peking Opera. In "Yangren," Chang added the phrase「學校的遊藝餘興」 [school funfair entertainment] as a metaphor that describes the cheerfully interactive atmosphere of Peking Opera.

By analyzing Peking Operas from what she perceives as the perspectives of Westerners and amateurs, Chang underscores the aesthetic features of this time-honoured art form with her distanciation of time, place, language, and culture. Given her lively descriptions and critical point of view, she highlights Peking Operas' conventions of quotation, accommodation of both classical and colloquial speech, and communal sentiments in order to recollect the past, reconstruct the present, and recreate memory for the future. The innovative adaptations of various cultural sources in Peking Operas, as well as the input of the audience during the performance, demonstrate the creativity of both performers and participants, the driving force that keeps this genre alive.

CHAPTER 11

Transformation: "Chinese Life and Fashions" and "Gengyiji" 〈更衣記〉 ("A Chronicle of Changing Clothes")

Transformation is inevitable in the process of cultural translation, as words and expressions, and their associated cultural connotations, are translated from the source language to the target language. New meanings are added, and some meanings are lost. Cultural values are challenged in the translation when different concepts and hierarchies of sociocultural relations, historical contexts, and political powers encounter one another. Walter Benjamin argues in "The Task of the Translator" that the source text achieves its "after-life" in the translation, which brings forth vitality by appropriating the source materials to facilitate understanding for the target audience. In the case of self-translation, self-translators, who enjoy more authorial freedom in translating their own works than outside translators, will have the space and ability to recreate the source text in the target language. As Susan Bassnett points out, "But if we think in terms of the text being the unit of significance, then we are better placed to accept the idea of translation as rewriting, albeit recognizable as rewriting because of the more across languages" ("The Self-translator as a Writer" 24). Self-translators show their power of creativity and the infinite possibility of remaking by making changes in their self-translation.

As a cultural translator and bilingual writer, Eileen Chang recounts the transformation of the sartorial culture of modern China in her literature, self-translations, and artworks. Modern Chinese women's fashion underwent a sea change in the early twentieth century with the onset of modernization and the shifts in political power. Western ideas imported to China slowly took root alongside traditional Chinese practices, thus leading to modifications of Chinese dress and blending of both Chinese and Western fashion trends during this era. Growing up in a declining aristocratic family in the transitional period of modern China, Chang developed an acute and remarkable observation and knowledge of modern Chinese women's fashion. This chapter explores Chang's depictions of the ongoing cultural negotiation in modern Chinese women's fashion of the early twentieth century, which embraced traditional and modern Chinese cultural elements as well as Western clothing styles, in her essays, fiction, and drawings. With her personal interest in clothes, Chang valorizes female agency through her famously eccentric style of dress that served as a

© JESSICA TSUI-YAN LI, 2025 | DOI:10.1163/9789004730052_013

TRANSFORMATION 185

response to, and a resistance against, the mainstream fashion trends in Shanghai at the time.

This chapter examines the literary imagery of Chinese women's fashion in Chang's works, along with Chinese vestiary history in modern China. Her English essay "Chinese Life and Fashions," (hereafter cited as "Fashions"), which was first published in the Anglophone journal *The xxth Century* in Shanghai in January 1943, traces Chinese design history from the Qing Dynasty (1644–1912) to the 1940s, and features 12 sketches of women's clothes, hairstyles, hats, and shoes. The essay explores how changing styles of fashion accompanied the transformation of China from imperial rule to modernization/Westernization in various aspects, such as social lifestyles, gender relations and politics, at the turn of the century. Chang translated her essay into Chinese as "Gengyiji" 〈更衣記〉, and this translation was first published in the Chinese journal *Gujin* 《古今》 in December 1943. In this essay, Chang showed a more ironic tone and culturally subtle style than in its English version. In 2003, Andrew F. Jones translated "Genyiji" into English as "A Chronicle of Changing Clothes." His translation reflects the aesthetic freedom of Eileen Chang as author and self-translator and her concerns for her readers' knowledge of and familiarity with Chinese fashion history. Chang also addresses the changes in fashion in the transitional period of the 1940s, specifically the incorporation of modern and traditional styles and of Chinese and Western styles, in her book *Duizhaoji: kan lao zhaoxiangbu* 《對照記：看老照相簿》 (*Mutual Reflections: Looking at Old Photo Albums*, 1994), which reproduces photographs of her family and herself, accompanied by autobiographical anecdotes. Furthermore, in her works of fiction such as "Qingcheng zhi lian" 〈傾城之戀〉 ("Love in a Fallen City," 1943), "Jinsuoji"〈金鎖記〉 ("The Golden Cangue," 1943), and "Stale Mates – A Short Story Set in the Time When Love Came to China" (1956), Chang depicts the colours, textures, and styles of women's fashion as manifestations of the female characters' psychological sophistication and sociohistorical circumstances. The analysis of the imagery of fashion in Chang's works provides readers with a fascinating picture of the culturally hybridized Chinese society in the early twentieth century.

In the Prelude to "Chinese Life and Fashions," Klaus Mehnert, editor of *The xxth Century,* points out:

> This article needs no recommendations to the ladies among our readers; for them, the word 'fashion' speaks for itself. But perhaps we should mention for the benefit of our male readers that the following pages contain more than just an essay on fashions. Indeed, they offer an amusing psychoanalysis of modern China.

54

Mehnert interprets this essay as not simply a discussion of modern Chinese fashion, but also a remarkable examination of people's ways of thinking and lifestyles, gender politics, and sociohistorical transformations. At the turn of the twentieth century, China experienced a paradigm shift in political power, from the Qing Imperial Court (1644–1911) to the establishment of the Republic of China (1912), and then to the Warlord Era (1916–1928), the New Culture Movement and the May Fourth Movement from the mid-1910s to the 1920s, the First Chinese Civil War (1927–1937), and the Japanese invasion (1937–1945). During these periods, modern Chinese women's fashions changed substantially as responses to new ideas and sociopolitical circumstances, such as the tightening of clothes for quick movements during political upheavals, the appearance of the *qipao* as an expression of women's rights, and the lowering of collars and the introduction of bras and white silk stockings from Western fashion. Nicole Huang comments in *Women, War, Domesticity* that Chang's

> impressionistic view of modern history highlights colors, lines, shapes, textures, and moods, which are all crystallized in the changing faces of women clothes. Chang's representation of modern history through the transformation of women's clothes has the effect of a museum of human fantasies, or a gallery of artifacts constantly in motion.
>
> 154

Chang presents a cultural history of Chinese modernity in her stories featuring changes in Chinese fashion, in both English and Chinese, from her positions as a transcultural and bilingual author and self-translator.

Speaking from the position of a Chinese cultural translator, Chang introduces Anglophone readers to the world of Chinese fashion, opening "Chinese Life and Fashion" with the welcoming remark, "Come and see the Chinese family on the day when the clothes handed down for generations are given their annual sunning!" (54); an exotic, to English readers, yet understandable custom. In "Gengyiji," Chang adopts a more nostalgic tone: 「如果當初世代相傳的衣服沒有大批賣給收舊貨的，一年一度六月裏晒衣裳，該是一件輝煌熱鬧的事罷。」(21) ["If all the clothing handed down for generations had never been sold to dealers in secondhand goods, their annual sunning in June would be a brilliant and lively affair" (Jones 428)]. She acknowledges the long history of Chinese civilization by advising her Chinese readers to keep their heritage clothes as reminders of happy moments in the past. Andrew F. Jones explains that his translation "attempts to mediate Chang's successive mediation between different languages, audiences, genders, and positions" (428) and thus to underscore the nuances and differences between the English and Chinese versions of her essay, particularly when addressing

Chinese readers from the perspective of a young Chinese intellectual woman of the 1940s.

Comparing the sociohistorical differences between China and the West, Chang comments:

> We find it hard to realize that less than fifty years ago it seemed a world without end. Imagine the reign of Queen Victoria prolonged to the length of three centuries! Such was the stability, the uniformity, the extreme conventionality of China under the Manchus that generation after generation of women clung to the same dress style.
>
> "Fashions" 54

She uses the reign of Queen Victoria, so familiar to Anglophone readers, as a point of comparison to the lengthy Manchu dynasty; however, the Chinese translation omits this historical reference in favour of a focus on the conventional style of women's dress in the Manchu era:「我們不大能夠想像過去的世界，這麼迂緩、安靜，齊整——在滿清三百年的統治下，女人竟沒有什麼時裝可言！」[We cannot really imagine the world of the past – so dilatory, so quiet, and so orderly that over the course of three hundred years of Manchu rule, women lacked anything that might be referred to as fashion ("Gengyiji" 21; Jones 429)]. In her Chinese essay, Chang characterizes the relatively static fashion of the Manchu period as a reflection of the restrictive conformity imposed on women and of the involution, tranquility, and impeccability associated with that time.

Chang's essay and its accompanying drawings give readers a taste of the classical style of Qing-era women's fashion, with the English version providing a comparison to equivalent Western designs:

> Almost throughout the Chin Dynasty (1644–1911), the classical ensemble was a jacket-and-trousers combination. In size and length the jacket corresponded to the modern swagger coat. The collar was very low; huge sleeves and trousers gave a feeling of statuesque repose. The sleeves measured over two feet in width but were later somewhat modified.
>
> "Fashions" 54

In the Chinese version, by contrast, she focuses on the compact posture of Qing-era women, and the obscuring of the female body under layers of clothing:「從十七世紀中葉直到十九世紀末，流行著極度寬大的衫袴，有一種四平八穩的沉著氣象。領圈很低，有等於無。」("Gengyiji" 21) ["From the middle of the seventeenth century all the way until the end of the nineteenth, jackets with huge sleeves were perennially popular, giving their wearers an air of statuesque repose. The jacket collar was very low, nearly nonexistent" (Jones 429)]. The Chinese translation emphasizes the valuing of discretion as the most desirable quality for women of the time, which is less noticeable in the English version.

Chang's analysis of the colours and designs of women's skirts, and the restraints they imposed on women, reminds her readers of the use of fashion in the Qing Dynasty as a marker of women's social and familial positions. For instance, bridal skirts were not only pleated, but also ornamented with numerous sashes from which little bells would hang down vertically: "The idea was to walk in such a manner that there was but a faint tinkle, like that of the bells on a distant pagoda in a dying wind" ("Fashions" 55). She translated this passage into Chinese as 「行動時只許有一點隱約的叮噹，像遠山上寶塔上的風鈴。」 [The bride was to emit no more than a faint chime as she moved, like the sound of bells coming on the wind from a distant pagoda ("Gengyiji" 22; Jones 431)]. The sound of bells ringing from a pagoda becomes an analogue to the tinkling of the small bells attached to a bride's dress, with the English phrase "in a dying wind" serving as an ominous reminder of the confinement of married women in a patriarchal society. This oppressive mood is conveyed in the Chinese text with the imagery of bells in a pagoda on a faraway mountain, associated with various Chinese legends, such as those of the Monkey King and the Green Snake, whose protagonists are confined as punishment for their transgressions. The Chinese text does not include a subject in this sentence, but the meaning is still understandable; however, Jones adds a subject, the bride, to his translation of this passage to clarify its meaning for Anglophone readers.

Chang's discussion of Chinese women's fashion trends between 1890 and 1910 corresponds to the social and cultural transformations occurring in modern China, brought on by foreign invasions, national cultural, political and educational reforms, and internal uprisings such as the first Sino-Japanese War (1894–1895), the Hundred Days' Reform (1898), the Boxer Rebellion (1900–1901), and an invasion by the Eight-Nation Alliance (1901). She notes in "Chinese Life and Fashions" that these sociopolitical upheavals inspired the move toward tight-fitting clothes for women that would allow for quicker movement:

> slim straight lines flaring a little of the knees, whence issued tiny trouser legs which dropped a timorous hint of even tinier shoes apologetically attached to the ground. There was something infinitely pathetic about those pencil-slim trousers, and in Chinese poetry the terms "lovely" and "pitiful" were identical.
>
> 57

TRANSFORMATION   189

In "Gengyiji" this passage reads:

> 長襖的直線延至膝蓋爲止，下面虛飄飄垂下兩條窄窄的袴管，
> 似腳非腳的金蓮抱歉地輕輕踏在地上。鉛筆一般瘦的袴腳妙在
> 給人一種伶仃無告的感覺。在中國的詩裏，『可憐』是『可
> 愛』的代名詞。

> A slim, straight robe would fall to the knees, from whence two tiny trou-
> ser legs dropped a timorous hint of even tinier shoes attached apologeti-
> cally to the ground. There was something infinitely pathetic about those
> pencil-slim trouser legs. In Chinese poetry, "pitiful" is just another way of
> saying "lovely."
>
> "Gengyiji" 24; Jones 433

Chang interprets the fashion for "pencil-thin trousers" as a style that does not
show off the curves of the female figure, but rather makes it unobtrusive and unre-
markable; the connotations in Chinese poetry of the words "pitiful" and "lovely"
further emphasize the inferior position of women in traditional Chinese society.
In her English essay, she describes the trousers as "pathetic," an observation from
an external perspective. However, in her Chinese version, she personifies the trousers as if they give the impression of 「伶仃無告」 [loneliness and helpless-
ness], which indirectly illuminates the psychological aspects of the wearer.

In the English text, Chang describes women's lotus shoes as "tinier shoes,"
focusing on their small size, but in the Chinese translation she uses the
phrase 「金蓮」 [golden lotus shoes] to focus on their aesthetic quality. The
practice of foot-binding was known in China as early as the tenth century. It
became popular among the elite classes during the Song Dynasty (960–1279)
and spread to the lower classes during the Qing Dynasty (1636–1912). Golden
lotus shoes for bound feet are elaborately decorated, even on the soles, reflecting the aesthetic preferences of the Chinese leisurely classes. However, with
foreign invasion and modernization in the late nineteenth century and onward,
the discourse surrounding bound feet and lotus shoes took on a more negative tone. Some May Fourth intellectuals, such as Lu Xun 魯迅 (1881–1936),
Chen Duxiu 陳獨秀 (1879–1942), and Hu Shi 胡適 (1891–1962), blamed traditional Chinese culture for the nation's failure in international policies, and
with this in mind, the idealized imagery of *tianzu* 天足 [natural or heavenly
feet] replaced the more dismissive imagery of *chanzu* 纏足 [bound feet] (Ko,
Cinderella's Sisters 14–15). The significance of footbinding dramatically shifted
from an appreciation of femininity, motherhood, morality, and modesty into a
symbol of backwardness, oppression, condemnation, and pity.

As part of a significant nationalistic project, the abolition of footbinding was seen as crucial to the modernization of China. Women with natural feet would be more capable of joining the labour force in order to increase national productivity. In his essay "Lun nüxue" 〈論女學〉 ("On Women's Education," 1896–1897), reformer Liang Qichao (1873–1929) argued that "yu qiangguo bi you nüxue" 「欲強國必由女學」 [women's education was the prerequisite for strengthening the country] (43). He claimed that strong nations, such as the United States of America, Britain, France, Germany, and Japan, promoted education for women, and that gender equality and collaboration were essential and important for nation building. He advocated abolishing footbinding for the sake of women's mobility and education and, by extension, the strengthening of China (J.T.Y. Li, "Ibsen's Nora" 248–249). Liang's essay was an example of the juxtaposing of women's rights and national salvation that paradoxically displaced women's liberation in a different subjugating discourse of nationalism.

More recent scholarship has nevertheless re-evaluated the discourse on foot-binding and golden lotus shoes. For instance, in *Every Step a Lotus: Shoes for Bound Feet* (2001), and *Cinderella's Sisters: A Revisionist History of Footbinding* (2007), Dorothy Ko examines the origin, purpose, and spread of this custom in Chinese society from the third century to the late twentieth century, mostly to engage women's own perspectives to reconstitute the implication of this practice in their lives:

> I feel strongly that we should understand footbinding not as a senseless act of destruction but as a meaningful practice in the eyes of the women themselves. This stance, adopted throughout this book, has led me to focus on the lotus shoes themselves instead of the crushed bones. As carriers and expressions of family values, women's handiwork, good wishes, and regional cultures, lotus shoes of all sizes, shapes, and colors are not only beautiful but also deeply meaningful.
>
> *Every Step a Lotus* 127

In traditional Chinese society, women with bound feet were seen as symbols of feminine ideals; however, the late nineteenth century saw a re-evaluation of, and a new meaning constructed for, the female body. Modern interpretations of the practice of footbinding tend to see it as an irreversible and undesirable bodily mutilation. However, in complementing the progressive analysis of footbinding, the perspectives of women with bound feet should also be considered in their Confucian domestic culture (J.T.Y. Li, "Ibsen's Nora" 252).

At the turn of the twentieth century, natural feet denoted emancipation, education, and modernization, as opposed to the more negative view of bound feet. Huang Suqiong 黃素瓊 (Huang Yifan 黃逸梵 1893–1957), Eileen Chang's mother, had bound feet in her childhood, but unbound them later. Unfortunately, the process of binding feet cannot be reversed, as the bones have already been twisted. As a new woman of the time, Huang, nonetheless, managed well in skiing in the Swiss Alps (Chang, *Mutual Reflections* 20), an activity that showcased the female body as a battlefield of old and new ideas. Zhang Maoyuan 張茂淵 (1898–1991), Eileen Chang's aunt, had natural feet, in part due to having been dressed as a boy and addressed as "little master" even though she was a girl. Her younger relatives called her "uncle" rather than "aunt." Chang notes that her aunt's childhood cross-dressing implied a vague idea of feminism, with the hope of promoting female agency in marriage prospects (Chang, *Mutual Reflections* 50–52), as discussed in the first chapter of this study.

Another late Qing-era fashion Chang discusses and illustrates in "Chinese Life and Fashion" is the "'Sycee collar,' a still collar reaching to the level of the nose. A long neck of swanlike grace was consequently much admired" ("Fashions" 57); or, in "Gengyiji," 「『元寶領』這東西產生了——高得與鼻尖平行的硬領，像緬甸的一層層疊至尺來高的金屬香圈一般，逼迫女人們伸長了——脖子。」(26) ["Sycee collar, a tall, stiff affair that reached nearly as far as the nose and, like the Burmese neck rings made of gold that are piled one atop the other until they are almost a foot tall, forced women to stretch and distend their necks" (Jones 434)]. The English text depicts the Sycee collar in a positive light as an exotic fashion, but the Chinese text takes a more cynical and distanced attitude by parallelling it with Burmese neck rings and emphasizing its effects on the female body, inviting her readers to rethink the body as a gendered battleground. Chang notes that the rather top-heavy collar was meant as a contrast to the woman's slender limbs and torso, producing a disproportionate and unbalanced effect in keeping with the sentiments of the time.

The "Sycee collar" is depicted as an indication of feminine beauty in Chang's novel *Yuannü* 《怨女》 and her English translation *The Rouge of the North*: "The ermine lining showed white around the edges of her high collar cutting across the deep pink plane of the cheek" (*RON* 72); or 「她的出鋒皮襖元寶領四周露出銀鼠裹子，雪白的毛托著濃抹胭脂的面頰。」(*Yuannü* 77). The English passage emphasizes the "ermine lining" as defining both the high collar and the cheek, but the Chinese version merely presents the Sycee collar as a fashion associated with wealthy women of the late Qing Dynasty. While describing the public gaze on Yindi's fashion, the narrator becomes a member of the onlookers but from a critical distance commenting on this scene's "theatrical look" (72). Feminist scholars have similarly remarked that "Women have been traditionally associated with the flesh, nature, and the body, and as a result, they have been denigrated, objectified, and afforded less social, political, and social moral values than their male counterparts" (Fischer and Dolezal 3). Yindi provides an instance of how outward appearance was constructed by late-Qing-era fashion and reiterated in performance as she parades in the street.

After the overthrow of the Qing Dynasty, China witnessed the New Culture Movement and the May Fourth Movement in the mid-1910s and 1920s. These movements advocated democracy, free love, and other modern ideals, as Chang notes in her description of the changes in the fashion of the time: "The 'Trumpet Sleeve' like the Western bishop sleeve, only shorter, began tight and ended a little below the elbow, large, breezy, and fluttering. The jacket reached only to the hips. The waist was beautifully molded" ("Fashions" 59). In "Gengyiji," this passage reads, 「『喇叭管袖子』飄飄欲仙，露出一大截玉腕。短襖腰部極爲緊小。」 ["Trumpet sleeves" fluttered fairylike, affording a view of the pale jade of a woman's wrists. Abbreviated jackets fit prettily around tiny waists" (26; Jones 434)]. Chang compares the "trumpet sleeves" of the Chinese fashion to those worn by Western bishops to provide a familiar image for Anglophone readers, but in Chinese, she uses the phrase 「飄飄欲仙」 [fluttering fairylike], to describe the sensual excitement triggered by the revealing of a woman's wrist and the sight of her beautifully shaped tiny waist. This Chinese idiom, moreover, denotes leaving the earthly world to become immortals and is often associated with erotic ecstasy aroused by carnal pleasure, a meaning that would be obvious for readers who know the reference in Chinese literature. These nuanced linguistic differences between Chang's source text and her self-translation reflect different concepts of and social expectations for women's dress codes in the West and in China, particularly the expectation of Chinese fashion of the modern era to be courageous and provocative, in keeping with the revolutionary period.

During the early Republican years of the 1910s and 1920s, when Western ideas were imported into China, Western fashion provided much inspiration to the changing styles of clothes in China:

> The collar was at first reduced in height, then practically done away with. The open collar, round, square, heart-shaped, diamond-shaped; white stockinet scarves for all seasons; white silk stockings with black embroideries crawling up the ankles: these were taken directly from European fashions of the day.
>
> "Fashions" 59

TRANSFORMATION

This passage appears in "Gengyiji" as:

「民國初年的時候，大部份的靈感是得自西方的。衣領減低了不算，甚至被蠲免了的時候也有。領口挖成圓形，方形，雞心形，金剛鑽形。白色絲質圍巾四季都能用。白絲襪腳跟上的黑銹花，像蟲的行列，蠕蠕爬到腿肚子上。」

71–72

Much of the inspiration for fashions in the early years of the Republic derived from the West. The collar was first reduced in height and then practically eliminated altogether. Necklines became round, square, heart-shaped, diamond-shaped; white silk scarves became suitable for all seasons, as were white silk stockings with embroidered designs that crawled up the legs like insects.

JONES 434

Chang interprets the changes in Chinese women's fashion in the first two decades of the twentieth century as results of Westernization, though she places this statement at the beginning of the Chinese version of this passage to emphasize it for her Chinese readers. In "Gengyiji," she provides a more vivid and disconcerting image of the embroidery on the stockings than in the English text by adopting the simile 「像蟲的行列，蠕蠕爬到腿肚子上」 [like insects in rows, slowly crawling up the calf of the leg] (72), which shows her mastery of the Chinese language.

The New China experienced a state of political unrest that resulted in the Warlord Era (1916–1928), during which Chinese fashion changed quickly in order to keep up with the equally rapid social transformations of the time. For example, hems on jackets changed from square, to round, to V-shaped, and eventually hexagonal, and these changes can be understood in terms of Porter and Robinson's observation that "[h]ermeneutics has become a way of describing our encounters with art and our own self-understandings as historical beings" (297). In her understanding of the correlation between Chinese fashion and history, Chang argues in "Chinese Life and Fashions" that these changes do not necessarily imply intellectual flexibility: "Quite the contrary, it may show general inactivity, frustration in other fields of action so that all the intellectual and artistic energy is forced to flow into the channel of clothes" (60). Her Chinese translation of this passage reads: 「恰巧相反。它可以代表呆滯；　由於其他活動範內的失敗，所有的創造力都流入衣服的區域裏去。」 [On the contrary. They may reveal instead a generalized apathy, for frustration in other fields may lead to the forced flow of intellectual and artistic energy into the domain of fashion ("Gengyiji" 27; Jones 435)]. Chang translates the word "inactivity" as 「呆滯」 [inactive/lethargic/sluggish], a phrase that indicates a state of behaviour. She theorizes that people who felt incapable of improving their situations in the face of political unrest would instead make changes in things they could control, such as their clothing; furthermore, people in different places and times may be more confident in some aspects of their lives than in others. Whether there is any causal relationship between a lack of political voice and an indulgence in fashion, however, is debatable. Ways of seeing significantly affect people's interpretations of their social circumstances; perhaps those perspectives reflect the subjectivity of the speakers and from which positions they speak.

According to Chang, Han Chinese women's sudden adoption of Manchu long gowns was not due to a desire for restoration after the overthrow of the Qing Dynasty, but to a desire to imitate men ("Fashions" 60). *Qipao* 旗袍, sometimes called *cheongsam* 長衫 or *cheongpao* 長袍, was a long gown for women introduced in the 1920s. The word *qi* 旗 means "banner"; *cheong* 長 means "long"; and *pao* 袍 means "gown." Manchu women typically wore stiff and masculine gowns in contrast to Han Chinese designs; indeed, for political reasons, Manchu women were forbidden from imitating Han Chinese fashions such as softer jackets. Traditionally, Han Chinese women's clothes are divided into two pieces, a "blouse and skirt," while men's clothes are made in one piece without a break at the waist. During the modernization movement of the 1920s, women in China were fascinated by the idea of gender equality. However, the socioeconomic situation of the time did not allow women to assert themselves, so women sought to reject femininity and dress like men, as Chang notes in "Chinese Life and Fashions": "Idealism and dainty escapism could not forever maintain themselves in the face of repeated national disasters. The fashions now had a curt, tightened look" (60). In "Gengyiji," she translates this passage as 「政治上，對內對外陸續發生的不幸事情使民眾灰了心。青年人的理想總有支持不了的一天。時裝開始緊縮。」 (27). Jones retranslates this passage into English as:

> The political misfortunes that befell the nation one after another, within and without its borders, could not help but leave the people disillusioned. There came a day when youthful idealism could no longer maintain itself in the face of unremitting disaster. Fashions began to retract, taking on a curt, tightened look.
>
> "A Chronicle" 436

Though both of Chang's versions discuss the adoption of "a curt, tightened look" in 1920s fashion, her English text simply attributes this design choice to the inability of "idealism and dainty escapism" to stand up to "repeated national

TRANSFORMATION

disasters," while her Chinese text addresses 「青年人的理想」 [young people's ideal/dream/vision] and elaborates on those young people's disillusionment with the political changes. Her Chinese self-translation/rewriting thus assesses national politics for her fellow Chinese readers in a relatively positive, even conciliatory, light.

Qipao was probably established as a nationalist style of dress by Soong Ch'ing-ling 宋慶齡 (1893–1981), also known as Madame Sun. As the wife of Dr. Sun Yatsen 孫逸仙 (1866–1925), she made frequent public appearances during the Republican era. Accompanying Dr. Sun to a meeting for the reorganization and consolidation of the Kuomintang (Nationalist Party) along the principles of the Communist Party of the Soviet Union in 1923, Soong Ch'ing-ling adopted Chinese gowns. American journalist Helen Foster Snow reported that "After this one never saw an adult Chinese woman in foreign dress even in the treaty-ports. It was Madame Sun who set the nationalist fashion, presumably as an 'anti-imperialist' new look" (119). Photographs of Soong Ch'ing-ling depict her changing dress styles over the ten years since her marriage to Sun. In her wedding photograph taken in 1915, she wore "big picture hats with feathers, curled her hair, and appeared in American-style dresses and suits, with collars and cuffs and lacy frills" (Snow 119). In the early 1920s, Soong Ch'ing-ling was seen in a "Chinese skirt and wide-sleeved jacket-blouse typical of the May Fourth era. In Beijing in 1925, she appeared in a simple, A-line *qipao* of dark cloth. The garment had wide sleeves, just like the jacket-blouse, and fell to just above her ankles" (Finnane 143). After that, she typically wore *qipao* until after the establishment of the Communist Regime, the People's Republic of China, in 1949. Soong Mei-ling 宋美齡 (1898–2003), Soong Ch'ing-ling's younger sister and wife of Chiang Kai-shek 蔣介石 (1887–1975), further popularized *qipao* in China during the Republican years.

In her various writings, Chang depicts the continuously evolving styles of *qipao* in the 1930s; for instance, "The Golden Cangue" features hybrids of Chinese and Western fashions, such as those that Ch'ang-hsing gives her cousin Ch'ang-an for her blind date: 「耳朵上戴了二寸來長的玻璃翡翠寶塔墜子，又換上了蘋果綠喬琪紗旗袍，高領圈，荷葉邊袖子，腰以下是半西式的百摺裙。」("Jinsuoji" 274); Ch'ang-an "wear[s] 'glassy-green' jade-ite earrings with pagoda-shaped pendants two inches long and change into an apple-green georgette gown with a high collar, ruffled sleeves, and fine pleats below the waist, half Western style" ("TGC" 178). Ch'ang-an's clothes coincidentally match the cross-cultural background of her future fiancé, who has just returned from overseas studies, and thus reflect the intercultural aesthetic and intellect of the time.

With the rise of women's liberation advocacy, organizations such as the Yongjia Women's Association promoted natural breasts in opposition to the age-old practice of breast-binding, which was perceived as unhealthy and backward. In 1937, a medical student wrote in *Shenbao* 申報, an early Chinese newspaper published in Shanghai between 1872 and 1949, about the risk of diseases related to the practice: "[t]he new women of today seek novelty in everything, but maintain old practices when it comes to breastbinding" (qtd. in Finnane 165). He criticized married men who were "lacking in common medical knowledge [and] they thoughtlessly rub and mishandle their wives' breasts, causing considerable discomfort and frequently resulting in the formation of lumps which develop into abscesses" (Finnane 165). The changing attitudes about breast-binding in the 1920s and 1930s were part of the desire for healthy and strong women rather than the "fragile beauty" preferred in the imperial era.

In the 1940s, *qipao* underwent notable design changes, such as removing sleeves, reducing collar height, and reducing dress length. Chang interprets those changes as the subtraction of all essential and non-essential ornaments to respect the principle of functionality. She contends that fashion in China in those days was not an industry dominated by a few fashion entrepreneurs, but a collective imagination that changes over time. It is impossible and unimportant to trace the original because Chinese people regard imitation as a compliment; for instance, people in Shanghai attributed the 1940s fashion of wide three-quarter sleeves to Hong Kong, while people in Hong Kong credited the fashion to Shanghai. Chang depicts modern Chinese women's fashion in her short story "Qingcheng zhi lian" 〈傾城之戀〉 ("Love in a Fallen City," 1943), whose protagonist Fan Liuyuan 范柳原, an overseas returnee bachelor, flirts with Bai Liusu 白流蘇, a Shanghainese divorcee, in the Repulse Bay Hotel in Hong Kong, saying to her:

> 我第一次看見你,就覺得你不應當光著膀子穿這種時髦的長背心,不過你也不應當穿西裝。滿洲的旗袍,也許倒適合一點,可是線條又太硬。
>
> 201

> The first time I saw you, you were wearing one of those trendy tunics, and I thought you shouldn't bare your arms like that. But Western-style clothes aren't right for you either. A Manchu-style cheongsam might suit you better, if its lines weren't so severe.
>
> KINGSBURY 143

Fan appreciates Bai's femininity, which cannot be confined in any kind of clothes or defined by any styles or standards, such as those popular in both Shanghai and Hong Kong at that time.

TRANSFORMATION

Modern Chinese fashions particularly flourished in the city of Shanghai, which was the pioneering producer and major center of the cotton trade in China. Li Hongzhang 李鴻章 (1823–1901), Eileen Chang's great-grandfather, established China's first cotton textile industry in Shanghai in 1890. By the end of the 1900s, Shanghai housed "eight foreign, four Chinese, and three Sino-foreign mills, out of a total of twenty-eight in China as a whole" (Finnane 107). Apart from textiles production, Shanghai was also a shopping center for modern fashion:

> a number of multistory department stores in the International Settlement – in particular the 'Big Four' of Xianshi 先施 (Sincere), Yong'an 永安 (Wing On), Xin Xin 新新 (Sun Sun), and Daxin 大新 (Sun Company), all built with investment from overseas Chinese businessmen – had become great attractions for the Chinese. With their escalators leading to variegated merchandise on different floors, together with dance halls and rooftop bars, coffeehouses, restaurants, hotels, and playgrounds for diverse entertainments, these edifices of commerce combined the functions of consumerism and recreation.
>
> L.O. LEE 13

All of these commercial and recreational warehouses contributed to the vital and colourful sartorial and cultural landscapes of Shanghai in the early twentieth century.

Chang portrays the metropolis of Shanghai as the center of modern Chinese fashion in the Republican years; for instance, in her essay "Daoluyimu" 〈道路以目〉 ("Seeing with the Streets," 1943), she describes the distinctive window displays and neon lights on Avenue Joffre (now known as Huaihai Road): 「四五年前在隆冬的晚上和表姐看霞飛路上的櫥窗，霓虹燈下，木美人的傾斜的臉，傾斜的帽子，帽子上斜吊著的羽毛。」 [On a bitter cold winter night four or five years ago, I went to look at the shop windows on the Avenue Joffre with my cousin. Under neon lights, hats slanted across the slanted faces of the wooden beauties, atop which slanted feathers (62; Jones 67)]. These displays of colourful garments epitomized the urban culture of this Chinese cosmopolitan center. Chang also depicted other landmark clothing stores of Shanghai in her short stories, such as in "Se, Jie" 〈色，戒〉 ("Lust, Caution"):

> 對面就是剛才那家凱司令咖啡館，然後西伯利亞皮貨店，綠屋夫人時裝店，並排兩家四個大櫥窗，華貴的模特兒在霓虹燈後擺出各種姿態。
>
> 199

Opposite was Commander K'ai's Café again, with the Siberian Leather Goods Store and the Green House Ladies' Clothing Emporium next, each fronted by two large display windows filled with glamorously dressed mannequins bent into all manner of poses beneath neon signs.

LOVELL 32

This passage provides a detailed description of the urban scenery of Jing'an shi Road (named after the Temple of Tranquility; now known as West Nanjing Road) in the 1930s and the early 1940s.

Based on her personal experience, Chang expresses her special insight on clothes in her literary works. For example, when she was nineteen years old, she wrote in "Tiancaimeng" 〈天才夢〉 ("Dream of Genius," 1940), 「生命是一襲華美的袍，爬滿了蝨子。」 [Life is a splendid and beautiful gown, crawling with loads of lice] (10). This image can be understood as a representation of the decline of her aristocratic family, who appeared extravagant on the surface but became rotten underneath. In *Mutual Reflections: Looking at My Old Photo Album*, Chang recalls her unhappy childhood in which she was forced to wear her stepmother's old clothes, some of which were worn out at the collar. Studying at St. Mary's Hall, a noble missionary girls' school in Shanghai, while wearing her stepmother's hand-me-downs upset her very much, and in her later life she became "clothes-crazy" (32) to compensate.

As a performative expression, Chang sometimes wore peculiar outfits that were meant to shock her audience. For instance, in *Mutual Reflections*, Chang included a photo of herself in a Qing-style jacket over a *qipao* (62). The jacket was loose with wide sleeves, padded and puffy, knee-length, decorated with black piping and an S-shaped *ruyi* 如意 [wishful] knot. The photo was taken in 1944, when Qing-era imperial clothes were seen as archaic and had been replaced decades earlier by more modern fashions. Chang's costume expresses her insight about the constant changes in modern Chinese society and her eagerness to enjoy the present. Her drawing of this eccentric ancient fashion, representing her appreciation of her ancestors and their heritage, became the cover image of both her 1944 edition of *Liuyan* and this book.

Chang's younger brother Zhang Zijing 張子靜 (1921–1997) alludes to her idiosyncratic dress styles in his book *Wo de zizi Zhang Ailing* 《我的姊姊張愛玲》 (*My Elder Sister Eileen Chang*, 1944).[1] He notes that Eileen enjoyed wearing unusual attire, such as, in one instance, a low collared qipao, with big blue and white flowers on a sharp red background, and without any buttons on either side, a very unconventional and daring fashion choice for the time

---

1 Zhang Zijing's "Wo de zizi Zhang Ailing" ("My Elder Sister Eileen Chang") was first published in the first edition of the journal *Biao* (*Whirlwind*) in September 1944.

(Z. Zhang 165). He confesses that he had never seen such a dress, and that he also heard people say that at a friend's wedding Eileen wore an old Qing-era embroidered jacket and pants, attracting much visual attention. Chang's eccentric style of dress may be interpreted not only as an expression of her passion for her ancestors and the past, but also as her subversion of the conventions of fashion and codes of behavior, and as her way of asserting her subjectivity in the transitional era of the 1940s.

Chang's self-translation challenges the preconception of gender inequality in Chinese culture, as Porter and Robinson note: "As a way of both seeing and resolving, when possible, the many obstacles that stand in the way of understanding someone or something else, hermeneutics represents an ongoing challenge to our preconceptions, beliefs, and ideals" (298). In "Gengyiji," Chang uses clothes as a metaphor to subvert the long-established patriarchal ideology that prevails in Chinese society, calling back to the Chinese proverb 「兄弟如手足，妻子如衣服。衣服破，尚可縫；手足斷，安可續？」 [Brothers are like limbs; wives are like clothes. Torn clothes can be repaired; how can broken limbs be mended?]. This comment was made by Liu Bei (161–223), a heroic warlord in the Three Kingdoms Period (220–280), depicted in Luo Guanzhong's (c. 1330–1400) *Romance of the Three Kingdoms*, Chapter 15. In subverting this misogynist idea, Chang ironically argues that women are more passionate for clothes than for men:

> 可是如果女人能夠做到『丈夫如衣服』的地步，就很不容易。有個西方作家（是蕭伯納麼？）曾經抱怨過，多數女人選擇丈夫遠不及選擇帽子一般的聚精會神，慎重考累。再沒有心肝的女子說起她『去年那件織錦緞夾袍』的時候，也是一往情深的。
>
> "GENGYJI" 29

> It will be very difficult indeed for women to reach the point when husbands are like clothes. One Western author (was it Bernard Shaw?) once explained, "Most women will wax passionate when she starts to speak of 'last year's quilted silk gown.'"
>
> JONES 440

The comments of Bernard Shaw "add a foreign flavor to the metaphorical description" (H. Meng 8). Employing the technique of parody, Chang appreciates women's passion for clothes while also reversing the patriarchal analogy of women as disposable clothes into a feminist metaphor of men as less valued than clothes.

As a cultural translator, Chang maps out a sartorial cultural history of modern China in the early twentieth century in her essays, fiction, drawings, and personal style of dress. Her English essay "The Chinese Life and Fashion" describes the transformation of women's fashion from the Qing Dynasty to the 1940s with elaboration of the sociohistorical and political backgrounds of these changes for her Anglophone readers. In her self-translation "Gengyiji," she re-evaluates the Chinese cultural assumptions embedded in vestural discourse, often accompanied by acute challenges to those assumptions in sometimes ironic and sometimes gracious tones. For Chang, women's fashion of the Qing Dynasty was burdened by restrictions such as special colours indicating different social or familial positions or bells attached to wedding dresses. During the period of political unrest between 1890 and 1910, tight-fitting clothes were favoured. The modern discourse of natural feet, encouraged by missionaries and by Chinese nationalistic discourse, gradually replaced the traditional Chinese aesthetics of bound feet. The advocacy of gender equality during the modernization movement of the 1910s and 1920s also led to the promotion of natural breasts and to the appearance of *qipao*. The introduction of bras and stockings and the lowering of collars were inspired by Western fashion, while the *qipao* was redesigned from a puritan look to a more audacious revelation of the female body. The mixing of Chinese and Western, as well as traditional and modern, women's fashions showcase the cultural mediation in Chinese sartorial history during this transitional period.

Overall, Chang performs the role of cultural translator in order to facilitate transcultural understanding and produces new meanings in her bilingual writings and self-translations/ rewritings. While interpreting Chinese cultural values and practices regarding folk religion, Peking operas, and fashion trends in her English essays, she re-evaluates those well-established cultural discourses in her Chinese self-translations. She offers innovative insights in her bilingual works through linguistic and cultural distanciation and comparative perspectives. Her appropriation tactics demonstrate her creativity in her writing and her appeal to her readers in both languages. All of these bilingual writings and self-translations contribute to deconstruct stereotypes of the Chinese and of Chinese culture, but not without self-criticism. Chang's English essays and Chinese self-translations published in Shanghai in the 1940s thus provide vivid pictures of the mobility and production of cultural ideas emerging from the modernization of early twentieth-century China.

PART 4

Political Ambivalence

∵

CHAPTER 12

Authenticity Reconsidered: *The Rice-Sprout Song – A Novel of Modern China* and *Yangge* 《秧歌》

In the manuscript for her speech "Chinese Translation: A Vehicle of Cultural Influence," Chang enigmatically crossed out a paragraph by hand:

> The May Fourth has set the tone for a rather sterilized view of the West as mentor, and now Hong Kong and Taiwan have perforce become part of the picture of worldwide Americanization, only more so because of their precarious existence – without the disinterested exploratory enthusiasm of the May Fourth. Imagination needs room, it needs distance and an absence of pressure.
>
> "A Vehicle of Cultural Influence" 498

Chang points out the paradoxical dilemma of freedom and censorship that both Hong Kong and Taiwan have experienced: on the one hand, they lean toward the United States in search of freedom, but on the other, they are still subject to political censorship. Similarly, Chang's self-censorship uncannily signals a "reminder of the translator's tenuous position" in the U.S." (C. Lee, "Introduction" 489).

Under political censorship originating in different political camps, Chang's novels written under the sponsorship of the Hong Kong Branch of the United States Information Services, *The Rice-Sprout Song – A Novel of Modern China* (1955) and *Yangge* 《秧歌》 (1954), as well as *Chidi zhi lian* 《赤地之戀》 (*The Love of Redland*, 1954) and *Naked Earth – A Novel about China* (1956), were banned in mainland China for their anti-Communist messages and edited by Taiwanese publishers to remove mentions of the Nationalist Party leaders of the time. Also, Chang noted that her travelogue "A Return to the Frontier" (1963) was published a year later because *The Reporter* thought that the PRC might collapse in a year, but her essay indicated otherwise (Chang, "Letter to Mae Fong Soong," February 22, 1963; *To My Beloved Friends* 1.107). Her essay "Chongfang biancheng" 〈重訪邊城〉 was only published posthumously in 2008 in *Crown* magazine in Taiwan due to the continuous revisions she made during her lifetime; likewise, "The Spyring/Ch'ing k'ê! Ch'ing k'ê!" was first sent to Richard McCarthy in Hong Kong in the early 1950s but was only published posthumously in 2008, as the ambiguity of the political stance presented in

© JESSICA TSUI-YAN LI, 2025 | DOI:10.1163/9789004730052_014

the story might have been too controversial during the Cold War period (Kowallis 53). The postponement of the publication of "Se, Jie" 〈色，戒〉 in Taiwan may also have been because of the story's political nature and its implicit engagement with Hu Lancheng 胡蘭成 (1906–1981). As her unsaid words suggest, creativity and innovation require freedom from political pressure.

Whether historical narratives or fiction can reproduce or represent reality is a controversial topic in both historiography and literary criticism. Hayden White argues that historical narratives "succeed in endowing sets of past events with meanings, over and above whatever comprehension they provide by appeal to putative causal laws, by exploiting the metaphorical similarities between sets of real events and the conventional structures of our fictions" (White 1473). According to White, historical narratives do not provide descriptions or images of history, but rather give directions for readers to associate feelings about historical figures or events. Authenticity is highly contested and negotiated in historical narratives and fiction, which depict their characters and events using literary techniques, styles, selection, omission, and addition by authors with specific perspectives. I further argue that self-translation of historical narratives and fiction destabilize the authenticity of the past they construct through writing and translation.

This chapter[1] discusses the negotiation of authenticity in both *The Rice-Sprout Song – A Novel of Modern China* (1955; hereafter cited as *RSS*) and *Yangge* (1954), arguing that *Yangge* oscillates between faithfulness towards and betrayal of the letter and spirit of *The Rice-Sprout Song*. The chapter investigates the context in which these two novels were produced and the ideologies they present, as well as the debate among critics in the United States and various Chinese communities over the novels' authenticity. It also explores the revision of representations of the female body in the two versions of the tale, with reference to the female protagonist Yuexiang 月香 (Moon Scent)'s physical beauty, her earthy and materialist personality, her relationship with her husband, and her political confrontations. Chang deliberately changes her self-translation into Chinese to make Moon Scent more resourceful and self-sufficient than she is in the earlier English text, thus destabilizing the authenticity of patriarchal rules in Chinese culture.

Both versions tell the story of the Tan family, who live in a village near Shanghai during the Communist Land-Reform Movement (1950–1953)[2] in

---

1 Part of this chapter has been based on the following previously published article: Li, Jessica Tsui-yan. "Female Body Revisited: Eileen Chang's *The Rice-Sprout Song* and *Yangge*." In Reeta Tremblay ed. *Asia: Local and Global Perspectives*. Montréal: Canadian Asian Studies Association. 272–289.

2 The story depicts the destruction that the land-reform movement brought to a southern Chinese village in the early 1950s. The land-reform movement was a radical agricultural

the early years of the People's Republic of China. The story begins with the hardworking peasant Gold Root marrying off his sister Gold Flower to a man from a nearby village. After the Communist-style wedding party, Gold Root's wife Moon Scent returns home after having worked as a domestic helper in Shanghai for three years to financially support her family in the village. To her shock, Moon Scent realizes that the villagers are suffering from severe famine, even though Big Uncle and Big Aunt were boasting about the good harvest and weather, all thanks to the benevolence of the Land-Reform Movement. In the first few days after her arrival, numerous villagers visit Moon Scent to borrow small amounts of money, but she refuses them all, including her mother and Gold Flower. Along with having to give their crops to the Party, the Tan family and other villagers are frequently requested to participate in political meetings. A literary cadre, Comrade Ku, comes from Shanghai to live with the Tan family in order to collect materials for his propaganda film.

Comrade Wong, a Communist cadre who supervises all aspects of the villagers' life, demands that all families donate half a pig and New Year cakes, or the equivalent in money, to the militia's families. Though Gold Root declares that he has neither pigs nor money to donate, Moon Scent surrenders her secret money to Comrade Wong and is beaten by Gold Root. On the day that the cakes are to be donated, the peasants ask the village government to borrow some food for the New Year. A riot starts when the militia fires at the peasants. Gold Root and Moon Scent's daughter Beckon is trampled to death, and Gold Root is shot in the leg. Moon Scent asks Gold Flower to help, but in vain, and then finds that Gold Root has left his coat for her and drowned himself. She then returns home. A woman is seen running near the grain storage that is set on fire; she is then chased into the fire by guards. The story ends with the villagers being forced to participate in a mass dance, known as "The Rice-Sprout Song."

After moving to Hong Kong in 1952, Eileen Chang worked for the Hong Kong branch of the United States Information Services (USIS) as a freelance writer and translator. The USIS was a local branch of the United States Information Agency (USIA), a United States government agency established in 1953 in order to publicize American ideologies around the world. One objective of the agency was to control the spread of Communism in Asia during the Cold War period. The director of the Hong Kong branch of the USIS, Richard McCarthy, recounted in an interview in 2003 that he aimed to publish remarkable literature that harmonized with United States foreign policy: 「香港美新處同仁比較關切出版我們認爲是文學類的出色作品。幾種不同的

---

policy implemented by the early Chinese Communist Party, that was meant to re-distribute agricultural land from landowners to peasants, and subsequently to lead to the liberation of the Chinese people's mindset.

個人與官方的興趣快快樂樂會合起來。」 [The officers of the USIS in Hong Kong were concerned with the publication of what we considered literary masterpieces. Several different personal and political interests happily joined together] (Kao, *Eileen Chang Reconsidered* 244).

Under the sponsorship of the USIS, Chang translated a series of Western novels and short stories into Chinese. She also wrote the novels *The Rice-Sprout Song* (1955), *Yangge* (1954), *Chidi zhi lian* 《赤地之戀》 (*The Love of Redland*, 1954), and *Naked Earth – A Novel about China* (1956). She wrote *The Rice-Sprout Song* and then translated it by herself into Chinese as *Yangge*, which was serialized in the magazine *Jinri shijie* 《今日世界》 (*The World Today*)[3] in 1954, while the English version was published by Charles Scribner's Sons in New York in 1955. The novel was reprinted by Dragonfly Books in Hong Kong in 1963 and again by the University of California Press in 1998. It was adapted into an American television drama directed by Sidney Lumet and broadcast on CBS *Studio One* in 1957; however, on seeing the film years later, Chang dismissed it as *"canburendu"* 「慘不忍睹」 [too disastrous to bear watching] (Q. *Song* 113). The copyright of *The Rice-Sprout Song* was extended to twenty-three foreign translations. For example, a Japanese translator, Namikawa Ryō 並河亮 (1905–1984), translated the English version into Japanese as *Nōmin Ongakutai* 《農民音樂隊》 (*Peasants' Band*; hereafter cited as *NO*), published in Tokyo by Jiji Tsūshinsha 時事通信社 (Jiji Press), in 1956.

While working with the USIS in Hong Kong, Chang wrote and self-translated two novels that expressed the anti-Communist sentiments that the office expected; however, she had previously published two pro-Communist novels, *Shiba chun* 《十八春》 (*Eighteen Springs*, 1950–1951)[4] and *Xiao Ai* 《小艾》 (*Little Ai*, 1951), when she was in Shanghai. After moving to the United States in 1955, she removed the leftist content from those novels and retitled *Shiba chun* as *Banshengyuan* 《半生緣》 (*Half a Lifelong Romance*, 1968). Both *Banshengyuan* and *Xiao Ai* were published by the Taiwan Crown Publishing Company, Ltd. Although she seemed to have adopted more rightist politics after leaving Shanghai, she married Ferdinand Reyher, a Communist, in New York in 1956. Her changing political stance was probably driven by acute economic and political circumstances; as David Der-Wei Wang 王德威 notes in the "Foreword" to *The Rice-Sprout Song*, "Chang's movement from the leftist to the rightist camp in the short span of five years is certainly of significance.

---

3 *Jinri Shijie* was a propaganda magazine sponsored by the USIS and circulated among the Chinese communities in Asia, Europe, and North and South Americas. It praised the achievements of the Nationalist government in Taiwan and condemned the Communist regime in the People's Republic of China.

4 *Shiba chun* was serialized in the Chinese newspaper *Yibao* 《亦報》 in 1950–1951, under her pseudonym Liang Jing 梁京, in Shanghai.

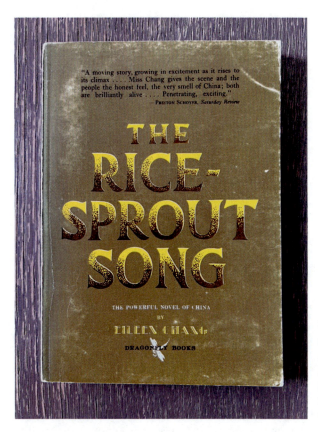

FIGURE 18

Chang, Eileen. *The Rice-Sprout Song – A Novel of Modern China.* New York: Scribner's, 1955
PHOTO CREDIT: JESSICA TSUI-YAN LI

It bespeaks, however, not her opportunism but her predicament as a Chinese writer trapped in the drastic imperatives of an ideological age" (XIV). I further argue that her ideological shifts can paradoxically be seen as representing her general aloofness toward politics, albeit somewhat confined by political censorship.

Though *The Rice-Sprout Song* was intended to promote the USIS's expected anti-Communist message, Chang exercised her aesthetic freedom of authorship in manipulating the ideologies she presented in the novel. She deliberately blurred the identities of different political parties, thus producing an ambiguous ideological position. For instance, Big Aunt confuses *Gongchandang* 共產黨 [the Communist Party] with *Kêmingtang* 革命黨 [Revolutionaries] and even *Kuomintang* 國民黨 [the Nationalist Party], thus betraying her political ignorance, while giving a speech in the complimentary manner that is expected in the surveillance environment of the time:

> Ai, everything is fine now! The poor have turned! Now things are different from before. If not for Chairman Mao we would never have this day! We

will go on suffering, I don't know how long, if our comrades in Kêmingtang had not come!

    RSS 15

咳！現在好嘍！窮人翻身嘍！現在跟從前兩樣嘍！要不是毛主
席，我們哪有今天呀？要不是革命黨來了，我們窮人受罪不知
道受到哪年呵！

    Yangge 18

In the English version, Chang further, painstakingly, explains the different
political stances of the three parties:

> Big Aunt mixed up Kunch'antang, Communists, with Kêmingtang, rev-
> olutionists, which only meant the early revolutionaries who had over-
> thrown the Manchu dynasty, back when Big Aunt was a young girl. So
> she persisted in referring to the Communists as Kêmingtang and some-
> times even as Kuomintang, the Nationalists who had been chased over to
> Formosa.
>
>   *RSS* 15

Although the Romanized Chinese names and the explanations of the three
parties' positions were potentially confusing for Anglophone readers, they
do highlight the peasants' shaky grasp of politics and obscure the boundaries
between the parties, thus defeating the rightist message the novel was meant
to convey. In the Chinese translation, Chang omits the clumsy explanations of
the political parties' positions because they are well known to Chinese readers,
who would similarly recognize the ignorance of the peasants.

Chang's ideological indifference can be further seen in her account of the
devastation of a small village, which a peasant named Chow Pa-kê recounts to
Comrade Wong: "This was one of those unfortunate areas which were alter-
nately raided by the Japanese, the Communists, the Peace Army of the puppet
government, and all sorts of nondescript troops who owed nominal allegiance
to the government in Chungking" (*RSS* 75) [這是一個不辛的『三不管』
的區域，被日本兵、共產黨、和平軍、與各種雜牌軍輪流蹂躪著。
(*Yangge* 80)]. The English version clearly identifies "the Peace Army of the
puppet government" and notes that they "owed nominal allegiance to the government in Chungking," while the Chinese version omits these details on the
grounds that they are already familiar to Chinese readers. This speech signifies
that even though the armies represent various political camps and act on different motives, all of them have had the same effect on the village; thus, from

AUTHENTICITY RECONSIDERED

Chow's viewpoint, their specific identities and political orientations are insignificant to the peasants. The indistinctness of Chang's portrayal of the various political parties is further demonstrated in Chow's questioning of Comrade Wong's political orientation: "Chow was in a quandary. The man pronounced himself a Communist but there was no telling which side he really belonged to" [「趙八哥左右爲難起來了。這人自己說他是個共產黨，但是誰知道他究竟是那一方面的。」(*RSS* 77; *Yangge* 82)]. The obscurity of Comrade Wong's identity shows the ambivalence of the political position presented in the novels.

The cultural values of individual and collective identities are respectively manifested in the English and Chinese versions. In the English version, Comrade Wong frightens Chow into speaking the truth: "If you hide anything, it is at your own peril" (*RSS* 77). Comrade Wong intimidates Chow alone in the English text; however, in the Chinese version, he further elaborates on this threat by mentioning Chow's family as well: 「扯了謊給我們對出來了，我們的黑名單上有了你的名字，一家子都不要想活著。」[If we find out that you tell lies, we will have your name in our black list; your whole family will not want to live] (*Yangge* 82). The recontextualization of the story presents a glimpse of the privilege of collective identity in Chinese society and the importance of the idea of individuality in Western culture. The Chinese version moves both towards and away from the English version, thus once again producing that familiar space of in-betweenness.

The Rice-Sprout Song was praised by critics in the United States upon its first publication for its "authenticity" and "honest reporting" of agricultural life under the Chinese Communist Regime. For instance, *Time* magazine describes the novel as "perhaps the most authentic novel so far of life under the Chinese Communists" ("Slavery & Hatred" 118). The *Yale Review* considers it a "good story that gives every evidence of being shrewd and honest reporting" (Pickrel 639). The *Saturday Review* claims that "Miss Chang gives the scene and the people the honest feel, the very smell of China; both are brilliantly alive" (Schoyer 18). The novel, embodying Chinese ethnographic features and written by a native Chinese woman writer in the United States, was obviously exploited as a propaganda tool.

Namikawa Ryō, who translated *The Rice-Sprout Song* into Japanese as *Nōmin Ongakutai*, stresses the novel's focus on peasant life in a Chinese village during the Land-Reform Movement under the Chinese Communist regime:

わたしがこの書を訳してみたいとおもつたのは、この小説には、中共が実現しようとしている大きい事業も、それの困難さも、共に[率] (sic.) 直に書かれていて、小説の内容がすべて事実に基いたものでないにしても、かなり現下の中国の実情を描いているのではないかとおもわれたからである。長い歴史と古い伝統をもつ中国農村の解放という事業は、実際並大抵のことではない。抜け切れぬ古い因習に縛られた中国農民の啓蒙と土地改革という事業が、いかに長期を要する至難事であるかを、この小説は如実に物語っている。

NO 1–2

I wanted to translate this novel because it presents straightforward descriptions of the large projects that Communist Party of China is trying to achieve and the difficulty in realizing them. Although the contents of the novel may not always be based on facts, the novel appears to contain a considerable number of depictions of real circumstances in contemporary China. It is an enormous task to liberate Chinese farm villages that have their long histories and old traditions. This novel realistically tells how difficult and laborious it is to educate Chinese farmers who are bound by old customs and to achieve the project of land reform.

Namikawa further claims that he consulted Chang for advice concerning the Japanese translation: 「邦訳に際しては、張愛玲女史に疑問の点を手紙で質し、女史から一 、懇篤な指示を受けた。」 [I contacted Miss Zhang Ailing by letter to ask questions about Japanese translations, and she kindly provided me with data and instructions] (*NO* 2). His contact with Chang is meant to signal that his rendition is a faithful version, and thus to highlight the authenticity of the novel, which purports the same political stance as the United States, given that Japan and the United States were political allies against Communist China during the Cold War period.

Where the American critical reviews and the Japanese translator's note emphasize the story's faithful representation of the Chinese social and historical circumstances it presents, most critics in mainland China denounce its claim to authenticity. *Yangge* had largely remained unavailable on the mainland until the revival of "Eileen Chang Fever" in the late 1980s and early 1990s. Its first publication was not well received. For example, Ke Ling 柯靈 condemns the story's fictional nature as 「意味著與祖國決裂了。」 [signifying her breaking away from the motherland] (Jiang 202). Yu Qing 于青 argues that Chang came from a decaying aristocratic family and her isolation from politics was understandable; furthermore, she wrote the novel for economic reasons, and it was, in Yu's opinion, 「對藝術的極大的背叛。」 [a great betrayal of art] (Yu 268). Fei Yong 費勇 praises the literary techniques Chang employed in the novel, but dismisses its theme of hunger: 「飢餓現象在50年代初曾經發生過, 但並不普遍。張愛玲以此作爲小說的核心也許含有某種偏見, 但純從藝術角度而言, 卻極具震憾性。」 [Famine happened in China in the early 1950s, but it was not phenomenal. Eileen Chang used it as the theme of the novel, which perhaps contained a certain bias. However, purely from the artistic viewpoint, it is impressive] (Fei 250).

In *A History of Modern Chinese Literature*, Hsia Chih-Tsing 夏志清 (1921–2013) disregards the novel's ideological stance and comments on its subtle portrayal of humanity, declaring that Eileen Chang "was no student of Communist horror in humane rather than dialectical terms, to focus her attention on ordinary humanity as it struggles helplessly to maintain its loyalties and affections under the crushing weight of an alien system" (417). Hu Shi 胡適 (1891–1962) points out the story's theme of hunger and praises its delicate, faithful, gentle, composed and natural characteristics ("Foreword" to *Yangge*). David Der-wei Wang argues that "Chang did not write the novel on behalf of any ideology" ("Foreword" to *Yangge* VIII) and analyzes the novel's hunger motif on different levels. He also claims that recent historical studies have revealed that at least thirty million Chinese people died between 1958 and 1962 from the famine caused by Maoist ideology. When Chang wrote the novel, "she had neither the intention nor the resources to predict the forthcoming horrors, but in an uncanny way her novel foretold the cruel absurdities that would soon be imposed on the Chinese" ("Foreword" to *Yangge* XXIV). Su Weizhen 蘇偉貞, a Taiwanese critic, however, meticulously elaborates the tale's hunger motif according to the "actual sources" Chang recounted in the "Afterword" of *Yangge*.

In the "Afterword" of *Yangge*, Chang ironically exposes the fictitiousness of her sources by attempting to assert their authenticity: 「『秧歌』裡面的人物雖然都是虛構的, 事情卻都是有根據的。」 [Though the characters in *Yangge* are fictional, the events are based on actual sources] (*Yangge* 193). She claims that she read a story about "a peasant uprising" published in *Renmin wenxue* 《人民文學》 (*People's Literature*) by a young writer whose name she cannot recall. Other "actual sources" to which she refers include an experience told by a young girl who ate rice gruel and long grass in the village; rumors about intellectuals who brought large amounts of money with them to purchase food while working in the rural communities; gossip about peasants borrowing small amounts of money from each other; a hardly noticeable newspaper report on famine relief in Tianjin, about which she asked several people who claimed they did not see it; and a leftist propagandist film depicting the burning of a grain store, of which she claimed to have forgotten who the director was. These "sources" are far from convincing; their value turns out to be minimal, especially when she reveals the obscurity of those events in her memory. Chang's "Afterword" to *Yangge* was translated into Japanese, but is absent in the English version because of its contradictory messages that ultimately jeopardize its "authenticity."

Chang's "Afterword" to *Yangge* is what Gérard Genette calls a "paratext," which "binds the text properly speaking taken within the totality of the literary work" (64). It is intended to provide the reader with a context and commentary, whether official or not. Based on the ironic tone and skeptical attitude presented in Chang's writings, a double agenda underlying the "Afterword," seen as a part of the fiction, can be discerned. On the one hand, the afterword is a declaration of the authenticity of the events in the novels and the presentation of the sources fulfill the story's rightist mission; on the other hand, Chang exercises her authorial power with some irony to reveal the deception of the so-called realistic events presented in her texts, thus defeating the propagandist messages prescribed for the novels and exploited by different camps of reviewers. Chang's rejection of both propagandist and realistic values imposed on her works by various critics demonstrates her precarious position in between writerly autonomy and political restraints during the writing and translation processes.

Neither specifically adjusted to any particular political position nor adapted from any "actual sources," *The Rice-Sprout Song* and *Yangge* feature characters who struggle to survive in harsh sociopolitical conditions. The body, especially the female body, becomes the locus of both personal and political contestation, as do the relationships of women with other people and the world. Stereotypes of the female body are deconstructed and reconstructed in a way that foregrounds vitality and resourcefulness, and challenges the authenticity of Chinese traditional patriarchal culture. This section examines the revision of the female body in Chang's *The Rice-Sprout Song* and *Yangge*, with Namikawa's Japanese translation as a comparison point to Chang's practice of self-translation.

Gold Root's perspective of Moon Scent's body represents the stereotypical aesthetic ideal of the feminine, as he gazes upon her, and she is described, not only through the image of a newly wedded bride but also as a divine figure: "She made him think of some obscure goddess in a broken-down little temple. He remembered seeing an idol like that sitting daintily behind the tattered and begrimed yellow curtains in a neglected shrine" [她使他想起一個破敗的小廟裡供著的一個不知名的娘娘。他記得看見過這樣一個塑像, 粉白脂紅, 低著頭坐在那灰黯的破成一條條的杏黃神幔裡。 (*RSS* 31–32; *Yangge* 34–35)]. Gold Root imagines Moon Scent as a goddess, with holy qualities in humble circumstances. In *Yangge*, Chang takes advantage of her privileges as author and self-translator to modify the imagery used to describe Moon Scent, choosing the Chinese phrase "buzhiming de niangniang" 「不知名的娘娘」 to translate the English phrase "obscure goddess." In the Chinese context, "buzhiming" means "unknown," while "niangniang" can be used to refer to an elderly woman, a respectable woman, or an immortal with divine power, associated with a female idol in a Chinese temple. In the English context, the phrase "obscure goddess" is rather ambiguous, and may remind Anglophone readers of a Greek goddess. In both versions of the story, Moon Scent is described in a manner that perpetuates the idealized imagery of the female body in either Chinese or Western cultures, and in so doing authenticates the female body as both a corporeal substance and a spiritual essence.

The meaning of Yuexiang 月香 or Moon Scent's name contrasts to that of her husband Jingen 金根 or Gold Root. Their Chinese names are not written in the English version in *pinyin* or romanization, but are translations that carry with them certain images and meanings. Moon Scent's name is abstract, because scent does not have a physical or tangible manifestation, while Gold Root's name contains a concrete and literally down-to-earth image. The divine beauty of Moon Scent's body is also juxtaposed with the carnal physicality of Gold Root's body. For instance, when Moon Scent offers a cake to Gold Root, "in the candlelight she saw that his hand that held the cake was trembling. There was a moment of absolute stillness in her mind, followed by a rush of anger and tenderness" [在燭光中，她看見他捏著餅的手顫抖得很厲害。她先還不知道那是飢餓的緣故，等她明白過來的時候，心裏突然像潮水似地漲起一陣憤怒與溫情。 (*RSS* 37; *Yangge* 40)]. Where the English text describes "a moment of absolute stillness in her mind," the Chinese version adds more details of what Moon Scent understands: 「她先還不知道那是飢餓的緣故，等她明白過來的時候 … 」 [She did not know it was because of hunger. Then when she understood ...] The Chinese version is a close translation of the English version apart from the addition of Moon Scent's realization of Gold Root's suffering from severe hunger, thus underscoring Gold Root's realistic bodily need and the scarcity of food in the village. However, even later, when Moon Scent has been living in the hunger-stricken village for a while, she remains beautiful without showing signs of weakness, which suggests her extraordinary ability to survive in a difficult situation.

This idealized image of Moon Scent, however, is put into question by her pragmatic personality. For example, when the Tan family is having dinner, Moon Scent secretly takes some vegetables: "Moon Scent scarcely touched the vegetable. It was unseemly for a woman to be too interested in tasty things. But when Gold Root turned to refill his bowl she quickly took some of it, twice" [月香幾乎碰都沒碰那鹹菜。彷彿一個女人總不應當饞嘴，人家要笑

話的。但是金根吃完了一碗，別過身去盛粥的時候，她很快地夾了些菜，連夾了兩筷。 (*RSS* 59; *Yangge* 62)]. The Chinese version adds the phrase 「人家要笑話的」 [people will laugh at her], indicating Moon Scent's concern about other people's perception of her. Her constraining herself from openly taking the vegetables reflects the social taboo of women's self-fulfillment, and serves as a reminder that women tend to suffer from physical deprivation to remain obedient to men (fathers, husbands, and sons) – a manifestation of social control over the female body in terms of constantly deferred desire for material food and, by extension, spiritual food. In famine-stricken families, women are supposed to yield food to men and children. In Western culture, gluttony, or overindulgence in eating, is one of the seven deadly sins specifically mentioned in the Bible, and this taboo applies to people of all genders. Moon Scent's daring move can be seen as a slight transgression of the virtue of self-restraint that is deeply rooted in both Chinese and Western cultures, thus showing her practical strategy for survival and challenging the authenticity of the idealized image imposed on women.

Instead of a poor hungry woman, Moon Scent appears to be the most resourceful member of her family, and in this way she becomes a new image of Chinese femininity. While working in Shanghai for three years, she plays the role of breadwinner in the family. Her working experience makes her not only financially empowered but also culturally superior to her husband Gold Root. Gold Root recalls an unpleasant experience he had when he visited her in Shanghai and was treated as if he were an unwelcome guest, looked down upon by the modern city dwellers: "His heart was a trodden and squashed thing that stuck to the bottom of his soles. He wished he had never come to the city" [他的心是一個踐踏的稀爛的東西，黏在他鞋底上。不該到城裏來的。 (*RSS* 25; *Yangge* 27)]. The second sentence in the Chinese text has no subject, which is possible in Chinese syntax. In this context, the psychological activity belongs to Gold Root, whose heart is figuratively detached from his body, a symbol of the blows to his dignity from his inability to earn a living for his family, his feelings of inadequacy over his inability to fulfill his role in the family, and his lower social status. Moon Scent's considerable economic superiority destabilizes the conventional power relations between wife and husband, and therefore repudiates the authenticity of the stereotypical depiction of women as culturally and financially inferior that is often seen in mainstream May Fourth literature, such as Lu Xun's 魯迅 "Zhufu" 〈祝福〉 ("New Year Sacrifice," 1924), Rou Shi's 柔石 "Wei nuli de muqin" 〈爲奴隸的母親〉 ("Slave Mother," 1930), and Xiao Hong's 蕭紅 *Shengsiqiang* 《生死場》 (*The Field of Life and Death*, 1935).

AUTHENTICITY RECONSIDERED

The female body, however, is still vulnerable to violence, as demonstrated by Gold Root's attack on Moon Scent, provoked by his feelings of inferiority: "Suddenly she felt her hair grabbed from behind. Gold Root slapped her right and left and she kicked and fought back wildly" (*RSS* 120); in Chinese, the passage reads, 「她突然覺得一陣疼痛，頭髮被人一把抽住了，往後面一拖。金根連接幾個耳刮子，打得她眼前發黑。她拼命掙扎著, 悶聲不響地踢他, 咬他。」 [She suddenly felt a burst of pain, and someone grabbed her head and dragged her back. Jingen snapped her a few times, which made her eyes roll back. She used all her might to struggle, silently kicked him, bit him] (*Yangge* 129). Gold Root exercises his power over Moon Scent's body, granted to him by patriarchal culture and greater physical strength. Domestic abuse is often depicted in Chinese literature as a social convention; for instance, Xi Menqing 西門慶 legitimately beats his wives several times in *Jinpingmei* 《金瓶梅》 (*The Plum in a Golden Vase*, c. 1610), a text that both constructs and perpetuates men's power over women's bodies. In response to Gold Root's displays of chauvinism, Moon Scent resists fiercely but in silence, a reaction that transgresses the stereotype of the passive, weak, and inferior woman. The actual strength of her body is emphasized here as well. The Chinese version preserves the couple's fighting as in the English text, but their conflict is depicted in more detail than in the source, and Moon Scent appears stronger and more furious.

Moon Scent's experience of physical assault is immediately followed by a detailed description of the slaughtering of a pig. Just as Gold Root attacks Moon Scent from behind, the peasants attack the pig from the back: "Suddenly it uttered a loud cry – one of Big Uncle's neighbors had grabbed it by its hind legs. Somebody else came to help drag it, and presently it was turned on its back, lying on a raised wooden frame" (*RSS* 125); in Chinese, the passage reads, 「忽然之間，牠大叫起來了——有人拉牠的後腿。牠叫著，叫著，索性人來得更多了，兩三個人七手八腳捉住了牠。」 [Suddenly, it screamed, and someone pulled its hind legs. It screamed, screamed, and more people came, and two or three people caught it with seven hands and eight feet] (*Yangge* 134). The Chinese translation/rewriting emphasizes the sound of the victim being butchered, and both versions juxtapose Moon Scent's beating with the pig's slaughter to underscore the vulnerability of both the female and the animal body.

Moon Scent's body is compared to that of an animal; and, just as animals are generally considered lesser beings than humans, women occupy a lesser status than men in the traditional Chinese gender hierarchy. The pig's feet are explicitly compared to a Chinese woman's bound feet: "The little snow-white ankle ending in a tiny pink sole looked as if it belonged to a woman with bound feet, where the toes were all bunched together" [那雪白的腿腕，紅紅的攢聚的腳心，很像從前的女人的小腳。] (*RSS* 126; *Yangge* 135). Though the English version more obviously makes this comparison, the Chinese version describes the pig's feet as resembling 「從前的女人的小腳。」 (women's small feet in the old days), with rather nostalgic and aesthetic connotations. Chang's posthumously published story "Yixiangji" 〈異鄉記〉 ("A Record of Foreign Land" (2010) similarly includes a description of the butchering of a live pig. Chang probably wrote "Yixiangji" during her trip to Wenzhou (Y. Song, "Guanyu 'Yixiangji'" 196) to seek Hu Lancheng, who was in exile in 1946. Her experience in the countryside provided valuable inspiration for her fictional depictions of rural life. Taiwanese writer Li Ang 李昂, who describes herself as a loyal fan of Chang, also uses the metaphor of butchering a pig as a parallel to the rape of a woman in her novel *Shafu* 《殺夫》 (*The Butcher's Wife*, 1983). Li's story ends with the victimized woman murdering her husband, like butchering a pig, as an act of revenge and a subversion of the male enactment of violence on the female body.

Although women's rights have been advocated in China since the May Fourth Movement and have been enshrined in law by the Communist government, the authenticity of these actions has been challenged by traditional Chinese patriarchal and patrilineal culture. Women seem on the surface to have been emancipated from the traditional feudal system, but underneath the modern reforms are another, but a different, patriarchal system: that of Communism. In the story, after Gold Root marries off Gold Flower, Big Aunt criticizes Gold Flower's mother-in-law, calling her a bad-tempered woman. Gold Root points out the establishment of the Women's Association that is supposed to protect women's interests, but this only reminds the Tan family of the mistreatment of one particular woman:

> They all remembered the case of that woman in Peach Creek Village who had gone to complain of cruel treatment by her in-laws, asking for a divorce. She was tied up to a tree and beaten with a rod by the *kan pu*, who was old-fashioned enough not to take the New Marriage Law too seriously.
> *RSS* 20

> 他們大家都記得桃溪的那個女人，到村公所去告她婆婆虐待，請求離婚。被幹部把她綑在樹上打了一頓，送回婆家去。
> *Yangge* 23

Chang closely translates this episode, but adds the rationale of the "*kan pu*" 幹部 [cadre] for Anglophone readers, and in so doing highlights the discrepancy between the New Marriage Law and the social practices and ideology of law enforcement in mainland China in the early 1950s. The male cadres continued to exercise patriarchal control over women, not through the traditional feudal system, but, ironically, through the so-called Women's Association, so that the female body also becomes a site of sociopolitical contestation.

The Chinese version translates only these ideas about the maltreatment of the woman by her in-laws and the cadres, eliminating much of the English text's elaboration of the Chinese cultural perspective on the authenticity of the Communist government's new measures. Thus, this presentation of the psychology of the villagers depicted in the English version is omitted in the Chinese translation:

> The people in the villages had previously been frightened by propaganda spread by the old government about the sharing of wives under Communist rule, the loose morals and easy divorces. So they were greatly reassured by the measures taken by this *kan pu* to uphold the old standards. Of course it was a most improper thing to do to ask for a divorce.
>
> *RSS* 20

The prevailing patriarchal beliefs about the lesser position of women in a feudal family are fully explained in the English text, making the critical tone apparent. When the story is recontextualized in Chinese, the villagers' mindset is expected to be understood by the Chinese reader, and thus it is unnecessary to express it openly. The absence of the male-dominated mindset in this version paradoxically mocks the old rules that, under the new regime, are taken for granted.

The female body is given multiple meanings in this episode. First of all, in personal and gendered terms, Gold Root beats Moon Scent to claim his right over her body as granted by patriarchal discipline, and her retaliation shows her female desire for control over her own body. On an economic level, their fight is provoked by Gold Root's anger over Moon Scent's stronger financial position. After he has declared his inability to donate food or money to the militia's families, as we have seen, she surrenders her secret money to Comrade Wong, which humiliates Gold Root, who is supposed to be the most resourceful person in the household. On a social level, their fighting over money and food shows the scarcity of resources and the physical suffering of peasants in China in the 1950s. On an ideological level,[5] their position also comments

---

5 As Terry Eagleton points out in *Ideology: An Introduction*, ideology may signify "ideas and beliefs which help to legitimate the interests of a ruling group or class specifically by distortion and dissimulation" (30). It may function to "unify a social formation in ways convenient for its rulers; that is not simply a matter of imposing ideas from above but of securing the complicity of subordinated classes and groups, and so on" (30).

upon the Communist ideological position on hunger: hunger not only makes people realize their class status and thus drives them into revolution, but it also tests people's ability to endure the hardship that is inevitable during the Communist revolution. In a religious sense, in both Buddhist and Christian doctrines, the endurance of hunger signifies the disciples' capability to transform the desire of their corporeal bodies into spiritual power (Wang, "Foreword to *Yangge*" XIX).[6]

From her critical perspective, Moon Scent observes the self-censorship the peasants have imposed on themselves, and, contrary to official propaganda, recognizes the true results of the Land Reform Movement in the city and the village. Upon her arrival from Shanghai, the Tan family defends the weather and crops, an action that contradicts the peasants' constant complaining in the past, meant as protection against jealous gods or exploitation by the government and landlords. While her family members are praising the crops that are supposed to be good after the Land Reform Movement, Moon Scent despises their exaggeration and questions the cultural myth of the redistribution of land in the village:

> She whispered, "Everybody said it is good in the country, good in the country, good in the country. The cities are poor now and people cannot afford servants, but they do not allow employers to dismiss servants. So my employer was always telling me, 'It is good now in the country. If I were you I would go home and work on the land.' Now I realize I have been fooled."
>
> *RSS* 38

> 她低聲說，『人人都說鄉下好，鄉下好。現在城裏是窮了，差不多的人家都僱不起傭人。又不許東家辭傭人。所以我們那東家老是告訴我，「現在你們鄉下好嘍！我要是你，我就回鄉下去種田。」現在我才曉得，上了當了！』
>
> *Yangge* 42

The English version repeats the phrase "good in the country" three times to emphasize the intensity of the rumour, while the Chinese version only repeats the phrase twice. Moon Scent rejects the authenticity of the propaganda that the government promotes and the city dwellers and villagers believe. She also considers earning her own livelihood more important than being with Gold

---

6 See David Der-Wei Wang's Foreword to *The Rice-Sprout Song* for a thorough analysis of the ideological meaning of hunger.

Root, thus privileging financial security over marriage. Her pragmatic personality, on the one hand, repudiates the stereotype of a sentimental and weak woman who depends on her husband's support and, on the other hand, constructs the image of a self-sufficient woman who is capable of reason.

The political troubles Moon Scent encounters not only make her aware of her physical body, but also allow her to translate her corporeal experience into mental activity; for instance, when she and Gold Root escape the militia, "she was conscious of her body as never before, feeling naked and vulnerable all over. But it could not be really serious, she felt, when they were running hand in hand like children in a game" (*RSS* 150). On one level, when her corporeal body is in danger, Moon Scent becomes more conscious of its existence and vulnerability, something to which she has not paid much attention generally. On another level, in her mind, she re-imagines the experience of escape as a children's game, which transforms her dangerous situation and anxiety about being killed into a more bearable experience of childhood. In the Chinese translation, the description is more metaphorical than in the English text:

> 她從來沒有像這樣自己覺得有一個身體，彷彿渾身都是風颼颼地暴露在外面，展開整大塊的柔軟的平面，等待著被傷害。 但是同時又有一個相反的感覺，覺得不會當真被傷害，因為它們這樣手牽手跑著; 像孩子在玩一種什麼遊戲。
> *Yangge* 164

> She has never felt she has a body as now, feeling like her whole body were frostily displaying outside, spreading a huge piece of soft horizontal dimension, and waiting to be hurt. However, in the meantime, she has a contradictory feeling, feeling that she would not really be hurt, because they were running hand in hand, like children playing a game.

In the English version, Moon Scent's awareness of her physical body is simply described as "feeling naked and vulnerable all over," and the workings of her mind are condensed into the two words "she felt." The Chinese translation, however, appears more figurative and sophisticated than the English text, partly thanks to Chang's greater familiarity with the Chinese language and her fuller understanding of Chinese culture. Most importantly, when the story is recontextualized in the Chinese language, the Chinese concept of the body, which refers simultaneously to the corporeal body, the mind, and one's relationship with other people and the world, is apparent. It is in these ways that *Yangge* oscillates between faithfulness to, and undercutting of, *The Rice-Sprout Song* in its presentation of the authenticity of the female body.

Moon Scent's authentic sensual experience further testifies to her perception of Gold Root's psychological conditions. The touch of Gold Root's hand on Moon Scent's ankle symbolizes their communication at the fleeting moment when he hovers between life and death. After Moon Scent has settled Gold Root under a tree, "The feel of his fingers around her ankle was so real and solid, the moment was so close at hand and yet forever out of reach, it drove her nearly frantic" [他的手指箍在她的腿腕上，那感覺是那樣真確，實在，那一剎那的時間彷彿近在眼前，然而已經是永遠無法掌握了，使她簡直難受得要發狂。 (*RSS* 161; *Yangge* 176)]. Chang's close translation of this scene underscores Moon Scent's "real" bodily experience of Gold Root's tangible touch, which indirectly sends the message to Moon Scent of his hesitation about leaving her. Her feelings about his fingers around her ankle remain even after his disappearance. The authenticity of their physical connection, therefore, metaphorically bespeaks their spiritual connection.

Shijing 《詩經》 (*The Classics of Poetry*) includes the poem 「死生契闊, 與子相悅。 執子之手, 與子皆老。」 [Life, death, separation, with thee there is happiness. Thy hand in mine, we will grow old together], which draws on, while also altering, the image of holding hands to signify love. In Chang's "Qingcheng zhi lian" 〈傾城之戀〉 ("Love in a Fallen City," 1943), Fan Liuyuan 范柳原 recites this poem to his beloved Bai Liusu 白流蘇 to declare his philosophy of love in a skeptical way – life, death, and separation are significant events that human beings cannot control, even though people declare that they would remain together forever as though they could assert such control over their lives (Chang, "LFC" 216). Fan doubts the authenticity of the idea of eternal love presented in this classical Chinese poem and interprets it with a sense of desolation. Chang also mentions this poem in her "Ziji de wenzhang" 〈自己的文章〉 ("Writing of One's Own," 1944). She claims that this is a sad poem, but appreciates its positive attitude towards life ("Ziji de wenzhang" 18). The sentiment of desolation present in "Love in a Fallen City" and "Ziji de wenzhang" can be associated with the meaning of Gold Root's love for Moon Scent in *The Rice-Sprout Song* and *Yangge* during their life-and-death farewell. Though he cannot resist eternal separation from her, he still declares the authenticity of his everlasting love to her through his subtle bodily gesture.

Both versions of the story portray a courageous image of women that is contrary to the traditional Chinese feminine ideal of passivity and humility. After Gold Root's disappearance, Moon Scent audaciously heads home, while a guard reports that he has chased a woman into the fire: "One of them [militiamen] claimed he had seen a woman sneaking away when the blaze first started and he had chased her right into the fire" [內中有一個民兵堅持著說剛起火的時候，他曾經看見一個女人在黑影裏奔跑著，一直把她趕到火

裏去了。] (*RSS* 170; *Yangge* 186–187). The English version uses the phrase "sneaking away," while the Chinese version describes the woman as 「在黑影裏奔跑著」 [running in the shadow]. Although the woman is not explicitly named, it is strongly implied to be Moon Scent; she is represented as unafraid of fighting injustice even at the cost of her own life, rather than as weak or cowardly as women were stereotypically thought to be.

Gold Flower's apparently contradictory behaviour towards her older brother Gold Root is an instance of the nature of humanity fashioned by social values. After they were orphaned at a young age, Gold Root took care of Gold Flower all his life, to the extent of arousing Moon Scent's jealousy. However, when Moon Scent begs Gold Flower to accommodate Gold Root, who is wanted by the government for his offense, Gold Flower first considers the welfare of her husband and her in-laws' family and refuses to help him. The end of *The Rice-Sprout Song* includes a lengthy account of Gold Flower's psychological state which is not present in the Chinese text. When Gold Flower is asked to identify Gold Root's corpse, she is not allowed to show any authentic emotion upon seeing her brother's dead body under political surveillance. However, she is dedicated to him in her heart: "She promised her brother's spirit then and there that she would arrange for the recitation of prayers and also the adoption of a boy child for his heir, that he might be mourned properly" (*RSS* 175). In the face of political oppression, Gold Flower betrays her brother and cares more for her husband and his family's safety. As prescribed by Chinese Confucian doctrines, women are supposed to follow their husbands, and no longer owe allegiance to their birth family. However, Gold Flower's promise toward Gold Root does show her filial piety and her desire to uphold patriarchal tradition by raising a boy to ensure the continuity of his family line. Chang explains this aspect of Chinese ethics and values in her English text for readers who may be unfamiliar with Chinese views of the family. Gold Flower's self-contradictory attitudes towards Gold Root indicate that ordinary people have both flaws and strengths that are shaped by social conventions and cannot be simply categorized as either absolutely good or absolutely bad people; they also form an example of Chang's favourite literary device, the "equivocal contrast."

The English version of the story also describes Moon Scent's dead body in a manner that is omitted in the Chinese translation. In *The Rice-Sprout Song*, to their shock and awe, the villagers find a female corpse as a "seated figure [suggesting] one of the bald, slim images of Arhans lined up on both sides of a temple" (*RSS* 176). Big Aunt speculates that the corpse belongs to Moon Scent, whose former life should be a monk, a characterization that empowers her memory by linking it to a spiritual figure, resembling Jia Baoyu 賈寶玉 as an incarnate monk in *Dream of the Red Chamber*. Big Aunt's imagination also echoes Gold Root's idealization of Moon Scent's image as a goddess in a temple upon her arrival from Shanghai. However, in contrast to the idealized eulogy over Moon Scent's body, the wild dogs in the cemetery fight over eating her, a brutal deconstruction of Big Aunt's hagiographical image. Big Aunt then provides a secular perspective on Moon Scent's body: "She certainly can't do anybody any harm," she thought, "if she can't even protect her own bones" (*RSS* 178–179). Big Aunt's incoherent comments release her from the psychological burden of fearing that Moon Scent would come after her with magical power, and also repudiate the authenticity of the idealized woman as a spiritual figure imposed on Moon Scent.

Chang creates several mysteries near the ending of the story so as to let readers reconsider the authenticity of the narrative she claims in the "Afterword" of *Yangge*. For instance, the discovery of Gold Root and Moon Scent's dead bodies is absent from the Chinese text. It is implied that Gold Root has drowned himself, but no evidence has been found to prove it; similarly, Moon Scent is not openly mentioned after her return to the village. Based on the description of her individualistic and shrewish personality, it is not difficult for the reader to relate the "woman" mentioned by the militiaman to Moon Scent. However, the uncertainty within the story is significant: the report given by the guard without identifying the woman may not be reliable, even if the reader trusts his claim. All these uncertainties, on the one hand, work to challenge the authenticity of the events narrated in the story and the authoritative tone of the narrator. On the other hand, they leave readers more space for their imagination and also help to soften the impact of the story. This transformation in the Chinese translation corresponds to Chang's philosophy of desolation, which she discusses in "Ziji de wenzhang" ("Writing of One's Own" 18), as offering a moderate comparison rather than a sharp contrast of extremities.

Though Chang wrote *The Rice-Sprout Song* and *Yangge* when she worked for the USIS, I join others in arguing that she deliberately blurred the identities of different political groups, thus defeating the novels' anti-Communist message. Moreover, the "Afterword" of *Yangge* skillfully subverts the authenticity of the events narrated in the two texts, pointing to aesthetic, rather than political concern, driving Chang's fictional world. Written neither to promote any single ideology nor in a realistic style, these two versions of the story simultaneously present and challenge stereotypes of the female body in Chinese and Western cultures. Chang, in general, closely translated *The Rice-Sprout Song* into *Yangge* with slight modifications. The Chinese culture highlighted in *The Rice-Sprout Song* provokes an open critique from a new perspective, while the re-evaluation of Chinese customs in *Yangge* paradoxically shows its legitimacy in Chinese society, making the novel's mocking tone more apparent.

The figurative elaborations in the Chinese version show Chang's mastery of the Chinese language and understanding of Chinese culture, as well as the Chinese concept of the body implied in the language itself. The omission from *Yangge* of the discovery of Gold Root and Moon Scent's bodies reshapes the story to produce a greater sense of desolation. The Chinese translation oscillates between faithfulness toward, and betrayal of, the English version, as well as of traditional representations of the female body in Chinese and Western thought, thus showing the possibilities of challenging patriarchal ideologies and establishing new feminist territory.

CHAPTER 13

Postmodern Intertextuality: *Chidi zhi lian* 《赤地之戀》 (*The Romance of the Redland*) and *Naked Earth – A Novel about China*

Postmodern intertextuality intermingles the literary world and social reality. While traces of the past can be seen in fiction interwoven with history, the past is constructed through the text, whether fictional or historical; as Linda Hutcheon argues in *A Poetics of Postmodernism*, "[T]he intertexts of history and fiction take on parallel status in the parodic reworking of the textual past of both the 'world' and literature. The textual incorporation of these intertextual pasts as a constitutive structural element of postmodernist fiction functions as a formal marking of historicity – both literary and 'worldly'" (124). Hutcheon points out the constitutive aspects of postmodernist fiction in the making of both fictional and historical worlds. In the case of Eileen Chang's historical novels and self-translation, the intertextuality of fiction and history creates potentially heterogeneous and infinite transformations and interpretations of hegemonic discourses.

This chapter discusses Chang's Chinese novel *Chidi zhi lian* 《赤地之戀》 (*The Love of Redland*, 1954; hereafter cited as CDZL) and her self-translation into English as *Naked Earth – A Novel about China* (1956; hereafter cited as NE). It argues that both *Chidi zhi lian* and *Naked Earth* demonstrate a postmodern intertextuality. By paradoxically using the rhetorical form of parody to "emphasize" the conventional trust in truth and to "overthrow" the idea of correspondence between the authenticity and worth of a novel, Chang establishes an intertextual relation between fiction and reality in her novels. This chapter studies the construction of the female body as a site of sociopolitical contestation in *Chidi zhi lian* and *Naked Earth*. It discusses the pre-determination of the novels' plot and certain publication issues, and focuses specifically on the construction of the female body in both versions of the story, with reference to political dissatisfaction and self-destruction as political protest.

The title of the Chinese version, *Chidi zhi lian*, refers to the love of the Redland, to the love affairs of Liu with Erh Nu, Ko Shan, and Huang Juan (Su Nan) under the Communist regime, and to Chinese people's love for their country (Kao, *Zhang Aling xue* 207). The title of the English translation is *Naked Earth: A Novel about China*, with the reference to nakedness alluding to the exploitation

© JESSICA TSUI-YAN LI, 2025 | DOI:10.1163/9789004730052_015

POSTMODERN INTERTEXTUALITY

of the land, and by extension, the country and the people living on it. The subtitle is a marketing device that emphasizes the novel's Chinese ethnographic credentials for Anglophone readers outside the country.

The two versions of the tale are both set during the early years of the Chinese Communist regime, from "Tudi gaige yundong" 土地改革運動 (the Land Reform Movement, 1948–1950), "Kangmei yuanchao yundong" 抗美援朝運動 (Resist America, Aid Korea, 1954–1958), and "Sanfan yundong" 三反運動 (the Three-Antis Movement, 1951) – "fan tan" 反貪 (anti-corruption), "fan langfei" 反浪費 (anti-waste), and "fan fubai" 反腐敗 (anti-bureaucracy) – to the end of the Korean War (1950–1953).

Narrated from the viewpoint of Liu Ch'uen 劉荃, the story follows a group of university graduates travelling to a northern village for land reform work. Living with the family of the honest landlord Tang, Liu is attracted to Tang Zhankui's 唐占魁 daughter Erh Nu 二妞, and vice versa. Though no feudal exploiting landlord can be found in the village, the cadres brutally humiliate and kill a number of landlords, including Tang. Liu not only fails to save the innocent Tang, but also believes that he has killed Tang himself as a form of self-protection amidst political turmoil. Having become totally disillusioned with the Communist myth, Liu and his colleague Huang Juan 黃絹 (renamed Su Nan in the English version) find a common bond and fall in love with each other.

During the Resist America, Aid Korea campaign, Liu is assigned to participate in propagandist work in Shanghai. On his first day of work, he is caught in a struggle over a material possession, a desk, between two senior female cadres, Zhou Yubao 周玉寶 (renamed Chu Ya-mei in the English version) and Lai Xiuying 賴秀英 (renamed Ma in the English version). He also meets a senior female cadre, Ko Shan 戈珊, who suffers from tuberculosis, but because of her devotion to the Communist Party in her youth, pays for her own medicine in return. Ko orders Liu to fabricate evidence against the United States and seduces him during their work. Having been betrayed by Ko, Liu breaks up with her and reunites with Huang/Su, who is then assigned to work as a reporter in Shanghai after a temporary job in Jinan 濟南.

When the Three-Antis Movement begins, Liu's supervisor, Zhao Chu 趙楚 (renamed Tsui Ping in the English translation) is betrayed by his best friend Cui Ping 崔平 (renamed Liang Po in the English translation) and executed. Associated with Zhao/Tsui, Liu is sent to jail. Ko sets Huang/Su up to become a mistress of a senior male cadre in order to obtain Liu's release from prison. After learning of Huang/Su's sacrifice for his sake, Liu joins the army to fight in the Korean War, hoping to use physical wounds to mask his psychological injuries. When the war is over, Liu is taken as a hostage, and then decides to return to China to pursue anti-Communist underground work.

Like *The Rice-Sprout Song* and *Yangge*, *Chidi zhi lian* was allegedly commissioned by the Hong Kong branch of the United States Information Service (USIS). Chang then translated it into English under the title *Naked Earth*, retaining its basic plot but making significant alterations to certain details in the story. The plot of *Chidi zhi lian* was for this reason said to be pre-determined. For example, in "Siyu Zhang Ailing" 〈私語張愛玲〉 ("Private Words with Eileen Chang," 1976), Song Qi 宋淇 (Lin Yiliang 林以亮, 1919–1996), a translator who had worked at the Hong Kong branch of the USIS, claims that 「(《赤地之戀》的) 大綱是別人擬定的, 不由她自由發揮, 因此寫起來不十分順手。」 [*Chidi zhi lian*'s plot was pre-determined; she was forbidden to freely develop it. Therefore, she found it difficult to write] (Lin 114). In "Chan–Yefang Zhang Ailing" 〈蟬——夜訪張愛玲〉 ("Cicada–Visit Eileen Chang at Night"), Taiwanese literary critic Shuijing 水晶 similarly claims:

> 她主動告訴我:『赤地之戀』是在『授權』 (Commissioned) 的情形下寫成的, 所以非常不滿意, 因為故事大綱已經固定了, 還有什麼地方可供作者發揮的呢?
>
> SHUIJING 27

She took the initiative to tell me: *Chidi zhi lian* was written under commission; therefore, she was very dissatisfied with it. Since the plot was fixed, was there still any room for the author to develop it?

Contrary to the views of both Song Qi and Shuijing that the plot of *Chidi zhi lian* was pre-determined, Richard McCarthy, the director of the Hong Kong branch of the USIS, declared in an interview[1] many years later that the USIS hired Chang to translate American literature. It was Chang herself who suggested writing novels and who had offered the basic ideas of their plots:

> 她是作家, 你不能規定或提示她如何寫作。不過, 因我們資助她, 難免會詢問進度。她會告訴我們故事大要, 坐下來與我們討論。
>
> KAO 241

She is a writer; you cannot restrict or give hints to her how to write. However, since we sponsored her, we could not avoid asking about her progress. She would tell us the plot summary and sat down to discuss it with us.

---

1 McCarthy spoke in English in the interview, and the interviewer, Kao Chuan C. 高全之, translated and recorded the conversation in his Chinese book *Zhang Ailing xue.*

POSTMODERN INTERTEXTUALITY

Both sides of the debate over the plot of *Chidi zhi lian* sound possible, but both only just fall short of bias. Since the USIS aimed to curb the spread of Communism in the world, it supported writers who produced anti-Communist projects. Under the sponsorship of the USIS, the agents may well have attempted to divert *Chidi zhi lian*'s development, according to the USIS's policies, during their discussions with Chang, though McCarthy has not admitted if this was true. However, even if the design of *Chidi zhi lian*'s plot had been interfered with, Chang as the author still retained certain creative power in the writing process of the novel, rather than being left powerless, as Shuijing had suggested. The plot of *Chidi zhi lian* can therefore be said to be situated in a state of in-betweenness, a condition resulting from the power struggle between the USIS's political demands and Chang's personal preferences.

Chidi zhi lian was first published by Tianfeng chubanshe 天風出版社, a Hong Kong publisher, in 1954, while *Naked Earth* was published by Union Press, also a Hong Kong publisher, in 1956, after Chang had moved to the United States in the previous year. Kashiwa Kensaku 柏謙作 translated the story into Japanese, based on the English version, with reference to the Chinese text, as *Akai Koi* 《赤い恋》; the Japanese translation was published by Seikatsusha 生活社 in 1955. The Hong Kong Union Press was formed by a group of young people who liked neither the Chinese Communist Party nor the Chinese Nationalist Party. Yan Guilai 燕歸來 (邱然 Maria Yen), a member of this group, wrote the Preface to *Naked Earth* (Gao 242–243). The sale figures for the Chinese version were reasonable; however, sales of the English translation were low, perhaps in part because of its poor print quality, as Song Qi has suggested.

The unsatisfactory sales of both versions of the story, in fact, were due not only to the print quality of the novels, but also to their poor reception. Since the novels communicated a prescribed anti-Communist message, some critics from mainland China denounced them. For instance, in "Sending Far Away to Eileen Chang" 〈遙寄張愛玲〉, Ke Ling 柯靈 criticizes the novels' unrealistic depictions of their characters and settings:

> 《秧歌》和《赤地之戀》的致命傷在于虛假，描寫的人、事、情、境，全都似是而非，文字也失去作者原有的美。無論多大的作家，如果不幸陷于虛假，就必定導致在藝術上繳械。
>
> Ke 25

Yangge and *Chidi zhi lian*'s fatal flaw is fictitiousness; their depicted characters, events, feelings, and environment may appear to be true and yet are false, their language also loses the writer's original beauty. No matter how great the writer is, [the works] will yield their weapons artistically if [they] unfortunately fall into fictitiousness.

Ke further argues that Chang had no rural experience and thus failed to reflect rural life in her novels. However, biographical studies of Chang have pointed out that she had stayed in rural areas near Wenzhou 溫州, while visiting her then-husband Hu Lancheng 胡蘭成 in exile. She also joined the Land Reform Movement and worked in a suburban area near Shanghai for a few months (Feng 391; Xiao 171). Nevertheless, Ke judges *Yangge* and *Chidi zhi lian* based on the assumption that they were not good works because they could not truly reflect Chinese reality. However, novels are creative works that are positioned somewhere between fictional and real worlds, narrated from writers' specific sociohistorical perspectives. It is, therefore, unfair to make judgments on *Chidi zhi lian* based on its degree of purported authenticity alone.

In her Preface to *Chidi zhi lian*, Chang says that a story will probably be highly appreciated if the author declares its authenticity: 「其實一個故事的真假當然與它的好壞毫無關係。」 [In fact, whether a story is true or false of course is totally unrelated to its quality] (*CDZL* 3). She then ironically asserts a belief in truth: 「不過我確是愛好真實到了迷信的程度。」 [However, I really love truth to the extent of being superstitious] (*CDZL* 3). Chang's claims about the irrelevancy of the relationship between authenticity and a novel's value seem to contradict her almost-religious preference for truth. Her self-undermining declaration, in fact, parodies the general belief in truth and mocks the criticisms of her novel as fictitious. The double coding of her preface echoes Linda Hutcheon's idea of postmodernism:

> In general terms [postmodernism] takes the form of self-conscious, self-contradictory, self-undermining statement. It is rather like saying something whilst at the same time putting inverted commas around what is being said. The effect is to highlight, or "highlight," and to subvert, or "subvert," and the mode is therefore a "knowing" and an ironic – or even "ironic" – one. Postmodernism's distinctive character lies in this kind of wholesale "nudging" commitment to doubleness, or duplicity.
>
> *The Politics of Postmodernism* 1

In applying Hutcheon's concept of postmodern intertextuality to Chang's preface, I argue that Chang's self-contradictory argument adopts the rhetorical mode of parody to "highlight" the general belief in truth and to "subvert" the idea of equivalence between the authenticity and value of a novel.

Chang further explains her ideas of the intertextual relation between fiction and reality in her novels as follows:

> 『赤地之戀』所寫的是真人真事，但是小說究竟不是報導文學，我除了把真正的人名與一部份的地名隱去, 而且需要把許多小故事疊印在一起, 再經過剪裁與組織。
>
> CDZL 3

> What *Chidi zhi lian* depicts are real people and real events. However, novels are not reporting literature. Apart from hiding some people and places' names, I need to assemble many anecdotes, and tailor and organize them.

Chang's claim of combining reality and fiction, and her practices of editing, reorganizing, and re-creating the events about which she wrote, suggest that readers cannot read her novels as though they are accurate reports of historical events.

Ke's criticism of *Yangge* and *Chidi zhi lian* was perhaps based not only on his assumption about the novels' degree of authenticity, but also on his self-censorship in light of the Communist political circumstances in mainland China. The majority of Chang's works have been revived in mainland China since the late 1980s and early 1990s, but these two novels, with their strong anti-Communist messages, were not included. In a similar vein, but this time because of censorship in Taiwan, the section on Ke's criticism of these two novels was erased from his article "Sending Far Away to Eileen Chang," collected in Zheng Shusen's 鄭樹森 *Zhang Ailing de Shijie* 《張愛玲的世界》 (*Eileen Chang's World*) and published by Taiwanese publisher Yunchen wenhua 允晨文化.

Chidi zhi lian was not only denounced by leftist critics in mainland China, but also censored by rightist publishers in Taiwan. When her complete works, including *Yangge*, were published by the Taiwanese publisher *Huangguan chubanshe* 皇冠出版社 (Crown Publishing Company Ltd.) in the 1960s, *Chidi zhi lian* was not included for political considerations. Ping Xintao 平鑫濤, the publisher of the Crown Publishing Company, noted in an interview:

> 小說中描寫共產黨員辱罵國民黨政府, 甚至對先總統蔣公也頗有譏諷, 在當時的書刊檢查制度下難獲通過, 若大幅刪改那些敏感的部分又傷害了原著的精神, 以出版社的立場而言, 委實兩難。
>
> S. PENG 180

The novel depicts Communist Party members insulting National Party members, and even considerably mocks the former president Mr. Jiang. Under the publication censorship system during that period of time, [the novel] can hardly be approved. If one largely eliminates and revises those sensitive sections, it will harm the original's spirit. From the publisher's standpoint, it is a dilemma.

Having simultaneously received opposition from leftist critics in mainland China and rightist publishers in Taiwan, *Chidi zhi lian* is situated in an ambivalent position between the different political stances of the Chinese Communist Party and the Chinese Nationalist Party.

Chidi zhi lian was later republished by two Taiwanese publishers: Huilong chubanshe 慧龍出版社 in 1978 and Huangguan chubanshe 皇冠出版社 (Crown Publishing Company) in 1991, but with slight alterations to the text, based on political concerns; for instance, the name of the former president of the Republic of China, Chiang Kai-shek 蔣介石, was removed from the Taiwanese editions. For example, Chiang's name was mentioned in Chapter Seven of the Chinese (Hong Kong) Tianfeng edition and the English Union Press edition:

> 劉荃和機關裡的一個通訊員一同推著一輛囚車，囚車裡是孔同志扮的杜魯門。另一輛囚車裡是張勵扮的*蔣介石*。樂隊的調子一變，杜魯門與*蔣介石*從檻車裡衝了出來，戴著巨大的彩色面具跳跳蹤蹤，像西藏的「跳神」儀式。
>
> *CDZL* 131 [1978]; my emphasis

> Liu helped a Communications Officer push a small prisoner's van with Comrade Ho [in the Chinese version, his surname is Kong] huddled inside it, masked and dressed as President Truman. Chang Li as *Chiang Kai-shek* crouched inside another van, bandaged and plaster-crossed to show the People had defeated him. At the sound of a gong they both crashed up against the bars and pranced around, posturing like Tibetan devil dancers, now threatening, now leaping away frightened. Their bodies dwarfed by their enormous hook-nosed, shiny pink masks that reached down to their chests, they were as jerky and unreal as coloured paper cutouts appliquéd on to the drab, crowded scene.
>
> *NE* 155 [1964]; my emphasis

In the Taiwanese Weilong and Crown editions, "Chiang Kai-shek" 「蔣介石」 was changed into 「反革命」 ["anti-revolutionary"] (*CDZL* 137 [1978]; *CDZL* 122 [2004]). The Crown publisher Ping probably refers to this scene in his claim

POSTMODERN INTERTEXTUALITY

that Chinese Communist Party members insulted Chinese Nationalist Party members in the novel.

Chiang is also mentioned in Chapter Nine of the (Hong Kong) Tianfeng edition and the Union Press edition: 「有一張舊報紙上刊出一張模糊的照片，是他謁見蔣介石呈遞國書的時候拍攝的」 (*CDZL* 172 [1978]; my emphasis) ["[In an old newspaper, a] blurred photo showed him presenting his papers to *Chiang Kai-shek*" (*NE* 202 [1964]; my emphasis)]. In the Taiwanese editions, "Chiang Kai-shek" 「蔣介石」 was changed to 「國民政府的首腦」 [the head of the Nationalist Party] (*CDZL* 178 [1978]; *CDZL* 158 [2004]). Later in the same chapter of the (Hong Kong) Tianfeng edition, Ko Shan 「心裡想如果根據這篇文字就證實黎培里是勾結蔣政府的特務」 ["thinks if [she] used this article, [she would] prove Li Peili was a spy working for *Jiang's government*" (*CDZL* 172 [1978]; my emphasis)]. The English translation was simplified so that this sentence was omitted. In the Taiwanese editions, 「蔣政府」 [Chiang's government] was changed to 「國民政府」 [Nationalist government] (*CDZL* 178 [1978]; *CDZL* 158 [2004]).

The present version of *Chidi zhi lian* is a product of the political struggle of various institutional forces and of Chang's personal preferences. The USIS sponsored Chang to write *Chidi zhi lian* in accordance with its anti-Communist policy; however, her novels do not appeal to any specific political party. The edition of *Chidi zhi lian* available nowadays is the one that was republished and revised by the Taiwanese Crown Publishing Company. Other editions of the Chinese version and the Union edition's *Naked Earth* are not widely available, but can be found in specialized academic libraries at some universities.

Chang might have tried to publish the English version in the United States, but it was never published during her lifetime (Q. Song 115). Even when the University of California Press republished Chang's English novels *The Rice-Sprout Song* and *The Rouge of the North* in 1998, *Naked Earth* was not republished. *Naked Earth* was eventually republished by New York Review Books in 2015. This study draws mainly upon the Crown (2004) and Union (1964) editions. The publication issues and various editions of *Chidi zhi lian* and *Naked Earth* set the politically fraught base for the discussion of postmodern intertextuality in both versions of the story.

Both *Chidi zhi lian* and *Naked Earth* portray the female body as a site of soci-opolitical battlefield. In *Naked Earth*, Ko exercises social and economic power over Liu. For example, in a scene unique to the English text, she pays for the meal when she dines out with him:

> When she called the waiter after they had finished eating and told him "*Cong tang*, close the account," the waiter seemed unsure of whom to

bring the bill. Liu did not like to see Ko Shan do the paying. He knew he ought not be affected by the convention of the old society which always expected a man to pay, but he had a bad moment wondering if the waiter might think he was a kept man, especially as she was older than he.

176 [1964]

Ko's paying for the meal for Liu and herself subverts the social convention that in a patriarchal society, the man is supposed to be the breadwinner and thus is expected to be responsible for expenditures. Since Ko is older than Liu, their dating also destabilizes the general practice of an older man and a younger woman making up a couple. Liu's concern about the waiter's view of him as "a kept man" shows his worries about his social and economic inferiority compared to Ko. In contrast to the Chinese version, the English translation reinterprets Ko as, rather than an object of carnal desire for Liu, a socially and economically self-sufficient subject.

In both *Chidi zhi lian* and *Naked Earth*, Ko uses her power and status to manipulate her male subordinate, while Huang Juan/Su Nan, as a recent university graduate, experiences sexual harassment at the hands of her male supervisor, Chang Li 張勵. When Huang/Su is copying out propaganda, Chang attempts to take advantage of her:

> 他的手就此按在她的肩膀上了 … … 他一面說著, 已經把她按在紙上的左手握在手裡, 但是又被她爭脫了 … … 他又撫摩著她的手, 並且漸漸的順著胳膊往上溜 … … 這一次她很突兀的把手一縮了回去, 跟著就往上一站。
>
> *CDZL* 33 [2004]

> His hand rested on her shoulder ... As he spoke he took her left hand which was resting on the paper. But she withdrew it quickly ... His hand was again on hers, fondling her wrist, sliding up her forearm ... This time she pulled away abruptly and stood up.
>
> *NE* 36 [1964]

Since Huang/Su is situated at the bottom of the political hierarchy, she is easily subjected to sexual exploitation. Chang's hand touches her body again and again to test the limits of her tolerance. Though she is politically inferior, she stands up and protects herself from further humiliation, thus showing her determination to assert control over her body.

Under severe political pressure, Huang/Su and Liu derive strength from loving each other. In *Chidi zhi lian*, their physical contact helps them to form a psychological union against the difficulties they both face:

> 他擁抱著她，這時他知道，只有兩個人在一起的時候是有一種絕對的安全感, 除此以外, 在這種世界上, 也根本沒有別的安全。只要有她在一起，他什麼都能忍受，什麼苦難都能想辦法度過。他一定要好好地照顧她，照顧他自己，他們一定要設法通過這兇殘的時代。
>
> *CDZL* 92 [2004]

> He was hugging her. He knew it then. Only when two people were together, was there an absolute sense of security. Apart from that, in this kind of world, there was basically no other security. Only when she was there, he could bear anything, and find the way to go through anything difficult. He must take good care of her, and take care of himself. They must find the way to pass through this brutal era.

Huang/Su and Liu's bodily caressing of each other becomes emotional strength that is enhanced in the face of danger. Narrating from his patriarchal perspective, Liu is eager to protect Huang/Su and himself from political harm.

In *Naked Earth*, Liu's heroic enthusiasm gives way to his dream of forming a familial bond with Huang/Su:

> They turned to look at each other. Liu could not help thinking that if the smooth mud wall were to tilt back to become the k'ang, and he were to see her face like this every night and every morning, his days would be safely locked in happiness at both ends and it would not matter what happened in between.
>
> 111 [1964]

The English text features peaceful and supportive imagery of a marriage between the two protagonists, rather than Liu's heroic desire to save both of them from danger, though both versions present this passage from Liu's viewpoint. In comparison to his embracing of Huang/Su, Liu regards his flirtation with Ko as a simultaneous dream and nightmare: 「他自己不知道抱得多麼緊，只覺得在黑暗中她壓在他胸膛上，使他不能呼吸，像一個綺麗而恐怖的噩夢。」("[he] did not realize he was holding her too tight.

It seemed to him she was a beautiful and horrible nightmare, sitting heavy on his chest so he could not breathe" (*CDZL* 141 [2004]; *NE* 181 [1964]). This is a close translation except for some differences in sentence structure: the Chinese version presents Liu's feeling first and then provides the metaphor of a nightmare, while the English version presents the metaphor first and then explains it. The young and innocent Huang/Su provides Liu with light and comfort, while the middle-aged and experienced Ko gives him sexual pleasure and excitement.

Liu's relationships with Huang/Su and Ko parody Tong Zhenbao's 佟振保 relationships with Meng Yanli 孟烟鸝 and Wang Jiaorui 王嬌蕊 in Chang's other Chinese novella, "Hong meigui yu bai meigui" 〈紅玫瑰與白玫瑰〉 ("Red Rose and White Rose," 1944; hereafter cited as *RRWR*):

> 振保的生命裡有兩個女人，他說的一個是他的白玫瑰，一個是他的紅玫瑰。一個是聖潔的妻，一個是熱烈的情婦——普通人向來是這樣把節烈兩個字分開來講的。
>
> *RRWR* 130

> In Zhenbao's life, there were two women. He called one his white rose, and the other his red rose. One was a pure wife, the other was a passionate mistress – ordinary people are used to explain these two combined words, pure and passionate, separately.

The Chinese phrase *jielie* 節烈 [pure and passionate] is usually used to describe women who bravely sacrifice themselves in the name of virtuousness. Through postmodern intertextual rhetoric, Chang playfully separates these two words and ironically manipulates their meaning to signify men's entanglements with two different types of women: where Liu's pure white rose is Huang/Su and his passionate red rose is Ko, Tong's white rose is Meng, his red rose Wang.

In "Hong meigui yu bai meigui," Chang sarcastically elaborates on her idea of men's changing attitudes toward the passionate mistress and pure wife through a series of metaphors of metaphors:

> 也許每一個男子全都有過這樣的兩個女人，至少兩個。娶了紅玫瑰，久而久之，紅的變了牆上的一抹蚊子血，白的還是『床前明月光』2; 娶了白玫瑰，白的便是衣服上沾的一粒飯子，紅的卻是心口上一顆硃砂痣。
>
> *RRWR* 130

---

2 The phrase 『床前明月光』 [moonlight in front of the bed] comes from the poem "Jingye shi" 〈靜夜詩〉 ("Thoughts on a Tranquil Night") written by the Chinese poet Li Bai 李白 (701–762) during the Tang Dynasty.

POSTMODERN INTERTEXTUALITY

Maybe every man has had two such women – at least two. Marry a red rose and eventually she'll be a mosquito-blood streak smeared on the wall, while the white one is "moonlight in front of my bed." Marry a white rose, and before long she'll be a grain of sticky rice that's gotten stuck to your clothes; the red one, by then, is a scarlet beauty mark just over your heart.

KINGSBURY, *Love in a Fallen City* 255

The contrasting images of "a mosquito-blood streak smeared on the wall" and "a scarlet beauty mark just over your heart," as well as "moonlight in front of the bed" and "a grain of sticky rice that's gotten stuck to our clothes," supplement the metaphors of "red rose" and "white rose" for the respective stereotypes of passionate mistress and pure wife. The desired but unattainable woman is romanticized, while the reachable woman is demeaned. This technique of intertextual comparison echoes the philosophy of writing that Chang outlines in her essay "Ziji de wenzhang" 〈自己的文章〉 (Writing of One's Own,1944):「我喜歡參差的對照的寫法,因爲它是較近事實的。」[I like writing by way of equivocal contrast because it is relatively true to life (18; Jones 19)]. The "equivocal contrast" between the "red rose" and the "white rose" rhetorically presents the dynamic feelings of Chang's male protagonists, Liu and Tong, toward their respective women in *Chidi zhi lian*/*Naked Earth* and "Hong meigui yu bai meigui."

Considering Huang/Su his desired yet unattainable pure beloved, Liu is worried about the impossibility of their union. In *Chidi zhi lian*, Liu reflects on the institution of marriage under the Chinese Communist regime:

這一類的故事劉荃聽得多了, 常常有年輕的男女一同參加革命, 兩人發生了愛情, 但是男方不能結婚, 需要耐心等待, 慢慢地熬資格。然而事實卻不容許女方等待那樣久。無論她怎樣強硬, 組織上總有辦法『說服』她, 使她嫁給一個老幹部。

CDZL 117 [2004]

He had heard a lot of these kinds of stories. Very often a young man and a young woman joined the revolution together. They fell in love with each other, but the man could not get married. He needed patience to wait and to meet the criteria slowly. However, reality did not allow the woman to wait for so long. No matter how tough she was, the association always had means to "persuade" her, making her marry an old cadre.

Liu's narration is a reminder that at the time, marriage was controlled by the Communist Party; members had to acquire certain qualifications in order to choose their own partners. The arrangement of marriages in Communist

China for political reasons was in many ways similar to the tradition in feudal China of families arranging marriages in order to merge their social and financial power. Young men and women from the lower ranks of the power structure were deprived of their right to marry the person of their choice, so that a union that is meant to be personal became political.

In *Naked Earth*, Liu's reflections on marriage are slightly transformed. The young male cadre's qualification is omitted, and the focus is shifted onto the young female cadre:

> He had heard stories of girl *kan-pu* [cadre] cajoled into marrying old *kan-pu* who had given up much for the Revolution and ought to get their rewards now. Sometimes the girl was engaged already. The Organization would send some Big Old Sister to talk to her, talk and talk and talk, night and day, for days on end. Eventually she had to agree.
>
> 151 [1964]

Since power often lies in the hand of senior male cadres, young women, especially those who are considered beautiful, are manipulated; likewise, young women were often deprived of their choices because of their lack of power in patriarchal society. The Chinese and English versions of this passage complement each other to provide fuller accounts of young male and female cadres' perspectives on the politics of marriage.

Liu's worry about Huang/Su's exploitation comes to fruition when Ko sets her up to become a concubine for an old Communist cadre, Sheng Kai-fu 申凱夫, in order to save Liu's life: 「戈珊介紹她去見他, 本來也就是這意思:『一石殺二鳥,』犧牲了這女孩子, 又救了劉荃。」 [Then she did have some vague idea of killing two birds with one stone – introducing the girl to Sheng and getting Liu out (*CDZL* 204 [2004]; *NE* 304 [1964]). Chang describes Ko's abuse of Huang as 「犧牲」 [sacrificing] in *Chidi zhi lian*, but uses the word "introducing" in *Naked Earth*. Huang/Su's body becomes a token of exchange, a transaction that matches Liu's earlier reflection on the institutionalization of marriage in the Communist economy. Ko's role in framing Huang/Su for bodily exploitation parodies Gu Manlu's 顧曼璐 role in trapping her younger sister Gu Manzhen 顧曼楨 for bearing her husband Zhu Hongcai's 祝鴻才 child by force in Chang's other novel, *Shibachun* 《十八春》 (*Eighteen Springs*, 1950–1951), which was later revised into *Banshengyuan* 《半生緣》 (*Half a Lifelong Romance*, 1968). Both serve as examples of how women in power can manipulate other women who are in inferior positions, and of how the female body becomes a site of sociopolitical contestation.

POSTMODERN INTERTEXTUALITY

Though she is trapped, Huang/Su is determined to sacrifice her body as a token of her love. She struggles between life and death when she visits Liu in prison:

> 她今天很奇怪，她那樣迫切地抱著他的脖子，但是她是冰冷的。
> 她像一個石像掙扎著要活過來，但是一種永久的寂靜與死亡已經
> 沁進她的肌肉裡。他彷彿覺得他是吻著兩瓣白石的嘴唇，又像吻
> 著一朵白玫瑰，花心裡微微吐出涼氣來。
>
> *CDZL* 211 [2004]

> She was very strange today. She was so eager to cuddle his neck, but she was cold. She was like a stone statue struggling to come to life, but a kind of utter stillness and death had already invaded her muscles. He seemed to feel that he was kissing two pieces of stony lips, and also seemed to kiss a white rose, with cold air blowing out gently from its centre.

Her body's liveliness during her temporary union with Liu contrasts with its deadness in her impending sacrifice to Sheng. The beautiful yet unemotional images of "stone statue" and "white rose with cold air" echo the idea of "equivocal contrasts" to which Chang refers in "Writing of One's Own." The "white rose" metaphor in *Chidi zhi lian* is an intertextual reference to that in "Hong meigui yu bai meigui," but with an added sense of lifelessness.

The account of Huang/Su's meeting with Liu in prison is different in *Naked Earth,* with his feelings about her body replaced by her question "'This is all that matters, isn't it? What's between us,' she said. 'Nothing else counts. No matter what happens'" (292 [1964]). She is eager to make sure he will not mind the trading of her body. With dramatic irony, he misunderstands her, thinking she knows about his romantic relationship with Ko: "He did not speak. It must be that she knew now about Ko Shan and him. What else could she mean? She had been seeing Ko Shan to get her help, and Ko Shan must have told her" (292 [1964]). The Chinese version emphasizes the representation of Huang/Su's body from Liu's perspective, while the English version focuses on her interrogation of his thoughts, thus turning her from an object of desire into a subject who takes the initiative to speak her mind and request an answer.

In terms of her self-translation styles, Chang generally translated *Chidi zhi lian* in conjunction with *Naked Earth,* with some omissions and additions due to her considerations of her target audience's linguistic and cultural backgrounds, political censorship, and reconstruction of gender relations. The transformation of the story in the English version highlights the futility of

Huang/Su's sacrifice, as well as the humiliation and pain she has endured, thus presenting her self-destruction as a form of political protest. The final plots of the Chinese and English versions and the Taiwanese editions of the Chinese text are the product of political struggles and of Chang's personal choices. In a similar vein, the female bodies presented in *Chidi zhi lian* and *Naked Earth* are sites of sociopolitical contestation. In the deliberate revision of *Chidi zhi lian* into *Naked Earth*, the women are no longer objects of desire but become subjects protesting against bodily exploitation. These two texts complement each other to reconstruct the female body from wider transcultural perspectives.

CHAPTER 14

Transcultural Hospitality: "A Return to the Frontier" and "Chongfang biancheng" 〈重訪邊城〉

In *On Translation*, Paul Ricœur recognizes the discrepancy between the meanings denoted by different languages, thus leading to the impossibility of an ideally equivalent translation. He defines the ethics of translation as a "linguistic hospitality," which he explains as a phenomenon in which "the pleasure of dwelling in other's language is balanced by the pleasure of receiving the foreign word at home, in one's own welcoming home" (*On Translation* 10). Here I build on Ricœur's idea of "linguistic hospitality" into what I call "transcultural hospitality," which, as I argue, acknowledges the plural and fluid cultural interactions across frontiers, sometimes in harmony and sometimes in conflict. Mutual understanding is achieved by engaging with other cultures and embracing new discourses and knowledge systems into new forms of cultures, which subsequently empowers the individual's continuous self-reconstruction.

This chapter focuses on Eileen Chang's travelogue "A Return to the Frontier" (1963; hereafter cited as "ARTF") and her own translation and rewriting into Chinese as "Chongfang biancheng" 〈重訪邊城〉, 2008; hereafter cited as "CFBC"). I argue that Chang breaks down various boundaries and dichotomies to cultivate "transcultural hospitality" in these works. In particular, she transgresses geopolitical, cultural, linguistic, and personal frontiers in "A Return to the Frontier" and "Chongfang biancheng," both of which retell her experiences travelling from the United States to Taiwan and Hong Kong between October 1961 and March 1962. By adopting the literary techniques of equivocal contrast, cultural and linguistic hybridity, and symbolism, Chang depicts her transcultural imaginary homelands to deconstruct Cold War literary polarization and enrich the complexity of Chineseness. Through the practice of self-translation, Chang produces a "transcultural hospitality" that fosters a sense of hope and cross-cultural understanding and ultimately reconstructs her revolving self.

The titles of the essays refer to Chang's trips to Taiwan and Hong Kong in the early 1960s. In "Chongfang biancheng," Chang says of these two cities that "Tong shi biancheng" 「同是邊城」 [Both are frontiers] ("CFBC" 35). Geographically, the main island of Taiwan is located around 180 kilometres across the Taiwan Strait from the southeastern coast of mainland China, and Hong Kong is situated on mainland China's southern coast on the eastern Pearl River Delta of the South China Sea. In the political arena of the 1960s, Taiwan was

© JESSICA TSUI-YAN LI, 2025 | DOI:10.1163/9789004730052_016

mainly ruled by the Nationalist Party and Hong Kong was ruled by the British government, in contrast to the mainland, which was ruled by the Communist Party. On a personal level, Chang regarded Shanghai as her hometown and lived in the United States, but was visiting Taiwan as a tourist for the first and only time; she also revisited Hong Kong, a place that had once nurtured her literary inspiration, to reconcile with her youthful experience and move on to her middle-aged life.

"A Return to the Frontier" was first published in the biweekly American magazine *The Reporter* on March 28, 1963. Max Ascoli (1898–1978), publisher and editor of *The Reporter*, wrote in its Editorial, "Our belief is in liberalism ... We cannot pursue anti-Communism as an end in itself, and yet there is no greater threat to the human race than the consolidation and spread of Communism" (12). He therefore proclaims that the political agenda of *The Reporter* is to promote American liberalism and to denounce Communism. Chang's essay appears on the surface to conform to this aim, given its account of the contrasts between the more desirable capitalist societies present in Taiwan and Hong Kong and the unpleasantness of Communism on the mainland. However, a closer reading shows that Chang uses her writerly authority to resist American hegemonic dominance by describing her liminal experience and presenting her understanding of both sides in the Cold War.

On her trip to Taiwan, Chang was well-received by Richard McCarthy, the director of the United States Information Services (USIS) at the time, and several Taiwanese literary writers and scholars. The day after she arrived in Taiwan,[1] McCarthy invited her for lunch with his wife and several Taiwanese authors including Kenneth Hsien-yung Pai 白先勇, Chen Ruoxi 陳若曦, Dai Tian 戴天, Hong Zhihui 洪智惠, Ouyang Zi 歐陽子, Wang Wenxing 王文興, Wang Zhenhe 王禎和, Wu Luqin 吳魯芹, and Yin Zhang Lanxi 殷張蘭熙 (Kao, *Zhang Ailing xue* 256; Chen 39–40) in the Suzhou restaurant Shijia 石家 near Ximending 西門町 in Taipei (K. Cao 36). Before she went to Taiwan, Chang read Wang Zhenhe's essay "Gui, Beifeng, Ren" 〈鬼，北風，人〉 ("Ghost, North Wind, Human") and became captivated by Wang's portrayal of the natural landscape and culture of Hualien 花蓮 on the east coast of Taiwan. When Chang arrived in Taiwan, Wang Zhenhe invited her to stay at his mother's house in Hualien and gave her a tour of his hometown.[2] Chen Ruoxi and Yin Zhang

---

1 According to Chen Ruoxi 陳若曦, Richard McCarthy said Eileen Chang would arrive in Taiwan on October 13, 1961, and McCarthy had invited Chang and some Taiwanese scholars for lunch on October 14, 1961 ("Zhang Ailing yipie" 39).

2 In their daily conversation, Eileen Chang spoke in Japanese with Wang Zhenhe's mother (Huang, *Hong Kong Connections*; 241).

Lanxi came along as companions for a short while. Together with Richard McCarthy and his wife, they watched the Taiwanese aboriginal performance of "Kiloma'an" 阿美族豐年祭 ("Ami Harvest Festival") in Hualien.[3]

After "A Return to the Frontier" was published in the United States, several Taiwanese writers and critics were disappointed. For instance, in an interview, Wang Zhenhe points out that Shuijing 水晶 disagreed with Chang about her reference in the essay's title to Taiwan as a "frontier," because doing so would symbolically position mainland China as the centre and relegate Taiwan to a marginal status. Shuijing also questioned Chang's mention of bedbugs in Taiwan. Wang Zhenhe said he had the same reaction under the influence of Shuijing's "patriotic stimulation" and then wrote a letter to Chang to protest these issues. In response to the question of bedbugs, Chang humorously wrote, 「臭蟲可能是大陸撤退到台灣帶來的。」 [Perhaps the bedbugs were brought to Taiwan during the retreats from the mainland] (Y. Qiu 4–5). Chang made notable expansions and transformation to her Chinese translation of ARTF[4] and continued to revise CFBC in 1983.[5] She might not respond to those negative comments per se, but in fact to the changing political situation of the time. Through self-translation and rewriting, Chang situates her experience of Taiwan and Hong Kong on the inside and the outside, and in so doing destabilizes the rigid boundaries of the Cold War polarization.

Chang subtly revises the naming of "Formosa" as "Taiwan" in her self-translation as a way to unpack Western imperialism and colonialism. In "A Return to the Frontier," she uses the name "Formosa," from the Portuguese "Ilha Formosa," meaning "Beautiful Island" (*Britannica: History of Taiwan*), first used in 1517 by the crew of a Portuguese ship passing through the Taiwan Strait, and later used as the Western name for the island. In "Chongfang biancheng," however, she reverses the Western imperialist naming choice by using the Chinese name Taiwan 台灣, the ethnonym of a tribe that lived near Ping'an in the southeast part of the island. A Dutch missionary transliterated the tribal name as Taiouwang in 1636, while the Portuguese called this region Tayowan, Taiyowan, Tyvon, Teijoan, Toyouan, and other variations (see Ban). By using a

---

3 Chen Ruoxi mentioned that she accompanied Eileen Chang, along with Wang Zhenghe, Yin Zhang Lanxi, Richard McCarthy and his wife, to watch "Kiloma'an" on October 15, 1961 in Hualien. Chang moved from the platform to sit on the lawn right in front of the performance for a better view ("Zhang Ailing yipie" 40).

4 Roland Soong claimed that Eileen Chang probably knew and was concerned about Taiwanese readers' reactions to ARTF. Therefore, she rewrote the essay in Chinese twenty years later as a response ("Song Yilang faju 'Chongfang biancheng' de guocheng" 84–85).

5 "Chongfang biancheng" includes a note quoted from *Shibao zhoukan* 《時報週刊》 (*China Times Weekly*), dated December 1982 (CFBC 20–21). Also, in her letters to Mae Fong Soong and Stephen Soong dated April 7, 1983 and October 10, 1983, Eileen Chang mentioned that she was still revising "Chongfang biancheng" (*To My Beloved Friends* 1.145).

name that refers to Taiwanese aboriginal people, Chang serves a decolonizing agenda in her self-translation that rewrites the historical narratives and identities of Taiwan.

Chang revises her critical comments on Taiwan's political dynamics with the United States in her self-translation, offering a complementary and ongoing interpretation of her earlier version. Upon her arrival at the Taipei airport, Chang is unexpectedly greeted by "an efficient-looking man in neat western clothes," who asks her in English, 'You are Mrs. Richard Nixon?'" ("ARTF" 62). After enquiries about this incident with Mr. Chu (Richard McCarthy), Chang realizes that this man was always at the airport greeting American celebrities. Adhering to the friendly Taiwanese/American relationship, she notes that she "[goes] under Formosa's huge wave of wistful yearning for the outside world, particularly America, its only friend" (ARTF 63). She retells this incident in "Chongfang biancheng," but her comment has slightly changed: 「隨即被一陣抑鬱的浪潮淹沒了，是這孤島對外界的友情的渴望。」 [immediately overwhelmed by a wave of depression, which is this lonely island's yearning for friendship with the outside world] ("CFBC" 12). Her earlier comment on America as "Taiwan's only friend" has been replaced by a description of Taiwan's situation as "a wave of depression." In the early 1960s, when Chang wrote "A Return to the Frontier," the United States and Taiwan were close allies against the People's Republic of China (PRC). This political dynamic dramatically changed when United States president Richard Nixon visited the PRC in 1972, and the United States and the PRC started to establish full diplomatic relations in 1979, further isolating Taiwan in the international political arena. Therefore, when Chang wrote "Chongfang biancheng" in the 1980s, she adapted her essay to take Taiwan's precarious position in world politics into consideration. This critical revision engages in dialogue with the previous version from new temporal and spatial angles.

As with her depiction of Taiwan, Chang revises her account of Hong Kong in her self-translation as a response to the dynamics between Hong Kong and the mainland in the latter half of the twentieth century. In "A Return to the Frontier," Chang describes the Lo Wu Bridge, located at the border across Sham Chun River between Hong Kong and the mainland city Shenzhen, as a "fateful bridge" that symbolizes the mythical "Naiho Bridge between the realms of the living and the dead" ("ARTF" 74). This comparison seems to comply with the American ideal of Hong Kong as a place of freedom and prosperity in contrast to the unfree and poorer mainland in the early 1960s. The metaphor of the "Naiho Bridge" disappears in "Chongfang biancheng," a decision that can be attributed to the PRC's economic reforms in the late 1970s that helped to make the socioeconomic disparities between the mainland and Hong Kong less severe than they had been two decades prior.

TRANSCULTURAL HOSPITALITY

In both "A Return to the Frontier" and "Chongfang biancheng," Chang juxtaposes the cases of young women in mainland China and Hong Kong, with similar characteristics yet different outcomes, as an equivocal contrast to remind her readers of the American Cold War ideology of polarization. Chang's landlord in Hong Kong tells her that in mainland China

> "[h]er younger sister is a doctor assigned to work in the country. She has to go out on sick calls at night, where it's pitch-dark and the ground is uneven and she's afraid of snakes. You know how young girls are," she said, just as she apologized for her daughters in Hong Kong monopolizing the bathroom: "You know how young girls are."
> "ARTF" 70–71

Her landlord's comment "You know how young girls are," on the one hand, calls back to the common grounds young women in different places share, and on the other, compares the landlord's sister, who experiences dangerous working conditions on the mainland, to his daughters, who enjoy extravagant lifestyles in Hong Kong. This reported speech provides "facts" in the literary information battlefield that tend to prove more persuasive than unsupported propaganda; as Ascoli states in the Editorial of *The Reporter*, "This liberal publication, of necessity, must be always objective and never impartial. Objectivity means a rounded, conscientious study of facts, so as to determine their causes and their weight" ("The Liberal Magazine – An Editorial" 13). As a cultural insider, Chang's writing appears to support *The Reporter*'s "factual approach" to American propaganda.

Chang's personal anecdote, however, provides a rather incoherent narrative that subverts *The Reporter*'s Cold War discourse by highlighting her unique voice and individual case. She recalls that when she crossed the border from mainland China to Hong Kong in 1952, a young Communist soldier urged her and other people waiting in line under the hot sun to stand in the shade. Deeply touched by the Communist soldier's compassion for her, she says, "Still, for a moment I felt the warmth of race wash over me for the last time" ("ARTF" 74). On a personal level, Chang recognizes the Chinese race as part of her collective self, represented by the Communist soldier whose fellowship has transcended the geopolitical frontier between mainland China and Hong Kong.[6]

---

6   In her essay "Betrayal, Impersonation, and Bilingualism: Eileen Chang's Self-Translation," Shuang Shen comments that "Chang's essay, while influenced by the ideologies of race and politics, nonetheless conveys a complex psychology of anxiety about belonging, which ultimately undermines the political self-assuredness that is a prerequisite for propaganda" (Louie 110).

Her individual encounters and experiences underscore the kindness and sociability of ordinary people in spite of geopolitical divisions and American hegemonic narratives.

Analyzing the cultural and linguistic frontier in Chang's essays requires a discussion of Chineseness. In reaction to Western imperialism in the late nineteenth and early twentieth century, Chineseness has often been essentialized as a homogeneous ethnicity bound to mainland China as a standardized Mandarin language and a coherent Han Chinese literature. However, such a perspective on a unified Chineseness neglects the multiplicity of Chinese ethnicities, languages, cultures, and locations; Rey Chow argues that "Chineseness can no longer be held as a monolithic given tied to the mythic homeland but must rather be understood as a provisional 'open signifier'" ("Introduction" 37). Tang Chun-I 唐君毅 (Tang Junyi, 1909–1978) uses the metaphor of drifting flowers and fruits to represent members of the Chinese diaspora who foster languages and cultures, and perpetuate values such as Zhongyong 中庸 (the Middle Way, or Way of Centrality), filial piety, and respect, in the new soil of their adopted countries (110). Challenging Tang's definition of Chineseness as both an ethnic and a cultural heritage, Lisa See uses personal and family anecdotes to illustrate that Chineseness is indeed a cultural practice rather than a mere biological inheritance (xx). While Kuehn, Louie, and Pomfret contend that Chineseness has been "re-embedded in the process of diasporic relocation" (7), Sereno Fusco suggests that Chineseness is a "transnational cultural category" (6). To reimagine Chineseness in the world at large, I argue that Chineseness incorporates Chinese ethnic and cultural heritage, which is characterized by transcendence, diversity, and fluidity rather than by essentiality, homogeneity, and stability, and is situated in specific temporal and spatial spectrums.[7]

In her travelogues, Chang depicts transborder Chineseness using her own boundary-crossing experience as an example. When she arrives at the Taipei airport from the United States, she has a dream-like illusion that she is returning to mainland China, her imagined homeland that only exists in her memory: "I looked around the crowded airport and it really was China, not the strange one I left ten years ago under the Communist but the one I knew best and thought had vanished forever" ("ARTF" 64). She feels connected with the Chinese people through their appearance and Mandarin voices that she encounters in Taiwan. For instance, Chu asks her, "How does it feel to be back?" ("ARTF" 63); she replies, "'It feels like dreaming.' And taking in all the familiar

---

7 See my discussion of Chineseness in the "Introduction" of *The Transcultural Streams of Chinese Canadian Identities*.

faces speaking in tones of homeland" ("ARTF" 64). In "Chongfang biancheng," she adds a personal touch with her description of the back of a middle-aged lady in a bulky black *qipao*, with a hair bun and liberated feet, struggling to climb up the stairs of a temple, who reminds her of her high-school classmate's mother ("CFBC" 12–13). The common racial features, language, bodily practice, and fashion that Chinese people share all contribute to the characteristics of Chineseness that cross the geopolitical borders between Taiwan and mainland China. Chang further tells the stories of people who have risked their lives to escape from mainland China to Hong Kong, but are willing to travel back and forth to bring essential food and clothes to their relatives who have been left behind ("ARTF" 70–71; "CFBC" 36–37). These portrayals show that the affective bond of Chineseness transgresses the rather permeable frontier between Hong Kong and mainland China and negotiate an imaginary border-crossing homeland.

Seeing Chineseness as ever-increasingly heterogeneous, Chang depicts its cultural diversity in her essays. In Taipei, she stays in a General's Suite in a mountain inn furnished with Japanese tatami flooring, a vase, and a picture-scroll, "almost next door to that Christian and Confucian founder of the New Life Movement" ("ARTF" 65), which bears the imprints of Japanese colonial history, the May Fourth Movement, and Western influence. While touring the countryside, she sees "a glimpse of a *shanti*, or a mountain dweller, a gray little wraith with whiskers tattooed on her cheeks carrying a baby on her back and loitering outside a shop along the highway" ("ARTF" 66). On the one hand, she is fascinated by the exoticism of the Taiwanese aboriginals; on the other, she appreciates the beauty of the young women of the Ami tribe in Hualien 花蓮 ("CFBC" 35). The ancient Chinese temple near the modern Taipei airport and the Americanized well-to-do homes in Hong Kong all contribute in their own ways to Chang's vivid account of the cultural plurality of Chineseness and of her position both in between and across boundaries.

Chang's essays are further enriched by code-mixing and elements of orality, which cater to multiple cultural environments. Her stories feature intermingling of languages such as English, "You are Mrs. Richard Nixon?" ("ARTF" 62); Mandarin ("ARTF" 64); Japanese, "Chigaru ["sic; Chigau'"] yo!" ("ARTF" 67); and Shanghainese "Huh-yee-ya!" "HA?" "Ah?" ("ARTF" 67). In "Chongfang biancheng," she uses the Hong Kong Cantonese combined words "*lengzai*" 「靚仔」 [handsome boy], rather than the Mandarin "*shuaige*" 「帥哥」 [handsome guy], to describe a Hong Kong policeman at the Lo Wu Bridge ("CFBC" 40). The linguistic hybridization in her texts signifies translational mimesis that represents multiple languages existing on both story and discourse levels (Klinger 116). Chang's description of the multiplicity of tongues in Chinese communities inevitably reminds readers of her constant existence across porous boundaries. The semantic mapping of realities in Taiwan and Hong Kong in her travelogues portrays the linguistic diversity embedded in Chineseness, which is further enhanced by the colonial histories of these two cities and the fast rate of globalization.

The fluidity of Chineseness can be seen in Chang's depiction of Hong Kong's evolving cultures between the 1940s and the 1960s in her essays. Chang first visited Hong Kong between 1939 and 1942 as a student at the University of Hong Kong. She returned in 1952 when she worked for the USIS, and remained there until 1955. Between October 1961 and March 1962 she wrote screenplays for the Motion Picture & General Investment Company (MP & GI Co.). Her travels to Hong Kong were multi-dimensional rather than linear, which enabled her to reflect on the transformation of Hong Kong with a heightened sensibility enhanced by her broadening of experience over a life span of twenty-four years. In "A Return to the Frontier," published in 1963, she compares her impression of the city in the 1960s with those from the 1950s: "From Formosa I went on to Hong Kong, which I had not seen for six years. The city was being torn down and rebuilt into high apartment buildings" ("ARTF" 68). She also notices the new settlement of refugees from mainland China, the younger generation who prefer to speak Cantonese rather than any other dialects, and the Americanized materialistic lifestyles that the new generation favour ("ARTF" 69). In "Chongfang biancheng," she also includes an observation of Hong Kong in the 1940s, when only babies would wear traditional colourful print cloth and even poor children preferred to wear Western-style clothes ("CFBC" 56). Her records of Hong Kong's transformation in terms of its infrastructures, common language, lifestyles, and fashion from the 1940s to the 1960s represent the intercultural dynamics inherent in cultural interactions in Hong Kong, which continuously produce both harmony and difference, and thus contest any fixed concepts of Chineseness.

Chang's travelogue and self-translation trace her encounters in Taiwan both as a significant in-transit moment of her life story and a self-reconstruction of her past. In "A Return to the Frontier," she simply says, "I got off the plane in Taipei on my way to Hong Kong" to indicate her transition;[8] in "Chongfang biancheng," she also includes a memory of passing Taiwan in 1942: 「我以前

---

8 On her trip to Taiwan, Eileen Chang also planned to interview Peter Hsueh Chang (1901–2001), a former warlord of Manchuria (1928–1936), who was under house arrest and could not accept any interview at that time, for her book *The Young Marshal*. She referred to this plan in a letter to Mae Fong Soong" dated October 2, 1961 (*To My Beloved Friends* 1.102). *The Young Marshal* remained unfinished during her lifetime and was published posthumously in 2015.

沒到過台灣，但是珍珠港事變後從香港回上海，不靠岸，遠遠的只看見個山。」[I have never been to Taiwan. However, when I returned to Shanghai from Hong Kong after the Pearl Harbour Incident, the Japanese ship I embarked took a meandering route and passed Taiwan. It did not dock. I saw a mountain from far away] ("CFBC" 133). Chang was amazed by the sublime scenery of high mountains in Taiwan, which she compares to Chinese landscape paintings during her narrow escape from war-torn Hong Kong, which she first discusses in her essay "Shuangsheng" 〈雙聲〉 ("Double Voices"). In her semi-autobiographical novel *The Book of Change,* she reworks this experience as follows: "She pressed against the rails and poked her head out. Two distant peaks hung high in the sky, brilliant green mountains veined and whittled down to the slim sculptured shapes you only see in Chinese painting, out of the waist by mist" (*BOC* 294). Her reflections on passing through the Taiwanese Strait are mediated through an ongoing process of interpretation, self-translation, and rewriting.

From Taiwan to Hong Kong, Chang further describes her diasporic sentiments of nostalgia. Through self-translation, she both reconnects with and distances herself from her experience in Hong Kong by means of expanded thought and broadened perspectives in her mother tongue:

> 我學生時代的香港，自從港戰後回上海，廢學十年，那年再回去，倒還沒怎麼改變，不過校園後面小山上的樹長高了，中間一條磚砌小徑通向舊時的半山女生宿舍，比例不同了，也有點『面熟陌生』。
>
> "CFBC" 41

> Hong Kong during my student years had not changed much since I returned to Shanghai after the Battle of Hong Kong and my abandoning of school for ten years. I went back that year, the place had not changed much, but the trees on the hill behind the campus had grown taller, and a brick path in the middle leading to the old mid-levels girls' dormitory had different proportions, and looked a bit "déjà vu."

In this passage, Chang reflects on her revisiting the vicinity of the University of Hong Kong, where she spent her youth in the pursuit of knowledge and dreams. The Hong Kong of her undergraduate memory is familiar, but no longer the same. The equivocal contrast between now and then in Hong Kong evokes her sentimental feelings about herself. In a stream-of-consciousness passage, she returns to the street market of Hong Kong in the early 1940s, where she purchased a piece of cloth printed with pink flowers, which she took to Shanghai to make her own clothes, in an act of independence, uniqueness, and individuality. She constructs and reconstructs her individual self through the symbol of the pink flowered print cloth; in contemplating her past, she reshapes the idealist self of her youth into a convoluted self that has travelled to many foreign places and has now returned to herself, recalling Paul Ricoeur's *Soi-même comme un autre* (*Oneself as Another,* 1990). Chang's individual self has been transformed and enlarged by crossing the boundaries of space and time. While her past studying and working in Hong Kong ceaselessly informs her present of revisiting, her present global experience and vision reinterpret her past and guide her future. Rewriting her past in her future empowers her to transgress her personal frontier between her own past, present and future.

Chang's dynamic points of view provide her with a means of representing her thoughts and feelings that have been captured in her self-translations and lead to her self-reconstruction. In *CFBC*, Chang rhetorically adds her reflections on Hong Kong at the end of her trip: 「忽然空中飄來一縷屎臭。」 [Suddenly a stink of shit drifted in the air] (*CFBC* 60). She considers this repulsive odour a gift from Hong Kong that comforts her nostalgic feelings and allows her to bid it farewell. In the past, she dealt with her transition from adolescence into adulthood in Hong Kong. Then, she faced challenges of tackling poverty and caring for a stroke-stricken husband, Ferdinand Reyher, in her middle age in the United States.[9] In a letter to Reyher dated March 2, 1962, she describes her suffering during this last visit to Hong Kong as a "total mess & a fitting end to the 5 most wretched months in [her] life" (Kao, *Zhang Ailing xue* 403). The offensive smell of feces serves as a symbol of the adversities she has endured during different stages of her life in Hong Kong, the dazzlingly magnificent "Pearl of the East." This equivocal contrast shows that no matter how glamorous the city of Hong Kong is, the difficulties in her life in this city at that time represented by the foulness drag her into the abyss of the unbearable that she cannot escape, and the strong sense of desolation that prevails in most of her works. Seeing herself from both inside and outside of Hong Kong in different spaces, times, and languages, she no longer perceives her world simply from a Shanghainese perspective, but from a global perspective, which continuously reconstructs her transcultural and transfrontier self through self-translation.

---

9 The main purpose of this trip to Hong Kong was to write the screenplays for *Dream of the Red Chamber* I and II for MP&GI Company on a promised commission of eight hundred dollars, which could have sustained her living expense with Reyher in the United States for some time. Unfortunately, her screenplays were not accepted and her hard work went unpaid. She then wrote another screenplay during her stay in Hong Kong that was finally accepted. See Chang's "Letter to Ferdinand Reyher" dated February 20, 1962, and "Letter to Ferdinand Reyher" dated March 2, 1962.

CHAPTER 15

Transgressing Boundaries: "The Spyring or Ch'ing k'ê! Ch'ing k'ê!" and "Se, Jie" 〈色，戒〉 ("Lust, Caution")

Bilingual writers who are also self-translators translate/recreate their own works from one linguistic and cultural system into another, transgressing boundaries of language, culture, gender, historical perception, ideologies, religious conceptions, and political thoughts; as Jan Walsh Hokenson argues, "Bilingual writers as self-translators in dual discourse can infuse one literature with new materials from the other, using one to innovate in the other, and then reverse the process, thereby enriching and challenging the dominant in both" (Cordingley 40). Hokenson points out the potential of bilingual writers and self-translators to enhance and subvert hegemonic ideas in their writing and self-translation. Such a paradoxical capacity opens infinite possibilities of boundary crossing within and beyond the source texts and self-translation.

This chapter focuses on Eileen Chang's English short story "The Spyring/ Ch'ing k'ê! Ch'ing k'ê!" (2008; hereafter cited as "The Spyring"), and her Chinese short story "Se, Jie" 〈色，戒〉 ("Lust, Caution," 1977). The plots and characters of these stories are similar, with slight modifications. It is unknown whether Chang wrote the English or the Chinese version first, both simultaneously, or alternatively, all of which are possible; but in these stories, she blurs the boundaries of history and fiction, performance and performativity, and personal and poetic memories. "The Spyring" and "Se, Jie" tell the story of an amateur female spy, Shahlu Li/Wang Chia-chih, who commits to an assassination plot to seduce and entrap a collaborator with the Japanese during the second Sino-Japanese War, also known as the War of Resistance against Japan (1937–1945), but tips him off to escape at the critical moment, leading to the execution of herself and her comrades in the end.

The story went through several revisions over twenty-five years before it was published as the Chinese version of "Se, Jie" in 1977. Chang started devising the plot in 1953 ("Preface to *Xuji*" 7), a year after her second sojourn in Hong Kong. In the upper left-hand corner of the typewritten manuscript of "The Spyring," the addressee was Richard McCarthy, the director of the United States Information Service in Hong Kong at the time. Chang probably finished writing the English version by 1955, as she mentioned in a letter to Mae Kwong dated December 18, 1955, that she sent out "The Spyring" to Frillmann, who worked at the Taplinger

© JESSICA TSUI-YAN LI, 2025 | DOI:10.1163/9789004730052_017

Publishing Company, for publication (*To My Beloved Friends* 1.30–31). In her "Wangrangji" 〈惘然記〉 ("A Record of Bewilderment"), Chang said that "Se, Jie" was written in the 1950s and revised several times even after it was published ("Wangranji" 4). "Se, Jie" was first published in issue 48, number 4, of the Taiwanese edition of Huangguan 皇冠 (Crown) in December 1977. It was then published in issue 20, number 1, of the American edition of *Huangguan* in March 1978. A month later, it was published again in the "Renjian fukan" 〈人間副刊〉 (Human Realm Literary Supplement) of *Zhongguo shibao* 《中國時報》 (*China Times*) on April 11, 1978 (Cai, *Se Jie Ailing* 20). The Chinese version was subsequently republished and reprinted several times by Crown Publishing in Taiwan and Hong Kong. The English version, "The Spyring," however, was published posthumously in *Muse*, a Hong Kong magazine, in April 2008.

Both "The Spyring" and "Se, Jie" feature characters who may have been inspired by historical individuals. For instance, in her letter to Stephen Soong, dated April 1, 1974, Chang wrote: 「那篇〈色戒〉 ("Spy, Ring") 故事是你供給的。」 [The story of "Se, Jie" ("Spy, Ring") was provided by you] (*To My Beloved Friends* 1.232). Chang also mentioned Ding Mocun 丁默村 (1901–1947) in her discussion of this story in a letter addressed to Mae Fong Soong and Stephen Soong dated August 5, 1977 (*To My Beloved Friends* 1.258). Ding Mocun joined the Communist Youth League of China in 1924; in 1932, he became chief of the intelligence team directly under Shanghai Investigation Division of Kuomintang's Central Organization Department, and in 1939, he became the director of the Secret Services of Wang Zhengwei's government in Shanghai. He is considered the prototype of Mr. Tai/Mr. Yee, who is the head of the Secret Services in Wang's government during the second Sino-Japanese war. Zheng Pingru 鄭蘋如 (1918–1940) is similarly considered the prototype of Shahlu Li/Wang Chia-chih. Zheng was half-Chinese and half-Japanese and was fluent in both Mandarin Chinese and Japanese. With her beauty and talent, she worked as a spy, gathering intelligence on the Imperial Japanese Army for Kuomintang's Central Organization during the second Sino-Japanese war. After an unsuccessful attempt to assassinate Ding Mocun, she was executed (Cai, *Se Jie Ailing* 76–81). Zheng's spy work resembles that of Shahlu/Chia-chih, who faces execution after her assassination plot against Mr. Tai/Mr. Yee fails.

In addition to Ding Mocun and Zheng Pingru, other historical people and events have been identified as sources for Chang's story. In his letter to Chang dated March 14, 1977, Stephen Soong recalled a few assassinations of *hanjian* 漢奸 (national traitors) in the north during the second Sino-Japanese war, conducted by high school and university students who made connections

TRANSGRESSING BOUNDARIES

251

with and worked for Dai Li 戴笠 (1897–1946), head of Kuomintang's Military Intelligence Service. Soong also mentioned the story of two Shi sisters who spied for Dai Li. When the Japanese collaborators discovered and searched for them, they had already left two days ago. The younger Shi sister married her high school classmate later on, and still looked like a student (*To My Beloved Friends* 1.349). The Shi sisters and other student spies became the inspiration for the Lingnan University students in "Se, Jie" who concoct assassination plots against Mr. Yee and are recruited by Old Wu, a Kuomingtang underground worker. Moreover, Shahlu/Chia-chih also shows similarities to Guanlu 關露 (Hu Shoumei 胡壽楣, 1907–1982), who acted in the drama *Sai Jinhu*a 《賽金花》, produced by the League of Left-wing Dramatists in 1932, and then became an actual spy for the Communist Party in 1939 against Li Shiqun 李士群 (1905–1943), head of Wang's government's Intelligence Service Division in Shanghai. Guanlu once went shopping with Li Shiqun's wife as a way to get close to Li (Y. Zhuang 47–48). While in Chang's story, Shahlu and Chia-chih befriend Mr. Tai and Mr. Yee, respectively, Chia-chih acts in a patriotic drama at Lingnan University and then extends her acting into reality.

The historical encounter between Zheng Pingru and Ding Mocun has been rewritten several times. For example, Zheng Zhenduo's 鄭振鐸 (1898–1958) essay "Yige nüjiandie" 〈一個女間諜〉 ("A Female Spy"), published in *Zhoubao* 《週報》 (*Weekly Magazine*) on October 6, 1945 honoured Zheng Pingru's patriotic resistance against the Japanese (Cai, *Se Jie Ailing* 112). Jin Xiongbai's 金雄白 (1904–1985) *Wang Zhengquan de kaichang yu shouchang* 《汪政權的開場與收場》 (*The Opening and Ending of Wang's Political Power*), published in the Hong Kong magazine *Chunqiu* 《春秋》 (*Spring Autumn*), between October 1957 and February 1964, features a chapter titled "Zheng Pingru mouci Ding Mocun dianmo" 〈鄭蘋如謀刺丁默村顛末〉 ("The Climactic Ending of Zheng Pingru Assassinating Ding Mocun") (Cai, *Se Jie Ailing* 113). Gaoyang's 高陽 (Xu Yanpian 許晏駢, 1922–1992) *Fenmo Chunqiu* 《粉墨春秋》 (*The Times of Powder Ink Spring Autumn*), published in the "Renjian funkan" 〈人間副刊〉 ("Human Realm Literary Supplement") of *Zhongguo shibao* 《中國時報》 (*China Times*) between June 1, 1979 and September 30, 1980, includes a chapter titled "Hongfen jinge" 〈紅粉金戈〉 ("Rouge Powder and Golden Sword"), a fictionalized retelling of the story of Zheng and Ding (Cai, *Se Jie Ailing* 117). All of these male authors emphasize history more than fiction, upholding the ideologies of Chinese patriotism and nationalism in the face of Japanese invasions. Eileen Chang's story, however, highlights female subjectivity and agency and dramatically changes the ending of the story, focusing on the female protagonist's psychological upheavals and thus subverting

252   CHAPTER 15

the established hierarchy in which nationalistic discourse is placed above individual desire.[1]

Whether the reconstructed stories can be perceived as history or fiction is controversial. After Ang Lee's film *Lust/Caution*, an adaptation of Eileen Chang's "Se, Jie," was released in 2007, Zheng Jingzhi hosted a press conference in Los Angeles to protest the film's inaccurate portrait of her sister, Zheng Pingru, in which she stated: "Since you [Ang Lee] want to shoot a historical story, you have to learn a bit more about history" (Liu 18). Zheng Jingzhi insisted that Zheng Pingru did not fall in love with the national traitor Ding Mocun, further explaining, "I can say that all my family members are patriots" (Liu 18). Her reaction demonstrates her view of the story of *Lust/Caution* as a historical reflection of Zheng Pingru's life experience, and her perception that the film's erroneous depiction of the history has damaged her family's reputation. In making the film, Ang Lee meticulously reproduced the historical details of the setting, such as the curtains, jewels, tables, chairs, and glasses (Hui), and even hired a consultant to ensure that the setting was reproduced as accurately as possible (mrbrown). In her discussion of Lee's film, Rey Chow states that Lee aims to "[provide] the original with a representational frame" to "reveal, to suggest, that things were really like that" (*Entanglements* 179); however, Lee claims that what he attempted to reconstruct was the bygone China of his father's generation ("Interview with Ang Lee," *Lust/Caution* DVD). The anti-Japanese history Lee recreated in this film was what Lee perceived as "the collected memory of both Taiwanese mainlanders and native Taiwanese" (H. Peng 157); nonetheless, since he produced the film from a specific male Taiwanese American perspective, he does appropriate the history for his own purposes.

Whether these reconstructions are presented as history, historical fiction, or fiction, they all reframe, adapt, edit, and appropriate the original history, so that readers cannot simply take the reproduction as history per se, but should rather see them, to a certain extent, as fiction. In her "Preface" to *Xuji* 《續集》 (*Sequel*), Chang points out that many readers cannot distinguish between the authors and their characters and often mix them up. She further notes that, as an ordinary person, she would not be able to obtain inner information about the political struggles of Wang's government's Secret Services, and this fact implicitly urges readers to perceive her story as fiction instead of history (*Xuji*

---

1   Haiyan Lee argues that "*Lust, Caution* is a deliberate deformation of Zheng's story precisely because the latter is easily absorbed into the archetypal national narrative that defers individual purposes and subsumes them into the totalizing ideology of national liberation, a teleology that justifies the instrumentalization of the individual body, particularly the female body" (650).

7). Chang gathered the plot from Stephen Soong, who provided source material covering various historical events. She might also have heard stories from her first husband Hu Lancheng, a Japanese collaborator, and received inspiration from other sources as well. However, she used her imagination and applied literary techniques to fictionalize the historical sources in her original works, self-translations, and rewritings, thus blurring the boundary between history and fiction and opening up infinite possibilities of (re)interpretation and (re)construction.

Chang's protagonists find life-fulfillment through performance and performativity in an ongoing debated political context. Soon after Chang had published "Se, Jie," the American-based Taiwanese writer Zhang Xiguo 張系國, using the pseudonym Yuwairen 域外人, wrote a critique of the story in his essay "Bu chi la de zenmo hudechu lazi – ping 'Se, Jie'?" 〈不吃辣的怎麼胡得出辣子？——評〈色，戒〉〉 ("You Can't Win if You Can't Eat Chili: On 'Se, Jie'"), published in *Zhongguo shibao – renjian* 《中國時報——人間》 (*China Times – Literary Supplement*) on October 1, 1978. In this essay, Zhang criticizes Chang's portrayal of the lustfulness and treachery of the female spy Wang Chia-chih, who 「像洗了個熱水澡，把積鬱都沖掉了。」 [felt cleansed, as if by a scalding hot bath (*"Se, Jie,"* 21; Lovell 27)] after having sex with the Japanese collaborator Mr. Yee. In defending her political and moral integrity, Chang responds to Zhang in her essay "Yangmao chuzai yang shengshang – tan "Se, Jie" 〈羊毛出在羊身上——談〈色，戒〉〉 ("Lamb's Wool Came From the Lamb: Discussing 'Se, Jie'"; hereafter cited as "Yangmao"), first published in *Zhongguo shibao – renjian* on November 27, 1978. In her response, Chang dismisses Zhang's negative assessment of Wang Chia-chih as overlooking the character's psychological struggle and the story's development. She argues that Chia-chih "felt cleansed" after having consummated her relationship with Mr. Yee because what she did became meaningful without sacrificing her virginity in vain in the first place. In their previous plan, Chia-chih and her fellow Lingnan University students had pretended to be Mrs. Mai and her family members. In order to lure Mr. Yee into an affair, Chia-chih "practices" sexual intercourse with a classmate she dislikes, Liang Runsheng 梁潤生, who has had sexual experience with prostitutes. Their plan fails when Mr. Yee and his family abruptly leave Hong Kong for Shanghai. Chia-chih then thinks of herself as an "idiot" who might have been set up for being raped. It is only when she resumes her role as Mrs. Mai again in Shanghai that she feels her life has a purpose and thus becomes the character she is performing. Instead of a shameless spy, Chia-chih demonstrates that she is a sophisticated character who, despite being an amateur, displays experience in undercover work.

254   CHAPTER 15

Chang also defends herself against Zhang's accusation that her depiction of Mr. Yee's "mousy face" ("Se, Jie" 12; "The Spyring" 4) as a sign of commanding prominence and wealth portrays a known national traitor in a positive light. In "Yangmao" she explains that stereotypical espionage stories often depict national traitors as repugnant and licentious, and that the heroine usually dies and thus retains her virginity before she is sexually humiliated. Although he has a "mousy face," Mr. Yee appears presentable, which accounts for why Chia-chih suddenly feels moved and confused in the jewelry shop, as if he truly loves her. Moreover, Chang argues that the interpretation of Mr. Yee's "mousy face" as a sign of fame and prosperity cannot be taken seriously. This compliment was probably given by some opportunistic fortune tellers after Mr. Yee has acquired his power ("Yangmao" 22–23). Accordingly, Zhang's critique of "Se, Jie" as a positive depiction of a national traitor cannot be justified; there is no substantial evidence with which to accuse Chang of depicting a Japanese collaborator in order to culturally facilitate the Japanese colonization of China.

I argue here that what Eileen Chang emphasizes in both "The Spyring" and "Se, Jie" is her depiction of human nature, especially its weakness, in her characters, whether they are performing the roles of patriotic spies or national traitors. Chang claims that the characters she wrote were not professionally trained secret agents as those portrayed in John le Carré's *The Spy Who Came in from the Cold* (1963); rather, her characters have the human nature and weaknesses of ordinary people. Otherwise, they would become stereotypes, falling into the pigeonholes of the heroic images portrayed in Communist propaganda ("Yangmao" 19–20). Chang's spy story focuses on the frailty of ordinary people rather than the strength of heroes. Her writing style distinguishes her story from stereotypical propaganda works, and that, paradoxically, has led to the enduring popularity of her works among readers in different times and places.

The weaknesses of the characters in "The Spyring" and "Se, Jie" are presented in their performative acts on stage and in the story's reality. Shahlu/Chia-chih, the story's protagonist is enchanted by "Jie," the second word in the Chinese title, that means *ring* or *caution*. The story begins with Shahlu/Chia-chih playing mahjong with Mrs. Mai/Mrs. Yee and two other ladies. Before introducing any of the characters, Chang highlights the symbolic significance of the ring, as "[d]iamond rings flashed in their wake" ("The Spyring" 1). This sentence helps to foreground the preference of materiality to humanity that is present in the story. In "Se, Jie," Chang adds more details of Chia-chih's feelings about the ring: though she is a spy pretending to be one of those ladies, Chia-chih cannot help but feel ashamed of her lack of a diamond ring: 「只有她沒有鑽戒，戴來戴去這隻翡翠的，早知不戴了，叫人見笑——正都看不得她。」["every pair of hands glinting ostentatiously – except hers. She should have left her jadeite ring back in its box, she realized; to spare herself all those sneering glances" ("Se, Jie" 13; trans. Lovell 9)]. In Chang's self-translation, Chia-chih unconsciously becomes the character she is supposed to play instead of remaining distanced from the role she is performing. The boundaries between acting and reality, as well as those between Chia-chih's double identities as a spy and Mrs. Mai, become blurred.

Shahlu and Chia-chih, the respective protagonists of "The Spyring" and "Se, Jie," perform their roles differently, as indicated by the slight discrepancy in their identities that Chang creates through self-translation and rewriting. In "The Spyring," Shahlu is merely portrayed as a spy who is obscurely connected to some nationalists covertly operating at Yu Hsing Plumbers and Electricians, and little background information is given about her. In "Se, Jie," Chia-chih is further depicted as a Lingnan University student disguised as Mrs. Mai, joining her classmates in an assassination plot against Mr. Yee with the help of Old Wu, a secret agent of the Nationalist party.

In "The Spyring," Shahlu explicitly asks Mr. Tai to purchase her a diamond ring in order to lure him to the jewelry shop: "I'm looking for a ring. Just now at the mah-jong table I nearly died of shame – look at the size of their diamonds and look at mine! You saw now ... I tell you I've never felt so cheap in my life. Just to be near you I have to put up with all those women with their grand airs. And then you kept me waiting here the whole afternoon. Really I'm such a fool" ("The Spyring" 9). In "Se, Jie," however, Chia-chih reflects internally on the connotations of diamond rings: 「首飾向來是女太太們的弱點」 [jewelry is always a weakness of ladies] ("Se, Jie" 17). She convinces herself that her plan will not raise Mr. Yee's suspicion because she, as a woman, is "naturally" perceived as a lover of diamonds.

"The Spyring" also features a rather loose and mysterious Shahlu, who adds a sense of suspense to this simplified version of the tale and makes this culturally Chinese story more accessible to Anglophone readers. After almost three decades of revision, "Se, Jie" presents a more discreet Chia-chih and provides further information about the university students' mission and their engagement with a Nationalist secret agent. These reworkings are more accessible to Sinophone readers with deeper background knowledge of Chinese politics and cultures.

Immersed in her playacting, Chia-chih is carried away by her persona, Mrs. Mai, and deeply engaged with the materiality of high society. She is self-conscious of her material and social insufficiency, as she demonstrates when she leads Mr. Yee to a jewelry shop that does not appear to be a high-class establishment and she feels embarrassed for having brought him there ("Se, Jie" 25). When the shop assistant brings out a pink diamond, Chia-chih feels relieved because the shop has saved her pride. Though she knows that she is in disguise, she is concerned about losing face as though she might look like a *"da xiangli"* 「大鄉里」 ("Se, Jie" 27), a Cantonese expression for a country bumpkin, here referring to someone who has come from a village in Guangdong to the metropolitan Shanghai. Nonetheless, she cannot repudiate these petty thoughts, which shows her awareness of the socially constructed stereotypical significance of vanity and social status associated with diamond rings.

Aside from the vanity of the elite social lifestyle, Shahlu/Chia-chih is also consumed by the emotional engagement of the theatricality of her own performance. In "Wangranji" 〈惘然記〉 ("A Record of Bewilderment"), Chang notes that 「演員沉浸在一個角色裏，也成爲自身的一次經驗。」 [Actors indulge in a role, which will become their own experience] ("Wangrangji" 3). Alongside their material and social connotations, diamond rings also represent commitment to love: in Western traditions, a diamond ring is a betrothal gift given by a man to his prospective wife when he proposes marriage. The durability of diamonds represents eternity, and the round shape of the ring stands for togetherness. This custom has been adopted by and become popular among the Chinese, especially in the cosmopolitan Shanghai in the 1940s. "Se, Jie" discusses Chia-chih's indulgence in the cultural significance of diamond rings; for instance, when Chia-chih and Mr. Yee consummate their relationship, Mr. Yee declares that he will buy her a ring to commemorate the occasion (17). The diamond ring then becomes a metonymic device of seduction, generosity, and social bondage. While carrying out her mission, Chia-chih is dazzled by the romantic significance of the diamond ring: 「只有一千零一夜裏才有這樣的事。用金子，也是天方夜譚裏的事。」 [She registered a twinge of regret that it was to be no more than a prop in the short, penultimate scene of the drama unfolding around it ... The entire – transaction – trading gold for diamonds – felt like another detail stolen from the Arabian Nights ("Se, Jie" 28; trans. Lovell 40–41)]. The diamond ring, at this moment, functions as a prop but still dazzles Chia-chih with its beauty, as well as its time-honoured symbolism of love.

Shahlu/Chia-chih is fascinated by the romantic atmosphere associated with the diamond ring, as she and Mr. Yee perform the roles of lovers in a fantasy world: 「這一刹那間彷彿只有他們倆在一起。」 [At this moment, it seems that they are the only two together] ("Se, Jie" 28). In "The Spyring," entrapped by her own roleplay, Shahlu thinks to herself, "This man really loves me" (14). In both versions of the story, Shahlu/Chia-chih feels a great shock and then a sense of loss. Such confusion and emotional turbulence eventually prompt her to warn Mr. Tai/Mr. Yee to escape, at the expense of her own life. Perhaps her weakness is her naïveté about love that leads to her misunderstanding of Mr. Tai/Mr. Yee's gift of jewelry in exchange for her sexuality as a token of love. Shahlu/Chia-chih's illusion is aggravated by the symbolic meanings of diamond rings, such as romance, love, devotion, value, social status, vanity, which have been socially constructed over generations. Shahlu/Chia-chih's misperception of Mr.Tai/Mr. Yee's affection for her leads her to terminate the assassination plot, which ultimately costs her own life.

Chang's self-translation and revision of the story underscores the psychological bewilderment of her female protagonists. In "The Spyring," after tipping Mr. Tai to escape, Shahlu passes by "a cobbed street lined with paper shops displaying brocade-trimmed gilt-patterned scarlet wedding certificates in their dark, unlit [shop windows]" ("The Spyring" 14). The street that displays "wedding certificates," signifying the institution of marriage is contrasted by the streetwalkers in its immediate vicinity; Shahlu's adventure on this street symbolizes her disguising herself as a married woman but acting like a prostitute for Mr. Tai. Afterwards, she rushes into a Soochow embroidery shop in which she encounters a homey scene of "[t]he shopkeeper's family and the assistant and apprentice [...] sitting down to dinner at the rear end of the shop. They made an incredibly homey scene around the crimson round table-top shiny with grease under the yellow electric light" ("The Spyring" 14). This scene, to some extent, reflects Shahlu's deep-seated desire for the family love that she may lack. She is unable to obtain the love she desires, as she is immediately chased out of the shop. During her escape from the assistant who tries to take advantage of her sexually, she defends herself by using the diamond ring to cut his face. In this moment, the ring becomes a weapon, and its many significances of value, social status, vanity, romance, and devotion all vanish. Shahlu's unfulfilled yearning for family love produces a sense of melancholia that haunts her to her death. This scene, however, is absent in "Se, Jie"; in her letters to Stephen Soong dated April 25, 1975, Chang states that she decided that Chia-chih in "Se, Jie" should have left the diamond ring in the shop before she escapes, because she lets him go due to her belief that he really loves her. If she took the ring away, it would seem that she allowed him to escape in exchange for money, thus making the theme unclear (*To My Beloved Friends* 1.266). After multiple revisions, in "Se, Jie" Chang highlights Chia-chih's confusion about Mr. Yee's illusory love with his presentation of a diamond ring, rather than simply aiming for the ring itself.

While the weakness of Shahlu/Chia-chih is symbolized by "jie," that of Mr. Yee is signified by "se," the first word in the Chinese title. The Chinese word "se" has multiple meanings, one of which is "lust." Mr. Tai/Mr. Yee demonstrates strong desires for power and money, which his service as head of the spy agency for Wang's puppet government supporting Japan's occupation of China during the second Sino-Japanese war demonstrates. Mr. Tai/Mr. Yee's lust for female sexuality is particularly magnified in the story, whose main plot focuses on his entrapment by the assassins due to his falling for Chia-chih's feminine beauty. Mr. Tai/Mr. Yee's infamous fondling of women can be seen in Shahlu/Chia-chih's reflection on him: "He was so numbed by the excessive demands on his attention that she had to literally stand over him and dangle her breasts at him" ("The Spyring" 8). The breasts, depicted as the female sexual organs, are alienated from the female body and subjectivity, and this objectification underscores Mr. Yee's lust. In "Se, Jie," Mr. Yee's desire for sex is embodied in his harassment of Chia-chih and his eagerness to touch her breasts while hypocritically upholding his "upright" posture ("Se, Jie" 23).

"Se" (lust, colour, phenomena) and "Jie" (ring, caution) are two sides of the same coin, reflecting the double roles played by Shahlu/Chia-chih and Mr. Tai/Mr. Yee. In "Se, Jie," Chang adds the metaphor of hunter and prey to represent the reciprocal relationship between Chia-chih and Mr. Yee: Chia-chih sets up a trap to assassinate Mr. Yee, but he executes her instead, so that the hunter becomes the prey and vice versa: 「他們是原始的獵人與獵物的關係，虎與倀的關係，最終極的佔有。她才生是她的人，死是他的鬼。」 ["And now he possessed her utterly, primitively, as a hunter his quarry, a tiger his kill. Alive, her body belonged to him; dead, she was his ghost" ("Se, Jie" 34; trans. Lovell 54)]. Chia-chih continues to submit to Mr. Yee even after she becomes a ghost, as hinted at in the Chinese expression "weihuzuochang" 「爲虎作倀」 [playing jackal to the tiger] ("Se, Jie" 34), with Mr. Yee as the tiger and Chia-chih as the ghost. After Chia-chih has surrendered to Mr. Yee as though she is already dead, she exposes the whereabouts and plans of her comrades, thus allowing Mr. Yee to destroy their spy network.

Chang rhetorically describes the power dynamics between Shahlu and Mr. Tai in "The Spyring." After letting Mr. Tai escape, Shahlu walks through a shop: "She skidded over a little heap of herbal dregs just outside the door. Somebody was sick in this house and they had thrown the black dregs of the medicinal brew out in the lane, hoping that passers-by would tread on it and catch the disease, thereby curing the patient" ("The Spyring" 15). In this superstitious setting, Shahlu unfortunately steps on a carrier of misfortune and symbolically takes over the curse from a patient; in a similar vein, she falls into her own trap that she set up for Mr. Tai, replacing him as the prey, and dies. This analogy of encountering the herbal dregs is not present in "Se, Jie." Considering the cultural knowledge background of her Anglophone readers in the 1950s when she wrote "The Spyring," Chang explains the Chinese folk belief in the transference of bad luck to others through herbal dregs. After revising the story for almost three decades and finally publishing "Se, Jie" in Taiwan in 1977, she removed the account of this superstition, which would have been well-known to her Sinophone readers.

In both "The Spyring" and "Se, Jie," Chang uses a paper windmill as a metonymic device to represent the Chinese *feng shui* belief of change, and thus Shahlu/Chia-chih's yearning for hope. While escaping, Shahlu/Chia-chih takes a pedicab with a paper windmill: "The pedicab driver wheeled around and peddled swiftly towards her. He was young and he had tied a little red-green-and white paper windmill on his handbar so that it whirled prettily when it went fast. Shahlu jumped on to the seat" ("The Spyring" 16). In Chinese culture, a paper windmill is associated with the Eight Diagrams windmill, an instrument said to have been invented by Jiang Ziya 姜子牙 (1156 BC–1017 BC) during the Zhou Dynasty (1046 BC–256 BC) to conquer demons; the windmill thus symbolizes transformation, childhood innocence, and wish fulfillment. In "Se, Jie," Chang portrays the pedicab driver as a *baima qishi* 白馬騎士 [white knight] who rides quickly, making the windmill turn, metaphorically rescuing Chia-chih from danger. However, soon afterwards the district is locked down: "The pedicab driver drew up just short of the line. He gave his paper windmill an exasperated twirl and turned to smile at her helplessly" ("The Spyring" 16–17). The pedicab driver's last effort to turn the windmill signifies Shahlu/Chia-chih's unattainable quest for hope.

Though Shahlu/Chia-chih turns from a hunter into prey, Mr. Tai/Mr. Yee plays the roles of both hunter and prey in Sino-Japanese politics. As a Japanese collaborator, he is extremely cautious and aggressive in hunting for Chinese resistance against Wang's government and the Japanese military aggression in China; meanwhile, he is being hunted by the assassination groups organized by the Nationalist government centred in Chungking. Moreover, he is himself prey to Wang's government and the Japanese military in China, serving their agenda at the cost of his own life: "When the Chungking government came back at the end of the war, he was arrested and executed" ("The Spyring" 19). He understands well the Chinese saying, "'T'eh wu pu fung chia, special agents are all one family,' because they could switch sides with ease" ("The Spyring" 18). Mr. Yee embodies the characteristics of change or trade signified by the Chinese word Yee (Yi) 易 in his surname. The changing nature of secret agents can also be seen in the representation of the yin and yang symbol in Taoist metaphysics, which shows the dialectics of the two opposites with a portion of the other element in each section. The paradoxical and ambiguous double roles of both Shahlu/Chia-chih and Mr. Tai/Mr. Yee blur the boundaries between spy and traitor, hunter and prey, and tiger and its ghost, and all of this undermines their fundamental premises of patriotism and nationalism.

Apart from lust for sex, money, and power, the Chinese word "se" also refers to the phenomena of all visible and non-visible things in the world of senses defined by Buddhist doctrines. *The Heart of the Perfection of Transcendent Wisdom* (*The Heart Sutra*), the best-known Buddhist scripture, states that "Shariputra, the characteristics of Blank Essence of all these things are: neither born nor deceased, neither dirty nor clean, neither increasing nor decreasing. Therefore in Blank Essence there are no phenomena, no feeling, conceptualization, motivation, consciousness" (trans. Lin Yutang). This core teaching of Mahāyāna Buddhism explicates the emptiness of the phenomenon of the sensory world. This illusory sense of "se" is seen in "The Spyring"/"Se, Jie" as both Shahlu/Chia-chih as a spy in disguise and Mr. Tai/Mr. Yee as the head of the collaboration government's secret agency, as well as their "romantic" relationship, are all deceptive and imaginary to both the characters themselves and to the readers as observers.

The Chinese saying *rensheng ru xi, xi ru rensheng* 人生如戲，戲如人生 [life is like a drama; drama is like life] points to the notion of performance and performativity in both versions of Chang's story. Shahlu/Chia-chih only finds her true self through performance, which exposes the performative spectrum of patriotism and nationalism, the apparent cause of her spy activities. In her "Preface" to *Xuji* (1988), Chang states that she is happy to see that the short story she began to construct in 1953 has found its imitation in real life (*Xuji* 7). In "Se, Jie," Chia-chih, performing her role as a seductive spy, realizes that she has been let down by Kuang Yumin, Liang Rusheng, and other students who might have tricked her for sexual advancement in the first place, and by Old Wu, who manipulates her for his political agenda at the cost of her sexuality and her life. Her disappointment in the integrity of the assassination group and the mastermind behind the scenes deconstructs the nationalistic patriotism to which she is subjugated. Confused by Mr. Tai/Mr. Yee's love for her, Shahlu/Chia-chih chooses to honour her individual desire and forsake the collective responsibility, which abruptly subverts the ideology of self-sacrifice for the sake of national benefits in Chinese culture.

Chang translated and revised her narrative multiple times. In her letter to Stephen Soong dated April 1, 1974, she notes that she planned to revise the plot again because she spotted some scenes perplexing after having reread it many years later: 「等改寫完了譯成英文的時候，又發現有個心理上的 gap [坎]沒有交代」 [I discovered a psychological gap that had not been explained after having finished the revision and translated into English] (*To My Beloved Friends* 1.232). Though it is unclear whether Chang wrote the Chinese version before the English or vice versa, it is evident that she had rewritten both versions simultaneously and alternatively, more than once and many times for the

Chinese version. Which version was composed first is irrelevant for this discussion; what is important here is that her creation process involved numerous instances of translation and rewriting. Hence, her practice of self-translation deconstructs the linear process of translation and the conventional hierarchy between the source text and the translation.

In "Wangranji," Chang points out that she wrote "Se, Jie" in the 1950s but had revised it many times even after its first publication in 1977. The major reason for the long process of revision is that this story had once shocked and moved her, and she was therefore willing to revise it repeatedly for more than twenty years. Even when she looked back, she could only remember the surprise and happiness in acquiring the materials and the experience of rewriting, without acknowledging the passage of almost thirty years during the process:「愛就是不問值不值得」[Love is not to ask if it is worth it or not] ("Wangrangji" 4). She further relates her passion for "Se, Jie" to poetry:「此情可待成追憶，只是當時已惘然。」[This affection in pursuit has already become a memory, though dazed and confused at that time] ("Wangrangji" 4). These two verses are derived from the Chinese poem "Jinse"〈錦瑟〉("Adorned Zither"), written by the late Tang poet Li Shangyin 李商隱 (813–858). Li's poem contains several allusions to classical Chinese literature and history that represent the poet's feelings of sorrow and frustration due to his failures in love and career pursuit, which have been haunting him throughout his old age. The last two verses of this poem convey a sense of melancholia, which is also present in "The Spyring"/"Se, Jie." Even though Shahlu's/Chia-chih's identity, her relationship with Mr. Tai/Mr. Yee, and her petty thoughts about the vanity of diamond rings are deceptive, as the historical and fictional references in Li Shangyin's "Jin Se" serve to indicate, Shahlu/Chia-chih is bewildered and continues to indulge in the illusion.

Similarly, Chang's constant revisions to the story were themselves driven by the sense of melancholia she had been feeling for almost thirty years, possibly deriving from her relationship with her first husband, Hu Lancheng. Chang had once been so deeply in love with Hu that she married him despite the disapproval of her family, including her beloved aunt, and of society. She was also willing to subsidize Hu several times when he was in exile, even after acknowledging his extramarital affairs. Hu's repeated betrayal of Chang's affection led to the latter's feelings of pursuing unattainable love, a sentiment that is echoed in "The Spyring" and "Se, Jie." Both Hu and Mr. Tai/Mr. Yee were collaborators with the Japanese during the second Sino-Japanese war, and both Chang and Shahlu/Chia-chih had studied at the University of Hong Kong, before they graduated due to the Japanese occupation of Hong Kong in 1941. Moreover, while Chang devoted her first passionate love to Hu who in return was unfaithful to her, Shahlu/Chia-chih thought Mr. Tai/Mr. Yee loved her and therefore saved him, but was ultimately killed at his hand (Lovell, "Foreword" xix). All of these similarities, and the sense of melancholy present in both stories, underscore the theme of illusory and unobtainable love that the allusions to Li Shangyin's "Jin Se" further serve to illuminate.

As a diasporic intellectual in the United States, Eileen Chang served as a hybridized cultural translator in (post)colonized crossroads, thus effectively connecting the colonial and the global. She became a global subject who was more open to (post)colonial hybridization and capable of taking an *avant-garde* role in search of an alternative global bourgeois modernity. Instead of serving as a representative of so-called Chinese traditions, Chang produces a "transcultural hospitality" that bridges various cultural divisions and transgresses established parameters of nationality, race, ethnicity, cultures, languages, history, fiction, performance, and performativity, as well as personal and poetic memories. Through her multiple self-translation and rewriting, Chang recreates her perception of history, her life experience, and her individual and collective selves, as a way to continuously reconstruct her cross-cultural self-conception.

CONCLUSION

The Performativity of Eileen Chang's Self-Translation

Translation in Chinese literary history occupies a core position in the exchange of language and culture and the destabilization of linguistic, cultural, ethnic, and national boundaries. For instance, Buddhist Sutras, ancient medicine, astronomy, and mathematics texts from India have been translated into Chinese since the Eastern Han Dynasty (AD 25–AD 220). The Bible has been translated since AD 300, with the first written record in AD 635 during the Tang Dynasty (618–907). Translations of Arabic medical science and Italian Jesuit missionary Matteo Ricci's (1552–1610) introduction of world geography were produced during the Ming Dynasty (1368–1644), and translations of science and technology were encouraged as part of a national salvation project in the late Qing dynasty.

Since the mid-nineteenth century, substantial translations of Western science, technology, literature, social sciences, and various ideologies and discourses, including liberalism, pragmatism, nationalism, anarchism, socialism, and feminism, into Chinese have been produced by translators such as Yan Fu 嚴復 (1854–1921), Lin Shu 林紓 (1852–1924), Lu Xun 魯迅 (1881–1936), and Zhou Zouren 周作人 (1885–1967). Their translations brought forth new ideas that revolutionized the vernacular Chinese language, narrative modes, and literary genres of fiction, essays, poetry, and drama, and literary techniques and themes such as stream of consciousness, realism, and romanticism, while challenging traditional ethics, principles, and practices, especially the Confucian doctrines of human relationships, family values, and gender hierarchy, as well as folk cultural superstitions, legal systems, and political perspectives.

Influential Chinese translation theories arose in the late nineteenth century and afterward. Most significantly, Yan Fu published his translation principles of *xin* 信 [faithfulness], *da* 達 [fluency], and *ya* 雅 [elegance] in 1898, and these principles laid the foundations on which future Chinese translators would follow, criticize, and expand. In the 1950s and 1960s, Fu Lei 傅雷 (1908–1966) proposed the translation theory of *shensi* 神似 [resemblance of spirit], and Qian Zhongshu 錢鐘書 (1910–1998) suggested the translation condition of *huajing* 化境 [a state of sublimity]. Modern scholars of Chinese translation history and theory include Xie Tianzhen 謝天振 (1944–2020), Wang Ning 王寧 (b. 1936), Xu Jun 許鈞 (b. 1955), and Lawrence Wang Chi Wong 王宏志.

© JESSICA TSUI-YAN LI, 2025 | DOI:10.1163/9789004730052_018

Western translation theories have continued to evolve and change; for instance, the debate between word-for-word and sense-for-sense translation dates back to the days of the Roman orators. The trend of foreignizing translation became popular in Germany in the eighteenth and nineteenth centuries as a strategy to enrich the German language and literature. From the twentieth century onward, Western translation theories have incorporated numerous theories and methodologies, pragmatics, computerized technology, perspectives on the process and outcomes of translation, and critical discourses such as poststructuralism, postcolonialism, feminism, Marxism, and globalization. Self-translation as a distinctive practice has received more attention in the twenty-first century. Representative works of academic discussion on self-translation include Jan Walsh Hokenson's and Marcella Munson's *The Bilingual Text: History and Theory of Literary Self-Translation* and Anthony Cordingley's anthology *Self-Translation: Brokering Originality in Hybrid Culture* (2013).

Self-translation activities often take place when authors in a newly established political state welcome foreign literature to enrich their own language and culture while also reaching out to foreign readers to promote their literature to the world. Sometimes authors are coerced to write in politically dominant languages due to imperialism or colonialism, but then self-translate their own works in their mother tongue when they are allowed to do so. Authors in exile in foreign countries due to political turmoil, wars, or religious persecution at home also write and translate their own works in their mother tongue and in the languages of their adopted countries. Globalization has promoted migration and travel, and has also made self-translations more accessible for readers in different linguistic and cultural zones. Charles d'Orléans (1394–1465), Sor Juana Inés de la Cruz (1648–1695), Carlo Goldoni (1707–1793), Giuseppe Ungaretti (1888–1970), Vladimir Nabokov (1899–1977), Samuel Beckett (1906–1989), and Rosario Ferré (1938–2016) are but a few of the many self-translators throughout history (Cordingley 45–54).

Chinese and English bilingual writers, in particular, who translated their own literary works have flourished since the twentieth century; some of these include Lin Yutang 林語堂 (1895–1976), Xiao Qian 蕭乾 (1910–1999), Yu Kwang-chung 余光中 (1928–2017), Kenneth Hsien-yung Pai 白先勇 (b. 1937), and Leung Ping-kwan/Yasi 梁秉鈞/也斯 (1949–2013). The newly established Republic of China (1919–1948) embraced foreign literature and learning, which not only strengthened the national culture but also encouraged Chinese bilingual writers. Writers who have migrated, been exiled, or traveled to other countries due to wars and political instability at home, economic opportunities abroad, personal lived experiences, or other circumstances, translate their own

CONCLUSION

works from one language into another to reach readers in different linguistic and regional markets, as well as for personal literary ambitions.

These translation histories and theories provide glimpses of the sociohistorical background of the study of Eileen Chang's self-translation. This project argues that Chang translates her conception of the self by rewriting her personal thoughts and feelings, lived experiences, and family sagas in her memoirs, semi-autobiographical novels, and family photo album so as to construct her individual, relational, and collective diasporic identities. Her personal and family narrative written during different times of her life can be seen as her ongoing lifelong process of self-exploration and self-healing. They demonstrate the changes in her thoughts and feelings towards her conception of the self, family members, friends, and historical events, which shows that the identities she constructs in her works are fluid rather than static, multiple rather than singular, and performative rather than essential.

Chang's writing and self-translation are interdependent. While her source texts provide the plot and characters for the creation of her self-translation, her self-translations shed new light on her source texts through additions, omissions, word choices, and changes in tones, styles, and techniques. Chang, as the author, has access to her authorial intention and the power of authorship to make changes in her self-translation. Her re-evaluation and re-contextualization of her source texts in the process of self-translation show her creativity and her consideration for the respective specific needs of Sinophone and Anglophone readers. Her multiple bilingual writings and self-translations destabilize the traditional linear process of translation and give rise to a multi-dimensional process of creation.

Chang performs the role of a cultural translator who constantly travels between the Sinophone and Anglophone worlds in her writing and self-translation. She interprets Chinese culture from her specific position of a Chinese woman, who came from a declining aristocratic family, with a transcultural higher education background and lived experience. Employing comparative perspectives, she acts as a native cultural insider giving insightful knowledge in her English writing and self-translation, while she distances herself from, and examines from alternative perspectives, Chinese culture in her Chinese writing and self-translation. Her translations transform the language, syntax, sentence, structure, meaning, and cultural connotations of her source texts and produce meaning from her own perspectives.

In her essays, short stories, novels, and self-translations written during and after the Cold War period, Chang creates a political ambivalence in her works that allows her to navigate through different sociopolitical circumstances and instances of censorship. She paradoxically claims the authenticity of the events depicted in her novels and self-translations set during the land reform movement in mainland China in the 1950s, but discloses the unreliability of her sources by revealing their fictionality. She also demonstrates her distancing from political ideologies and entities in her characterizations of Chinese peasants' confusion about the various political parties of the time. Using postmodern intertextuality, she parodies reality in her novels and self-translations and reconstructs meanings in each new version. I have proposed the term "transcultural hospitality" for the characteristic of Chang's self-translations that accommodates dynamic and plural cultural interactions across linguistic and cultural borders, whether in conflict or in harmony with one another. Her self-translations produce meanings that transgress borders between cultures, ethics, values, and hierarchies, as well as those between fiction and reality, author and self-translator, and the Sinophone and Anglophone worlds. Overall, this project argues that Chang's self-translations produce representations of meaning, identity, and agency as manifestations of their performativity.

1 Significance of Eileen Chang's Self-Translation

Eileen Chang's phenomenal fashion of self-translation is unique among writers and translators. Chang's self-translation is not mere repetition, but a way she finds to express herself in new linguistic and cultural realms. She translated her self into her essays, short stories, novels, photographic autobiography, which were mainly based on her life experience, family anecdotes, and the history in which she was situated. She was a Chinese-English bilingual writer and self-translator who translated her own writing from Chinese into English and vice versa. Most of all, her exercises of self-translation proliferated throughout her entire literary career. Chang used subjective languages and perspectives not only to translate her self and construct her identities, but also to revisit the past and heal traumatic experiences, to tackle the challenging dynamism of her immediate presence, and to deal with her sense of displacement from Shanghai to Tianjin, Hong Kong, Wenzhou, Japan, Taiwan, and the United States, spanning seven decades from the May Fourth Movement to the Second World War, the Cold War, and the post-Cold War era.

A thorough analysis of Chang's writing and self-translation as performative acts illuminates her reconstruction of individual, collective, gender, social, and cultural identities, of which she explores the constitutive factors in terms of gender hierarchy, social changes, cultural diversity, national transition and building, and global dynamics. Self-translation is Chang's interpretation of the

CONCLUSION

world in which she resided at a specific historical time, from the turn of the twentieth century nearly to its end.

In her works, Chang translates the conflicts of individualist self-identity imported from the West during the New Culture Movement in China in the 1910s and 1920s, and the Confucian collective identity defined as the sacrifice of individuals for collective goods. For example, Shahlu and Wang Chia-chih in the "The Spyring" (2008) and "Se, Jie" (1977), respectively, are required to surrender their bodies and sexualities for nationalistic missions, while disregarding their personal feelings and desires. Their psychological struggles of sensuality, suspicion, and confusion lead to their decisions to let the collaborators Mr. Tai and Mr. Yee escape, at the cost of their own lives. Shahlu and Wang Chia-chih, nevertheless, listen to their bodies and reject the patriotic assignments imposed on them, which turns the conventional hierarchy of nationalism over female sexuality upside down.

Gender identity in flux in Chinese society in the twentieth century is a significant topic in many of Chang's works and self-translations. She vividly translates in her works the changing power relationship between men and women, the controversial body politics, and the empowerment of women in modern China. In traditional patriarchal Chinese culture, men's interests are prioritized over women's, and the female body is largely seen as a commodity for consumption or sale. For instance, Ts'ao Ch'i-ch'iao in "Jinsuoji" ("The Golden Cangue," 1943) and "The Golden Cangue" (1971) and Chai Yindi in *The Rouge of the North* (1967) and *Yuannü* 《怨女》 (*Embittered Woman*, 1966) marry wealthy but paralyzed husbands to produce male heirs in exchange for materialistic returns at the expense of the fulfillment of love and sexual desires. Both Ch'i-ch'iao and Yindi are socially expected to rely on a strong husband to assert their position in society. They are, however, looked down upon by others partly because their husbands are invalids, and hope for change can only be seen in the younger generations.

Chang also translates her social identity in her writing. She was born and spent most of her childhood and teenage years in Shanghai. After studying at the University of Hong Kong, she expanded her horizon and wrote seven stories based on her Hong Kong experience after she returned to her birthplace. She claims in her essay "Daodi shi Shanghai ren" 〈到底是上海人〉 "Shanghainese, After All" (1943) that she wrote those stories from the perspectives of Shanghainese for Shanghainese readers (57), strongly asserting her Shanghainese identity at this stage in her writing career. After the Second Sino-Japanese War, she traveled to Wenzhou to seek her then-husband Hu Lancheng, with whom she lived a rural life. In the 1950s, she traveled to Hong Kong and Japan, then moved to the United States in 1955, and visited Taiwan and Hong

Kong briefly in 1961 and 1962. In her essays "A Return to the Frontier" (1963) and "Chongfang biancheng" (2008), she regards the political oscillation among Hong Kong, Taiwan, mainland China, and the United States from a broader viewpoint. Her essay "Yijiubaba zhi – ?" 一九八八 至——? [1988 to – ?, 1995] constructs her Chinese American diasporic identity that crosses the boundaries of the Chinese and English languages, Chinese and South Asian ethnicities in the United States, and the connection of natural scenery in the present and in her memory.

Chang's cultural identity is characterized by in-betweenness, her geographical moving between cities and countries, her perception between Shanghainese, Hong Kong, and Chinese American diasporas, and her code switching between Chinese and English languages. For example, in her English essay "Still Alive" (1943), she performs the role of cultural translator to translate Peking Opera in modern China, from her Chinese points of view, to Anglophone readers in Shanghai. In switching her language and viewpoint to translate this essay into Chinese as "Yangren kan jingxi ji qita" 〈洋人看京戲及其他〉 ("Westerners Watching Peking Operas and Other Issues," 1943), she speaks from what she claims as a "foreigner's" perspective to examine this significant Chinese performing art. Her analysis embraces the Chinese conventions of quotation, mixing of classical and vernacular speeches, collective memory, and the creativity of artists and audiences in the genre's ongoing transformation.

Chang took ownership of her self by breaking away from her social, cultural, and political comfort zones to embrace the challenges and changes in her life. She defines her new being by her conscious actions and decisions to cross boundaries. Her writing and self-translation show her adaptability and active responses to all of the demanding forces and transformations she faces at different stages of her life, as reflected in her works. For example, she depicts her encounter with Japanese encroachment during her undergraduate studies in Hong Kong in her memoir "Jinyulu" 〈燼餘錄〉 ("From the Ashes," 1944), which examines her psychological journey of the loss of innocence and her growing insight into human nature in her construction of a young female Chinese bourgeoise identity. Many years later in the United States, she recounts this experience in her English semi-autobiographical novel *The Book of Change* (2010), whose female protagonist, Lute, uses her wisdom and courage in heroically obtaining steerage boat tickets for her friends and herself so they can return to Shanghai (281–290). She revisits this episode in her Chinese semi-autobiographical novel *Xiao tuanyuan* 《小團圓》 (*Little Reunions*, 2009) but simply as enquiries about boat tickets without further elaboration (71), partly due to political sensibility.

CONCLUSION

Throughout her writing career, Chang experiences changes of perspective, constructions of identity, and evolutions of aspiration. In the 1940s, she wrote several Chinese short stories with distinctive literary styles, using devices such as metaphors, irony, and equivocal contrast, to seek self-expression and actualization. She was in a stage of finding her own voice and found her position as a writer. At this time she also wrote English cultural essays on Chinese vestural trends, Peking Opera, and Chinese religion and film criticism in the magazine *The xxth Century*. She tried out different voices and adopted different languages and perspectives to build up her reputation in Shanghai.

Chang wrote more works in English after having moved first to Hong Kong and then to the United States in the 1950s. She translated a number of American essays and novels from English into Chinese, and wrote *The Rice Sprout Song – A Novel of Modern China* (1955), *Yangge* 《秧歌》 1954), *Chidi zhi lian* 《赤地之戀》 (*The Romance of the Redland*, 1954), and *Naked Earth – A Novel about China* (1956), while working for the United States Information Services (USIS) in Hong Kong. In the United States, she explored a new Chinese American identity, as she catered to her direct readership in the United States, dedicated herself to writing in English, and aimed to establish her status as an international writer in the English-speaking world.

Her English publications did not enjoy wide popularity in the United States, and she acknowledged that the subject matter of her writing may not have fit into the stereotypes of Americans of the time:

> I have lived in the U.S. for the last ten years, largely occupied with two unpublished novels about China before the Communists, a third that I am still working on, and translations, film and radio scripts in Chinese. The publishers here seem to agree that the characters in those two novels are too unpleasant; even the poor are no better. An editor at Knopf's wrote that if things were so bad before, then the Communists would actually be deliverance.
>
> CHANG, "Chang, Eileen (Chang Ai-ling)" 297

The Chinese names and historical plots in her works might be too complicated for the reading public in the United States, and her bookish use of the English language was also a barrier to American readers. Her Chinese publications, however, have been very popular in Chinese communities in Hong Kong and Taiwan since the 1960s, and in mainland China since the late 1970s, due to their different political environments.

The performativity of Chang's writing and self-translation, as a result, exhibits a dynamic condition that is not in a well-defined and static state, but in a fluid situation. Chang always adjusted her self, identities, languages, perspectives, and worlds to where she resided at the time. All of these are reflected in her writing strategies, such as choices of themes, genres, and characters' psychological realms, to deal with various subject matters with which she was concerned, in response to changes in the geographical, social, cultural, and political realms. For instance, Fan Liuyuan 范柳原, the protagonist of her short story "Qingcheng zhi lian" 〈傾城之戀〉 ("Love in a Fallen City," 1943), experiences transformations as a character prompted by the changes in his environment. He progresses from keeping Bai Liusu 白流蘇 as a mistress to marrying her for the sake of convenience. For others, this seems a romantic love story, given that love exists in many different kinds and manifestations.

Chang adopted different genres in her writing and self-translation to adjust to her subject matter, a performative writing strategy that is not absolute, but flexible. She retells her childhood and adolescent memories in works such as "Siyu" 〈私語〉 ("Whispers," 1944), which she wrote in her young adulthood as a focus on an important part of her life. Later, she recreated her life experiences with her family, education, romances, marriages, abortion, and writing career in semi-autobiographical novels that allow her to include more detailed descriptions, characters, and plots. For her cultural and film analysis, she chose the genre of essays, in which she presents her arguments and debates with examples and comparison clearly. Most of her short stories, such as "Stale Mates: A Short Story Set in the Time When Love Came to China" (1956), "Wusi yishi – Luo Wentao sanmei tuanyuan" 〈五四遺事——羅文濤三美團圓〉 ("Regret after the May Fourth Movement: The Reunion of Luo Wentao and the Three Beauties," 1957), "Deng" 〈等〉 ("Waiting," 1944), "Little Finger Up" (1961), "Guihuazheng – A Xiao beiqiu" 〈桂花蒸——阿小悲秋〉 ("Steamed Osmanthus: Ah Xiao's Unhappy Autumn," 1944), and "Shame, Amah" (1962), focus on central incidents and changes in their characters' lives. She also uses her family photo albums in *Duizhaoji – kan lao zhaoxiangbu* 《對照記：看老照相簿》 (*Mutual Reflections – Looking at Old Photo Albums*, 1994) to unite visual images and written text, and thus performatively construct a pictorial autobiography.

This book's discussion of Eileen Chang's lifelong self-translation produces a fascinating picture of her construction of identity, as well as her linguistic and cultural translations of modern China through her continuous negotiations between family sagas and revisiting of images, and between personal reflection and public history amid transcultural hybridization in the twentieth century. Chang pays attention to the needs of her readers and to their respective linguistic and cultural backgrounds. Her earlier writings and self-translations on Chinese culture, covering subject areas such as Chinese religion, Peking Opera, and Chinese fashion, first published in Shanghai in 1943, create an alienating

CONCLUSION   271

effect in cultural translation. When self-translating her short stories and novels from Chinese into English, and vice versa, between the 1940s and the 1960s, she produces a state of in-betweenness in her themes, characters, languages, and literary styles. Her essays, short stories, and novels composed and self-translated during the Cold War period indicate her use of authorial power in navigating censorship by using political ambivalence. Her later self-translations of her semi-autobiographical novels revisit and reimagine the originals' plots, structures, and use of literary devices and display a rather loose translation technique that appears at first glance to be rewriting. All of her writings and self-translations demonstrate her fluid condition of being situated in, and constantly travelling between, different linguistic and cultural zones.

Chang's writing in both Chinese and English and her translations of her own works from one language into another were influenced by her sociohistorical contexts, lived experiences and circumstances, and personal literary ambitions. She grew up in Shanghai in the 1920s and 1930s when the Republic of China had been newly established and Chinese intellectuals were eager to enrich their literature and culture through translation. She had lived in cosmopolitan cities, such as Shanghai and Hong Kong, where she had the platform and potential readers for her English-language publications. Later, she immigrated to the United States, where she needed to write in English in order to reach her newly adopted country's readers. It was by writing in English that she established herself as a world writer. In "Siyu," Chang declared that she wanted to be more famous than her predecessor Lin Yutang 林語堂 (1895–1976), who published and translated novels into English (162). By using the English language to write what I have called culturally Chinese stories, Chang adopted a Western "instrument" to help globalize her writing, and thus managed to associate her works with Western modernity and modern literature.

Chang's English publication helped to move not only her own work, but arguably also modern Chinese literature and culture in general, from what some might perceive as the periphery to the centre of the world in the twentieth century. Chang's English writings are also experiments in using the English language to tell culturally Chinese stories for a specifically Anglophone reading public, though her dream of global literary fame would remain unfulfilled in her lifetime. There are several reasons for the unpopularity of her English works during her lifetime: her usage of English is fluent, but rather bookish, and sometimes sounds unnatural to Anglophone readers; the numerous Chinese names and characters in her stories, along with their complicated Chinese historical and political settings, may not appeal to Anglophone readers who are unfamiliar with Chinese culture and history; and, her stories that depict social issues in pre-Communist China do not conform to American ideology during the Cold War period: if pre-Communist China was not ideal, then the Communists did improve the country's situation, an unpopular, and officially discouraged, opinion among Americans of the time. In her late writing and translation stages, she conducted extensive research and incorporated her results into her (re)writing and (re)translation. Nevertheless, these stories serve as Chang's retrospective means of looking back at China's modernization efforts, as well as her own past in China, as her English works form parallels and contrasts with the modernization and Westernization movements in twentieth-century China. As mentioned above, Chang used Western means of production to critique Chinese culture, a reversal of the practice of using Western methods to preserve Chinese traditions. Her English texts, in a sense, are themselves already translations of her culturally Chinese stories.

In the case of Chang's subsequent Chinese translations, however, the English texts are the sources. Chinese culture cannot be fully represented in Chang's Anglophone texts because of the English/American cultural perspectives inherent in the English language, which may in fact contradict any possible ideological connotations embedded in the Chinese language. Since she was aware of her English-language readers' cultural background and its limits when she wrote her stories, Chang highlighted and expanded upon Chinese cultural elements in her translations in order to enable Anglophone readers to better understand the cultural contexts of her stories. On the other hand, she may sometimes have considered the Chinese language insufficient for expressing new ideas; therefore, she opted to use the English language and write from a Western perspective in order to draw attention to and criticize traditional Chinese cultural codes, particularly those that regulated gender relations. She therefore deliberately changed her culturally Chinese stories to recontextualize them in the English language and culture. In her own translations, she could rearticulate gender relations in a different language with new and additional meanings and perspectives.

Chang's English and Chinese writings and translations construct and give voice to the changing historical and cultural situations of China in the twentieth century, when new values challenged old ones and Western ideas encountered Chinese traditions. Chang makes the interactions of Western ideas and Chinese society clearer in her English texts so that her readers will better understand the specific contextual meanings of these interactions. The Chinese traditions she revisits and reimagines in her works are most visible and understandable in the Chinese texts intended for a Chinese audience. The combination of both the English and Chinese versions of Chang's works thus presents a more comprehensive picture of Westernization in China following the May Fourth Movement. Chang's Chinese and English translations during

CONCLUSION   273

the Cold War period also brought forth the possibility of global convergence. However, the implications are widely different for Sinophone and Anglophone readers who experience the stories in their respective languages, because words in different languages may carry dissimilar and even contradictory social and cultural connotations. Nevertheless, both versions of Chang's stories and essays interact to produce vivid images of the clash between Chinese and English languages, cultures, traditions, and values in twentieth-century China. In order to grasp the significance of different versions, the ideal reader would be, like Chang herself, a Chinese/English bilingual reader who also recognizes the nuances of differences between these cultures and languages.

The performativity of Eileen Chang's self-translation stands in the meaning-making attributes of language that empower her works in the construction of her individual, relational, and collective diasporic identities by bringing her conception of the self from the inside to the outside, from the unconscious to the conscious, and from the private to the public. She also rearticulates her voices in different languages and cultures by constantly occupying different linguistic and cultural spaces and traveling between these spaces. Her self-translation is not a mere literary curiosity, but a condition of in-betweenness entangling with various linguistic and cultural discourses, authorship, re-evaluation, re-contextualization, globalization, interpretation, distanciation, transformation, authenticity, postmodern intertextuality, transcultural hospitality, transgression, and metacommentary. Her bilingual writings and self-translations destabilize the boundaries between author and self-translator, Chinese and English languages and cultures, and Chinese and Western literary conventions. By performing the roles of bilingual writer and self-translator, Chang produces transcultural meaning in her source text and self-translation from her own perspectives derived from her specific sociohistorical position, and she uses her lifelong experiences in bilingual writing and in self-translation to performatively construct her fluid and plural identities.

Bibliography

Works by Zhang Ailing 張愛玲 (Eileen Chang)

Chang, Eileen, and Hu Lancheng 張愛玲, 胡蘭成. *Zhang ai Hu shuo* 《張愛胡說》 [*Zhang Loves Hu Speaks*]. Wenhui chubanshe 文匯出版社, 2003.

Chang, Eileen, Stephen Soong, and Mae Fong Soong 張愛玲, 宋淇, 宋鄺文美. *Zhang Ailing wanglai shuxinji: zhi duan qing chang* 《張愛玲往來書信集： 紙短情長》 [*To My Beloved Friends: Letters of Eileen Chang, Stephen Soong & Mae Fong Soong*], *Vol. 1, 1955–1979.* Crown, 2020.

Chang, Eileen, translator. "Ouniesi Haimingwei" 〈歐涅斯・海明威〉 ["Ernest Hemingway"]. *Meiguo xiandai qida xiaoshuojia* 《美國現代七大小說家》 [*Seven Modern American Novelists*], edited by William Van O'Connor, Jinri shijie chubanshe 今日世界出版社, 1967.

Chang, Eileen, translator. "Wutou qishi" 〈無頭騎士〉 ["The Legend of Sleepy Hollow"]. *The Legend of Sleepy Hollow,* by Washington Irving, 1953, Jinri shijie chubanshe 今日世界出版社, 1983, pp. 1–46.

Chang, Eileen, translator. *Aimosen xuanji* 《愛默森選集》 [*Selected Writings of Emerson*]. 1995. *Complete Works of Eileen Chang*, Vol. 16, 2004.

Chang, Eileen, translator. *Fool in the Reeds*, by Chen Chi-ying (Chen Jiying 陳紀瀅), Meiya chubanshe, 1976.

Chang, Eileen (Ai Zhen 愛珍), translator. *Haidi changzheng ji* 《海底長征記》 [*Submarine!*] by Edward L. Beach, Zhongnan ribao 中南日報 [Chung Nan Daily News], 1954.

Chang, Eileen, translator. *Haishanghua kai* 《海上花開》 [*The Blossoming of Flowers on the Sea*], by Han Bangqing 韓邦慶 (Han Ziyun 韓子雲), *Complete Works of Eileen Chang,* Vol. 10, 2004.

Chang, Eileen, translator. *Haishanghua liezhuan* 《海上花列傳》 [*The Sing-Song Girls of Shanghai*], by Han Bangqing 韓邦慶, Columbia UP, 2005.

Chang, Eileen, translator. *Haishanghua luo* 《海上花落》 [*The Falling of Flowers on the Sea*], by Han Bangqing 韓邦慶. *Complete Works of Eileen Chang*, Vol. 11, Paper Back, 2004.

Chang, Eileen, translator. *Laoren yu hai* 《老人與海》 [*The Old Man and the Sea*], by Ernest Hemingway, Jinrishijie chubanshe 今日世界出版, 1972.

Chang, Eileen, translator. *Luyuanchangchun* 《鹿苑長春》 [*The Yearling*], by Marjorie K. Rawlings, Jinri shijie chubanshe 今日世界出版社, 1963.

Chang, Eileen, translator. *Xiaolu* 《小鹿》 [*The Yearling*], by Marjorie K. Rawlings, Tianfeng chubanshe 天風出版社, 1962.

Chang, Eileen. "'On With the Show' and 'The Call of Spring.'" *The xxth Century,* vol. 5, no. 4, 1943, p. 278.

BIBLIOGRAPHY

Chang, Eileen. "'Song of Autumn' and 'Cloud Over the Moon.'" *The xxth Century,* vol. 5, no. 1, 1943, pp. 75–76.

Chang, Eileen. "Yijiubaba zhi – ?" 〈一九八八 至——?〉 [1988 to – ?]. 1995. *Zhang Ailing diancang 13: Duizhaoji – sanwen ji san: yijiujiuling niandai* 《張愛玲典藏13：對照記——散文集三：一九九0年代》 [*Eileen Chang Classics Collection 13: Mutual Reflections – Collected Works of Prose: 1990s*], Crown Publishing, 2020.

Chang, Eileen. "A Beating." *The Chinese Essay,* translated and edited by David Pollard, Hurst, 2000, pp. 292–293.

Chang, Eileen. "A Chronicle of Changing Clothes." Translated by Andrew F. Jones, *Positions: East Asia Cultures Critique,* vol. 11, no. 2, 2003, pp. 427–441.

Chang, Eileen. "A Return to the Frontier." 1963. *Zhang Ailing quanji: Chongfang biancheng* 《張愛玲全集：重訪邊城》 [*Complete Works of Eileen Chang: A Return to the Frontier*], Crown, 2008, pp. 62–80.

Chang, Eileen. "Biaoyi xiyi ji qita" 〈表姨細姨及其他〉 ["Biao Aunt, Little Aunt, and Other Issues"], 1979, *Zhang Ailing quanji: Xuji* 《張愛玲全集：續集》 [*Complete Works of Eileen Chang: Sequel*], Crown, 2000, pp. 25–32.

Chang, Eileen. "Chinese Life and Fashions." *The xxth Century,* vol. 4, no. 1, 1943, pp. 54–61.

Chang, Eileen. "Chinese Translation: A Vehicle of Cultural Influence." *PMLA,* vol. 130, no. 2, March 2015, pp. 490–498.

Chang, Eileen. "Chongfang biancheng" 〈重訪邊城〉 ["A Return to the Frontier"]. *Zhang Ailing quanji: Chongfang biancheng* 《張愛玲全集：重訪邊城》 [*Complete Works of Eileen Chang: A Return to the Frontier*], Crown, 2008, pp. 10–61.

Chang, Eileen. "Chuanqi zaiban zixu" 「傳奇再版自序」 ["Self-Preface to the Second Edition of *Romances*"]. 1947. *Zhang Ailing duanpian xiaoshuo ji* 《張愛玲短篇小說集》 [*The Collected Stories of Eileen Chang*], Huangguan chubanshe 皇冠出版社 [Crown Publishing Ltd.], 1980, p. 3.

Chang, Eileen. "Daoluyimu" 〈道路以目〉 ["Seeing with Streets"]. *Liuyan* 《流言》 [*Written on Water*], Crown, 2000, pp. 59–66.

Chang, Eileen. "Demons and Fairies." *The xxth Century,* vol. 5, no. 6, 1943, pp. 421–429.

Chang, Eileen. "Deng" 〈等〉 ["Waiting"]. 1944. *Complete Works of Eileen Chang,* Vol. 5, 2004, pp. 99–114.

Chang, Eileen. "Educating the Family." *The xxth Century,* vol. 5, no. 5, 1943, p. 358.

Chang, Eileen. "Eileen Chang at the University of Hong Kong: An Online Presentation of Images and Documents from the Archives." *University of Hong Kong,* 28 Sept. 2020, www.hku.hk/press/press-releases/detail/21623.html.

Chang, Eileen. "Gengyiji" 〈更衣記〉 ["A Chronicle of Changing Clothes"]. 1943. *Complete Works of Eileen Chang,* Vol. 3, 2004, pp. 67–76.

Chang, Eileen. "Gongyu shenghuo jiqu" 〈公寓生活寄趣〉 ["Notes on Apartment Life"]. 1943. *Zhang Ailing diancang 11: Huali yuan – sanwenjiyi: yijiusiling niadai* 《張愛玲典藏 11：華麗緣—散文集一：一九四0年代》 [*Eileen Chang Classics*

Collection 11: Splendid Serendipity: Collection of Short Stories – 1940s], Crown, 2020, pp. 35–40.

Chang, Eileen. "Guihuazheng: A Xiao beiqiu" 〈桂花蒸——阿小悲秋〉 ["Steamed Osmanthus: Ah Xiao's Unhappy Autumn"]. 1944. *Complete Works of Eileen Chang*, Vol. 5, 2004, pp. 115–137.

Chang, Eileen. "Huadiao" 〈花凋〉 ["Withering Flower"]. 1944. *Zhang Ailing diancang 02: Hongmeigui yu Baimeigui – duanpian xiaoshuoji er: yijiusisi – siwu nian* 《張愛玲典藏 02：紅玫瑰與白玫瑰——短篇小説集二：一九四四——四五年》 [*Eileen Chang Classics Collection: Red Rose and White Rose – Collection of Short Stories 2: 1944–45*], Crown, 2020, pp. 92–113.

Chang, Eileen. "Jie yindeng" 〈借銀燈〉 ["Borrowing the Silver Spotlight"]. *Complete Works of Eileen Chang*, vol. 3, 2004, pp. 93–96.

Chang, Eileen. "Jinyulu" 〈燼餘錄〉 ["From the Ashes"]. 1944. *Zhang Ailing Diancang 11: Huali yuan – sanwenjiyi: yijiusiling niadai* 《張愛玲典藏 11：華麗緣—散文集一：一九四〇年代》 [*Eileen Chang Classics Collection: Splendid Serendipity: Collection of Short Stories – 1940s*], Crown, 2020, pp. 64–76.

Chang, Eileen. "Letter to Ferdinand Reyher" (February 20, 1962). *Zhang Ailing xue* 《張愛玲學》 [*Eileen Chang Reconsidered*], Second Edition, edited by Kao Chuan Chih 高全之, Maitian, 2011, p. 401.

Chang, Eileen. "Letter to Ferdinand Reyher" (March 2, 1962). *Zhang Ailing xue* 《張愛玲學》 [*Eileen Chang Reconsidered*], Second Edition, edited by Kao Chuan Chih 高全之, Maitian, 2011, p. 403.

Chang, Eileen. "Letter to Hsia Chih-tsing 夏志清 dated April 6, 1988." *Zhang Ailing geiwodexinjian* 《張愛玲給我的信件》 [*Letters Given to Me by Eileen Chang*], edited by Hsia Chih-tsing, Lianhe wenxue 聯合文學, 2013, pp. 340–341.

Chang, Eileen. "Little Finger Up." *New Chinese Stories*, edited by Lucian Wu, Heritage P, 1961, pp. 65–83.

Chang, Eileen. "Mother and Daughter-in-Law." *The xxth Century*, vol. 5, no. 2–3, 1943, p. 202.

Chang, Eileen. "My Writing." Translated by Wendy Larson. *Modern Chinese Literary Thought – Writings on Literature 1893–1945*, edited by Kirk A. Denton, Stanford UP, 1996, pp. 436–442.

Chang, Eileen. "New England ... China." (title obscured), undated, Box: 12, Folder: 13.0. Ferdinand Reyher Papers, 0037 – LIT. Special Collections and University Archives, U of Maryland Libraries, archives.lib.umd.edu/repositories/2/arhival_objects/15152

Chang, Eileen. "Nüe er nüe" 〈謔而虐〉 ["Maltreatment Through Jokes"]. *Xishu jinghua* 《西書精華》 [*The Essence of Western Books*], vol. 6, 1941, pp. 168–173.

Chang, Eileen. "On the Screen: Wife, Vamp, Child." *The xxth Century*, vol. 4, no. 5, May 1943, pp. 392.

Chang, Eileen. "Poxi zijian" 〈婆媳之間〉 ["Between Mothers and Daughters-in-Law"]. Translated by Chen Bingliang 陳炳良, *Unitas*, vol. 3, no. 5, March 1987, pp. 46–47.

BIBLIOGRAPHY

Chang, Eileen. "Qingcheng zhi lian" 〈傾城之戀〉 ["Love in a Fallen City"]. 1943. *Complete Works of Eileen Chang*, vol. 5, 2004, pp. 187–231.

Chang, Eileen. "Qiuge he wuyun gaiyue" 〈秋歌和烏雲蓋月〉 ["Song of Autumn and Cloud Over the Moon"]. Translated by Lin Shuyi 林淑懿, *Unitas*, vol. 3, no. 5, March 1987, pp. 50–51.

Chang, Eileen. "Se, Jie" 〈色，戒〉 ["Lust, Caution"]. 1977. *Zhang Ailing quanji: Wangranji* 《張愛玲全集：惘然記》 [*Complete Works of Eileen Chang: A Record of Bewilderment*], Crown, 1999, pp. 10–36.

Chang, Eileen. "Shame, Amah!" *Eight Stories by Chinese Women*, edited by Nieh Hua-ling, Heritage P, 1962, pp. 91–114.

Chang, Eileen. "She Said Smiling." *Zhang Ailing Papers.* Special Collections, U of Southern California, 22 pages.

Chang, Eileen. "Siyu" 〈私語〉 ["Whispers"]. 1944. *Zhang Ailing diancang 11: Huali yuan – sanwenjiyi: yijiusiling niadai* 《張愛玲典藏 11：華麗緣——散文集一：一九四〇年代》 [*Magnificent Destiny: Collection of Short Stories – 1940s*], Crown, 2020, pp. 143–156.

Chang, Eileen. "'Song of Autumn' and 'Cloud Over the Moon.'" *The xxth Century*, vol. 5, no. 1, July 1943, pp. 75–76.

Chang, Eileen. "Stale Mates: A Short Story Set in the Time When Love Came to China." 1956. *Complete Works of Eileen Chang*, vol. 13, 2004, pp. 249–267.

Chang, Eileen. "Still Alive." *The xxth Century,* vol. 4, no. 6, 1943, pp. 432–438.

Chang, Eileen. "Taitai wansui" 〈太太萬歲〉 ["Long Live My Wife"]. 1946. *Zhang Ailing wenji • buyi* 《張愛玲文集・補遺》, edited by Zitong and Yiqing 子通, 亦清, Zhongguo huaqiao chubanshe 中國華僑出版社. 2002, pp. 3–39.

Chang, Eileen. "Tan nüren" 〈談女人〉 ["Speaking of Women"]. 1944. *Complete Works of Eileen Chang*, vol. 3, 2004, pp. 79–91.

Chang, Eileen. "The Golden Cangue." *Twentieth-Century Chinese Stories*, edited by Hsia Chih-Tsing and Joseph S. M. Lau, Columbia UP, 1971, pp. 138–191.

Chang, Eileen. "The Opium War." *The xxth Century,* vol. 4, no. 6, 1943, p. 464.

Chang, Eileen. "The Spyring/Ch'ing k'ê! Ch'ing k'ê!" *Muse*, April 2008.

Chang, Eileen. "The Young Marshal." *Shao Shuai*, Crown, 2014.

Chang, Eileen. "Tiancaimeng" 〈天才夢〉 ["Dream of Genius"]. 1940. *Zhang Ailing diancang 11: Huali yuan – sanwenjiyi: yijiusiling niadai* 《張愛玲典藏 11：華麗緣—散文集一：一九四〇年代》 [*Eileen Chang Classics Collection 11: Splendid Serendipity: Collection of Short Stories – 1940s*], Crown, 2020, pp. 8–10.

Chang, Eileen. "Tongyanwuji" 〈童言無忌〉 ["From the Mouths of Babes"]. *Zhang Ailing diancang 11: Huali yuan – sanwenjiyi: yijiusiling niadai* 《張愛玲典藏 11：華麗緣——散文集一：一九四〇年代》 [*Eileen Chang Classics Collection 11: Splendid Serendipity: Collection of Short Stories – 1940s*], Crown, 2020, pp. 122–132.

Chang, Eileen. "Wangranji" 〈惘然記〉 [A Record of Bewilderment]. 1983. *Zhang Ailing quanji: Wangranji* 《張愛玲全集：惘然記》 [*Complete Works of Eileen Chang: A Record of Bewilderment*], Crown, 1999, pp. 3–5.

Chang, Eileen. "Wanzi qianhong yu yanyingchun" 〈萬紫千紅與燕迎春〉 ["On With the Show and The Call of Spring"]. Translated by Chen Bingliang, *Unitas,* vol. 3, no. 5, 1987, pp. 52–53.

Chang, Eileen. "Wo de Tiancaimeng" 〈我的天才夢〉 ["My Dream of Genius"]. *Xifeng* 《西風》 [*The West Wind Monthly*], vol. 48, 1940, pp. 542–543. Rpt. in *Zhang kan* 《張看》 [*Zhang's Outlook*], Huangguan, 1977, pp. 277–279.

Chang, Eileen. "Wo kan Su Qing" 〈我看蘇青〉 ["My View on Su Qing"]. 1945. *Zhang Ailing diancang 11: Huali yuan – sanwenjiyi: yijiusiling niadai* 《張愛玲典藏 11：華麗緣——散文集一：一九四〇年代》 [*Eileen Chang Classics Collection 11: Splendid Serendipity: Collection of Short Stories – 1940s*], Crown, 2020, p. 271–286.

Chang, Eileen. "Writing of One's Own." *Written on Water*, translated by Andrew F. Jones, coedited with an introduction by Nicole Huang, Columbia UP, 2005, pp. 15–22.

Chang, Eileen. "Wusi yishi – Luo Wentao sanmei tuanyuan" 〈五四遺事——羅文濤三美團圓〉 ["Regret after the May Fourth Movement – The Reunion of Luo Wentao and the Three Beauties"]. 1957. *Complete Works of Eileen Chang*, vol. 13, 2004, pp. 249–267.

Chang, Eileen. "Xiangjianhuan" 〈相見歡〉 [A Joyful Rendezvous]. 1978. *Zhang Ailing diancang 03: Se, Jie – Duanpian xiaoshuoji san: yijiusiqi nian yihou* 《張愛玲典藏 03：色，戒——短篇小說集三：一九四七年以後》 [*Eileen Chang Classics 03: Lust, Caution – Collection of Short Stories 03, 1947 and Afterwords*], Crown, 2020, pp. 212–268.

Chang, Eileen. "Yangmao chuzai yang shengshang – tan 'Se, Jie'" 〈羊毛出在羊身上—談〈色，戒〉〉 ["Lamb's Wool Came from the Lamb: Discussing 'Se, Jie'"]. *Zhang Ailing quanji: xuji* 《張愛玲全集：續集》 [*Complete Works of Eileen Chang: Sequel*], Crown, 2000, pp. 17–24.

Chang, Eileen. "Yangren kan jingxi ji qita" 〈洋人看京戲及其他〉 ["Westerners Watching Peking Operas and Other Issues"]. 1943. *Complete Works of Eileen Chang*, vol. 3, 2004, pp. 107–116.

Chang, Eileen. "Yapian zhanzheng" 〈鴉片戰爭〉 ["The Opium War"]. Translated by Chen Bingliang, *Unitas*, vol. 3, no. 5, 1987, pp. 48–49.

Chang, Eileen. "Yi Hu Shizhi" 〈憶胡適之〉 ["Remembering Hu Shizhi"]. 1968. *Zhang Ailing dianchang 12 – Wangran ji: sanwenji er: yijiuwuling – baling niandai* 《張愛玲典藏12：惘然記——散文集二：一九五〇——八〇年代》 [*Eileen Chang Classics Collection: A Record of Bewilderment: Collection of Short Stories 2: 1950s – 80s*], Crown, 2010, pp. 12–26.

Chang, Eileen. "Yingong jiuxueji" 〈銀宮就學記〉 ["Attending a Film School"]. *Complete Works of Eileen Chang*, vol. 3, 2004, pp. 101–105.

BIBLIOGRAPHY

Chang, Eileen. "You jijuhua tongduzhe shuo" 〈有幾句話同讀者説〉["Have a Few Words with the Readers"]. 1946. *Zhang Ailing Diancang 11: Huali yuan – sanwenjiyi: yijiusiling niadai* 《張愛玲典藏 11：華麗緣——散文集一：一九四〇年代》 [*Elieen Chang Classics Collection 11: Splendid Serendipity: Collection of Short Stories – 1940s*], Crown, 2020, pp. 294–295.

Chang, Eileen. "Zhongguoren de zongjiao" 〈中國人的宗教〉["The Religion of the Chinese"]. 1944. *Complete Works of Eileen Chang*, vol. 14, 2004, pp. 15–39.

Chang, Eileen. "Ziji de wenzhang" 〈自己的文章〉["My Writing"]. 1944. *Complete Works of Eileen Chang*, vol. 3, 2004, pp. 17–24.

Chang, Eileen. "Ziji de wenzhang" 〈自己的文章〉["Writing of One's Own"]. 1944. *Zhang Ailing Diancang 11: Huali yuan – sanwenjiyi: yijiusiling niadai* 《張愛玲典藏 11：華麗緣——散文集一：一九四〇年代》 [*Eileen Chang Classics Collection 11: Splendid Serendipity: Collection of Short Stories – 1940s*], Crown, 2020, pp. 114–120.

Chang, Eileen. "Zixu" 〈自序〉["Preface"]. *Zhang Ailing quanji: Xuji* 《張愛玲全集：續集》 [*Complete Works of Eileen Chang: Sequel*], Crown, 2000, pp. 5–7.

Chang, Eileen. *Banshengyuan* 《半生緣》 [*Romance of Half a Life Time*]. 1968. *Complete Works of Eileen Chang*, vol. 7, 2004.

Chang, Eileen. "Chang, Eileen (Chang Ai-ling)." *World Authors, 1950–1970: A Companion Volume to Twentieth Century Authors*, edited by John Wakeman, H. W. Wilson, 1975, pp. 297–299.

Chang, Eileen. *Chidi zhi lian* 《赤地之戀》 [*Love in Redland*]. 1954. *Complete Works of Eileen Chang*, vol. 2, 2004.

Chang, Eileen. *Chidi zhi lian* 《赤地之戀》 [*Love in Redland*]. Huilong chubanshe 慧龍出版社, 1978.

Chang, Eileen. *Chuanqi* 《傳奇》 [*Romances*]. Shanghai shudian 上海書店, 1984.

Chang, Eileen. "Daodi shi Shanghai ren" 〈到底是上海人〉 "Shanghainese, After All." 1943. *Zhang Ailing quanji: liuyan* 《張愛玲全集：流言》 [*Complete Works of Eileen Chang: Written on Water*], Crown, 2000, pp. 55–57.

Chang, Eileen. *Duizhaoji – kan lao zhaoxiangbu* 《對照記——看老照相簿》 [*Mutual Reflections – Looking at Old Photo Albums*]. *Complete Works of Eileen Chang*, vol. 15, 2004.

Chang, Eileen. "Hong meigui yu bai meigui" 〈紅玫瑰與白玫瑰〉["Red Rose and White Rose"]. 1944. *Complete Works of Eileen Chang*, vol. 5, 2004, pp. 51–97.

Chang, Eileen. *Hongloumeng yan* 《紅樓夢魘》 [*Nightmare in the Red Chamber*]. *Complete Works of Eileen Chang*, vol. 9, 2004.

Chang, Eileen. "Jinsuoji" 〈金鎖記〉["The Golden Cangue"]. 1943. *Complete Works of Eileen Chang*, vol. 5, 2004, pp. 139–186.

Chang, Eileen. *Liuyan* 《流言》 [*Written on Water*]. 1945. *Complete Works of Eileen Chang*, vol. 3, 2004.

Chang, Eileen. *Love in a Fallen City*. Translated by Karen S. Kingsbury, New York Review Books, 2007.

Chang, Eileen. *Lust/Caution*. Translated by Julia Lovell, Anchor Books, 2007.

Chang, Eileen. *Naked Earth: A Novel about China*. Union P, 1964.

Chang, Eileen. *Shaoshuai* 《少帥》 [*The Young Marshal*], Crown, 2014.

Chang, Eileen. *Shibachun* 《十八春》 [*Eighteen Springs*]. 1950–1951. Zhongguo Huaqiao chubanshe 中國華僑出版社, 2003.

Chang, Eileen. "Siyu" 〈私語〉 ["Whispered Words"]. *Complete Works of Eileen Chang*, vol. 3, 2004, pp. 153–168.

Chang, Eileen. *The Book of Change*. Hong Kong UP, 2010.

Chang, Eileen. *The Fall of the Pagoda*. Hong Kong UP, 2010.

Chang, Eileen. "The Golden Cangue." *Twentieth Century Chinese Stories*, edited by Hsia Chih-Tsing, Columbia UP, 1971, pp. 138–191.

Chang, Eileen. *The Rice-Sprout Song – A Novel of Modern China*. Scribner's, 1955. Rpt. with foreword by David Der-wei Wang, U of California P, 1998.

Chang, Eileen. *The Rouge of the North*. London: Cassell, 1967. Rpt. with foreword by David Der-wei Wang, U of California P, 1998.

Chang, Eileen. *Tongxue shaonian du bu jian* 《同學少年都不賤》. *Complete Works of Eileen Chang*, vol. 17, 2004.

Chang, Eileen. *Traces of Love and Other Stories*. Edited by Eva Hung, Renditions, 2000.

Chang, Eileen. *Wangranji* 《惘然記》 [*A Record of Bewilderment*]. *Complete Works of Eileen Chang*, vol. 12, 2004.

Chang, Eileen. *Xiaotuanyuan* 《小團圓》 [*Little Reunions*]. Crown, 2009.

Chang, Eileen. *Xuji* 《續集》 [*Sequel*]. *Complete Works of Eileen Chang*, vol. 13, 2004.

Chang, Eileen. *Yangge* 《秧歌》. 1954. *Complete Works of Eileen Chang*, vol. 1, 2004.

Chang, Eileen. *Yuannü* 《怨女》 [*Embittered Woman*]. 1966. *Complete Works of Eileen Chang*, vol. 4, 2004.

Chang, Eileen. *Yuyun* 《餘韻》 [*Lingering Rhymes*]. *Complete Works of Eileen Chang*, vol. 14, 2004.

Chang, Eileen. *Zhang Ailing duanpian xiaoshuo ji* 《張愛玲短篇小說集》 [*The Collected Stories of Eileen Chang*]. Tianfeng chubanshe 天風出版社. 1954.

Chang, Eileen. *Zhang Ailing quanji* 《張愛玲全集》 [*Complete Works of Eileen Chang*]. 17 vols, edited by Fang Liywan 方麗婉, Huangguan chubanshe 皇冠出版社 [Crown Publishing Ltd.], 2004.

Chang, Eileen. *Zhang Ailing xiaoshuo ji* [*Chuanqi*] 《張愛玲小說集[傳奇]》 [*Collected Short Stories of Zhang Ailing* [*Romances*]]. Huangguan chubanshe 皇冠出版社 [Crown Publishing Ltd.], 1985.

Chang, Eileen. *Zhang kan* 《張看》 [*Zhang's Outlook*]. *Complete Works of Eileen Chang*, vol. 8, 2004.

Chang, Eileen, Stephen Soong, and Mae Fong Soong 張愛玲, 宋淇, 宋鄺文美. *Zhang Ailing wanglai shuxinji: zhi duan qing chang* 《張愛玲往來書信集： 紙短情長》 [*To My Beloved Friends: Letters of Eileen Chang, Stephen Soong & Mae Fong Soong*], *Vol. 1, 1955 – 1979*. Crown, 2020.

BIBLIOGRAPHY

Chang, Eileen, Stephen Soong, and Mae Fong Soong 張愛玲, 宋淇, 宋鄺文美. *Zhang Ailing wanglai shuxinji: zhi duan qing chang* 《張愛玲往來書信集： 紙短情長》 [*To My Beloved Friends: Letters of Eileen Chang, Stephen Soong & Mae Fong Soong*], *vol. 2, 1980–1995*. Crown, 2020.

Other References

《論語》 [*The Analects of Confucius*]. ctext.org/analects/zh.

"Alleged Breach of Lighting Rules." *Singapore Free Press and Mercantile Advertiser*, December 20, 1941, quoted in "Zhang Ailing muqin, Xinjiapo qingren" 〈張愛玲母親，新加坡情人〉 *Lianhe Zaobao* 《聯合早報》, February 21, 2021.

Ascoli, Max. "The Liberal Magazine – An Editorial." *The Reporter*, 21 Apr. 1955, pp. 12–13.

Austin, John Langshaw. *How to Do Things With Words*. Edited by J. O. Urmson and Marina Sbisa, 2nd Edition, Clarendon P, 1975.

Bakhtin, Mikhail Mikhailovich. *The Dialogic Imagination: Four Essays*. Edited by Michael Holquist, translated by Caryl Emerson and Michael Holquist, U of Texas P, 1981.

Ban, Zhao (Pan, Chao 班昭). "Nüjie" 〈女誡〉 ["Lessons for Women"]. Translated by Nancy Lee Swann, *The Columbia Anthology of Traditional Chinese Literature*, edited by Victor H. Mair, Columbia UP. 1994, pp. 534–541.

Barthes, Roland. "The Death of the Author." 1967. Translated and edited by Stephen Heath, *Image-Musica-Text*, Fontana, 1977, pp. 42–48.

Barthes, Roland. *Roland Barthes by Roland Barthes*. 1975. Translated by Richard Howard, 1994 [1997], monoskop.org/images/b/b3/Roland_Barthes_by_Roland _Barthes.pdf.

Bassnett, Susan. "The Self-Translator as a Writer." *Self-Translation: Brokering Originality in Hybrid Culture*, edited by Anthony Cordingley, Bloombury, 2013, pp. 13–25.

Bassnett, Susan. *Translation Studies*. 4th edition. Routledge Taylor and Francis Group, 2014.

Beardsley, Monroe C. *Aesthetics – From Classical Greece to the Present: A Short History*. Macmillan, 1966.

Bem, Daryl J. "Self-Perception Theory." *Advances in Experimental Social Psychology*, Vol. 6, edited by Leonard Berkowitz, Academic P, 1972, pp. 1–62.

Benjamin, Walter. "The Task of the Translator: An Introduction to the Translation of Baudelaire's Tableaux Parisiens." *A Translation Studies Reader,* edited by Lawrence Venuti, Routledge, 2000, pp. 15–25.

Benjamin, Walter. *Illuminations*. Translated by Harry Zohn, Schocken Books, 1968.

Berger, John. *Ways of Seeing*. British Broadcasting Corporation and Penguin Books, 1972.

Bhabha, Homi K. *The Location of Culture*. Routledge, 2004.

Breines, Winifred. *The Trouble Between Us – An Uneasy History of White and Black Women in the Feminist Movement*. Oxford UP, 2006.

Burke, Seán. *The Death and Return of the Author – Criticism and Subjectivity in Barthes, Foucault and Derrida, 2nd Edition.* Edinburgh UP, 1998.

Butler, Judith. *Bodies That Matter: On the Discursive Limits of "Sex."* Routledge, 1993.

Butler, Judith. *Gender Trouble: Feminism and the Subversion of Identity.* Routledge, 1990.

Butler, Judith. *The Judith Butler Reader.* Edited by Sara Salih and Judith Butler, Blackwell, 2004.

Cai Dengshan 蔡登山. *Se Jie Ailing* 《色戒愛玲》 [*Lust Caution Eileen*]. Comos Books, 2007.

Cao Xueqin 曹雪芹. *Hongloumeng* 《紅樓夢》 [*Dream of the Red Chamber*]. 1791. 4 vols. Beijing shifan daxue chubanshe 北京師範大學出版社, 1987.

Cao, Kefan 曹可凡. "Bai Xianyong tan Zhang Ailing" 〈白先勇談張愛玲〉 [Bai Xianyong Talking about Eileen Chang]. *Dongfang ribao* 《東方日報》 [*Oriental Daily*], 26 July 2009. Rpt. in *ESWN Cultural Blog*, "The Bilingual Eileen Chang, Part 1: A Return to the Frontier," pp. 35–37, www.zonaeuropa.com/culture/c20080407 _1.htm.

Chan, Leo Tak-hung. "What's Modern in Chinese Translation Theory? Lu Xun and the Debates on Literalism and Foreignization in the May Fourth Period." *Traduction, terminologie, redaction,* vol. 14, no. 2, 2001, https://doi.org/10.7202/000576ar.

Chen, Ruoxi 陳若曦. "Zhang Ailing yipie" 〈張愛玲一瞥〉 [A Glance at Eileen Chang], 22 Nov. 2010. *ESWN Cultural Blog*: "The Bilingual Eileen Chang Part 1: A Return to the Frontier," pp. 39–40, www.zonaeuropa.com/culture/c20080407 _1.htm.

Chow, Rey 周蕾. "Introduction: On Chineseness as a Theoretical Problem." *Boundary,* vol. 25, no. 3, 1998, pp. 1–24.

Chow, Rey 周蕾. *Entanglements, or Transmedial Thinking about Capture.* Duke UP, 2012.

Chunzi 淳子. *Zhang Ailing Ditu* 《張愛玲地圖》 [*Eileen Chang Map*]. Hanyu da cidian chubanshe 漢語大詞典出版社, 2003.

Cicero, M.T. *De inventions. De optimo genere oratorum, Topica.* Translated by H.M. Hubell, Harvard UP, 1949.

Confucius. *Liji* 《禮記》 [*The Books of Rites*], vol. 1. Translated by James Legge, University Books, 1967.

Confucius. *Yili* 《儀禮》 [*The Rites of Courtesy*]. Edited by Zheng Xuan 鄭玄, Taiwan Zhonghuashuju 台灣中華書局, 1996.

Confucius. *Zhouli* 《周禮》 [*The Rites of Zhou*]. Edited by Zheng Xuan 鄭玄, Xinxingshuju 新興書局, 1972.

Cordingley, Anthony, editor. *Self-Translation: Brokering Originality in Hybrid Culture.* London: Bloomsbury, 2013.

Couser, Thomas. *The Work of Life Writing: Essays and Lectures.* Routledge Taylor & Francis Group, 2021.

BIBLIOGRAPHY

Deppmann, Hsiu-Chuang. "Rewriting Colonial Encounters: Eileen Chang and Somerset Maugham." *A Journal of Postcolonial Studies,* vol. 5, no. 2, 2001, social.chass.ncsu.edu/jouvert/v5i2/hcdepp.htm.

Derrida, Jacques. "Des Tours de Babel." Translated by Joseph F. Graham. *Difference in Translation,* edited by Joseph F. Graham, Cornell UP, 1985, pp. 165–208.

Derrida, Jacques. "Signature Event Context." Translated by Samuel Weber and Jeffrey Mehlman, *Glyph,* vol. 1, 1977, pp. 172–197.

Derrida, Jacques. "What Is a 'Relevant' Translation?" *A Translation Studies Reader,* edited by Lawrence Venuti, Routledge, 2004, pp. 423–446.

Derrida, Jacques. *Of Grammatology.* Translated by Gayatri Chakravorty Spivak, Johns Hopkins UP, 1976.

Ding Ling 丁玲. *I Myself Am a Woman: Selected Writings of Ding Ling.* Edited by Tani E. Barlow with Gary J. Bjorge, Beacon, 1989.

Ding Ling 丁玲. *Shafei nushi de riji* 《莎菲女士的日記》 [*Miss Sophia's Diary*]. 1928. *Ding Ling wenji* 《丁玲文集》 [*Writings of Ding Ling*], Hunan renmin chubanshe 湖南人民出版社, 1982.

Dryburgh, Majorie, and Sarah Dauncey. "Chinese Life Writing: Themes and Variations." *Writing Lives in China, 1600 – 2010: Histories of the Elusive Self,* edited by Marjorie Dryburgh and Sarah Dauncey, Palgrave Macmillan, 2013.

Eagleton, Terry. "What Is Ideology?" *Ideology – An Introduction.* Verso, 1991, pp. 1–31.

Eco, Umberto, editor. *On Beauty.* Translated by Alastair McEven, Secker & Warburg, 2004.

Evangelista, Elin-Maria. "Writing in Translation: A New Self in a Second Language." *Self-Translation: Brokering Originality in Hybrid Culture,* edited by Anthony Cordingley, Bloomsbury, 2013, pp. 177–187.

Fei, Yong 費勇. *Zhang Ailing zhuanji* 《張愛玲傳奇》 [*The Legend of Zhang Ailing*]. Guangdong renmin chubanshe 廣東人民出版社, 2000.

Feng, Zuyi 馮祖貽. *Bainian jiazu – Zhang Ailing* 《百年家族——張愛玲》 [*Hundred Years Family – Eileen Chang*]. Lixu wenhua chubanshe 立緒文化出版社, 1999.

Finnane, Antonia. *Changing Clothes in China: Fashion, History, Nation.* Columbia UP, 2008.

Fischer, Clara, and Luna Dolezal. "Contested Terrains: New Feminist Perspectives on Embodiment. *New Feminist Perspectives on Embodiment*, edited by Clara Fischer and Luna Dolezal, Palgrave Macmillan, 2018.

Fitch, Brian T. "The Relationship Between *Compagnie* and *Company*: One Work, Two Texts, Two Fictive Universes." *Beckett Translating/Translating Beckett,* edited by Alan Warren Friedman et al., Pennsylvania State UP, 1987, pp. 25–35.

Foucault, Michel. "What Is an Author?" 1969. *Textual Strategies: Perspectives in Post-Structuralist Criticism,* translated and edited by Josué V. Harari, Cornell UP, 1979, pp. 141–160.

Foucault, Michel. *The History of Sexuality – An Introduction. Vol. 1.* Translated by Robert Hurley, Vintage Books, 1978.

Frueh, Joanna. *Erotic Faculties.* U of California P, 1996.

Fu, Lei 傅雷. "Gaolaotou chongyiben xu" 〈高老頭重譯本序〉 [Preface to the Second Translation of *Gaolaotou*]. 1951. *Fanyi lunji* 《翻譯論集》 [*Essays on Translation*], edited by Liu Jingzhi 劉靖之, Joint Publishing Co., 1985, pp. 68–69.

Fusco, Serena. *Incorporations of Chineseness: Hybridity, Bodies, and Chinese American Literature.* Cambridge Scholars Publishing, 2016.

Genette, Gérard. *Palimpsests: Literature in the Second Degree.* Translated by Channa Newman and Claude Doubinsky, U of Nebraska P, 1982.

Genette, Gérard. *Paratexts: Thresholds of Interpretation.* Translated by Jane E. Lewin, U of Nebraska P, 1997.

Gordon, Chad. "Self-Conceptions: Configurations of Content Structure." *Social Psychology of the Self-Concept,* edited by Morris Rosenberg and Howard B. Kaplan, Harlan Davidson, 1982, pp. 13–23.

Gunn, Edward. *Unwelcome Muse: Chinese Literature in Shanghai and Peking 1937–1945.* Columbia UP, 1980.

Halbwachs, Maurice. *On Collective Memory.* 1950. Edited, translated, and with an introduction by Lewis A. Coser, U of Chicago P, 1992.

The Heart of the Perfection of Transcendent Wisdom (The Heart Sutra). Translated by Lin Yutang, *DharmaNet International,* www.dharmanet.org/HeartSutra.htm.

"History of Taiwan." *Britannica,* 2006, www.britannica.com/place/Taiwan/Sports -and-recreation#ref404127.

Hokenson, Jan. "History and the Self-translator." *Self-Translation: Brokering Originality in Hybrid Culture,* edited by Anthony Cordingley, Bloombury, 2013, pp. 39–60.

Hokenson, Jan Walsh, and Marcella Munson. *The Bilingual Text: History and Theory of Literary Self-Translation.* St. Jerome Publishing, 2007.

Hoyan, Hang Fung 何杏楓. "On the Translation of Eileen Chang's Fiction." *Translation Quarterly,* vol. 18–19, 2000, pp. 99–136.

Hsia, Chih-tsing 夏志清. *A History of Modern Chinese Fiction, 1917–1957.* Yale UP, 1961.

Huang, Nicole 黃心村. "Afterword." *Written on Water,* edited by Andrew F. Jones and Nicole Huang, New York Review Books, 2023, pp. 239–244.

Huang, Nicole 黃心村. "Eileen Chang and Alternative Wartime Narrative." *The Columbia Companion to Modern East Asian Literature,* edited by Joshua S. Mostow, Kirk A. Denton, Bruce Fulton, and Sharalyn Orbaugh, Columbia UP, 2003, pp. 459–462.

Huang, Nicole 黃心村. *Yuanqi Xiangguang – Zhang Ailing de yixiang he shijie* 《緣起 香港——張愛玲的異鄉和世界》 [*Hong Kong Connections: Eileen Chang and Worldmaking*]. U of Hong Kong, 2022.

Hui, La Frances. "Director Ang Lee on the Making of *Lust, Caution* at The Asia Society." Interview video, 7 Dec. 2007, www.youtube.com/watch?v=irSY5l3BecU &lc=Ugh0XOt6iEu8k3gCoAEC.

BIBLIOGRAPHY

Hung, Eva 孔慧怡. "Translation in China: An Analytical Survey: First Century B.C.E. to Early Twentieth Century." *Asian Translation Traditions,* edited by Eva Hung and Judy Wakabayashi, St. Jerome Publishing, 2005, pp. 67–99.

Hutcheon, Linda, editor. *The Politics of Postmodernism.* 2nd Edition. Routledge, 2002.

Hutcheon, Linda. *A Poetics of Postmodernism: History, Theory, Fiction.* Routledge, 1988.

Hutcheon, Linda. *A Theory of Adaptation.* Routledge, 2006.

Hutcheon, Linda. *Literary Borrowing ... And Stealing – Theory & Practice of Intertextuality.* Canadian Scholars' P, 2003.

Ibsen, Henrik. *A Doll's House.* 1879. Dover, 1992.

Ignatieff, Michael. *Russian Album,* 2nd edition. Picador, 1977.

"Interview with Ang Lee." *Lust/Caution.* DVD. Focus Features Spotlight Series, Universal Studios, 2008.

Irigaray, Luce. "The Power of Discourse and the Subordination of the Feminine." *This Sex Which Is Not One,* translated by Catherine Porter with Carolyn Burke, Cornell UP, 1985, pp. 68–85.

Irigaray, Luce. "This Sex Which Is Not One." *This Sex Which Is Not One,* translated by Catherine Porter with Carolyn Burke, Cornell UP, 1985, pp. 23–33.

Isidore of Seville, Saint. *The Etymologies of Isidore of Seville.* Translated by Stephen A. Barney, et al., Cambridge UP, 2006.

Jerome. "Letter to Pammachius." Translated by Kathleen Davis, *The Translation Studies Reader,* 3rd Edition, edited by Lawrence Venuti, Routledge, 2012, pp. 21–30.

Jiang, Xun 江迅. "Ke Ling zhuiyi Zhang Ailing" 〈柯靈追憶張愛玲〉 [Ke Ling Recalling Eileen Chang]. *Zuobie Zhang Ailing* 《作別張愛玲》 [*Farewell to Eileen Chang*], edited by Chen Zishan 陳子善, Wenhui chubanshe 文匯出版社, 1996, pp. 200–203.

Jameson, Fredric. "Metacommentary." *PMLA,* vol. 86, no. 1, 1971, pp. 9–18. *JSTOR,* https://doi.org/10.2307/46996. Accessed July 11, 2024.

Jones, Andrew F., translator. "From the Ashes." Translation of "Jinyulu" 〈燼餘錄〉 by Eileen Chang, *Written on Water,* edited by Andrew F. Jones and Nicole Huang, New York Review Books, 2023, pp. 44–60.

Jones, Andrew F., translator. "From the Mouths of Babes." "Tongyanwuji" 〈童言無忌〉 by Eileen Chang. *Written on Water,* edited by Andrew F. Jones and Nicole Huang, New York Review Books, 2023, pp. 3–17.

Jones, Andrew F., translator. "Notes on Apartment Life." "Gongyu shenghuo jiqu" 〈公寓生活記趣〉 by Eileen Chang. *Written on Water,* edited by Andrew F. Jones and Nicole Huang, New York Review Books, 2023, pp. 27–33.

Jones, Andrew F., translator. "Peking Opera Through Foreign Eyes." Translation of "Yangren kan jingxi ji qita" 〈洋人看京戲及其他〉 by Eileen Chang, *Written on Water,* edited by Andrew F. Jones and Nicole Huang, New York Review Books, 2023, pp. 113–123.

Jones, Andrew F., translator. "Seeing with the Streets." Translation of "Daoluyimu" 〈道路以目〉 by Eileen Chang, *Written on Water,* edited by Andrew F. Jones and Nicole Huang, New York Review Books, 2023, pp. 64–71.

Jones, Andrew F., translator. "Whispers." Translation of "Siyu" 〈私語〉 by Eileen Chang, *Written on Water*, edited by Andrew F. Jones and Nicole Huang, New York Review Books, 2023, pp. 156–173.

Jones, Andrew F., translator. "Writing of One's Own." Translation of "Ziji de wenzhang" 〈自己的文章〉 by Eileen Chang, *Written on Water*, edited by Andrew F. Jones and Nicole Huang, New York Review Books, 2023, pp. 18–26.

Jones, Andrew F. and Nicole Huang, editors. *Written on Water*. New York Review Books, 2023.

Kano, Ayako. *Acting Like a Woman in Modern Japan: Theater, Gender, and Nationalism*. Palgrave. 2001.

Kao, Chuan C. 高全之. *Zhang Ailing xue: Piping, kaozheng, gouchen* 《張愛玲學: 批評, 考證, 鉤沉》 [*Eileen Chang Reconsidered*]. Yifang chuban youxian gongsi 一方出版有限公司 [iFRONT Publishing Company], 2003.

Kao, Chuan Chih 高全之. *Zhang Ailing xue* 《張愛玲學》 [*Eileen Chang Reconsidered*], Second edition. Maitian, 2011.

Kao, Chuan Chih 高全之. *Zhang Ailing xue xupian* 《張愛玲學續篇》 [*Eileen Chang: More Essays on Her Life and Works*]. Maitian, 2014.

Kashiwa, Kensaku 柏謙作, translator. *Akai Koi* 《赤い恋》. *Chidi zhi lian* 《赤地之戀》 [*Love in Redland*] by Eileen Chang, Seikatsusha 生活社, 1955.

Kato, Shuichi. *A History of Japanese Literature*, Vol. 1. Macmillan, 1979.

Ke, Ling 柯靈. "Yaoji Zhang Ailing" 〈遙寄張愛玲〉 [Sending Far Away to Eileen Chang]. *Siyu Zhang Aililng* 《私語張愛玲》 [*Whispered Words on Zhang Aililng*], edited by Chen Zishan 陳子善, Zhejiang wenyi chubanshe 浙江文藝出版社, 1995, pp. 15–25.

Ke, Ling 柯靈. "Yaoji Zhang Ailing" 〈遙寄張愛玲〉 [Sending Far Away to Eileen Chang]. *Zhang Ailing de shijie* 《張愛玲的世界》 [*Eileen Chang's World*], edited by Zheng Shusen 鄭樹森, Yunchen wenhua gufen shiye youxian gongsi 允晨文化股份實業有限公司, 1989, pp. 3–13.

Kearney, Richard. "Introduction: Ricœur's Philosophy of Translation." *On Translation*, by Paul Ricœur, Routledge Taylor & Francis Group, 2006, pp. VII–XX.

Kim, Hunggyu. *Understanding Korean Literature*. M.E. Sharpe, 1997.

Kingsbury, Karen S., translator. *Half a Lifelong Romance*, by Eileen Chang. London: Penguin Books, 2014.

Kingsbury, Karen S., translator. "Jasmine Tea." *Love in a Fallen City*, by Eileen Chang, translated by Karen S. Kingsbury, New York Review of Books, 2007, pp. 79–108.

Kleeman, Faye Yuan. *Under an Imperial Sun: Japanese Colonial Literature of Taiwan and the South*. U of Hawaii P, 2003.

Klimkiewicz, Aurelia. "Self-Translation as Broken Narrativity: Towards an Understanding of the Self's Multilingual Dialogue." *Self-Translation: Brokering Originality in Hybrid Culture*, edited by Anthony Cordingley, Bloomsbury, 2013, pp. 189–201.

BIBLIOGRAPHY

Klinger, Susanne. "Translated Otherness, Self-Translated In-Betweenness: Hybridity as Medium versus Hybridity as Object in Anglophone African Writing." *Self-Translation: Brokering Originality in Hybrid Culture*, edited by Anthony Cordingley, Bloomsbury, 2013, pp. 113–126.

Knapp, Steven, and Walter Benn Michaels. "Against Theory." *Critical Inquiry,* vol. 8, no. 4, 1982, pp. 732–742. Rpt. in *Against Theory: Literary Studies and the New Pragmatism,* edited by W.J.T. Mitchell, U of Chicago P, 1985, pp. 11–30.

Ko, Dorothy. *Cinderella's Sisters: A Revisionist History of Footbinding.* U of California P, 2007.

Ko, Dorothy. *Every Step a Lotus: Shoes for Bound Feet.* U of California P, 2001.

Kohlstruck, Michael. "Klaus Mehnert und die Zeitschrift *The xxth Century.*" *Exile Shanghai: Jewish Life in Emigration (1938–1947)*, edited by Georg Armbrüster, Michael Kohlstruck, and Sonja Mühlberger, Verlag Hentrich & Hentrich, 2000.

Korte, Barbara. *Body Language in Literature.* U of Toronto P, 1997.

Kowallis, Jon Eugene. "Sado-masochism, Steamy Sex, and Shanghai Glitter – What's Love Got to Do with It? A 'Philologist' Looks at Lust/Caution and the Literary Texts that Inspired It." *From Eileen Chang to Ang Lee*, edited by Xiaoyan Peng and Whitney Crothers Dilley, Routledge, 2014, pp. 51–63.

Kuehn, Julia, Kam Louie, and David M. Pomfret, editors. *Diasporic Chineseness after the Rise of China: Communities and Cultural Production.* U of British Columbia P, 2013.

Lee, Christopher. "Introduction to 'Chinese Translation: A Vehicle of Cultural Influence.'" *PMLA,* vol. 130, no. 2, 2015, pp. 490–498.

Lee, Haiyan. "Enemy under My Skin: Eileen Chang's *Lust, Caution* and the Politics of Transcendence." *PMLA,* vol. 125, no. 3, 2010, pp. 640–655.

Lee, Leo Ou-Fan 李歐梵. *Shanghai Modern: The Flowering of a New Urban Culture in China 1930–1945.* Harvard UP, 1999.

Lejuene, Philip. *On Autobiography.* U of Minnesota P, 1989.

Li, Ang 李昂. *Shafu* 《殺夫》. Lianhe baoshe, 1983.

Li, Ang 李昂. *The Butcher's Wife: Shafu: A Novel.* Translated by Howard Goldblatt and Ellen Yeung, North Point P, 1986.

Li, Jessica Tsui Yan 李翠恩. "The Politics of Self-Translation: Eileen Chang." *Perspectives: Studies in Translatology,* vol. 14, no. 2, 2006, pp. 99–106.

Li, Jessica Tsui-yan 李翠恩. "Ibsen's Nora Represented: Female Body and Identities in *China Doll.*" *Ibsen and the Modern Self*, edited by K.K. Tam, Terry S. Yip, and Frode Helland, Open U of Hong Kong P; Centre for Ibsen Studies, U of Oslo, 2010, pp. 298–310.

Li, Jessica Tsui-yan 李翠恩. "The Politics of Self-Translation: Eileen Chang." *Perspectives: Studies in Translatology,* vol. 14, no. 2, 2006, pp. 99–106, www.tandfonline.com /doi/abs/10.1080/09076760608669023.

Li, Jessica Tsui-yan 李翠恩. "Introduction: Interdisciplinary Approaches to Transcultural Negotiations of Chinese Canadian Identities." *The Transcultural Streams of Chinese Canadian Identities*, edited by Jessica Tsui-yan Li, McGill-Queen's UP, 2019, pp. 3–28.

Li, Junguo 李俊國 and Zhou Yi 周易. "Zhang Ailing 'Xiangjianhuan' yingwen yigao de faxian yu yanjiu" 〈張愛玲〈相見歡〉英文遺稿的發現與研究〉 ["The Discovery of and Studies on Eileen Chang's Xiang Jian Huan"]. *Comparative Literature in China*, 2020, vol. 0, issue 3, pp. 150–167.

Liang, Qichao 梁啓超. "Lun nüxue" 〈論女學〉 [On Women's Education], in "Bianfa tongyi" 〈變法通議〉 [General Discussion of Reform]. 1896. *Yinbingshi heji, wenji* 《飲冰室合集，文集》 [*Collected Works of Yingbing Shi*], by Liang Qichao, Zhonghua shuju 中華書局, vol. 1, no. 1, 1994, pp. 37–48.

Lim, Chinchown 林幸謙. "Castration Parody and Male 'Castration': Eileen Chang's Female Writing and Her Anti-Patriarchal Strategies." *Feminism/Femininity in Chinese Literature,* edited by Chen Peng-hsiang and Whitney Crother Dilley, Rodopi, 2002, pp. 127–143.

Lin, Yiliang 林以亮. "Cong Zhang Ailing de 'Wusi yishi' shuoqi'" 〈從張愛玲的《五四遺事》說起〉 [Speaking from Eileen Chang's 'Wusi yishi']. 1973. *Siyu Zhang Ailing* 《私語張愛玲》 [*Whispered Words on Zhang Ailing*], edited by Chen Zishan 陳子善, Zhejiang wenyi chubanshe 浙江文藝出版社, 1995, pp. 46–50.

Lin, Yiliang 林以亮. "Siyu Zhang Ailing" 〈私語張愛玲〉 [Whispered Words on Zhang Ailing]. 1976. *Siyu Zhang Ailing* 《私語張愛玲》 [*Whispered Words on Zhang Ailing*], edited by Chen Zishan 陳子善, Zhejiang wenyi chubanshe 浙江文藝出版社, 1995, pp. 32–45.

Lin, Yiliang 林以亮. "Cong Zhang Ailing de 'Wusi yishi' shuoqi'" 〈從張愛玲的《五四遺事》說起〉 [Speaking from Eileen Chang's 'Wusi yishi']. 1973. *Siyu Zhang Ailing* 《私語張愛玲》 [*Whispered Words on Zhang Ailing*], edited by Chen Zishan 陳子善, Zhejiang wenyi chubanshe 浙江文藝出版社, 1995, pp. 46–50.

Lin Yutang 林語堂. "Lun fanyi" 〈論翻譯〉 [Discussing Translation]. 1932. *Fanyi Lunji* 《翻譯論集》 [*Essays on Translation*], edited by Liu Jingzhi 劉靖之, Joint Publishing Co., 1985, pp. 32–47.Lin, Yutang 林語堂. *My Country and My People*. William Heinemann, 1936.

Liu, Lydia He 劉禾. *Tokens of Exchange: The Problem of Translation in Global Circulations.* Duke UP, 1999.

Liu, Wei. "A Misunderstood Passion." *China Daily*, 27 Sept. 2007, p. 18, www.chinadaily.com.cn/cndy/2007-09/27/content_6137460.htm

Louie, Kam ed. *Eileen Chang: Romancing Languages, Cultures and Genres*. Hong Kong UP, 2012.

Lovell, Julia. "Foreword." *Lust, Caution*, by Eileen Chang, translated by Julia Lovell, Anchor Books, 2007, pp. IX–XIX.

Lovell, Julia, translator. *Lust, Caution*, by Eileen Chang, Anchor Books, 2007.

BIBLIOGRAPHY

Loxley, James. *Performativity*. Routledge, 2006.

Lu Ling 路翎. *Ji'e de Guo Su'e* 《肌餓的郭素娥》 [*Hungry Guo Su'e*]. 1943. Beijing Renmin chubanshe, 1988.

Lu, Tonglin. "Introduction." *Gender and Sexuality in Twentieth-Century Chinese Literature and Society*, edited by Lu Tonglin, State U of New York P, 1993, pp. 1–22.

Lu Xun 魯迅. "Suowei guoxue" 〈所謂國學〉 [The So-called 'Scholar']. *Chenbao fukan* 《晨報副刊》, 4 Oct. 1922, www.millionbook.net/mj/l/luxun/rf/10.htm.

Lu Xun 魯迅. *Diary of a Madman and Other Stories*. U of Hawaii P, 1990.

Lu Xun 魯迅. *Kuangren riji* 《狂人日記》 [*Diary of a Madman*]. Luotuo chubanshe, 1998.

Lu Xun 魯迅. *Lu Xun Quanji* 《魯迅全集》 [*Complete Works of Lu Xun*]. Renmin wenxue chubanshe 人民文學出版社, 2005.

Lu Xun 魯迅. *Zhu fu* 《祝福》 [*The New Year's Sacrifice*]. 1924. Chao Yang, 1973.

Ma, Jianzhong 馬建忠. "Nishe fanyi shuyuan yi" 〈擬設翻譯書院議〉 ["On Establishing a Translation Institution"]. *Huangchao jingshiwen tongbian: juanliu, wenjiaobuliu, yishu* 《皇朝經世文統編：卷六，文教部六，譯書》 [*Collection of Dynasty Classical Essays: vol. 6, Literature and Teaching no. 6, Translation*], 1984, ctext.org/wiki.pl?if=gb&chapter=882612. Accessed July 11, 2024.

Mai Ke 邁克. "Benlaiwuyiwu" 〈本來無一物〉 ["There was Nothing Originally"]. "Keshehui zhuanlan" 《克社會專欄》, *Pingguo ribao* 《蘋果日報》 [*Apple Daily*], October 17, 2010.

Mai Ke 邁克. "Guannian tai luohou" 〈觀念太落後〉 ["Concept Too Outdated"]. "Keshehui zhuanlan" 《克社會專欄》, *Pingguo ribao* 《蘋果日報》 [*Apple Daily*], October 15, 2010.

Mai Ke 邁克. "Zhangkai dazuiba" 〈張開大嘴巴〉 ["Open the Big Mouth"]. "Keshehui zhuanlan" 《克社會專欄》, *Pingguo ribao* 《蘋果日報》 [*Apple Daily*], October 16, 2010.

Mair, Victor H. "How to Forget Your Mother Tongue and Remember Your National Language." 2003, pinyin.info/readings/mair/taiwanese.htm. Accessed 19 Nov. 2020.

Maugham, W. Somerset. "The Letter." 1927. *East and West: The Collected Short Stories of W. Somerset Maugham,* Doubleday, 1937, pp. 184–216.

Mehnert, Klaus. "Foreword" to "Demons and Fairies" by Eileen Chang. *The xxth Century*, vol. 5, no. 6, 1943, pp. 421–429.

Meng, Hui. "Awkward Betweenness and Reluctant Metamorphosis: Eileen Chang's Self-Tranlsation." *TranscUlturAl*, vol. 13, no. 1, 2021, pp. 2–22.

Meng, Yue, and Dai Jinhua 孟悅、戴錦華. *Fuchu lishi dibiao: Zhongguo xiandai nuxing wenxue yanjiu* 《浮出歷史地表: 中國現代女性文學研究》 [*Emerging from the Surface of History: The Study of Modern Chinese Female Literature*]. Shibao wenhua chuban shiye youxiangongsi 時報文化出版事業有限公司, 1993.

Mirzoeff, Nicholas. *Bodyscape – Art, Modernity and the Ideal Figure*. Routledge, 1995.

mrbrown. "See What Show: Interview with Ang Lee on *Lust, Caution*." Interview video, 24 Sept. 2007, www.youtube.com/watch?v=EtrUC-Oi6io.

Namikawa, Ryō 並河亮. *Nōmin ongakutai* 《農民音樂隊》. *Yangge* 《秧歌》 [*The Rice-Sprout Song – A Novel of Modern China*] by Eileen Chang, Jiji Tsūshinsha 時事通信社, 1956.

Pan, Jane Weizhen and Martin Merz, translators. *Little Reunions*, by Eieen Chang. New York: New York Review Books, 2018.

Parsons, Talcott. "An Approach to Psychological Theory in Terms of the Theory of Action." *Psychology: The Study of a Science, Vol. III*, edited by Sigmund Kock, McGraw-Hill, 1959, pp. 612–711.

Patton, Simon, translator. "Steamed Osmanthus Flower: Ah Xiao's Unhappy Autumn." "Guihuazheng: A Xiao beiqiu" 〈桂花蒸——阿小悲秋〉 by Eileen Chang, *Traces of Love and Other Stories*, edited by Eva Hung, Renditions Paperbacks, 2000, pp. 59–91.

Peng, Hsiao-yen. "Woman as Metaphor – How Lust/Caution Re/deconstructs History." *From Eileen Chang to Ang Lee*, edited by Xiaoyan Peng and Whitney Crothers Dilley, Routledge, 2014, pp. 155–164.

Peng, Shujun 彭樹君. 〈瑰美的傳奇・永恆的停格——訪平鑫濤談張愛玲著作出版〉 [Beautiful Romance ・ Forever Stop – Interview with Ping Xintao Talking about Eileen Chang's Works' Publication]. *Huali yu cangliang: Zhang Ailing jinian wenji* 《華麗與蒼涼:張愛玲紀念文集》, Huangguan chuban she 皇冠出版社 [Crown Publishing Company Limited], 1996, pp. 175–184.

Phelan, Peggy. *Mourning Sex – Performing Public Memories*. Routledge, 1997.

Pickrel, Paul. Review of *The Rice-Sprout Song – A Novel of Modern China*, by Eileen Chang. *Yale Review*, vol. 44, 1955, pp. 639–640.

Pollard, David, translator. "The Religion of the Chinese." Translation of "Zhongguoren de zongjiao" 〈中國人的宗教〉 ["The Religion of the Chinese"], by Eileen Chang, *The Chinese Essay*, translated and edited by David Pollard, Hurst & Co., 2000, pp. 283–292.

Porter, Stanley E., and Jason C. Robinson. *Hermeneutics: An Introduction to Interpretive Theory*. William B. Eerdmans, 2011.

Qian Zhongshu 錢鐘書. "Lin Shu de fanyi" 〈林紓的翻譯〉 [Lin Shu's Translation]. 1979. *Fanyi lunji* 《翻譯論集》 [*Essays on Translation*], edited by Liu Jingzhi 劉靖之, Joint Publishing Co., 1985, pp. 302–323.

Qiu, Yanming 丘彥明. "Zhang Ailing zai Taiwan – fang Wang Zhenhe" 張愛玲在台灣 ——訪王禎和 ["Eileen Chang in Taiwan – Interviewing Wang Zhenhe"]. *Unitas Magazine*, March 1987. Rpt. in *ESWN Cultural Blog*, "The Bilingual Eileen Chang Part 1: A Return to the Frontier," pp. 4–5, www.zonaeuropa.com/culture/c20080407_1.htm.

Qu Qiubai 瞿秋白. "Lu Xun he Qu Qiubai guanyu fanyi de tongxin: Qu, Qiubai gei Lu Xun de Xin" 〈魯迅和瞿秋白關於翻譯的通信 ：瞿秋白給魯迅的信〉 ["Letters about Translation between Lu Xun and Qu Qiubai: Qu Qiubai's Letter to Lu

Xun"]. 1931. *Fanyi Lunji* 《翻譯論集》 [*Essays on Translation*], edited by Liu Jing-zhi 劉靖之, Joint Publishing Co., 1985, pp. 3–10.

Ratner, Joshua. "Paratexts." *Early American Studies*, Special Issue: Keywords in Early American Literature and Material Texts, vol. 16, no. 4, 2018, pp. 733–740.

Reynolds, Stephen. "Autobiografiction." *Speaker*, new series, vol. 15, no. 366, 1906, pp. 28–30, blogs.kcl.ac.uk/maxsaunders/autobiografiction/transcription-of-reynolds-essay/

Ricœur, Paul. *Hermeneutics: Writings and Lectures*, Vol. 2, translated by David Pellauer, Polity, 2013.

Ricœur, Paul. *On Translation*. Routledge Taylor & Francis Group, 2004.

Ricœur, Paul. *Soi-même comme un autre* [*Oneself as Another*]. Seuil, 1990.

Rogers, Carl R. "A Theory of Therapy, Personality, and Interpersonal Relationships, as Developed in the Client-centered Framework." *In Psychology: A Study of a Science, Study 1: Conceptual and Systematic; Volume 3: Formulations of the Persona and the Social*, edited by Sigmund Kock, McGraw-Hill, 1959, pp. 184–256.

Rosenberg, Morris, and Howard B. Kaplan. "General Introduction." *Social Psychology of the Self-Concept*, edited by Morris Rosenberg and Howard B. Kaplan, Harlan Davidson, 1982, pp. XI–XV.

Ruan, Fang Fu. *Sex in China – Studies in Sexology in Chinese Culture*. Plenum P, 1991.

Rugg, Linda Haverty. *Picturing Ourselves: Photography & Autobiography*. U of Chicago P, 1997.

Santoyo, Julio-César. "On Mirrors, Dynamics and self-translations." *Self-Translation: Brokering Originality in Hybrid Culture*, edited by Anthony Cordingley, Bloombury, 2013, pp. 27–38.

Saunders, Max. "Autofiction, Autobiografiction, Autofabrication, and Heteronymity: Differentiating Versions of the Autobiographical." *Biography*, vol. 43, no. 4, 2020.

Schleiermacher, Friedrich. "On the Different Methods of Translating." Translated by Susan Bernofsky, *The Translation Studies Reader*, 3rd Edition, edited by Lawrence Venuti, Routledge, 2012, pp. 43–63.

Schoyer, Preston. "The Smell of a Hidden World." Review of *The Rice-Sprout Song – A Novel of Modern China*, by Eileen Chang. *Saturday Review*, 21 May 1955, p. 18.

Sedikides, Constantine, and Marilynn B. Brewer. "Individual Self, Relational Self, and Collective Self: Partners, Opponents, or Strangers?" *Individual Self, Relational Self, and Collective Self*, edited by Constantine Sedikides and Marilynn B. Brewer, Routledge, 2002, pp. 1–4.

See, Lisa. *On Gold Mountain: The One-Hundred-Year Odyssey of My Chinese-American Family*. St. Martin's P, 1995.

Shen, Shuang. "Betrayal, Impersonation, Bilingualism: Eileen Chang's Self-Translation." *Eileen Chang: Romancing Languages, Cultures and Genres*, edited by Kam Louie, Hong Kong UP, 2012, pp. 91–111.

Shengjing Heheben. 《聖經和合本》 [*Chinese Union Version Bible*], 1919.

Shui Jing. 水晶. "Chan – Yefang Zhang Ailing" 〈蟬——夜訪張愛玲〉["Cicada – Visit Eileen Chang at Night"]. *Zhang Ailing de xiaoshuo yishu* 《張愛玲的小說藝術》 [*The Art of Eileen Chang's Fiction*] (1973), 3rd Edition, Dadi chubanshe 大地出版社, 1976, pp. 17–32.

Sima, Xin 司馬新. *Zhang Ailing yu Laiya* 《張愛玲與賴雅》 [*Zhang Ailing and Reyher*]. Dadi chubanshe 大地出版社, 1996.

Simpson, J. A., and E. S. C. Weiner. *The Oxford English Dictionary*. Clarendon P, 1989.

"Slavery & Hate." Review of *The Rice-Sprout Song – A Novel of Modern China*, by Eileen Chang, *Time*, 24 Apr. 1955, p. 108.

Snow, Helen Forster. *Women in Modern China*. Mouton & Company, 1967.

Song, Qi 宋淇 (Lin Yiliang 林以亮, Stephen Soong). "Siyu Zhang Ailing" 〈私語張愛玲〉 ["Whispered Words on Zhang Ailing"]. *Huali yu cangliang: Zhang Ailing jinian wenji* 《華麗與蒼涼：張愛玲紀念文集》, Huangguan chubanshe 皇冠出版社 [Crown Publishing Company Limited], 1995, pp. 105–124.

Song, Yilang 宋以朗 (Soong, Roland). "Song Yilang faju 'Chongfang biancheng' de guocheng" 〈宋以朗發掘重訪邊城的過程〉 ["The Process of Roland Soong's Discovery of 'Chongfang biancheng'"]. *Zhang Ailing Quanji: Chongfang biancheng* 《張愛玲全集：重訪邊城》 [*Complete Works of Eileen Chang: A Return to the Frontier*], Crown, 2008, pp. 81–85.

Song, Yilang 宋以朗 (Soong, Roland). *Song Qi Chuanqi – Cong Song Chunfang dao Zhang Ailing* 《宋淇傳奇——從宋春舫到張愛玲》 [*The Legend of Song Qi – From Song Chunfang to Eileen Chang*], Oxford UP, 2014.

Song, Yilang 宋以朗 (Soong, Roland). "'Xiangjianhuan' jiujing xiang shuoshenme?" 〈〈相見歡〉究竟想說什麼？〉 ["What Exactly Does 'Xiangjianhuan' Want to Say?"] "The Eileen Chang Blog," *ESWN Culture Blog*, October 1, 2015. www.zonaeuropa.com/culture/ Accessed July 11, 2024.

Spivak, Gayatri Chakravorty. "Can the Subaltern Speak?" *The Post-Colonial Studies Reader,* edited by Bill Ashcroft, Gareth Griffiths, and Helen Tiffin, Routledge, 1995, pp. 24–28.

Spivak, Gayatri Chakravorty. "The Politics of Translation." *The Translation Studies Reader*, 3rd Edition, edited by Lawrence Venuti, Routledge, 2012, pp. 312–330.

Stavans, Ivans. *On Self-Translation: Meditations and Language*. State U of New York P, 2018.

Su Weizhen 蘇偉貞. *Gudao Zhang Ailing – Zhuizong zhang Ailing Xianggang shiqi (1952–1955) Xiaoshuo* 《孤島張愛玲——追蹤張愛玲香港時期 (1952–1955) 小說》 [*The Isolation of Eileen Chang – In Search of Eileen Chang's Hong Kong Period Fiction (1952–1955)*], Sanmin shuju 三民書局, 2002.

Sun, Longji. (Sun, Lung-kee 孫隆基). *Zhongguo wenhua de shenceng jiegou* 《中國文化的深層結構》 [*The Deep Structure of Chinese Culture*]. Jixianshe 集賢社, 1983.

BIBLIOGRAPHY

Tam, Kwok-kan 譚國根. "Introduction: Feminism and Gender Discourse in Mainland China, Taiwan and Hong Kong." *Gender, Discourse and the Self in the Literature: Issues in Mainland China, Taiwan, and Hong Kong*, edited by Kwok-kan Tam and Terry Siu-han Yip, Chinese U of Hong Kong P, 2010, pp. IX–XXX.

Tam, Kwok-kan 譚國根. "Xifang dui nüxing yishi de liangge lunshu moshi yu Zhongguo nüxing" 〈西方對女性意識的兩個論述模式與中國女性〉 ["Two Western Discourses of Femininity and Chinese Womanhood"]. *Nüxing yu Zhongguo wenxue*《女性與中國文學》 [*Women and Chinese Literature*], edited by Zheng Zhenwei 鄭振偉, Lingnan College, 1997, pp. 141–51.

Tang, Junyi 唐君毅. *Lun Zhonghua minzu zhi huaguo piaoling* 《論中華民族之花果飄零》 [*On the Floating About of the Chinese Nation's Flowers and Fruits*]. Samin shuju 三民書局, 1974.

Tang, Wenbiao 唐文標, editor. *Zhang Ailing ziliao daquanji* 《張愛玲資料大全集》 [*Complete Collection of Materials on Zhang Ailing*]. Shibao wenhua chubanshe 時報文化出版社, 1984.

Tyler, Alexander Fraser. *Essay on the Principles of Translation*. J. M. Dent; E. P. Dutton, 1971.

Van Doren, Mark, editor. *The Portable Emerson*. Viking, 1963.

Venuti, Lawrence, and Mona Baker, editors. *A Translation Studies Reader*. 1946. Routledge, 2000.

Venuti, Lawrence, editor. *The Translation Studies Reader*, 3rd Edition. Routledge, 2012.

Venuti, Lawrence. *The Scandals of Translation: Towards an Ethics of Difference*. Routledge, 1998.

Von Flotow-Evans, Luise. *Translation and Gender: Translating in the "Era of Feminism."* St. Jerome Publishing; U of Ottawa P, 1997.

Wakabayashi, Judy. "Translation in the East Asian Cultural Sphere: Roots, Divergent Paths?" *Asian Translation Traditions*, edited by Eva Hung and Judy Wakabayashi, St. Jerome Publishing, 2005, pp. 17–61.

Walker, Cheryl. "Feminist Literary Criticism and the Author." *The Death and Resurrection of the Author?* edited by William Irwin, Greenwood P, 2002, pp. 141–159.

Wang, Anyi 王安憶. *Jinxiugu zhi lian* 《錦繡谷之戀》 [*Love in the Valley of Splendor*]. Zhongguo dianying chubanshe, 2004.

Wang, David Der-wei 王德威. "Foreword." *The Rice-Sprout Song – A Novel of Modern China*, by Eileen Chang, U of California P, 1988, pp. VII–XXV.

Wang, David Der-wei 王德威. "Foreword." *The Rouge of the North*, by Eileen Chang, U of California P, 1998, pp. VII–XXX.

Wang, David Der-wei 王德威. "Luodi de maizi bu si – Zhang Ailing de wenxue yingxiangli yu Zhangpai zuojia de chaoyue zhi lu" 〈落地的麥子不死——張愛玲的文學影響力與張派作家的超越之路〉. *Huali yu cangliang: Zhang Ailing jinian wenji* 《華麗與蒼涼:張愛玲紀念文集》. Huangguan chuban she 皇冠出版社 [Crown Publishing Company Limited], 1996, pp. 196–210.

Wang, David Der-Wei 王德威. "Xin de lunlixue" 〈信的倫理學〉 "The Ethics of Letters." *Zhang Ailing geiwodexinjian.* 《張愛玲給我的信件》 [*Letters Given to Me by Eileen Chang*], edited by Hsiu Chih-tsing, Lianhe wenxue 聯和文學, 2013, pp. 392–400.

Wang, David Der-Wei 王德威. "Zhang Ailing chengle zushi nainai" 〈張愛玲成了祖師奶奶〉 ["Zhang Ailing Became Grand Mistress"]. *Xiaoshuo Zhongguo – wanqing dao dangdai de zhongwen xiaoshuo* 《小說中國—晚清到當代的中文小說》 [*Novels China – Chinese Novels from Late Qing to Modern*]. Maitian 麥田, 1993.

Wang, Xiaojue. "Memory, Photographic Seduction, and Allegorical Correspondence: Eileen Chang's *Mutual Reflections.*" *Rethinking Modern Chinese Popular Culture: Cannibalizations of the Canon*, edited by Carlos Rojas and Eileen Chow, Routledge, 2009, pp. 190–206.

White, Hayden. "The Historical Text as Literary Artifact." *The Norton Anthology of Theory and Criticism*, edited by Vincent B. Leitch. W. W. Norton, 2018, pp. 1463–1480.

Wimsatt, W. K., Jr., and Monroe C. Beardsley. "The Intentional Fallacy." *Sewanee Review*, vol. 54, no. 3, 1946, pp. 468–488. Revised in *The Verbal Icon: Studies in the Meaning of Poetry*, by W. K. Wimsatt Jr., U of Kentucky P, 1954, pp. 3–18.

Wong, Lawrence Wang-Chi 王宏志. "From 'Controlling the Barbarians' to 'Wholesale Westernization': Translation and Politics in Late Imperial and Early Republication China, 1840–1919." *Asian Translation Traditions*, edited by Eva Hung and Judy Wakabayashi, St. Jerome Publishing, 2005, pp. 109–131.

Woolf, Virginia. *A Room of One's Own*. 1928. London: Penguin, 1945.

Wu, Bangmou 吳邦謀. "Zhang Ailing yingwen chunüzuo xinfaxian" 〈張愛玲英文處女作新發現〉 ["New Discoveries of Eileen Chang's English Debut Writing"]. *INK yinke wenxue shenghuo zazhi: Zhang Ailing dansheng bainian jinian* 《INK 印刻文學生活雜誌:張愛玲誕生百年紀念》 [*INK Literary Monthly*], vol. 205, September 2020, 56–61.

Xiao, Guanhong 蕭關鴻. "Xunzhao Zhang Ailing" 〈尋找張愛玲〉 ["Finding Eileen Chang"]. *Lianhe wenxue* 《聯合文學》 (UNITAS), vol. 11, 1995.

Xiao, Hong 蕭紅. *Shangshijie* 《商市街》 [*Market Street: A Chinese Woman in Harbin*]. Translated with an introduction by Howard Goldblatt, U of Washington P, 1986.

Xiao, Hong 蕭紅. *Xiao Hong quanji* 《蕭紅專集》 [*Collected Writings of Xiao Hung*]. 2 vols. Harbin chubanshe 哈爾濱出版社, 1991.

Xiao, Hong 蕭紅. *Xiao Hong sanwen xiaoshuo Xuan* 《蕭紅散文小說選》 [*Prose and Novels of Xiao Hong*]. Edited by Li Shumin 李書敏 and Yan Ping 嚴平, Chongqing chubanshe 重慶出版社, 1999.

Xiaoxiaosheng 笑笑生. *Jinpingmei* 《金瓶梅》. Huayan jiaoxue chubanshe, 1993.

BIBLIOGRAPHY

Xiaoxiaosheng 笑笑生. *The Plum in the Golden Vase.* Translated by David Tod Roy, Princeton UP, 1993.

Xie, Tianzhen 謝天振. *Fanyi yanjiu xin shiye* 《翻譯研究新視野》 [*New Perspectives in Translation Studies*]. Qingdao chuban she 青島出版社, 2003.

Xie, Tianzhen 謝天振. *Zhongxi fanyi jianzhi* 《中西翻譯簡史》 [*A Brief History of Translation in China and the West*]. Waiyu jiaoxue yu yanjiu chubanshe 外語教學與研究出版社, 2010.

Xun Yu 迅雨 (Fu Lei 傅雷). "Lun Zhang Ailing de xiaoshuo" 〈論張愛玲的小說〉 ["On Zhang Ailing's Fiction"]. *Zhang Ailing yanjiu ziliao* 《張愛玲研究資料》 [*Research Materials on Zhang Ailing*], edited by Yu Qing 于青 and Jin Hongda 金宏達, Haixia wenyi chubanshe 海峽文藝出版社, 1994, pp. 115–130.

Yan, Fu 嚴復. "Tianyanlun yi liyan" 〈天演論譯例言〉 [Preface to *Tianyanlun*]. 1898. *Fanyi lunji* 《翻譯論集》 [*Essays on Translation*], edited by Liu Jingzhi 劉靖之, Joint Publishing Co., 1985, pp. 1–2.

Yan, Fu 嚴復. "Yu *Waijiao Bao* zhurenshu" 〈與外交報主人書〉 [Letter to the Proprietor of the *Waijiao Bao*]. *Yan Fu ji* 《嚴復集》 [*Works of Yan Fu*], Vol. III, edited by Wang Chi 王栻, 1986, pp. 557–565.

Yan, Zeya 顏擇雅. "Zhang Ailing yitisanxie – xi "Liuqing," "Xiangjianhuan," *Tongxueshaonian dou bujian*" 〈張愛玲一題三寫——析〈留情〉、〈相見歡〉、《同學少年都不賤》〉 ["Eileen Chang Writing One Topic in Three-Works – Analysis of 'Traces of Love,' 'Joyful Rendezvous,' and *Classmates when Adolescence Was Not Despicable*"]. *Jing Bao* 《晶報》, February 7, 2013.

Yi Shu 亦舒 (Nee Yeh-su 倪亦舒). "Hu Lancheng de xiazuo" 〈胡蘭成的下作〉 ["Hu Lancheng's Despicableness"]. *Ming Bao zhoukan* 《明報周刊》 [Ming Pao Weekly], 1976.

Yi Shu 亦舒 (Nee Yeh-su 倪亦舒). "Yuedu Zhang Ailing xinzuo yougan" 〈閱讀張愛玲新作有感〉 ["Feelings after Reading Eileen Chang's New Works"]. *Ming Bao zhoukan* 《明報周刊》 [Ming Pao Weekly], 1979.

Yip, Terry Siu-han 葉少嫻. "Faces of the Self in Modern Chinese Literature." *Garnering Diversities in Comparative Literature*, edited by Jessica Tsui-yan Li, Special Issue of *Canadian Review of Comparative Literature/Revue Canadienne de Littérature Comparée*, vol. 45, no. 2, 2018, pp. 275–289.

Yu, Qing 于青. *Zhang Ailing zhuan* 《張愛玲傳》 [*The Biography of Zhang Ailing*]. Tiandi tushu youxian gongsi 天地圖書有限公司, 1999.

Yuwairen 域外人 (Zhang Xiguo 張系國). "Bu chi la de zenmo hudechu lazi?" 不吃辣的怎麼胡得出辣子？——評〈色，戒〉 ["You Can't Win If You Can't Eat Chili: On 'Se, Jie'"]. "Renjian fukan" 〈人間副刊〉 ("Human Realm Literary Supplement"), *Zhongguo shibao* 《中國時報》 [*China Times*], 1 Oct. 1978.

Zelizer, Barbie. "Reading the Past Against the Grain: The Shape of Memory Studies." *Critical Studies in Mass Communication*, vol. 12, no. 2, 1995, pp. 214–239.

Zhang, Chufan 張春帆. *Jiuweigui* 《九尾龜》 [*Nine-Tailed Turtle*]. Guangya chuban youxian gongsi, 1984.

Zhang, Jie 張潔. *Fangzhou* 《方舟》. Beijing shiyue wenyi chubanshe, 1988.

Zhang, Jie 張潔. *The Ark. Love Must Not Be Forgotten*, China Books and Periodicals, 1986, pp. 113–201.

Zhang, Zijing 張子靜. *Wo de Jiejie Zhang Ailing* 《我的姊姊張愛玲》 [*My Elder Sister Zhang Ailing*]. Shibao wenhua chubanshe 時報文化出版社, 1996.

Zhong, Weihe. "An Overview of Translation in China: Practice and Theory." *Translation Journal*, vol. 7, no. 2, 2003.

Zhuang, Xinzheng 莊信正. *Zhang Ailing laixin qianzhu.* 《張愛玲來信箋註》 [*Annotations of Letters from Eileen Chang*]. INK yinke chuban youxian gongsi INK 印刻出版有限公司, 2008.

Zhuang, Yiwen 莊宜文. "Qipao xia de (fan) geming – Zhang Ailing he nü jiandie" 〈旗袍下的（反）革命—張愛玲和女間諜〉 ["(Counter)Revolutionary under Qipao – Eileen Chang and Female Spies"]. *Lianhe wenxue* 《聯合文學》 (UNITAS), no. 431, 2020.

Zitong and Yiqing 子通, 亦清, editors. *Zhang Ailing wenji · buyi* 《張愛玲文集 · 補遺》. Zhongguo huaqiao chubanshe 中國華僑出版社, 2002.

Index

A Doll's House 92
A Poetics of Postmodernism 53
"A Return to the Frontier" 8, 29, 203,
    239–243, 246, 268
    "Chongfang biancheng" 8, 29, 203, 239,
      241–243, 245, 246, 268
adolescence 48, 54, 72, 151
adulthood 15, 36, 53, 80, 84, 248
aesthetics 88–90, 95, 100, 106, 107, 128, 129,
    131, 132, 135, 200
afterlife 152, 172
"Against Theory" 24
Anglophone 55, 59, 64, 91, 97, 101, 102, 105,
    111, 115, 119–121, 124, 126, 129, 130, 133,
    153, 157–159, 161, 162, 167, 173, 176, 177,
    185–188, 200, 208, 213, 216, 225, 255,
    258, 265, 266, 268, 271, 272
analogy 37, 116, 176, 258
Akai Koi 227
Alec Wagstaff 58
Alfred Schenkman 118
Analects 161
Anhui wenyi chubanshe 118
    Anhui Literature and Art Publisher 118
Anthony Cordingley 62, 108
aristocratic 4, 60, 70, 80, 90, 91, 184, 198,
    210, 265
Augustine 19
authenticity 16, 203–205, 207, 209, 210–224,
    228, 265
author 111, 117, 118, 128, 134, 136, 137, 172, 185,
    186, 199, 213, 226–228, 266, 273
    authorial intention 23–25, 87, 111, 117,
      152, 172, 265
    authorship 3, 7, 25, 26, 28, 88, 108, 109,
      115, 117, 153, 273
autobiography 34, 36, 52, 53, 61, 69, 80, 266,
    270
autobiografiction 66
avant-garde 262

Ba Jin 35, 47, 170
baihua 164, 175
    vernacular Chinese 14, 141, 164, 170, 263,
    268
Banshengyuan 9, 54, 206, 236

Half a Lifelong Romance 9, 54, 206
Barbie Zelizer 181
Basil Hatim 20
Battle of Hong Kong 44, 53, 247
betrayal 23, 67, 106, 128, 133, 142, 204, 210,
    223, 243, 261
Bian Zhilin 16
"Biaoyi xiyi ji qita" 29, 136, 142, 148, 149
    "*Biao Aunt, Little Aunt, and Other
    Issues*" 29, 136
bilingual 2, 5, 16, 88, 116, 129, 135, 153, 164, 184,
    186, 200, 243, 249, 264, 265, 266, 273
body 45, 51, 56, 68, 78, 80, 88–95, 98–100,
    102–104, 106, 107, 110, 113–115, 120, 121,
    128–133, 135, 136, 149, 153, 166, 168, 175,
    187, 190, 191, 192, 200, 204, 209, 212–219,
    221–224, 232, 236–238, 258, 267
Boston 82, 83
boundaries 5, 11, 23, 29, 53, 56, 68, 87, 89, 93,
    105, 113, 128, 153, 208, 239, 241, 245, 246,
    248, 249, 251, 253, 255, 259, 261, 263,
    268, 273
bourgeois 10, 47, 92, 141, 262, 268
Boxer Rebellion 188
Brian T. Fitch 22
Buddhism 18, 160, 165–167, 171, 260

Calcutta 118, 121
Cannibalism 170
Cantonese 29, 64, 245, 246, 256
Carl R. Rogers 80
Carlo Goldoni 264
Cassell Company of London 90
Catford 20
cenci duizhao 37
    equivocal contrast 30, 37, 39, 221, 235,
    239, 243, 247, 248, 269
censorship 119, 121, 136, 203, 207, 218, 229,
    230, 237, 265, 271
Chad Gordon 45
Changde Apartment 41, 42
Changsha 73, 74
chanzu 189
    bound feet 49, 189–191, 200, 215
Charles d'Orléans 15, 264
Charles Scribner's Sons 206

INDEX

Chen Duxiu 170, 189
Chen Ruoxi 240
"Chenlun" 34
 "Sinking" 34
Chiang Kai-Shek 121, 195, 230, 231
Chidi zhi lian 8, 29, 203, 206, 224, 226–232,
 237, 238, 269
 Naked Earth 8, 10, 29, 203, 206, 224, 226,
 227, 231–233, 235–238, 269
Chinese civil war 15, 186
Chinese Imperial Examination 77
"Chinese Life and Fashions" 6, 157, 184, 185,
 193, 194
 "Gengyiji" 6, 29, 103, 157, 184–189,
 191–194, 199, 200
 "A Chronicle of Changing Clothes" 157,
 185
"Chinese Translation: A Vehicle of Cultural
 Influence" 9, 27, 203
Chineseness 101, 239, 244, 245, 246
Chiuhaitang 174
 Autumn Quince 165, 174
Christianity 11, 162, 165–167
Chuanqi 6, 63, 118
 Romances 6, 115, 118, 270
Chunqiu 251
 Spring Autumn 251
ci 140
 changduanju 140
Cicero 18, 19
cidiao 140
cige 140
cipai 140
codes of conduct 115
Cold War 2, 3, 7–9, 15, 29, 66, 83, 84, 119,
 204, 210, 239–241, 243, 265, 266,
 271–273
 post-Cold War 15, 266
colloquial speech 173, 175, 183
colloquialism 175
colonialism 15, 241, 264
coming-of-age 64
commentary 77, 152, 160, 161
Communism 7, 205, 216, 227, 240
concubinage 40, 66, 123, 124, 126, 127
Confucian 34, 50, 92, 93, 105, 106, 115, 116,
 129, 133, 134, 144, 159, 169, 190, 221, 245,
 263, 269
 Confucianism 14, 35, 88, 160, 161, 166,
 167, 170, 171

Confucius 50, 132, 161
 Neo-Confucianism 14
copyright 25, 26, 88, 109, 119, 153, 172, 206
cosmopolitan 50, 197, 256
cross-cultural 29, 195, 239
cultures 2, 4, 17, 21, 34, 35, 93, 119, 126, 128,
 129, 135, 149, 158, 166, 167, 173, 190, 213,
 214, 222, 239, 244, 246, 255, 262, 266,
 273

da 16, 263
 fluency 16, 17, 18, 263
"Daodi shi Shanghai ren" 267
 "Shanghainese, After All" 267
"Daoluyimu" 197
 "Seeing with the Streets" 197
Dai Li 251
Dai Tian 240
Dai Wangshu 16
Daryl Bem 47
David Der-wei Wang 51, 62, 91, 98, 206, 211
De doctrina Christiana 19
"Demons and Fairies" 29, 157, 159–161,
 163–165, 167, 168, 170, 171
 Zhongguoren de zongjiao" 6, 29, 157,
 159, 161, 163–169
 "The Religion of the Chinese" 6, 157, 159
"Deng" 6, 8, 28, 88, 118–127, 153, 270
"Des Tours de Babel" 26, 27
desolation 10, 37, 41, 50, 67, 104, 106, 112, 119,
 126, 220, 222, 223, 248
dialect 9, 29, 49, 102, 165, 246
dialectics 77, 259
diaspora 10, 51, 72, 244, 268
Ding Ling 35
Ding Mocun 250–252
discourse 1, 2, 20, 22, 23, 24, 26, 75, 104, 113,
 114, 136, 176, 189, 200, 224, 239, 243, 245,
 249, 252, 264, 273
distanciation 29, 158, 172, 178, 183, 200
Dragonfly Books 206
droit moral 25, 88, 109
Duizhaoji 7, 28, 69, 185, 270
 Mutual Reflections 39, 55, 67, 71, 75, 76,
 79, 80, 82, 83, 185, 191, 198

Egyptian theology 159, 166
Eight-Nation Alliance 188
Emerich de Vatel 12
Empress Dowager Cixi Taihou 13

INDEX

equivocal contrast   30, 37, 39, 221, 235, 239, 243, 247, 248, 269
Ernest Hemingway   7
   "Ouniesi Haimingwei"   7
Erotic Faculties   103
ethnicity   20, 34, 35, 244, 262
Etymologies of Isidore of Seville   100
Eurocentric   113
Eva Hung   109
Eve Kosofsky Sedgwick   21

fairy tales   171
faithfulness   16–18, 23, 106, 133, 204, 219, 223, 263
"fan fubai" (anti-bureaucracy)   225
"fan langfei" (anti-waste)   225
"fan tan" (anti-corruption)   225
fashion   6, 24, 29, 34, 39, 70, 98, 103, 104, 129, 131, 132, 157, 158, 181, 184–189, 191, 193–200, 245, 246, 266, 270
feminine   96, 105, 116, 145, 190, 191, 212, 220, 258
femininity   112, 116, 125, 132, 194, 196, 214
feng shui   259
Ferdinand Reyher   5, 50, 68, 82, 93, 206, 248
filial piety   59, 145, 163, 166, 169, 171, 221, 244
fluidity   27, 36, 38, 171, 244, 246
footbinding   189, 190
Formosa   208, 241, 242, 246
Fredric Jameson   136
Friedrich Nietzsche   19
Friedrich Schleiermacher   19, 33
Fu Lei   18, 37, 91, 263
Fu Ssu-nien   164
"Fuhua langrui"   139
   "Floating Flowers and Wavy Pistils"   139, 151
"Fuzheng"   120
   "Straighten Up"   120

G. Thomas Couser   36, 37
Gaolaotou   18
   Old Man Gao   18
Gaoyang   251
   Xu Yanpian   251
Gayatri Spivak   20, 114
gaze   79, 102, 103, 113, 115, 131, 191, 212
gender   1, 3, 6, 20, 21, 25, 34, 35, 43, 91–93, 103–105, 107, 112, 114, 119, 120, 124, 125, 127, 129, 133, 153, 157, 159, 185, 186, 190,

191, 194, 199, 200, 215, 217, 237, 249, 263, 266, 267, 272
George Bernard Shaw   38, 199
Gérard Genette   89, 160, 212
Giuseppe Ungaretti   15
globalization   1, 15, 20, 118, 246, 264, 273
Gongchandang   207
   Communist Party   140, 195, 204, 207, 210, 225, 230, 231, 235, 251
"Gongyu shenghuo jiqu"   48
   "Notes on Apartment Life"   28, 48
Gu Hungming   27
Guangdong   256
Guanlu   251
   Hu Shoumei   251
guanren   102
"Guihuazheng"   8, 28, 88, 108–112, 114, 116, 117, 153, 270
   "Shame Amah"   88, 153
   "Steamed Osmanthus"   8, 28, 88, 108–111, 270
Gujin   173, 185
   From Ancient to Present   173
guiyuan shi   96
   Boudoir Lament Poetry   96
Guo Moruo   35
guoyu   11, 175

Haishanghua liezhuan   9, 137
   Flowers of Shanghai   9
Haiguo tuzhi   13
   An Illustrated Gazetteer of the Maritime Countries   13
Han Bangqing   9, 49, 137
Han Gaozulun   38
   On Emperor Gaozu of Han   38
Hangzhou   72, 73
Hanjian   49, 250
Harriet Beecher Stowe   14
Heartbreak House   38
Henrik Ibsen   39, 92
Hermeneuin   158
hermeneutics   1, 33, 158, 179, 199
heterogeneous   93, 107, 173, 181, 224, 245
Hong Kong   2, 4, 6–8, 10, 15, 29, 36, 41, 44–50, 53, 55, 63–65, 78, 81–83, 91, 110, 118, 140–142, 164, 196, 203, 205, 206, 226, 227, 230, 231, 239–241, 243, 245, 246–251, 253, 261, 266, 269, 271

Hongloumeng 4, 11, 97
  Dream of the Red Chamber 4, 11, 97, 221, 248
Honoré de Balzac 18
"Hong meigui yu bai meigui" 234, 235, 237
  "Red Rose and White Rose" 234
Hong Zhihui 240
Hongzong liema 176
  Red-Maned Horse 176
Hošoi Gungnecuke Cin Wang 13
  Prince Gong 13
  Aisin Gioro Yixin 13
hospitality 29, 239, 262, 266, 273
Hsia Chih-tsing 10, 51, 90, 91, 211
Hsiung Shih-I 16
  Xiong Shiyi 16
Hu Lancheng 5, 10, 51, 66, 67, 150, 151, 204, 216, 228, 253, 261, 267
"Hu Lancheng de xiazuo" 150
  "Hu Lancheng's Despicableness" 150
Hu Shi 14, 28, 49, 50, 189, 211
"Huadiao" 60
  "Withering Flower" 60, 61
Huajing 263
  a state of sublimity 263
Hualien 240, 241, 245
Huang Dingchu 61
Huang Jiayi 61
Huang Suqiong 4, 69, 71, 73, 191
  Huang Yifan 4, 39, 58, 69, 92, 191
  Yvonne Whang 58
Huang Yisheng 4
Huangguan 28, 90, 118, 136, 230, 250,
  Crown 90, 91, 118, 119, 136, 140, 203, 206, 229–231, 250
Huayu 175
Huilong chubanshe 279
Hunan 73
Hundred-Day Reforms 73, 188
Hybridity 30, 118, 173, 175, 176, 239
Hybridization 37, 262, 270

Ian Mason 20
ideal self 35, 80
identity 1–3, 13, 21, 25, 28, 33–36, 45–49, 52, 81, 84, 98, 105, 111, 113, 114, 134, 147, 209, 261, 266–270
ideology 7, 95, 98, 129, 211, 216, 217, 222, 243, 252, 260, 272
idiom 9, 43, 95, 123, 125, 149, 192

imagination 37, 49, 51, 52, 55, 69, 74, 82, 163, 168, 196, 203, 221, 253
in-betweenness 2, 3, 8, 23, 26–28, 87, 89, 101, 106, 109, 117, 120, 132, 135, 136, 153, 173, 175, 176, 209, 227, 268, 271, 273
intentio 22
interdependence 22
interpretation 3, 11, 18, 19, 22, 24–27, 29, 33, 59, 62, 74, 87, 89, 108, 110, 124, 137, 145, 151–153, 158, 159, 163, 165–167, 170–173, 176–179, 181, 190, 194, 224, 242, 247, 253, 254, 266, 273
intertextuality 29, 30, 224, 228, 231
Isabel Nee Yeh-su 150
  Yi Shu 150, 151

Jacques Derrida 21, 23, 24, 26
Jan Walsh Hokenson 249, 264
Jerome 19
Jiang Ziya 259
Jiji Tsūshinsha 206
Jili 44
  Auspicious 44
Jiliu sanbu qu 170
  Trilogy of Turbulent Stream 170
"Jilong" 75
  "Chicken Coop" 75
Jin Xiongbai 251
Jing Bao 151
Jinpingmei 215
  The Plum in a Golden Vase 215
"Jinjiazhuang" 40
  "Homestead of the Jin" 40
Jinri shijie 7, 206
  The World Today 206
"Jinse" 261
  "Adorned Zither" 261
Jinsheng jinshi 150
  This Life, These Times 150
"Jinsuoji" 8, 28, 88–95, 97–99, 101, 104, 105, 153, 185, 195, 267
  "The Golden Cangue" 8, 28, 87–91, 93–95, 99, 101, 104, 106, 153, 185, 195, 267
"Jinyulu" 28, 46, 64, 268
  "From the Ashes" 28, 46, 64, 268
Joanna Frueh 103
Johann Wolfgang von Goethe 19
John Berger 102
John Donne 15
John Langshaw Austin 21, 136

INDEX

John le Carré   254
Judith Butler   21, 103, 104
Julio-César Santoyo   89

"Kan Zhang – 'Xiangjianhuan' de
    tantao"   148
    "Reading Chang – Discussion on 'Joyful
    Rendezvous'"   148
"Kangmei yuanchao yundong"   225
    Resist America, Aid Korea   225
Kang Youwei   12, 13
Kashiwa Kensaku   227
"Ke shehui zhuanlan"   151
    "Ke Society Column"   151
Kêmingtang   207, 208
    Revolutionaries   207, 208
Kenneth Hsien-yung Pai   16, 264
"Kiloma'an"   241
Kim Il-sung   83
Klaus Mehnert   157–161, 177, 185, 186
Korean War   225
Kuaile cun   46
    Happy Village   46
"Kuangren riji"   170
    "Diary of a Madman"   170
Kuomintang   195, 207, 208, 250, 251
    the Nationalist Party   195, 203, 207, 227,
    230, 231, 240, 255

Land-Reform Movement   204, 205, 209
Lawrence Venuti   19, 20, 25, 26, 118, 126
Le Droit des Gens   12
    The Law of Nations   12
Le Père Goriot   18
Letter to Pammachius   19
Li Ang   216
Li Hongzhang   4, 74, 75, 90, 197
Li Jouou   4, 75, 76
Li Shangyin   261, 262
Li Shiqun   251
Li Xianglan   79
    Yamaguchi Yoshiko   79
Li Yu   140, 141
    Li Houzhu   140
Liang Qichao   12, 13, 190
Liang Zongdai   16
Liangyou Huabao   92
    The Young Companion   92
Liji   133
Lin Shu   14, 263

Lin Yutang   14, 16, 17, 182, 260, 264, 271
Lin Zexu   12
Linda Hutcheon   53, 174
linear   27, 89, 91, 131, 140, 240, 261, 265
Ling Shuhua   16
    Su-hua Ling Chen   16
Liuyan   6, 198
    Written on Water   6
Los Angeles   51, 81, 252
"Lu wenxue zizhuan"   34
    "Autobiography of Imperial Instructor
    Lu"   34
Lu Xun   9, 17–19, 35, 47, 92, 170, 189, 214, 263
    Zhou Shuren   9, 17
Lu Yu   34
Lucian Wu   119
"Lun nüxue"   190
    "On Women's Education"   190

Ma Jianzhong   17
Mae Fong Soong   9, 60, 203, 241, 246, 249,
    250
Mandarin   9, 10, 29, 49, 64, 175, 244, 245, 250
manuscript   28, 50, 136–140, 142–148, 203,
    249
Mao Dun   47
Marcella Munson   264
Marjorie Dryburgh   34
Matteo Ricci   12, 263
Maurice Halbwachs   179
Max Ascoli   240, 243
May Fourth Movement   8, 10, 17, 37, 69, 84,
    89, 92, 128–130, 164, 170, 186, 189, 192,
    203, 245, 266, 270, 272
memoir   53, 55, 57, 58, 61, 84, 150, 268
memory   41, 49, 50, 55, 58, 70, 72–75, 97, 134,
    173, 174, 179, 181, 183, 221, 244, 246, 247,
    252, 262, 268
mendang hudui   99
    the matching of doors and families   99
metacommentary   29, 75, 136, 137, 142, 143,
    148, 149, 152
metaphors   110, 234, 235, 269
metonymic   256
metonymy   113
Michael Ignatieff   83
Michel Foucault   24, 25
Middle Ages   24
Mingbao zhoukan   150
    Ming Pao Weekly   150

modernization   2, 13, 14, 40, 90, 131, 170, 176, 184, 185, 189, 190, 194, 200, 272
"Moli xiangpian"   63
   "Jasmine Tea"   63
Monroe C. Beardsley   23
motifs   96, 176
Motion Picture & General Investment Company   197, 246
multi-dimensional   112, 246, 265

Namikawa Ryō   206, 209, 210
nationalism   1, 190, 251, 259, 260, 263, 267
Nationalist Party   203, 207, 227, 230, 231, 240, 255, 259
nationality   262
New Chinese Stories: Twelve Short Stories   119
New Criticism   23
New Culture Movement   267
"New England ... China"   28, 50
New Pragmatism   24
Nicole Oresme   15
Nicolas Perrot d'Ablancourt   19
Niehaihua   74, 75, 76
   A Flower in a Sinful Sea   74
Nishe fanyi shuyuan yi   17
   On Establishing a Translation Institution   17
Niu'er   70, 71
Nōmin Ongakutai   206, 209
   Peasants' Band   206
Nuola zouhou zenyang?   92
   What Happens After Nora Leaves Home?   92

Of Grammatology   24
Opium War   12
Orient Review and Literary Digest   118
original   2, 16–18, 19, 22, 25, 44, 62, 108, 139, 140, 145, 152, 172, 196, 227, 230, 252, 253
Ouyang Zi   240

P. Lal   118
palimpsests   89
Pan Gu   162, 163
Paratexts   89, 160
paratextuality   160
patriarchal   28, 43, 47, 66, 72, 96–98, 102–106, 124, 125, 129, 130, 133, 143, 177, 188, 199, 204, 212, 215–217, 221, 223, 232, 233, 236, 267

patriotism   251, 259, 260
Paul Ricœur   20, 21, 33, 53, 172, 239
"Peach Blossoms Spring"   49
Peking Opera   6, 29, 97, 157, 158, 170–183, 200, 268–270
performativity   16, 21, 29, 34, 36, 149, 249, 260, 262, 263, 266, 269, 273
peritext   160
personas   30, 37, 69, 167
Peyton Place   50
photo albums   33, 53, 69, 84
photographs   51, 69, 72, 73, 79–84, 185, 195
Ping'an   241
Ping Xintao   229
Pingguo ribao   151
   Apple Daily   151
Pliny the Younger   18
portrait   39, 72–76, 78, 82–84, 252
postcolonialism   1, 20, 25, 113, 264
poststructuralism   20, 23, 264
Protestant   159, 162, 166
Pu Yi   34
Putonghua   175

Qian Zhongshu   18, 263
qichu zhi tiao   133
   the Seven Out Rules   133
"Qiduan qingchang ji qita"   44
   "Short of Ambition, Everlasting Love, and Others"   44
"Qingcheng zhi lian"   6, 185, 196, 220, 270
   "Love in a Fallen City"   7, 185, 196, 220, 235, 270
qipao   80, 186, 194–196, 198, 200, 245
   cheongsam   194, 196
   cheongpao   194
   long gown   50, 71, 133, 194
Qu Qiubai   17
quanpan xihua   14
   wholesale Westernization   14
Quintilian   18
quotation   109, 110, 171, 173–175, 179, 180, 183, 268

Rabindranath Tagore   15
race   20, 35, 176, 240, 243, 262
Rebecca Hourwich   5, 93
reinterpretation   110, 173, 176, 181
re-evaluation   10, 20, 28, 88, 118–120, 124, 126, 158, 190, 265

INDEX

reconstruction 16, 26, 54, 72, 87, 104, 108, 110, 124, 173, 174, 237, 239, 246, 248, 252, 266

recontextualization 28, 88, 175, 209

relevance 23, 174

religion 6, 29, 34, 35, 157–163, 165–167, 170, 171, 200, 269, 270

Rémy Belleau 15

Renaissance 19

representation 2, 3, 21–23, 25, 26, 33, 34, 37, 51, 69, 70, 72, 80, 81, 84, 87, 89–92, 95–97, 101, 109, 117, 129, 153, 159, 176, 179, 180, 186, 204, 210, 223, 237, 252, 259, 266

Republic of China 8, 10, 15, 61, 121, 195, 205, 206, 230, 242, 264

rewriting 3, 29, 55, 57, 64, 72, 84, 89, 91, 92, 107, 117, 119, 125, 148, 152, 158, 173, 176, 184, 195, 200, 215, 239, 241, 247, 248, 253, 255, 261, 262, 265, 272, 283

Richard McCarthy 203, 205, 226, 227, 240–242, 249

Roland Barthes 24, 51, 81

Roland Soong 68, 140, 151, 152, 241

Roman orators 18, 264

Rosario Ferré 15, 264

Rou Shi 214

Sacred Scripture 19

Sai Jinhua 251

sancong side 132, 144

three obediences and four virtues 132, 144

Samuel Beckett 15, 22, 264

San Francisco 82, 83

"Sanfan yundong" 225

the Three-Antis Movement 225

Sanguo yanyi 176

The Tales of the Three Kingdoms 176

Sarah Dauncey 34

Saturday Review 10, 209

second Sino-Japanese war 5, 10, 13, 15, 49, 90, 108, 120, 188, 249, 250, 257, 259, 261

Seikatsusha 227

self 34–41, 44–46, 48–50, 52–54, 57, 59, 62, 67, 69, 72–77, 80–82, 84, 91, 113, 214, 239, 243, 248, 260, 266, 268, 269, 273

self-concept 33, 34, 36, 45, 46, 49, 66, 78–80, 84

self-determination 29, 43, 45, 46, 80, 147

self-esteem 35, 45, 46, 75, 80

self-exploration 265

self-healing 55, 265

self-image 28, 35, 78, 80

self-perception 35, 36, 47

self-portrait 82, 83, 84

self-translation 1–3, 6–9, 11, 14–16, 20–23, 25–28, 33, 34, 36, 43, 52, 62, 84, 87–89, 92, 108–112, 116, 118, 119, 125, 128, 129, 132, 134, 135, 140, 148, 152, 153, 157–159, 161, 163–169, 172, 180, 184, 192, 195, 199, 200, 204, 212, 224, 237, 239, 241, 242, 243, 246–248, 253, 255, 257, 261, 262, 264–271, 273

self-translator 1–3, 5, 7, 14–16, 21, 22, 23, 25, 26, 33, 34, 62, 84, 88, 89, 108, 118, 137, 153, 157, 158, 172, 173, 184, 185, 213, 249, 264, 266, 273

semi-autobiographical novel 7, 15, 36, 52, 53, 55, 57, 84, 115, 170, 247, 265, 268, 270, 271

sense-for-sense 19, 264

Shafu 216, 287

The Butcher's Wife 216, 287

"Shanhai yudi quantu" 12

"Complete Terrestrial Map" 12

Shanghai 3–7, 9, 10, 15, 29, 36, 38, 41, 42, 44–46, 48–50, 53, 57, 60, 64, 65, 78, 79, 81, 92, 95, 96, 102, 103, 107, 108, 112–115, 117, 118, 120, 121, 140–142, 151, 157–159, 164, 165, 173, 174, 185, 196, 197, 200, 205, 206, 214, 218, 222, 225, 228, 240, 247, 250, 251, 253, 266–271

Shanghai Evening Post 6

Shanghainese 196, 245, 248, 267, 268, 279

Shanhe tushu gongsi 118

Mountains and Rivers Books Company 118

Shao-shing Opera 165

Shenbao 196

Shengjing heheben 11

Chinese Union Version Bible 11

Shengsi 18

Shengsiqiang 214

The Field of Life and Death 214

Shenzhen 242

Shibachun 9, 54, 236

Eighteen Springs 9, 54, 236

Shijing 51, 220

The Book of Songs 51

The Classics of Poetry 51, 220

Shiyu 140

"Shuangsheng" 44, 247
  "Double Voices" 44, 247
Shuihu zhuan 176
  Water Margins 176
Shuping shumu 148
  Taiwan Review of Books 148
"Signature, Event, Context" 24
Sima Qian 34
Sinocentric 113
Sinophone 56, 59, 159, 255, 259, 265, 266, 273
"Siyu" 6, 28, 38, 90, 226, 270, 271
  "Whispers" 38, 39, 41, 43, 54, 105, 270
"Siyu Zhang Ailing" 90, 226
  "Private Words with Eileen Chang" 226
Soi-même comme un autre 21, 248
  Oneself as Another 248
Somerset Maugham 27, 113
Song Chunfang 27
Song Qi 226, 227
  Stephen Soong 60, 68, 81, 138, 139, 140, 150, 152, 241, 250, 253, 257, 260
  Lin Yiliang 134, 226
Soong Mei-ling 195
Sor Juana Inés de la Cruz 15, 264
St. Mary's Hall 4, 5, 6, 80, 198
"Stales Mates" 8, 28, 88, 128–130, 133, 135, 153, 185, 270
  "Wusi yishi" 131–135, 153, 270
Stefan George 15
stereotypes 118, 125, 126, 170, 171, 200, 212, 222, 254, 269
Steven Knapp 24
Stoicheia 12
  Jihe yuanben 12
  The Origin of Geometryi 12
stream-of-consciousness 247
Su Shi 178
subaltern 25, 114
Submarine! 7
  Haidi changzheng ji 7
Sun Yongfan 79
supernatural 171
superstitions 167, 263
Susan Bassnett 157, 184

Tableaux Parisiens 22
taboo 53, 56, 59, 68, 134, 148, 214
"Tai shigong zixu" 34
  "Autobiographical Afterword of the Grand Historian" 34
Taipei 119, 121, 240, 242, 244–246
Taiwan 8–10, 15, 16, 27, 29, 90, 119, 121, 136, 139, 141, 175, 203, 204, 206, 211, 229, 230, 239–242, 258, 266–269
  Taiouwang 241
  Taiyowan 241
  Tayowan 241
  Teijoan 241
  Toyouan 241
  Tyovon 241
Talcott Parsons 45
Tan Sitong 12
Tang Chun-I 244
  Tang Junyi 244
Tang Ouzhou 61
Tao Yuanming 34, 49
Taoism 111, 160, 165–167, 171
The Art of Poetry 19
The Bible 11, 19, 214
The Book of Change 7, 28, 52, 53, 55, 56, 58, 59, 63, 64, 84, 247, 268
The Cotton Weaver 182, 183
"The Death of the Author" 24, 51
The Fall of the Pagoda 6, 7, 28, 52–54, 58, 62–64, 84
The Heart of the Perfection of Transcendent Wisdom 260
  The Heart Sutra 260
"The Intentional Fallacy" 23
"The Legend of Sleepy Hollow" 7
  Wutou qishi 7
"The Letter" 113
The Old Man and the Sea 7
  Laoren yu hai 7
The Portable Emerson 7
  Aimoshen xuanji 7
The Reporter 203, 240, 243
The Rice-Sprout Song 8, 29, 203–207, 209, 212, 218, 220–222, 226, 269
  Yangge 8, 29, 49, 203, 204, 206, 208–216, 218–223, 226–229, 269
The Russian Album 83
The Scandals of Translation 118, 126

INDEX

"The Spyring" 9, 29, 203, 249, 250, 254–257, 260, 261, 267
   "Ch'ing k'ê! Ch'ing k'ê!" 249
   "Se, Jie" 9, 139, 197, 204, 249, 250–261, 267
   "Lust, Caution" 9, 139, 197, 249, 252
"The Task of the Translator" 22, 26, 184
The Translation Studies Reader 19, 20, 25
The xxth Century 157–159, 173, 185, 269
The Yearling 7
   Xiaolu 7
   Luyuan Changchun 7
The Young Marshal 9, 246
Thomas H. Huxley 13
   Evolution and Ethics 13
"Ti Xilinbi" 178
   "Written on the Wall at West Forest Temple" 178
tian 111
   Heaven 35, 111, 163–165, 189
Tian Han 35
"Tiancaimeng" 28, 45, 198
   "Dream of Genius" 28, 45,
Tianfeng chubanshe 7, 118, 227, 230, 231
Tianjin 3, 4, 15, 36, 44, 53, 71, 72, 73, 211, 266
tianrenheyi 111
   unity of Heaven and Human 111
tianzi 111
   Sons of Heaven 111
Tianyanlun 13, 16
   On Evolution 13
tianzu 189
   natural or heavenly feet 189
Tongwen Guan 13
   School of Interpreters 13
   Common Learning 13
"Tongyan wuji" 28, 62
   "From the Mouths of Babes" 28, 39, 40, 62
transcultural 1–5, 11, 15, 16, 23, 29, 35–38, 52, 53, 70–73, 79, 87, 88, 106, 118, 129, 131, 132, 135, 186, 200, 239, 244, 248, 262, 266, 270, 273
transformation 2, 28, 29, 35, 38, 50, 90, 92, 95, 128, 133, 153, 158, 159, 171, 181, 184–186, 188, 193, 200, 222, 224, 237, 241, 246, 259, 268, 270, 273
transgression 92, 105, 107, 188, 214, 273
transmigration theory 18

transtextuality 160
traumatic 1, 6, 54, 55, 62, 64, 72, 266
twentieth-century 30, 92, 96, 127, 129, 131, 170, 200, 272, 273
Twentieth Century Chinese Stories 91
"Tudi gaige yundong" 225
   the Land Reform Movement 218, 225

uncanny 63, 64, 211
Uncle Tom's Cabin 14
   Heinu yutian lu 14
   The Record of Negro Slave Calls Upon Heaven 14
Union Press 227, 231
United States Information Agency 7, 205
United States Information Services 7, 205, 226, 240, 249
University of California Press 90, 91, 206, 231
University of Hong Kong 4, 44, 45, 65, 110, 246, 261, 267
utterances 21, 136, 137

Vladimir Nabokov 15, 264

"Waiting" 8, 88, 118, 270
   "Little Finger Up" 8, 88, 118–121, 123–127
Washington, D.C. 82, 83
W. K. Wimsatt 23
W. W. Wagstaff 57, 58
Walter Benjamin 22, 26, 184
Walter Benn Michaels 24
Wang Jingwei 5, 120
Wang Wenxing 240
Wang Zhenhe 240, 241
Wangranji 29, 136, 139, 140, 148, 149, 250, 256, 261
   A Record of Bewilderment 29, 136, 139, 250, 256, 257
Ways of Seeing 48, 102, 194
"Wei nuli de muqin" 214
   "Slave Mother" 214
Wei Yuan 12
"*weihuzuochang*" 258
   playing jackal to the tiger 258
wenhua hanjian 49
   cultural traitor 49

wenyan 175
Wenzhou 15, 216, 228, 266, 267
William Somerset Maugham 27, 113
Wo de qian bansheng 34
   The First Half of My Life 34
   From Emperor to Citizen 34
Wo de zizi Zhang Ailing 198
   My Elder Sister Eileen Chang 198
"Wo kan Su Qing" 28, 44
   "My View on Su Qing" 28, 44
word for word 19
Wu Luqin 240
Wu Yu 170

Xianggang tianfeng chubanshe 7, 118, 227
   Hong Kong Sky and Wind Publisher 118
"Xiangjianhuan" 28, 29, 89, 136–141, 143, 144,
   145, 147–151, 153
   "A Joyful Rendezvous" 28, 148, 151
   "She Said Smiling" 28, 89, 136–138, 140,
     144, 147, 153
Xiao Ai 206
   Little Ai 206
Xiao Hong 214
Xiaotuanyuan 28
   Little Reunion 7, 52–60, 62, 65–67, 78,
     84, 268
Xie Bingying 34, 35
Xie Tianzhen 128, 263
Xifeng 45, 46
   West Wind 45, 46
xin 16, 18, 263
   faithfulness 16–18, 23, 106, 133, 204, 219,
     223, 263
"Xin de lunlixue" 51
   "The Ethics of Letters" 51
Xiyouji 11
   Journey to the West 11
Xu Dishan 63
Xu Guangqi 12
Xuji 249, 252, 260
   Sequel 252

ya 16, 18, 263
   elegance 16–18, 263
Yale Review 209
Yan Fu 13, 16–18, 263
Yan Guilai 227
yangwu yundong 13
   Westernization movement 13

Yanying 44, 78, 79, 110
   Fatima Mohideen 44, 109
   Modai 44
   Modai 44
   Momeng 44
"Yanying yipu" 44
   "The Spectrum of Yanying's Clothes" 44
"Yanying yulu" 44
   "The Sayings of Yanying" 44
Yi Baisha 170
"Yi Hu Shizhi" 28, 49
   "Remembering Hu Shizhi" 28, 49, 50
"Yi Xifeng" 46
   "Recalling *West Wind*" 46
Yige nübing de zizhuan 34
   A Woman Soldier's Own Story 34
"Yige nüjiandie" 251
   "A Female Spy" 251
"Yijiubaba zhi – ?" 28, 51, 268
   "1988 to – ?" 28, 51, 268
Yili 132
   The Book of Etiquette and Ceremonial 132
Yin Zhang Lanxi 240, 241
"Yingyi" 17
   "Strict Translation" 17
Yip Wai-lim 16
"Yixiangji" 216
   "A Record of Foreign Land" 216
"You jiju hua tong duzhe shuo" 49
   "Have a Few Words with the Readers" 49
Yu Dafu 34
Yu Kwang-chung 16, 264
Yuanbaoling 103
   the old Sycee collar 103
yuangao 139
   original text 16, 139
Yuannü 8, 28, 87–91, 93, 95, 96, 98, 100–103,
   105, 106, 153, 191, 267
   Embittered Woman 8, 88, 267
Yuanyang hudie pai 9
   Mandarin Ducks and Butterflies
     School 9, 10
"Yuedu Zhang Ailing xinzuo yougan" 149
   "Feelings after Reading Eileen Chang's
     New Work" 149, 150
Yuwai xiaoshuo ji 17
   Foreign Fiction Reader 17

Zazhi 118
   Magazine 118

INDEX   307

Zeng Pu   74

Zeng Xubai   74

Zhang Ailing duanpian xiaoshuo ji   118
    Collected Short Stories by Eileen
       Chang   118

Zhang Ailing Wenji   118
    Collected Works by Eileen Chang   118

Zhang Jiuling   83

Zhang Peilun   4, 70, 74–76

Zhang Renjun   70

Zhang Xiguo   253
    Yuwairen   253

Zhang Xueliang   8
    Peter Hsueh Chang   8

Zhang Zhidong   13

Zhang Zhiyi   4, 38, 69, 71
    Zhang Tingzhong   4, 38, 69

Zhang Zijing   6, 39, 57, 58, 61, 62, 69, 73, 198

zhanghui xiaoshuo   109

Zhangkan   6
    Chang's Outlook   6

Zheng Jingzhi   252

Zheng Pingru   250–252

Zheng Zhenduo   251

Zhili-Fengtian battles   72

Zhongguo shibao   250, 251, 253

China Times   250, 251, 253

"Zhongguoren de zongjiao"   6, 29, 157,
    159–165, 167–169, 171
    "The Religion of the Chinese"   6, 157, 159

zhongxue weiti, xixue weiyong   13
    Chinese learning as principles   13

Zhongyong   244
    the Middle Way   244
    Way of Centrality   244

Zhou Fohai   120

Zhou Zuoren   17, 18

Zhouli   133

"Zhufu"   214
    New Year Sacrifice   214

"Ziji de wenzhang"   28, 37, 220, 222,
    235
    "Writing of One's Own"   28, 37, 47, 220,
       237

"Zijiwen"   34
    "A Requiem for My Soul"   34

ziqiang yundong   13
    Self-Strengthening Movement   13

Zixiaoji   75
    The Legend of Purple Hairpin   75

Zhoubao   251
    Weekly Magazine   251

Printed in the United States
by Baker & Taylor Publisher Services